Japan Post Bank

Akira Uno

Japan Post Bank

Current Issues and Prospects

Springer

Akira Uno
Kyoto University
Kyoto, Japan

ISBN 978-981-15-1407-4 ISBN 978-981-15-1408-1 (eBook)
https://doi.org/10.1007/978-981-15-1408-1

This Springer imprint is published by the registered company Springer Nature Singapore Pte Ltd.
The registered company address is: 152 Beach Road, #21-01/04 Gateway East, Singapore 189721, Singapore

Preface

Between 2001 and 2006 the government abolished mandatory deposits of postal savings and pension reserves with the Ministry of Finance, implemented the FILP reform, and privatized policy-based financial institutions and postal services with the aim of changing Japan's financial system so it would serve its original purpose of complementing the private financial sector. These changes resulted in multifaceted structural reforms of the Japanese financial system, such as the revision of the Basic Law on Special Public Institutions Reform and privatization of public organizations by transforming them into stock companies.

Soon after these reforms, however, Japan was hit by a series of shocks, such as the collapse of Lehman Brothers, a change in ruling parties, and the Great East Japan Earthquake. Each time one of these unexpected events occurred, the government veered off track as it made revisions to laws that did away with the deadline for making its financial system complement the private sector. In the meantime, the ratio of government debt to GDP continued to climb. Although government debt is financed by household financial assets, national finances will eventually collapse.

Thirteen years ago, recognizing Japan's fiscal problems, I became involved in the privatization of postal services and started studying how household financial assets, which are the source of funds for both public and private financial services, were used. I discovered that different types of financial institutions had different asset portfolios and that the difference in portfolios between public and private financial institutions resulted in a profitability gap. I believed that these analytical findings would provide a theoretical rationale for privatizing public financial services, which is now stalled, and promote the reorganization of regional banks, which have hit a saturation point. The analytical findings notably suggest that the imbalance between Japan Post Bank's interest-bearing liabilities and earning assets causes low profitability and that the interest rate risk that the bank is likely to be exposed to may threaten its very existence. The analysis also found that regional banks must have enough assets to maintain a certain level of profitability and that regional restructuring, which includes mergers and consolidations, is a must in any future discussion of regional financial institutions.

Looking at the national wealth data in the government's Annual Report on National Accounts (Stock Accounts) and financial assets and liabilities by sector in the chart provided in the Bank of Japan's Flow of Funds Accounts Statistics, one sees that household financial assets are being used to repay government debt. For example, according to the financial assets and liabilities chart for the end of 2018 provided in the Bank of Japan's Flow of Funds Accounts Statistics, household assets totaling 1,779 trillion yen, which include deposits totaling 961 trillion yen, securities totaling 296 trillion yen, insurance and pension reserves totaling 522 trillion yen, are used to finance the government's securities (e.g., Japanese government bonds) and borrowings, which amount to 1,083 trillion yen and 159 trillion yen, respectively, through financial intermediaries such as banks and insurance companies, for example.

This situation is addressed in a Ministry of Finance document outlining Japan's fiscal status (published in October 2018) in the section highlighting the need for restoring Japan's fiscal health and related actions. The Ministry uses a graph of general government debt and household financial assets data that highlights the narrowing gap between government debt and net household financial assets (e.g., total financial assets excluding home mortgage loans) to illustrate that funds are running short and asks for public understanding.

The percentage of JGBs held by foreign investors is low at 11%, and the majority of them are denominated in the domestic currency and underwritten by financial intermediaries that use individual financial assets and insurance premiums as a source of funds. While these domestic-currency-denominated JGBs become assets of financial institutions, a 0% risk weight is applied when financial institutions calculate their capital adequacy ratio based on the international standard. Japanese financial institutions' long-term investments in low-risk but low-return JGBs, which are not risk-weighted assets, predate Japan's negative interest rate policy. Japan Post Bank and regional banks in particular hold a high percentage of JGBs, posing a problem in their portfolio makeup.

Facing the high ratings of domestic-currency-denominated bonds, the Cabinet Office's economic and fiscal projections for medium- to long-term analysis of January 30, 2019, make no projection regarding turning around the primary balance, despite the fact that the ratio of government debt to GDP has reached 230%. While both the government and the public are aware of Japan's financial crisis, no one has found a way out of it. It's like the fable of the boiling frog has come to life.

In this book I will analyze total assets (i.e., the operating foundation) and ROA) (i.e., profitability) of different types of financial institutions (public and private financial services) in Japan to get the big picture. Then, using ROA as an assessment indicator, I will look into ways for these institutions to optimize their portfolios to make the most of individual financial assets (especially deposits and savings) from a welfare economics point of view and formulate a theory of optimization. Financial institutions can optimize their ROA by using individual deposits and savings for total optimization to maximize their return on investment (in other words, ROA: Ordinary profit/Total assets (deposits and savings) = Ordinary profit/Total assets (deposits and savings) × Ordinary profit/Interest income).

To verify whether total optimization is achieved, I will estimate optimal figures for each bank based on their past data and change the composition of financial institutions by type. If the share of total assets by type of financial institution is optimized through mergers or vertical integration between different types of financial institutions, and if ROA is optimized overall as a result, the structure of financial institutions in Japan should be optimized. I will lay out institutional designs for financial institutions in Japan based on this positive analysis and theory.

Regional bank savings, postal savings, and agricultural cooperative savings, which are individual deposits and savings that are automatically used as collateral for government debt, are deposited with the Bank of Japan or invested in JGBs. If this practice is creating a low-profit economy, the best fix would be to optimize public and private financial institutions, which are financial intermediaries, through restructuring so that household deposits and savings can be used to generate higher profits in the public economic interest.

As of late 2018, the Bank of Japan holds 43% of JGBs, totaling 478 trillion yen. This yen figure is 86% of GDP, which is much higher than that of other advanced countries. Although the Bank of Japan has purchased JGBs that have been issued as a monetary easing measure, the proceeds from selling the government bonds owned by banks do not flow into the real economy. The money instead gets reinvested to the tune of 350 trillion yen in deposits with the Bank of Japan. Comparison of the flow of postal savings totaling 51 trillion yen deposited by the Japan Post Bank at the Bank of Japan (whose savings are invested in JGBs) with mandatory deposits reveals that this flow of money is very similar to the flow of funds deposited with the Ministry of Finance, which were invested in JGBs. That's why the three privatized banks should be restructured so that the 51 trillion yen currently deposited at the Bank of Japan can be used for lending; otherwise, they won't be able to generate funds in the public economic interest. The three privatized banks' expansion into the lending market is the key to the Bank of Japan's exit strategy. Another good step would be to fully privatize them as soon as possible (by selling all shares through public offerings as required by law).

If the economy grows, the government's tax revenue will increase, leading to healthy fiscal management and turning around the general account, and the national debt will be repaid. If the nation is to survive, the government should use tax revenues to pay down the national debt, which Hitotsubashi University Graduate School of Economics Professor Makoto Saito claims is the top priority for Japan, while household deposits and savings are automatically used as collateral for government debt, bolstering Japan's creditworthiness.

This book will focus on charting a road map to early full privatization of the three privatized banks and reorganization of regional banks.

Over the various stages of my life encompassing the private, public, and academic sectors, I have implemented concrete knowledge-based measures to solve problems in the private sector, gained practical public-sector experience in formulating rules and systems designed to create social change, and learned how to formulate theory through understanding history and analyzing the current situation in the academic sector.

The knowledge I gained through this experience has helped me construct a practical and well-substantiated methodology.

Stuck in a rut since the collapse of the economic bubble, the Japanese economy urgently needs a boost. As the huge amount of individual deposits and savings continues to be pooled in Japan Post Bank with a tacit understanding, that the bank is guaranteed by Japanese government—because government is the principal stockholder of Japan Post Holdings and it owns 89% of JP Bank's stock—full privatization of public financial institutions continues to experience delays, and the reorganization of regional banks remains untouched. I strongly believe that boldly addressing these issues will enable Japan's economy to get back on its feet.

Kyoto, Japan
April 2019

Akira Uno

Acknowledgements

This research was supported by DMG Mori Co. I would like to express my sincere gratitude to the company's president, Mr. Masahiko Mori, for helping to provide the financial assistance that made the work possible. I would also like to thank Mr. Hiroaki Tamai, executive vice president of DMG Mori, and Ms. Masami Hatano for taking time out of their busy schedules to lend a helping hand with the long-term translation project for this publication.

Finally, I would like to thank Mr. Yutaka Hirachi, senior editor of Springer Japan KK, for his warm encouragement, which helped me overcome the many obstacles to publishing this book. My special thanks goes to my wife, Fukuko, who patiently supported me over the last 4 years as I finished this research work.

Introduction Optimizing Japan's Financial Institutions

This book employs two analysis methods to approach its main theme, i.e., how Japan's financial institutions should be operated.

First, I analyze the total assets of private and public financial institutions in Japan to determine the optimal ratio of assets held by each type of financial institution to their combined total assets in order to create a free, fair, and efficient financial market. I would like to start off by defining the term "public financial services" as it's used in this book. Public financial services are generally described as part of the Fiscal Investment and Loan Program (FILP), which is designed to provide loans to local governments and private companies, for example, using funds deposited by individuals in an institution backed by the full faith and credit of the government. In this book, public financial services is used in a narrower sense and refers to nine financial institutions, i.e., the eight policy-based financial institutions[1] related to the policy-based finance reform laws (enacted in May 2007), which were based on the Act on Promotion of Administrative Reform for the Realization of Small and Efficient Government (the Administrative Reform Promotion Act) that went into effect in May 2006, plus Japan Post Bank. Following the reform of policy-based finance (October 2010), the eight financial institutions were merged and restructured into five organizations, i.e., Shoko Chukin Bank, the Development Bank of Japan, the Japan Finance Corporation, the Japan Bank for International Cooperation, and the Japan International Cooperation Agency (JICA). The six restructured public financial institutions can be further broken down into three privatized banks (Japan Post Bank, Shoko Chukin Bank, and the Development Bank of Japan) and three state-owned banks (the Japan Finance Corporation, the Japan Bank for International

[1]The eight financial institutions are the National Life Finance Corporation, the Agriculture Forestry and Fisheries Finance Corporation, the Japan Finance Corporation for Small and Medium Enterprise, the Okinawa Development Finance Corporation, the Japan Finance Corporation for Municipal Enterprises, Shoko Chukin Bank, the Development Bank of Japan, and the Japan Bank for International Cooperation.

Cooperation, and JICA), which are designed to complement the private sector and have been placed under full control of the government.

The combined total assets of financial institutions in Japan came to 1,640 trillion yen in the fiscal year ending March 31, 2017. Private financial services accounted for 82.2% (with Japan Agricultural Cooperatives (JA) accounting for 7.1%), while public financial services accounted for 17.8% (with the three privatized banks accounting for 14.6%). The share held by public financial services has been declining annually. Once the three privatized banks are fully privatized, more than 95% of financial institutions in Japan will be private financial services, and Japan's financial market will finally be a *free market*. However, privatization of public financial services, which began in 2007, is still at an early stage of development, even though over a decade has gone by since its inception. It was hampered by a host of legal restrictions over these years, and a road map to full privatization has still not been drafted. On top of all this, bank operations are governed by two different laws, the Banking Act, which applies to private banks, and special laws that apply to public financial services, preventing them from competing on an equal footing. Under such circumstances, increasing the percentage of assets held by private financial services will rapidly pave the way to a free and fair financial market.

Secondly, I analyze the share of total assets (i.e., the operating foundation) and return on assets (ROA) (i.e., profitability) of each type of financial institution in Japan to determine whether they have been optimized among different types of financial institutions. I also assess how good financial institutions in Japan are for the economy, finances, and national interest since their operating foundations and profitability vary from one type of financial institution to another. Most financial institutions in Japan are listed companies, and even unlisted banks operate under the supervision of the Financial Services Agency as well as the Bank of Japan and prepare financial statements in accordance with the disclosure requirements of the Ordinance for Enforcement of the Banking Act. That's why their financial information is extremely transparent. The earnings summary of a bank shows ordinary profit and ROA under operating results and total assets under financial standing at the beginning of the document. Ordinary profit and ROA are significant indicators, respectively demonstrating how well a company is doing and how profitable a company is relative to its total assets. While the assets-to-equity ratio is a key indicator of a company's financial standing, total assets are used to measure a company's position in its industry as well as demonstrate how solid the company's operating foundation is.

In this book, using the data of total assets and ROA by type of financial institution, I analyze chronological changes by type of financial institution and region to examine the trends among different types of financial institutions. I simulate a future scenario based on this examination and illustrate a process in which optimized figures (theoretical values) for respective types of financial institutions are used as targets. The book divides financial institutions into the following types: commercial banks, trust banks, regional banks, shinkin banks (regional financial cooperatives) and credit unions, and JA, all of which are private financial services, as well as three privatized banks, i.e., Japan Post Bank, Shoko Chukin

Bank, and the Development Bank of Japan, and three state-owned financial institutions, i.e., the Japan Finance Corporation, the Japan Bank for International Cooperation, and JICA, which are public financial services. To achieve an optimal balance among the different types of financial institutions, it is important to sort out the operations of the banks that constitute each type and consolidate them for an optimal combination of total assets and ROA indicators. When a company, including one not in finance-related industries, is looking to integrate its operations with another company's operations through integration under a holding company or a merger, it usually focuses on how the merger partner's assets (or market capitalization) will help it shore up its operating foundation by looking at the growth potential of the industry in which that company operates.

To increase its ROA, which is an indicator of profitability, the company would then implement various measures designed to increase efficiency and enable it to enjoy an advantage of scale. In the financial sector, repeating this process will lead to an optimal balance among different types of financial institutions. In the U.S. there are many cases where banks have optimized their corporate value through a vertical restructuring that leverages a merger or acquisition, such as a merger between a regional bank and commercial bank.

Optimizing the balance of different types of financial institutions means returning personal savings totaling 932 trillion yen as of the fiscal year ending March 31, 2017, which are automatically used as collateral for Japanese government bonds (JGBs), to the free and efficient financial market. In other words, strengthening financial intermediary operations that invest locally raised funds locally will put a stop to the current centralized and institutionalized investment practice. The bloated total assets of the three privatized banks should be split into independent business or regional companies that are capable of making quick business decisions to optimize their revenues by reducing the operating expense ratio and improving ROA. This optimization model has already been successfully demonstrated in Nippon Telegraph and Telephone Corporation's (NTT) restructuring.

In the meantime, small regional banks, which are suffering the brunt of a low-interest-rate policy in the face of a declining birth rate, graying population, and depopulation, are on the brink of extinction, and that is accelerating the reorganization of regional banks. A third of the 105 regional banks across Japan have undergone a reorganization to optimize their total assets and ROA. Another third of them have a solid enough operating foundation and sufficiently high profitability to keep them afloat, but the remaining third are likely to sink if they don't enter into some horizontal or vertical merger.

All types of financial institutions focus on collecting and investing personal savings as their primary business operations. Once the three privatized banks are restructured and fully privatized and after regional banks in crisis have completed some kind of merger and reorganization, the share of total assets and ROA by type of financial institution will be optimized. This will lay the foundation for creating *a free, fair, and efficient financial market in Japan* and reforming its financial structure.

Contents

Chapter 1
Paving the Way to the Privatization of Public Financial Services

1 The Birth of Public Financial Services and What Followed—Public Financial Services and a Financial Market under Interest Rate Control

1.1 From Early Meiji to the Post-Pacific War Period: The Age of Complementarity—Public and Private Financial Services under Government Control

Japan's public economy, i.e., the system in which taxpayers receive public services in return for their tax money, was the brainchild of Maejima Hisoka (1835–1919), also known as the father of the Japanese postal service.

On the premises of Ikebe Shrine, which is located in Maejima's hometown of Joetsu in Niigata Prefecture, a monument to the man stands with an inscription reading "a major architect of modern Japan" (M. Kobayashi 2009, *Shirarezaru Maejima Hisoka*, prologue). While Maejima was given the title of *danshaku* (baron) in 1902, the year marking the 25th anniversary of the Universal Postal Union, Kobayashi (2009) notes that it was the strides Maejima took across a broad spectrum of fields stretching beyond his achievement in founding the postal service that earned him the distinction of being one of modern Japan's primary architects.

In 1870, Maejima was sent to the United States and Great Britain to study their postal systems. Upon his return to Japan a year later, he was appointed head of the Bureau of Posts and began work on establishing Japan's postal service. Then, on May 2, 1875, Maejima launched the postal savings system. Appointed Vice-Minister of Communications in 1887, he established the Post and Telegraph Bureau and in 1892 transferred the Railway Bureau to the Ministry of Communications. In 1893, Maejima directed the sale of the mail steamer company, Yubin Kisen, to shipping giant Nippon Yusen. Upon enactment of the Railway Nationalization Act in 1907, he also created the national railway system using postal savings to fund the public service.

A. Uno, *Japan Post Bank*, https://doi.org/10.1007/978-981-15-1408-1_1

Postal savings were first deposited with the Ministry of Finance's Bureau of the Government Debt in 1878 with an eye toward investing the money in government bonds. The Ministry of Finance set up the Deposits Section in 1885 with the aim of expanding the scope of investment avenues to include special bank debentures and other types of bonds. This is how the mechanism of financing the public debt by investing postal savings deposited with the Ministry of Finance in government bonds and special bank debentures was created. To put this mechanism to work, the Japanese government established special banks designed to provide long-term industrial loans, including the Yokohama Specie Bank, Nippon Kangyo Bank, Hokkaido Takushoku Bank, Noko Bank, and the Industrial Bank of Japan.

Under the gun of Western powers to open up the country, Japan embraced a policy designed to boost national prosperity and military power in order to ensure its independence. Policies to develop industry and boost capital made building state-run factories as well as the transport and communications industries top priorities, all of which required one thing—money.

The Japanese government needed a public financial system for many reasons. One thing for sure was that, if it was to keep Western aggression in Asia in check and carry out its own colonial policy, it had to increase its national coffers, boost its military might, and build a foundation of industrialization that would put it on a course to modernization.

The Western powers were steadily expanding their colonial footprint across East Asia. The Netherlands established the Dutch East Indies in Indonesia in 1824. Britain colonized Malacca and included it in the Straits Settlement in 1826. France occupied Vietnam from 1874 to 1882. The British took control of Malaya (now Malaysia) in 1874 and annexed Burma as a province of British India in 1886. France added Cambodia to its colonial territories to form French Indochina in 1887 and later added Laos in 1889. Japan quickly followed in their footsteps as it embarked on a program of colonization over outlying territories and more. After taking control of Sakhalin as well as the Kuril and Ogasawara Islands in 1875, Japan annexed the Ryukyu Kingdom in 1879. This was followed by the annexation of Taiwan in 1895 at the end of the First Sino-Japanese War and the annexation of Korea in 1910. Under a colonial rule guided by a strategy to bring "civilization and enlightenment (growth)," Western countries introduced postal services, postal savings systems, railways, the telegraph, and other critical infrastructure (public financial services as well as fiscal investments and loans) that would modernize their colonies while using them as tools of control over its peoples.

Maejima was the first to introduce postal and postal savings systems as well as railway and telegraph service infrastructure to Japan after gaining a knowledge of these systems in Europe and the U.S. You could say that he single-handedly helped Japan escape the fate of Western colonization and become the only country in Asia to pave the way to "civilization and enlightenment" on its own. According to *Yubin chokin keizai shikan* [A look back at the history of postal savings] published by the Ministry of Communications' Bureau of Posts, Japan has a proud postal savings system history. Launching its postal savings system just 14 years after Great Britain did, Japan was the third in the world to have such a system, if all the countries of the

British Empire are treated as one. Back then the overall savings total was next to nothing since the majority of people rejected the idea of accumulating wealth and viewed money, not as something to be saved, but as something to be spent as soon as it was obtained. This set of circumstances posed a major obstacle that the Meiji government would have to overcome if it was going to generate the funds it needed for industrial development. As shown in Table 1.1 and Fig. 1.1, the balance of postal savings increased as the number of post offices offering financial services grew. After peaking at 5311 in 1884, the number of post offices subsequently hovered around 4500. The ratio of postal savings depositors to the total population continued to grow. The deposit balance peaked at 28 million yen and the number of depositors reached 1.25 million in the year after the First Sino-Japanese War ended in 1895.

Systems for generating funds, such as postal savings, national banks, and savings banks, were quickly developed in order to help get the government's industrial development policy off the ground.

Hailed as one of modern Japan's major architects, Maejima laid the foundation for Japan's telecommunications, railroad, and sea transportation systems, which are seen as symbols of progress. His work also contributed to Japan's technological and economic development as well as the formation of the public financial services that supported it. As postal savings balances stagnated after the First Sino-Japanese War, the government established special banks designed to provide long-term industrial loans. Enjoying government backing, these banks were granted the exclusive right to use postal savings to fund loans. The government launched Nippon Kangyo Bank in 1897, Noko Bank in 1898, and the Industrial Bank of Japan in 1902. The expansion of industrial loan offerings through these special banks, coupled with the establishment of public financial services as well as commercial, savings, and central banks, paved the way to building Japan's first banking system over the following decade. This banking system, however, left Japan with a legacy of postal savings and policy-based finance, the likes of which the world had never seen. While countries in the West and the rest of Asia also saw the emergence of public financial services over the course of development, they have either been shifted to private services or downsized over the last hundred some years.

Today you can see shades of colonial rule over East Asia in the colors of its mailboxes. I visited the rapidly growing countries of Southeast Asia (Vietnam, Indonesia, Malaysia, Thailand, Myanmar, Cambodia, Laos, and the Philippines) to study their postal savings systems.

The color of mailboxes in Indonesia, Malaysia, Myanmar, Japan, Taiwan, and Korea descended from the Dutch red mailbox or the British Royal Mail post box (the Japanese mailbox is believed to have originated from Scotland by way of Japan's Satsuma Domain). The yellow mailboxes in Vietnam, Cambodia, and Laos mirror France's. China uses three colors with dark green mailboxes labeled "regular mail" in yellow and red boxes labeled "express mail" in yellow. The use of these three colors seems to reflect the influence of both Britain and France.

Public financial services that use postal savings for policy-based finance are unique in the way they raise funds. An increase in postal savings is attributed to the number of post offices and applicable interest rates. The Japanese postal service

Table 1.1 Balances of postal savings over its 140-year history (May 1875–March 2014)

Year		Balance	Year		Balance	Year		Balance	Year		Balance
	Meiji		1910	43	169×10^{6}	**1944**	19	303×10^{9}	1980	55	61×10^{12}
1875	8	30×10^{3}	1911	44	192×10^{6}	**1945**	20	471×10^{9}	1981	56	69×10^{12}
1876	9	60×10^{3}		Taisho		1946	21	53.3×10^{9}	1982	57	78×10^{12}
1877	10	210×10^{3}	1912	1	201×10^{6}	1947	22	53.5×10^{9}	1983	58	86×10^{12}
1878	11	390×10^{3}	1913	2	199×10^{6}	1948	23	80.5×10^{9}	1984	59	94×10^{12}
1879	12	620×10^{3}	1914	3	202×10^{6}	1949	24	122.0×10^{9}	1985	60	102×10^{12}
1880	13	740×10^{3}	1915	4	240×10^{6}	1950	25	154.7×10^{9}	1986	61	110×10^{12}
1881	14	940×10^{3}	**1916**	**5**	328×10^{6}	1951	26	200.8×10^{9}	1987	62	117×10^{12}
1882	15	1.51×10^{6}	**1917**	**6**	458×10^{6}	1952	27	266.7×10^{9}	1988	63	125×10^{12}
1883	**16**	4.14×10^{6}	**1918**	**7**	605×10^{6}	1953	28	355.0×10^{9}		Heisei	
1884	**17**	6.74×10^{6}	**1919**	**8**	740×10^{6}	1954	29	455.1×10^{9}	**1989**	**1**	134×10^{12}
1885	**18**	11×10^{6}	**1920**	**9**	884×10^{6}	1955	30	538.2×10^{9}	**1990**	**2**	136×10^{12}
1886	**19**	15×10^{6}	1921	10	901×10^{6}	1956	31	656.9×10^{9}	**1991**	**3**	155×10^{12}
1887	20	18×10^{6}	1922	11	994×10^{6}	1957	32	756.6×10^{9}	**1992**	**4**	170×10^{12}
1888	21	19×10^{6}	1923	12	1.1×10^{9}	1958	33	853.8×10^{9}	**1993**	**5**	183×10^{12}
1889	22	20×10^{6}	1924	13	1.1×10^{9}	1959	34	986.6×10^{9}	**1994**	**6**	197×10^{12}
1890	23	19×10^{6}	1925	14	1.1×10^{9}	1960	35	1.1×10^{12}	1995	7	213×10^{12}
1891	24	21×10^{6}		Showa		1961	36	1.3×10^{12}	**1996**	**8**	224×10^{12}
1892	25	22×10^{6}	1926	1	1.2×10^{9}	1962	37	1.5×10^{12}	**1997**	**9**	240×10^{12}
1893	26	26×10^{6}	**1927**	**2**	1.6×10^{9}	1963	38	1.8×10^{12}	**1998**	**10**	252×10^{12}
1894	27	25×10^{6}	**1928**	**3**	1.8×10^{9}	1964	39	2.2×10^{12}	**1999**	**11**	259×10^{12}
1895	28	28×10^{6}	**1929**	**4**	22×10^{9}	1965	40	2.7×10^{12}	**2000**	**12**	249×10^{12}
1896	29	28×10^{6}	**1930**	**5**	24×10^{9}	1966	41	3.3×10^{12}	2001	13	239×10^{12}
1897	30	26×10^{6}	1931	6	28×10^{9}	1967	42	4.1×10^{12}	2002	14	233×10^{12}
1898	31	22×10^{6}	1932	7	27×10^{9}	1968	43	5.1×10^{12}	2003	15	227×10^{12}
1899	32	24×10^{6}	1933	8	29×10^{9}	1969	44	6.3×10^{12}	2004	16	214×10^{12}

1900	33	24×10^6	1934	9	30×10^9	1970	45	7.7×10^{12}	2005	17	200×10^{12}
1901	34	27×10^6	1935	10	32×10^9	1971	46	9.6×10^{12}	2006	18	186×10^{12}
1902	35	30×10^6	1936	11	34×10^9	1972	47	12×10^{12}	2007	19	181×10^{12}
1903	**36**	32×10^6	1937	12	38×10^9	1973	48	15×10^{12}	2008	20	177×10^{12}
1904	**37**	43×10^6	1938	13	47×10^9	1974	49	19×10^{12}	2009	21	175×10^{12}
1905	**38**	56×10^6	1939	14	61×10^9	1975	50	24×10^{12}	2010	22	174×10^{12}
1906	**39**	81×10^6	**1940**	**15**	79×10^9	1976	51	30×10^{12}	2011	23	176×10^{12}
1907	**40**	97×10^6	**1941**	**16**	99×10^9	1977	52	37×10^{12}	2012	24	176×10^{12}
1908	**41**	112×10^6	**1942**	**17**	130×10^9	1978	53	44×10^{12}	2013	25	176×10^{12}
1909	**42**	133×10^6	**1943**	**18**	189×10^9	1979	54	51×10^{12}	2014	26	177×10^{12}

Source: Ministry of Posts and Telecommunications 1968. *Yusei hyakunenshi (shiryo)* [Centenary history of the postal service (data)]

Bold: Growth period

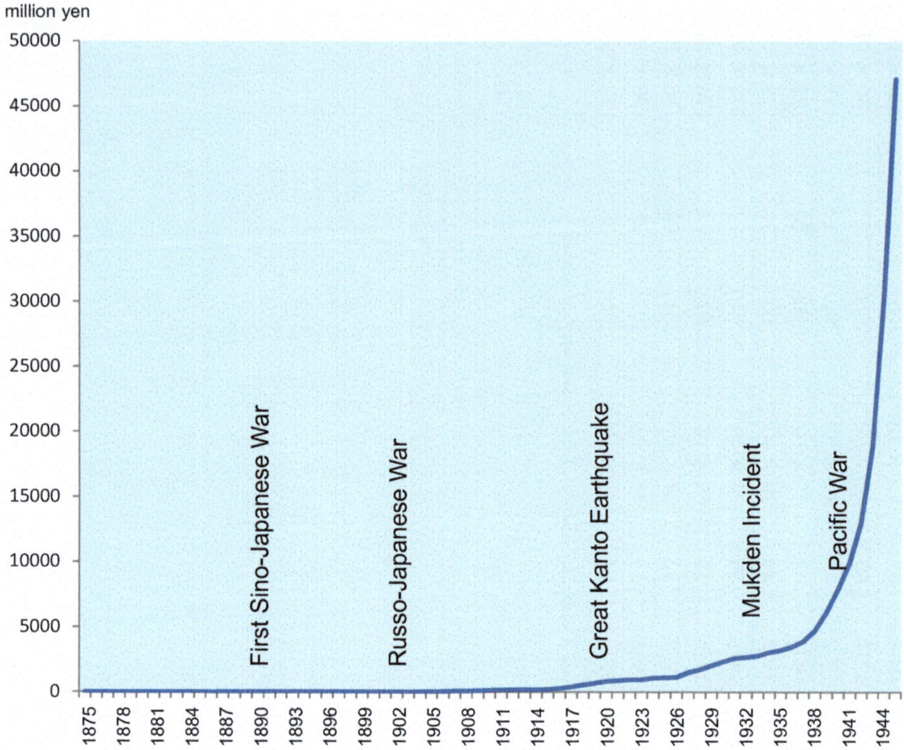

Fig. 1.1 Balance of postal savings (1875–1945)

was given more preferential terms than private financial institutions in opening new locations and offered account holders higher interest rates. To put the brakes on this preferential treatment, the government put a cap on postal savings deposits. By limiting the deposit amount per customer, the government tried to prevent postal savings deposits from becoming bloated. The deposit cap was modeled after the British system's cap and was set at 500 yen when the postal savings system was introduced in 1875.

Unique to Japan's postal service were grade 3 post offices (called special post offices after 1940), in contrast to the grade 1 and grade 2 post offices (general post offices), operated by the Ministry of Communications, which provided mail collection and delivery functions. Table 1.2 and Fig. 1.2 show how post offices were springing up everywhere between the early Meiji period and World War II (WWII). The grade 3 post office system was widely used in the Meiji and Taisho periods as a way to increase the number of post offices by commissioning operations to landlords and prominent local figures (for a fee paid by the government). While government-guaranteed postal savings dramatically increased during the economic depression triggered by the 1927 financial crisis, military spending also increased, which gave postal savings greater importance as a source of funds for financing public debts.

Table 1.2 Expansion of number of post offices. Postal savings increased in step with the growing number of post offices. The opening of a new post office was approved according to a different set of rules applied to private-sector institutions

Year	Number	Year	Number	Year	Number	Year	Number
1871	179	1906	6428	1941	13,564	1976	22,204
1872	1159	1907	6685	1942	13,756	1977	22,414
1873	1500	1908	6854	1943	14,091	1978	22,627
1874	3244	1909	6918	1944	14,238	1979	22,810
1875	3815	1910	7054	1945	13,281	1980	23,005
1876	3895	1911	7141	1946	13,699	1981	23,134
1877	3946	1912	7243	1947	13,916	1982	23,250
1878	4090	1913	7244	1948	14,014	1983	23,391
1879	4584	1914	7242	1949	14,576	1984	23,513
1880	5036	1915	7334	1950	15,017	1985	23,633
1881	5177	1916	7506	1951	15,152	1986	23,713
1882	5585	1917	7623	1952	15,314	1987	23,793
1883	5663	1918	7739	1953	15,460	1988	23,886
1884	5311	1919	7877	1954	15,522	1989	23,994
1885	4795	1920	8002	1955	15,566	1990	24,107
1886	4692	1921	8207	1956	15,599	1991	24,190
1887	4524	1922	8477	1957	15,657	1992	24,303
1888	4190	1923	8546	1958	15,828	1993	24,419
1889	4088	1924	8633	1959	16,038	1994	24,521
1890	4134	1925	8705	1960	16,234	1995	24,587
1891	4240	1926	8916	1961	16,374	1996	24,638
1892	4251	1927	9114	1962	17,057	1997	24,693
1893	4275	1928	9393	1963	17,639	1998	24,736
1894	4250	1929	9690	1964	18,180	1999	24,768
1895	4240	1930	9954	1965	18,740	2000	24,778
1896	4260	1931	10,208	1966	19,285	2001	24,773
1897	4274	1932	10,322	1967	19,726	2002	24,752
1898	4325	1933	10,611	1968	20,093	2003	24,715
1899	4447	1934	10,891	1969	20,374	2004	24,678
1900	4798	1935	11,253	1970	20,643	2005	24,631
1901	5097	1936	11,667	1971	20,976	2006	24,574
1902	5485	1937	12,138	1972	21,408	2007	24,540
1903	5898	1938	12,621	1973	21,679	2008	24,539
1904	6078	1939	12,938	1974	21,871	2009	24,185
1905	6217	1940	13,278	1975	22,043	2010	24,248

Source: Ministry of Posts and Telecommunications 1968. *Yusei hyakunenshi (shiryo)* [Centenary history of the postal service (data)]
Growth
Meiji–Taisho (1868–1925): Increased by about 9000
Showa–End of war (1926–1945): Increased by about 5000
High economic growth period (1955–1970): Increased by about 5000
From low-growth period to bubble economy: Increased by about 4000
Two lost decades: No increase

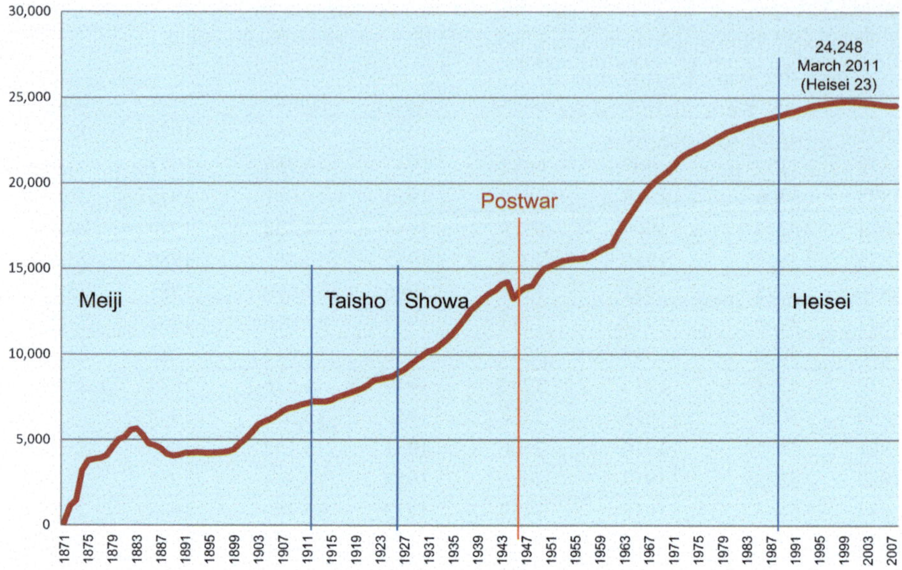

Fig. 1.2 Changes in number of post offices from Meiji to Heisei

Table 1.3 Historical data for postal savings interest rates (%)

Date	Ordinary savings	Deferred savings	Fixed-amount postal savings
Sept. 1, 1904 (Meiji 37)	5.04		
Apr. 1, 1910		4.2	
Apr. 1, 1915 (Taisho 4)	4.8		
Sept. 1, 1922	4.8	5.04[a]	
Oct. 1, 1930 (Showa 5)	4.2	4.44	
Oct. 1, 1932	3.0	3.24	
Apr. 1, 1937	2.76	3.036	
July 1, 1941	2.76	3.036	3.4[a]
Apr. 1, 1944	2.64	2.904	3.4

Source: Yucho Shikin Kenkyu Kyokai (2006) Part 3 Statistics. In *Yubin chokin no keiei doko heisei 18-nen ban* [Postal savings operation trends 2006]
[a]New product

Post offices numbered 9114 when Japan was hit by the financial crisis in 1927 but had grown to 13,281 by the time the war in the Pacific ended.

Postal savings typically offered higher interest rates than private savings, especially for ordinary savings accounts, as shown in Table 1.3. In 1922 postal savings started offering time deposits with a specified date of maturity that were comparable to time deposit products offered by private institutions. Giving preferential treatment to postal savings was necessary since savings helped Japan modernize: they supplemented government funding, especially during the years of economic depression and the war. During the Russo-Japanese War (1904–1905), postal savings interest rates were increased to match the interest rate for long-term government bonds in order to raise funds for the war. This resulted in a significant increase in postal savings that could be used to boost government funds. The postal savings deposit balance experienced some ups and downs during World War I and was hit hard by the 1923 Great Kanto Earthquake, while interest rates on private bank savings were drastically lowered in the wake of the 1927 financial crisis. Since the postal savings interest rate had not been touched since 1915, it remained higher than the interest rates offered by private banks.

In the wake of the Mukden Incident of 1931, the Japanese government maneuvered to weaken the yen, lower interest rates, and put monetary inflation policies in play. In 1932, deficit-covering bonds underwritten by the Bank of Japan were issued, triggering inflation. This paved the way for the 1936 attempted Imperial Army coup, known as the February 26 Incident, and the Second Sino-Japanese War the following year. Japan then put itself on a wartime footing with the enactment of the National Mobilization Law. The Emergency Armaments Expenditures Special Account Act also went into effect. In the meantime, the government established the Shoko Chukin Bank, a special bank designed to promote small and medium-sized enterprises in the export industry as an antirecession measure. The Ministry of Communications also launched a fixed-amount postal savings account in 1941 in order to raise money on a long-term basis to fund Japan's war effort. The fixed-amount postal savings account offered a fixed interest rate with a maximum deposit period of 10 years. Depositors could withdraw principal and collect interest whenever they wanted once a specific period of time had passed. Offering a higher contracted interest rate for a longer deposit period as well as a compound interest rate, it was a high-interest-rate product that no private bank had. Once Japan shifted to a wartime economy, postal savings were invested in government bonds and statutory companies that greased the war machine. The relationship between the government's financial condition and postal savings during and after the war is shown in Table 1.4. Deficit-covering bonds underwritten by the Bank of Japan were issued immediately after the outbreak of the Mukden Incident. Outstanding government bonds rose sharply from 3.2 billion yen in 1935 to 7.9 billion yen in 1940, and to 47.1 billion yen at the end of the war in 1945. The number of special post offices that did not collect or deliver mail jumped to 3305 by the end of the war.

One of the early studies on this topic can be found in *Waga kuni no kinyu seido* [The Japanese financial system] published by the Bank of Japan's Research Bureau in 1966, which on page 67 contains Schedule 5, "Ratio between Outstanding Government Bonds and Gross National Product (GNP)" Table 1.5. It analyzes how the balance of Japan's government bonds changed in relation to GNP over the course of the war and postwar years and clearly illustrates how the ratio between

Table 1.4 Government debt and balance of postal savings (100 million yen)

Year	Nominal GNE	Government debt	Balance of postal savings	No collection/delivery special post offices
1930	139	68	24.9	4240
1931	125	71	28.1	4367
1932	130	79	27.7	4469
1933	143	89	29.1	4639
1934	157	98	30.6	4785
1935	167	105	32.3	5027
1936	178	113	34.8	5337
1937	234	134	38.9	5750
1938	268	179	47.3	6073
1939	331	236	61.5	6372
1940	394	310	79.1	7516
1941	449	418	99.7	7803
1942	544	572	130.4	7983
1943	638	851	189.7	8226
1944	745	1520	303.7	8332
1945	–	1995	471.5	7532

Table 1.5 Ratio of outstanding government bonds to gross national product (100 million yen)

As of end of year (interval)	1930	1936 (6 years)	1944 (8 years)	1949 (5 years)	1959 (10 years)	1962	1963	1964 (5 years)
Outstanding government bonds, A	61	110	1095	5104	11,197	11,290	10,227	11,497
Long-term domestic bonds, B	44	92	1067	2908	4598	4137	4245	4332
Short-term securities	1	4	19	1190	5782	6671	5516	6555
Foreign bonds	14	13	8	1006	816	482	463	610
GNP, E	138	178	745	33,752	133,772	210,515	246,889	282,360
A/E ratio (%)	44.2	61.8	147	15.1	8.4	5.4	4.1	4.1
B/E ratio (%)	31.9	51.7	143.2	3.6	3.4	2.0	1.7	1.5

Bank of Japan and Toshihiko Yoshino (head of Research Bureau) (1966) *Waga kuni no kinyu seido* [The Japanese financial system]. p.67, Schedule 5 in Chapter 3, Finance, balance of payments, and financial services, Part 2 Japanese financial structure

the two was normalized during the postwar reconstruction period. I added an index to Schedule 5 indicating the relationship between general expenditures and postal savings to create a teaching resource that explains the fiscal conditions during the war and postwar years, which I used for a class I taught at Kyoto University in 2013

Table 1.6 Financial condition of wartime/postwar Japan (100 million yen)

As of end of year (Interval)	1930	1936 (6 years)	1944 (8 years)	1949 (5 years)	1959 (10 years)	1964 (5 years)
Long-term domestic bonds, A	44	92	1067	2908	4598	4332
Nominal GNP, B	138	178	745	33,752	133,772	282,360
A/B ratio (%)	31.9	51.7	143.2	8.6	3.4	1.5
General spending, C	15.5	22.8	198.7	6994	14,953	33,109
C/B ratio (%)	11.5	12.8	26.6	20.7	11.1	11.7
Balance of postal savings, D	23.4	34.8	303.7	1220	9866	22,000
D/B ratio (%)	66.9	19.6	40.6	3.6	7.3	7.8

Source: *Honpo shuyo keizai tokei* [Major Japanese economic statistics] Bank of Japan Statistics Bureau

The table on the *left* (1930–1944) is taken from Bank of Japan's Research Bureau (1966) p. 67, *Waga kuni no kinyu seido* [The Japanese financial system]. Data for general expenditures and balance of postal savings was added by author

(Table 1.6). As shown in this table, the factors that helped Japan reduce the excessive debt it carried immediately after the war and regain its fiscal health were the high inflation between 1945 and 1951, which slashed the real value of savings and deposits to a hundredth of their previous worth, and the Bank of Japan Notes Deposit Ordinance promulgated in 1946 (the deposit blockade), under which it became mandatory to deposit Bank of Japan notes worth 50 billion yen in some sort of financial institution. Another factor was the passage of the Act on Special Treatment of Losses Related to the Deposit Department of the Ministry of Finance in 1946, which made it possible to write off a loss of 6.2 billion yen. Postal savings were used partially as a reserve fund. Although they were returned in 1959, their value declined to virtually zero as a result of inflation.

The U.S. occupation authority, or General Headquarters (GHQ), forcefully implemented its own economic and financial policies. The Dodge Line was adopted in 1949, and financial and monetary contraction measures were implemented to help Japan achieve economic independence and stability. These policies focused on (1) controlling domestic consumption and promoting exports to reduce inflation, (2) rigidly balancing the federal budget, (3) giving priority to repaying Bank of Japan loans, (4) fixing the exchange rate to 360 yen to the U.S. dollar, and (5) easing wartime controls and promoting free competition. Then the tax reform proposed by the Shoup Mission was implemented the following year. It included (1) equalizing the tax burden, (2) imposing a direct taxation system (e.g., a progressive income tax, raising the maximum gift and inheritance tax rates), and (3) increasing the independence of local governments (expanding local tax revenue sources and specifying taxation and administrative responsibilities between the national and local governments).

Table 1.7 Development of postal savings and private savings deposits in relation to social conditions

Period	Postal savings	Private banks (savings deposits)
1875–1822	Postal savings system launched in 1875	Private savings deposits begin in 1879
1883–1886	First surge in savings	Growth stagnates due to financial instability
1887–1893	First wave of stagnation	Steady growth, good corporate performance
1894–1903	First Sino-Japanese War, second wave of stagnation	Quick increase in number of savings banks, outnumbering postal savings
1904–1913	Russo-Japanese War, second growth period	Depression in U.S., private savings stagnate
1914–1923	WWI, Great Kanto Earthquake, Third growth period	Significant increase along with postal savings
1924–1933	Fourth growth period 1927–1930	Stagnation due to Showa Depression
1934–1945	WWII, fifth growth period	

Source: Data created by author based on Bureau of Posts (1935) *60-nenkan ni okeru yubin chokin keizai shikan* [An economic history of postal savings, a 60-year retrospective] and *Cyokin-kyoku* (1942) *Zoku yubin chokin keizai shikan* [An economic history of postal savings, a 60-year retrospective Vol. 2]

As a result, while the number of post offices remained the same, postal savings kept on increasing until just after the end of the war, with the deposit balance going from 47.1 billion yen in 1945 to 200.8 billion yen in 1951. However, the real value of that balance was reduced to a hundredth of that figure due to inflation, making it worth only 2 billion yen, or around 4.3 percent of 47.1 billion yen. Deposits in private banks affiliated with the Japanese Bankers Association (JBA) totaled 1.5 trillion yen in 1951, which was 7.5 times the deposit balance in postal savings. That's why private financial institutions played a leading role in Japan's postwar economic recovery, taking over the role played by postal savings for the time being. It was also the end of public financial services at the expense of the public (public financial burden). The problem-solving process pointed out by the Bank of Japan's Research Bureau is the first fundamental lesson learned from the history leading up to the privatization of public financial services described in Sect. 1.1.

An overview of the changes in the balance of postal savings and private savings from the early Meiji period to WWII indicates a relationship between the market and government as well as small vs. big government.

Table 1.7 and Fig. 1.3 reveal a push for modernization that occurs particularly during times of war, economic crisis, or disaster, fueled by national pride and in defiance of Western powers. When it came to the government's financial and monetary support, the spotlight was on government guarantees, making public financial services one with national finances. As a result of Japan's defeat in WWII, the public was strapped with the burden of reducing government debt as

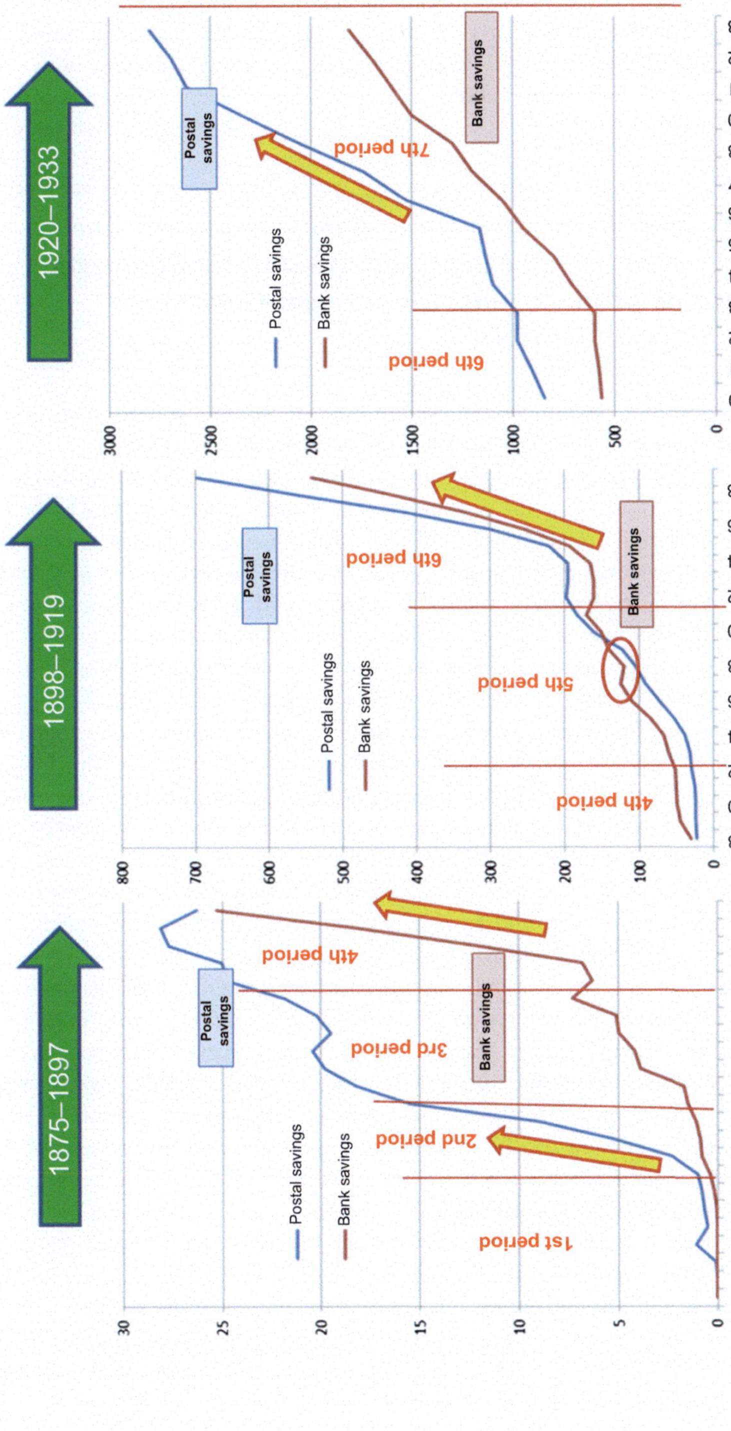

*Estimated on graphs

Fig. 1.3 Postal savings and private bank deposit balances (from Meiji to prewar period)
*Estimated in graphs
Source: Yusei-syo (1971) *Yusei hyakunenshi* [Centenary history of the postal service]. Cyokin-kyoku (1935) *60-nenkan ni okeru yubin chokin keizai shikan* [An economic history of postal savings, a 60-year retrospective]

their assets dropped to virtually zero as a result of inflation. Once Japan had weathered its postwar financial crisis, market forces began turning things around. Postal savings returned to being private savings, and private financial services dramatically expanded in step with Japan's economic growth. In tune with the times, it was an era in which public and private services complemented each other.

1.2 From Postwar Reconstruction to Bubble Economy: The Age of Coexistence and Coprosperity—Private Financial Services Competing against Government-Guaranteed Public Financial Services

The negative legacy of a postal savings system that served as a source of military spending was disposed of through postwar financial measures. Private financial institutions instead played the lead role in providing funds needed for Japan's reconstruction. In 1950, the Korean War broke out, resulting in a sharp increase in both domestic and foreign demand for funds. Due to a tremendous demand for funds needed to develop the general infrastructure and specifically rebuild the industrial infrastructure in Japan, the financial market was faced with an extreme shortage of funds. The Ministry of Finance's Deposits Section was placed under the control of GHQ after the war and was allowed to use funds only for government and municipal bonds. The way public financing worked was later completely overhauled with the revision of the Trust Fund Bureau Fund Act in 1951. As a result of the revision, postal savings deposited with the Ministry of Finance were used for the Fiscal Investment and Loan Program (FILP) as well as policy-based financial institutions. Postal savings came to be used to fund industry over the long run in the interest of the public. The government established policy-based financial institutions, including the People's Finance Corporation in 1949 and the Japan Development Bank in 1951. As well as the Agriculture Forestry and Fisheries Finance Corporation and the Japan Finance Corporation for Small and Medium Enterprise in 1953. In the same year FILP was included in the government budget, and postal savings, public pension funds, and other types of deposits were used to make loans and issue bonds to government agencies, special public institutions, and local governments, paving the way to Japan's rapid economic growth. Public works projects were also implemented to build infrastructure. The Japan Housing Corporation was established in 1955, followed by the establishment of the Japan Highway Public Corporation and the Forest Development Corporation in 1956, adding to the number of FILP-eligible special public institutions.

In 1949, the Ministry of Posts and Telecommunications revised the product features of fixed-amount postal savings accounts in order to revive the postal savings system. To compete with private banks, the ministry made it the highest-interest-rate product with its maturity period set at 6 months and the interest accrued after 6 months for up to 10 years at a fixed rate. The interest rate for ordinary savings was set at 2.76%, much higher than the 1.83% offered by private banks. Postal savings also offered an advantage because the interest earned was nontaxable.

The government had to keep expanding its postal savings system in order to meet growing capital demand and over a period of a decade added 3174 post offices to the 15,566 that had existed in 1955. The government also doubled the deposit cap from 100,000 to 200,000 yen in June 1955 and increased it to 300,000 yen in 1957, and to 500,000 yen in 1962, making it five times the original amount in a relatively short period of time. The cap was then raised all the way to one million yen in 1965. That is a tenfold increase in just 10 years. As a result, the balance of postal savings, which stood at 538.3 billion yen in 1955, soared to five times that amount in 1965 to total 2.7 trillion yen. In the meantime, the outstanding FILP balance continued to grow since its launch in 1953, reaching 5.1 trillion yen in 1965. The balance of loans by policy-based financial institutions also jumped 2.7 trillion yen in 10 years, going from 685.3 billion yen in 1955 to 3.3 trillion yen in 1965. This quick recovery of postal savings was the engine driving the recovery of Japan as well as its industrial development policy aimed at catching up with Western countries and served as funding for FILP as well as newly established policy-based financial institutions.

At the same time, private financial institutions, which had deposits on hand that they collected by taking advantage of Japan's economic boom and used for loans, engaged in fierce competition with post offices. Back then the Ministry of Finance would authorize a line of credit depending on the amount of deposits and fixed the profit margin under interest rate control. That meant financial institutions' profitability depended on the volume of transactions, so financial institutions sought to expand their branch networks across the country. While private financial institutions had to obtain the Ministry of Finance's authorization when opening a new branch, the Ministry of Posts and Telecommunications imposed no restrictions on opening a new post office location. Since private financial institutions had to surmount an extra hurdle to open a new branch, they fell behind in the race to build up deposits.

As the economic boom heated up, the Ministry of Finance and the Bank of Japan controlled the amount of currencies via window guidance and adjusted interest rates by changing the discount rate and reserve ratio with an eye toward controlling private financial institutions' loans. Plagued by strict compliance requirements imposed by the authorities, departments at private financial institutions responsible for lines of credit did everything they could to stay on top of loan requests from their branch offices. Since there was no such thing as an online system for monitoring deposits and loans, personnel at each branch office would notify the head office's line of credit personnel about its loan balance by phone at the end of each day (this practice was known as *denkoku* or phone reporting). Any bank that violated the line of credit requirements would be penalized by the authorities, and its line of credit would be reduced to a lower level than that of other banks for subsequent loans. This was a matter of life and death for banks, which is why they were nervous about retaining their line of credit. The threat of being penalized loomed large in the imagination of every bank employee from branch manager on down. That threat is what continually kept quantity, rather than quality, foremost in everyone's mind when making a new loan. When it came to deposits, however, there was no ceiling, and banks with more deposits would be authorized for a higher line of credit, which made the competition for deposits cutthroat.

Interest rates were regulated and set equally for all banks. Gifts given out to customers as incentives were regarded as virtual interest, so the JBA imposed voluntary regulations to limit the value of gifts in accordance with the guidance of regulatory authorities and the Act against Unjustifiable Premiums and Misleading Representations.

Different interest rates were set for different types of private financial institutions, such as commercial banks, trust banks, and long-term-credit banks. Since demand for long-term capital investment funds was high, financial institutions tried to come up with ways to secure deposits. This is clearly evident in the fact that the deposit balance and loan balance increased in lock step with each other (Table 1.8) (Figs. 1.4 and 1.5).

The government regulated public financial services, which used postal savings as a source of funds, in light of private financial services. It was a time when the government was stepping up its control over monetary and financial systems, which is mockingly referred to as the Ministry of Finance's "convoy system." Things were different then from today in that the economic cycle was in the development stage and monetary and financial systems were driven by Japan's economic boom.

Both public and private financial services provided critical support for the Japanese economy during its high growth period, with the former helping implement public works projects and public services while the latter contributed to the growth of private corporations with large capital needs. It was an age where public and private financial services existed and prospered together.

Consequently, nominal GDP showed a phenomenal increase, going from 853.8 billion yen in 1955 to 33 trillion yen in 1965. After the 1964 Olympic Games in Tokyo, Japan continued to experience economic growth. Dubbed the "Izanagi boom," the economy continued to skyrocket until 1970, and Japan's GDP became the second highest in the world in 1969, following the United States.

After the 1973 oil crisis that followed on the heels of the Nixon shock in 1971, the growth of the Japanese economy slowed down. Japan then shifted gears. Overhauling its industrial structure with the incorporation of labor-saving automation, information, and other cutting-edge technologies, Japan transformed itself into a technological superpower with the automobile, electrical, and precision machinery industries at its core.

Faced with mounting energy and environmental problems, Japan had no choice but to alter its underlying industrial structure, yet it continued to enjoy economic growth, albeit at a slower pace, by enhancing labor-saving technology, efficiency, and more. In the meantime, with increasing household financial assets as well as external assets, Japan as a nation became more powerful. Both public and private financial services continued to play an essential role in the monetary and financial systems that supported Japan's sustained economic growth. While Japan joined the world's most powerful economies club, it was faced with foreign currency issues that were critical to international trade.

Table 1.8 Public financial institutions and outstanding government bonds vs. private financial institutions (JBA-affiliated private banks) deposit and loan balance in postwar Japan (trillion yen)

	Balance of postal savings	Outstanding loans of government-affiliated financial institutions	Outstanding government bonds	FILP balance	JBA-affiliated private bank deposits	JBA-affiliated private bank loan	Nominal GDP	Remarks
1946[a]	0.05	0.002	Zero		0.144	0.146	0.047	Constitution of Japan promulgated in November, *zaibatsu* dissolved
1947	0.05	0.046	↓		0.234	0.168	0.130	Antimonopoly act enacted in April, issuance of deficit-covering government bonds prohibited
1948	0.08	0.113	↓		0.505	0.381	0.266	Occupation policy shifted from demilitarization to economic recovery
1949	0.12	0.111	↓		0.792	0.679	0.337	Dodge Line (economic stabilization policies)
1950	0.15	0.100	↓		1.048	0.994	0.394	Special procurement boom, Korean War (June)
1951	0.20	0.130	↓		1.506	1.517	0.544	Treaty of Peace with Japan signed in September, Export-Import Bank of Japan established
1952	0.26	0.318	↓	FILP launched	2.223	2.128	0.637	Enterprise Rationalization Promotion Act passed Japan Development Bank established
1953	0.35	0.467	↓	0.34	2.707	2.671	0.752	Korean War ends in July – antimonopoly act revised
1954	0.45	0.602	↓	0.29	3.036	2.911	0.782	(-Factors behind economic growth)
1955	0.53	0.685	↓	0.32	3.724	3.195	0.853	Jinmu Boom (Dec. 1954–Jun. 1957)
1956	0.65	0.775	↓	0.35	4.764	4.066	0.979	
1957	0.75	0.916	↓	0.40	5.504	5.024	1.116	Prolonged recession

(continued)

Table 1.8 (continued)

	Balance of postal savings	Outstanding loans of government-affiliated financial institutions	Outstanding government bonds	FILP balance	JBA-affiliated private bank		Nominal GDP	Remarks
					deposits	loan		
1958	0.85	1.096	↓	0.44	6.484	5.812	1.168	Iwato Boom (Jul. 1958–Dec. 1961, 42 months)
1959	0.98	1.293	↓	0.57	7.413	6.802	1.379	
1960	1.1	1.5	↓	0.6	8.8	8.1	16	
1961	1.3	1.8	↓	0.8	10.3	9.7	20	
1962	1.5	2.1	↓	1.0	12.1	11.4	22	1962 recession
1963	1.8	2.4	↓	1.3	15.6	14.5	26	Olympic boom (Nov. 1962–Oct. 1964)
1964	2.2	2.8	↓	1.4	17.8	16..8	30	Tokyo Summer Olympics
1965	2.7	3.3	0.2	1.8 (5.1 outstanding)	20.6	19.2	33	1965 recession, deficit bonds issued, Izanagi Boom (Nov. 1965–Jul. 1970)
1966	3.3	3.9	0.8	2.1	23.7	22	39	Construction bonds introduced
1967	4.1	4.6	1.5	2.5	26.6	25.3	46	
1968	5.1	5.4	2.0	2.7	31.0	29.0	54	
1969	6.3	6.4	2.4	3.2	35.9	33.7	64	
1970	7.7	7.5	2.8	3.8	41.3	39.4	74	(Economic slowdown)
1971	9.6	8.9	3.9	5.0	50.6	49	80	Nixon Shock, recession due to strong yen ($)
1972	12	10	5.8	6.4	61	61.5	94	
1973	15	12	7.5	7.5	68.6	71.8	117	First oil shock
1974	19	15	9.6	9.1	74.8	79.6	138	First negative growth in real terms after war (2 trillion yen tax cut)
1975	24	18	14	10.7 (42.8 outstanding)	85.5	88.7	152	(Economic slowdown)
1976	30	22	22	11.3	96.9	98.6	169	Positive finance with current account surplus

1977	37	26	31	13.9	108	108	186	(Economic slowdown)
1978	44	30	42	15.5	122	119	206	Bonn summit, positive finance for 7% growth
1979	51	35	56	16.8	131	127	228	
1980	61	41	70	18.2	141	136	246	
1981	69	47	82	19.5	158	151	261	(Global economic recession)
1982	78	53	96	20.7	169	167	274	Zero-based budgeting
1983	86	58	109	22.9	182	186	286	"Minus ceiling" budgeting
1984	94	62	121	21	197	210	306	Fiscal reforms implemented
1985	102	65	134	20.8	217	237	327	Plaza Accord, devaluation of dollar
1986	110	67	145	22.8 (167 outstanding)	279	300	341	Maekawa Report (expanding domestic demand/easing trade friction)
1987	117	71	151	28.2	334	337	359	Bubble economy (Nov. 1986–Mar. 1991), interest-rate deregulation
1988	125	76	156	30.1	375	372	386	Leveraging revenue from sale of Nippon Telegraph and Telephone Corp. NTT
1989	134	83	160	207 outstanding	429	412	414	Stock prices hit record high of 38,915 yen, 3% consumption tax introduced in April
1990	136	91	166	228	468	443	449	Money management, land speculation, real estate loans
1991	155	97	171	250	459	462	472	Heisei recession (economic bubble bursts)

Source: Yucho Shikin Kenkyu Kyokai. *Yubin chokin no keiei doko* [Postal savings operation trends]; Ministry of Finance, Cabinet Office's GDP statistics, and Japanese Bankers Association's statistical data
[a]Showa 21

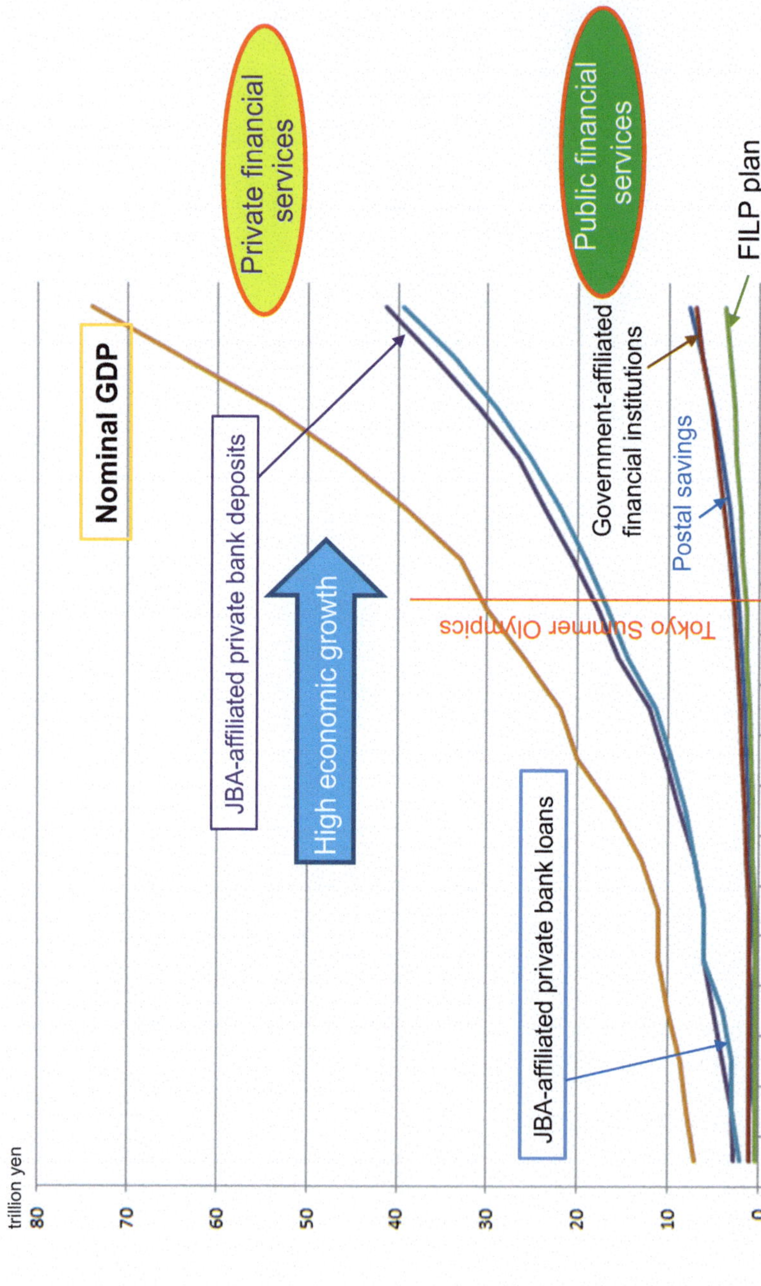

Fig. 1.4 Deposit/loan balance of public financial institutions and JBA-affiliated private banks, 1953–1970
Source: Yucho Shikin Kenkyu Kyokai, Ministry of Finance, Cabinet Office, and Japanese Bankers Association's statistical data

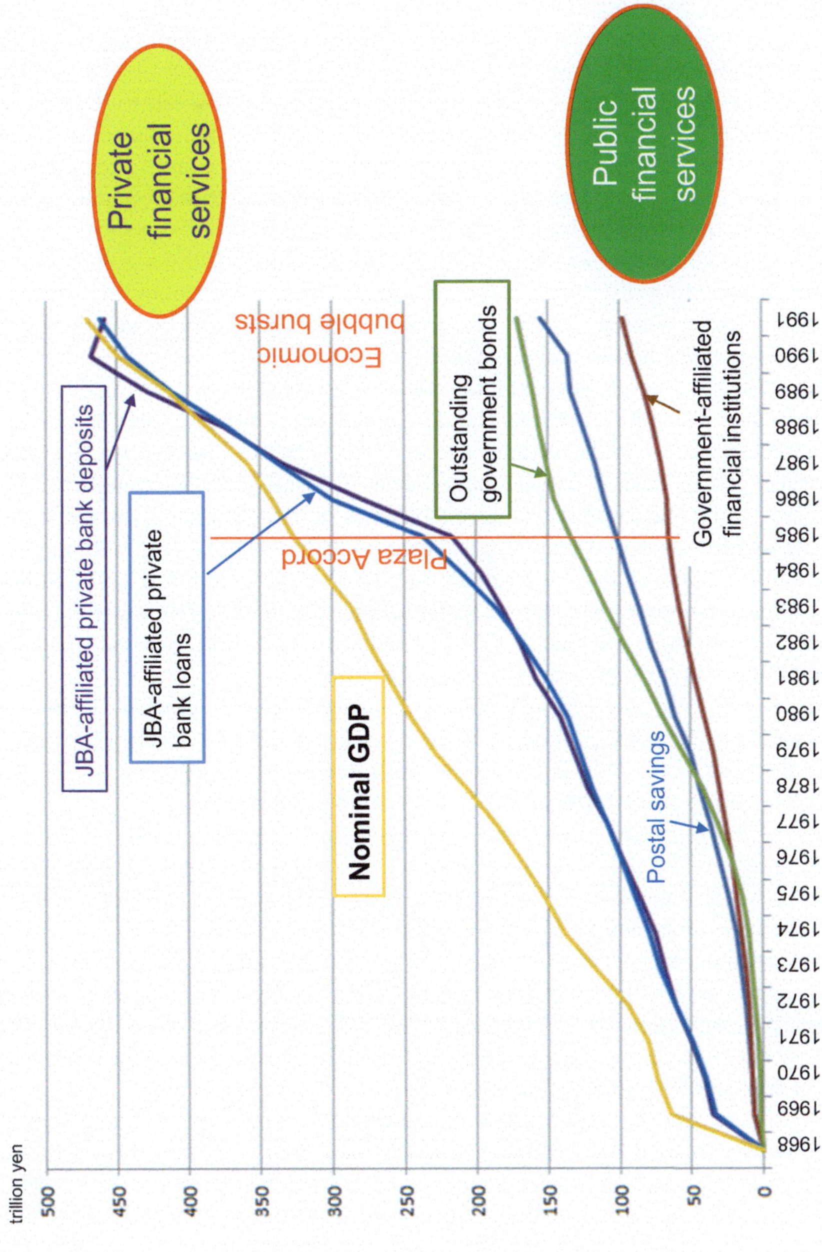

Fig. 1.5 Deposit/loan balance of public financial institutions and JBA-affiliated private banks 1971–1991

In August 1971, U.S. President Richard Nixon suspended the convertibility of the dollar into gold and imposed an import surcharge to protect the dollar. Then the fixed exchange rate system was replaced by a floating exchange rate system. In February 1973, the floating exchange rate system was adopted for the Japanese yen, and the exchange rate dropped from 360 to 264 yen to the dollar. Export companies were hit hard by this sudden appreciation of the yen.

Then in October 1973, the outbreak of the Yom Kippur War led to the first oil crisis. The price of crude oil, which was below $3 a barrel, skyrocketed to $11 in January of the following year. The hike in crude oil prices caused the prices of petroleum products to soar. The economies of developed countries around the world hit rock bottom due to mounting production costs on top of the Nixon shock and oil crisis. Japan, however, saw its public works boom continue under the government's "plan for remodeling the Japanese archipelago." As the amount of currency increased, inflation soared, and at one point skyrocketing prices coupled with increasing wages resulted in a higher GDP.

At the same time, postal savings and private deposits kept on growing, although at different rates. The balance of household financial assets, which totaled 332 trillion yen in 1979, increased to 982 trillion yen in 1989, 1389 trillion yen in 2000, and 1567 trillion yen in 2012. In 1971, the balance of postal savings amounted to 9.6 trillion yen, while the combined deposit balance in JBA-affiliated private banks totaled 50.6 trillion yen, and their loan balance totaled 49 trillion yen, with nominal GDP at 80 trillion yen. In 1985, the balance of postal savings amounted to 102 trillion yen (a 10.6-fold increase). The bank deposit balance stood at 217 trillion yen (a 4.3-fold increase), the loan balance at 237 trillion yen (a 4.8-fold increase), and the nominal GDP at 327 trillion yen (a 4.1-fold increase).

In September 1985, the Plaza Accord was signed at the meeting of G5 finance ministers and central bank governors, and G5 countries agreed to rectify the excessively high value of the U.S. dollar. As a result, the dollar depreciated (or the yen appreciated), going from 230+ yen to 168 yen to the dollar (Fig. 1.6).

In light of the appreciating yen, the government came out with a policy to expand domestic demand. The policy fueled private real estate investment and public works investment, which created Japan's bubble economy. This was the dawn of a new era where monetary policy would trump the old economic growth policy.

The government's general account tax revenue, which stood at 38.2 trillion yen in 1985, surged to 50.8 trillion yen in 1988 and 60.1 trillion yen in 1990 as a result of real estate purchases and sales, for example. When you compare these figures with the general account tax revenue figure of 40.9 trillion yen for 2011, you get a clear picture of the bubble economy that it was.

In post-Plaza Accord Japan, JBA-affiliated private bank loans increased by 162 trillion yen to total 462 trillion yen in 4 years from 1987 to 1991 when the economic bubble burst. Deposits also increased 187 trillion yen for a balance total of 459 trillion yen. On the other hand, government-affiliated financial institutions increased their combined loan balance by a mere 30 trillion yen, and the FILP balance grew by just 45 trillion yen. This resulted in a balance of 97 trillion yen and 250 trillion yen, respectively. Postal savings increased 55 trillion yen, with the

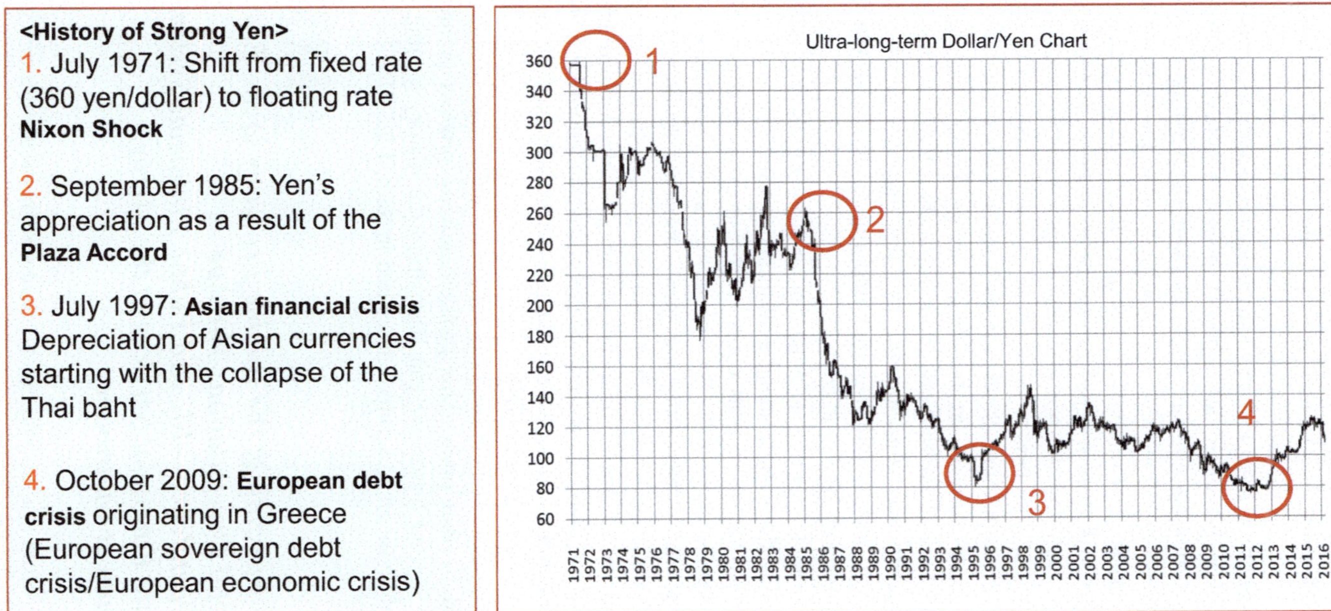

Fig. 1.6 Foreign exchange liberalization in Japan and yen-dollar rates after the war. Japanese companies shifted their focus from exports to overseas production (hollowing out of industry)

balance totaling 155 trillion yen in 1991. The share price hit a record high of 38,915 yen at the end of 1989. Looking back, you can say that it was a lending race officially endorsed by the Ministry of Finance, with private financial institutions taking the lead.

I had the opportunity to meet Harvard University professor Dr. Andrew Gordon in 2012. He noted how economic development in East Asia had begun to pick up steam just as Japan's postwar era came to an end with the bursting of the bubble—and how unfortunate it was that Japan had not invested in the Asian market more aggressively. His earlier study on the definition and demarcation of Japan's postwar era as well as analysis of postwar Japan can be found in *Postwar Japan as History* published in 1993. Defining the postwar era as spanning the years 1945–1990, Dr. Gordon writes that "the essays in this book have shown that postwar Japan can be divided very roughly into three periods." He also states that no one today would think that the bursting of the bubble economy in 1990 was the milestone marking the end of Japan's postwar era. Noting that the Meiji Restoration and the Pacific War and occupation constitute the two revolutionary epochs of modern Japanese history, the book emphasizes the importance of seeing the history of postwar Japan in a broader historical context.

In light of this view, Dr. Gordon told me that, after the bubble burst, Japan stuck to its policy of fueling domestic demand as it turned a blind eye to the fact that its postwar economic growth had run its course and that the market was shifting its focus to Asia's emerging economies. He was saying Japan should have shifted the focus of its policies from increasing the gross domestic production (GDP) to increasing the gross national income (GNI). In dividing the historical periods leading up to the privatization of public financial services, I have viewed the "age of coexistence and coprosperity" as the end of the postwar economic growth period. Preoccupied with cleaning up the mess left in the wake of the burst economic bubble, Japan failed to turn its attention to GNI.

The ages of coexistence and coprosperity for public and private financial services had already ended by that point. This problem-solving process pointed out by Dr. Gordon is the second lesson we can learn from the history leading up to the privatization of public financial services described in Sect. 1.2.

1.3 From the Bursting of the Bubble Economy to the Era of Financial Deregulation: The Age of Interdependence—Bloated Public Financial System and Private Financial Services at the Mercy of Government Guarantee

After the Japanese economic bubble burst, private financial institutions were hard-pressed to write off nonperforming loans. They reached into the equity capital they had accumulated during the economic boom and liquidated all hidden assets to cover the loss.

During this process a large amount of deposits flowed out of private financial institutions that had lost credibility and into postal savings. The government was also busy dispelling uncertainties about the financial system. The first to be hit hard were nonbank financial institutions. After the government bailed out seven housing loan companies to the tune of 685 billion yen, Nichiei Finance went bankrupt in 1996. This was followed by the collapse of Nissan Life, Sanyo Securities, the Hokkaido Takushoku Bank, and Yamaichi Securities in 1997, then the bankruptcy of the Long-Term Credit Bank of Japan and Nippon Credit Bank in 1998. In February 1998, the government spent 1.42 trillion yen to buy preferred stocks and subordinated bonds from 17 commercial banks and take other actions under the Act on Emergency Measures for the Stabilization of Financial Functions. In October of that year, the Act on Emergency Measures for the Revitalization of the Financial Functions and the Act on Emergency Measures for Early Strengthening of Financial Functions (systems for increasing capital by using public funds) were enacted, and a Minister of State for Financial Reconstruction was appointed.

The period from the bursting of the economic bubble in 1991 until 2000 is referred to as the "lost decade." While the balance of JBA-affiliated private bank deposits remained flat during this period, individual accountholders flocked to the postal savings system. The balance of postal savings almost doubled in 10 years, going from 136 trillion yen in 1990 to 249 trillion yen in 2000, an increase of 113 trillion yen. The postal savings balance peaked in 1999 at 259 trillion yen (Table 1.9, Fig. 1.7).

To suppress asset inflation, the Bank of Japan raised the discount rate four times for a total of 3% in 1989. It also regulated loans (the total amount) to stop asset prices from inflating. As mentioned earlier, however, private financial institutions were facing a growing mountain of bad loans that cast a long shadow of uncertainty. In July 1991, the discount rate hit 6% and deposit interest rates rose along with it. As a result, on top of concerns over the credibility of private financial institutions, there was a likelihood that their time deposits would bottom out. This triggered a stampede of customers to the post office to open fixed-amount postal savings accounts, which offered high long-term fixed interest rates. The contracted interest rate for the fixed-amount postal savings account in 1991 was 6.33%, with a final yield of 8.65% after 10 years (Fig. 1.8).

As shown in the figure, the ratio of postal savings balances to GDP started to climb quickly in 1992 and remained at over 40% until 2004. The shift from private financial institutions to postal savings not only caused the financial intermediary function of private financial institutions to degrade but also resulted in the expansion of government-affiliated financial institutions and special public institutions as the increased postal savings provided funds for FILP.

At the same time, while private financial institutions' loans stagnated as a result of the restrictions imposed by capital adequacy requirements, as well as a loss of corporate credibility, the loan balance of policy-based financial institutions increased by 71 trillion yen, from 91 trillion yen in 1990 to 162 trillion yen in 2000, over the

Table 1.9 Public financial institutions and outstanding government bonds vs. private financial institutions (JBA-affiliated private banks) deposit and loan balance in two lost decades Japan (trillion yen)

	Balance of postal savings	Outstanding loans of government-affiliated financial institutions	Outstanding government bonds	FILP balance	JBA-affiliated private banks		Nominal GDP	Remarks
					deposits	loans		
1992	170	105	178	277 outstanding	443	508	483	Stock prices fall below 15,000 yen in May
1993	183	117	192	308	446	513	482	Economic boom (IT bubble)
1994	197	129	206	339	453	510	489	
1995	213	132	225	356	470	514	497	
1996	224	137	244	377	469	513	509	
1997	240	143	257	394	474	515	513	Deposit of postal savings with Ministry of Finance ends, Yamaichi and Hokkaido Takushoku Bank bankruptcies, consumption tax raised to 5%
1998	252	147	295	400	464	507	503	Negative GDP growth (2nd time), LDP trounced in Upper House election in July, Obuchi Cabinet formed
1999	259	162	331	414	479	484	499	(Act on Emergency Measures for the Revitalization of Financial Functions, Act on Emergency Measures for Early Strengthening of Financial Functions – injection of public money)
2000	249	162	367	417	475	475	504	Mori Cabinet formed in April, U.S. economic slowdown, zero-interest-rate policy
2001	239	160	392	410	500	442	493	Koizumi Cabinet formed in April, financial reforms implemented, discretionary use of postal savings
2002	233	154	421	390	505	422	489	Structural reform policy

2003	227	146	456	354	514	410	493	
2004	214	138	499	322	521	400	498	
2005	200	128	526	299	527	409	503	Election focused on postal privatization in September, Postal Service Privatization Act passed in October
2006	186		531	275	533	412	510	Abe Cabinet
2007	181		541	245	542	417	515	Postal service privatized in October Fukuda Cabinet
2008	177		546	216	556	435	494	Collapse of Lehman Brothers in September (global financial crisis) Aso Cabinet
2009	175		592	208	570	424	476	Democratic Party becomes ruling party in September

Source: Yucho Shikin Kenkyu Kyokai. *Yubin chokin no keiei dōkō* [Postal savings operation trends]; Ministry of Finance, Cabinet Office's GDP statistics, and Japanese Bankers Association's statistical data

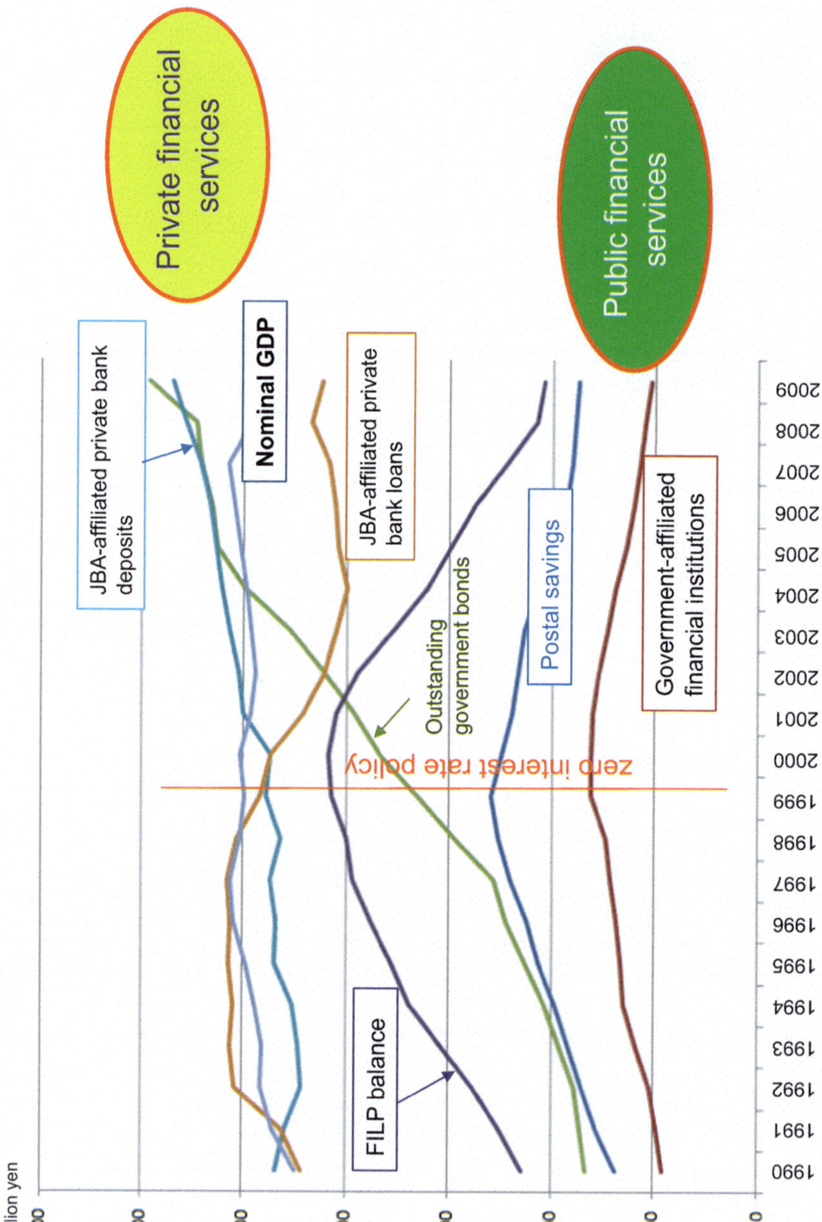

Fig. 1.7 Deposit/loan balance of public financial services and JBA-affiliated private banks, 1991–2009

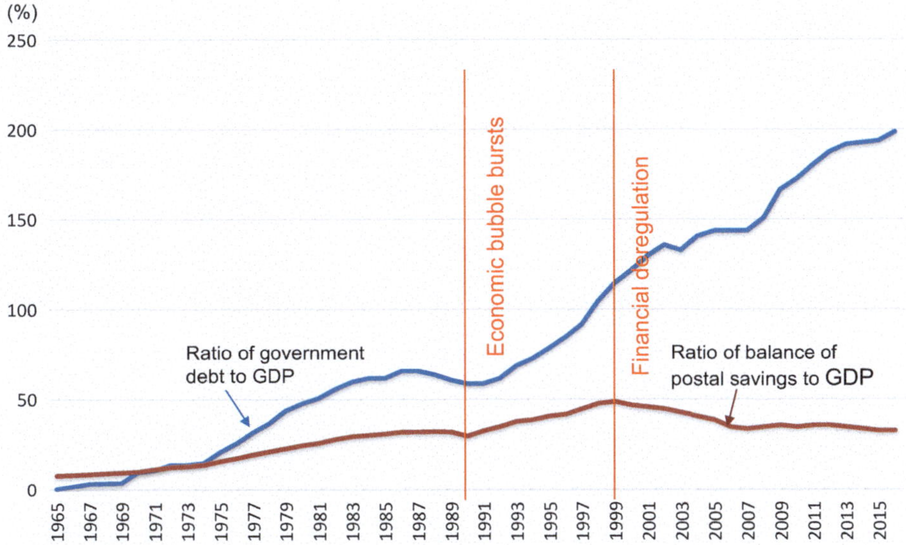

Fig. 1.8 Ratio of government debt to GDP and ratio of balance of postal savings to GDP (1945–2016)

period of the lost decade. Likewise, the FILP balance, which was 228 trillion yen in 1990, rose a whopping 189 trillion yen to total 417 trillion yen in 2000.

The factors behind these increases included the government's economic stimulus package, which was also designed to mitigate the impact of the government's bad-loan write-offs on the macro economy. The government implemented public works projects and tax cuts under its big-spending economic stimulus plans, known as the Comprehensive Economic Measures and the Emergency Economic Measures, over 8 years from 1992 to 1999, with a total spending of 118 trillion yen. Public financial services, which saved private financial services from crisis, raised funds from postal savings, postal life insurance premiums, and pension funds.

The government also issued construction bonds and deficit-covering bonds to support Japan's economy in a number of ways through general and special accounts.

As a result, the outstanding balance of government bonds increased by 201 trillion yen, from 166 trillion yen in 1990 to 367 trillion yen in 2000.

As shown in Fig. 1.9, after peaking in 1990 at 60.1 trillion yen, general account tax revenue started to fall with the bursting of the economic bubble and dropped to 38.7 trillion yen in 2009 following on the heels of the collapse of Lehman Brothers. In the meantime, expenditures kept on increasing due to bad-loan write-offs, economic measures, and mounting social security costs for Japan's graying population. The expenditure total went from 69.3 trillion yen in 1990 to 101 trillion yen in 2009. Private companies and individuals that were hurt by the bursting of the economic bubble tried various means to cover their losses, for example, leveraging public fund injections, selling private real estate, drawing from retained earnings, or generating yearly profits, in an effort to restore their balance sheets.

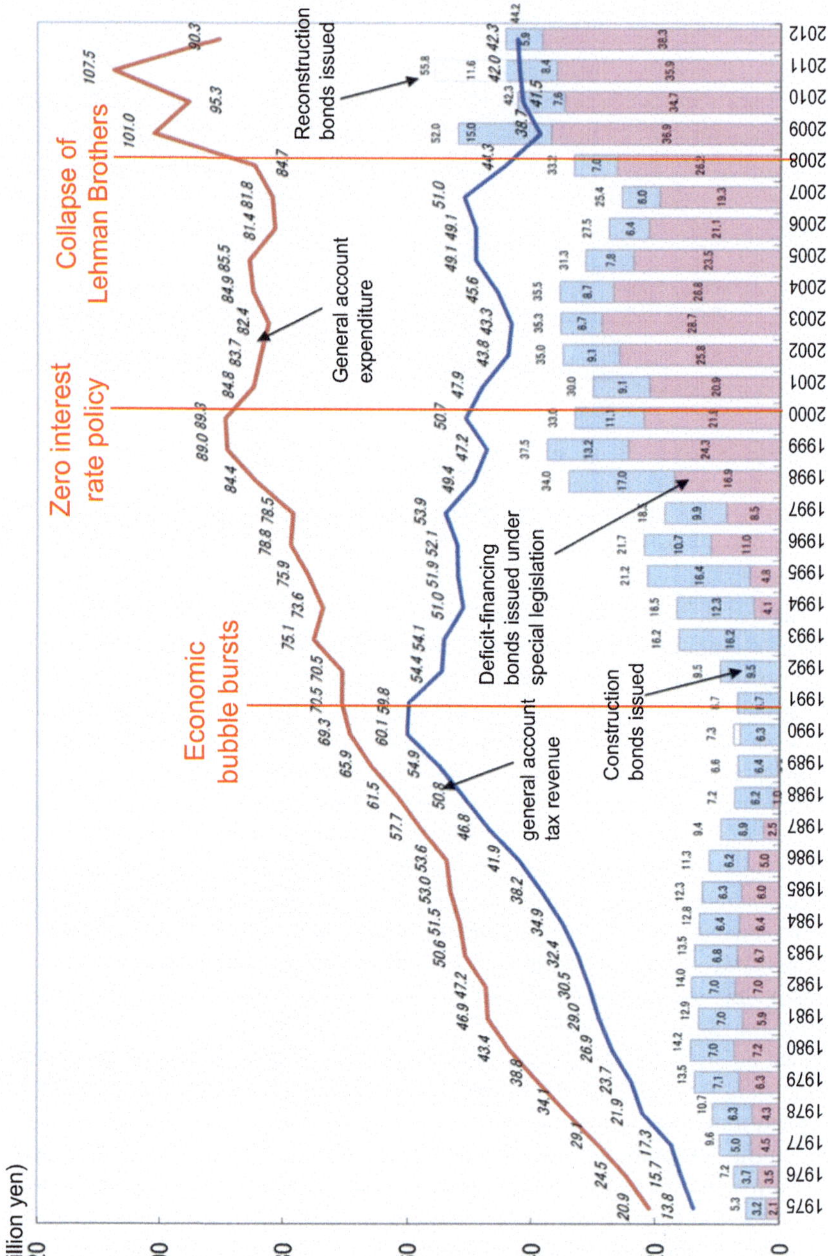

Fig. 1.9 Why does Japanese public finance continue to deteriorate? Reasons behind increasing public debt. General account tax revenue, total spending, and government bonds issued

The government, which earned money from tax revenue, and private financial institutions, which made a profit from lending, both ended up spending those earnings during the lost decade.

Once the economic bubble burst, the government proposed to reform FILP at the third meeting of the Provisional Council on Administrative and Fiscal Reform in October 1993. In December 1997 the government, under Prime Minister Ryutaro Hashimoto, abolished mandatory deposits of postal savings with the government and introduced the discretionary use of postal savings under the Basic Act on Central Government Reform (Fig. 1.10). In December 1999, the Ministry of Finance announced an outline of its proposal to drastically reform FILP, which included abolishing mandatory deposits of postal savings and pension funds with the government, complementing the private-sector with FILP, and ensuring redemption of government bonds. Fiscal reconstruction was urgently needed and the government had no time to lose.

While the deposit balance of private financial institutions continued to drop due to a growing lack of trust resulting from the collapse of financial institutions in the wake of the economic bubble's collapse, postal savings, backed by a government guarantee, grew. This is the same picture of public and private financial services we have seen since the Meiji period. In feeding funds to FILP, the bloated postal savings system facilitated the expansion and upsurge of government-affiliated special public institutions (totaling 163 organizations), such as the Japan Regional Development Corporation and Land Development Corporation, making for a tight market. Once the FILP reform was implemented in 2001, the FILP balance started to decline from its peak of 417 trillion yen in 2000 and dropped by half in 2011 to total 181 trillion yen. After peaking in 1999 at 259 trillion yen, the balance of postal savings also fell by nearly half, hitting 175 trillion yen in 2011. The 2001 FILP reform and the Reorganization and Rationalization Plan for Special Public Institutions, on which I'll go into detail later, changed the flow of FILP funds, which would typically come from postal savings and go to FILP and policy-based finance, to a more flexible system, marking a shift from a regulated market to a free market.

Japan's financial deregulation started with the establishment of the Japan-U.S. Yen-Dollar Committee in 1984 and gained momentum with the introduction of large time deposits in 1989. While depositors expect government guarantees when interest rates are regulated, they make deposits at their own risk when they're not regulated. In other words, public financial services backed by government guarantees are not fit for deregulation. The Ministry of Finance held that fixed-amount postal savings were not economically rational as products and were not in line with market principles. Naturally, private financial institutions demanded that the interest rates on liquid funds be deregulated and that the interest rate difference with ordinary postal savings be 1% so that they could compete on an equal footing. This led to the deregulation of interest rates on liquid funds in 1994 and full deregulation of interest rates.

Under the 2000 zero-interest-rate policy, the postal savings system lost its deposits to private financial institutions, which regained their credibility, and its deposit balance continued to dwindle. The FILP reform also resulted in a significant decrease in the FILP balance each year. Although the public financial system played

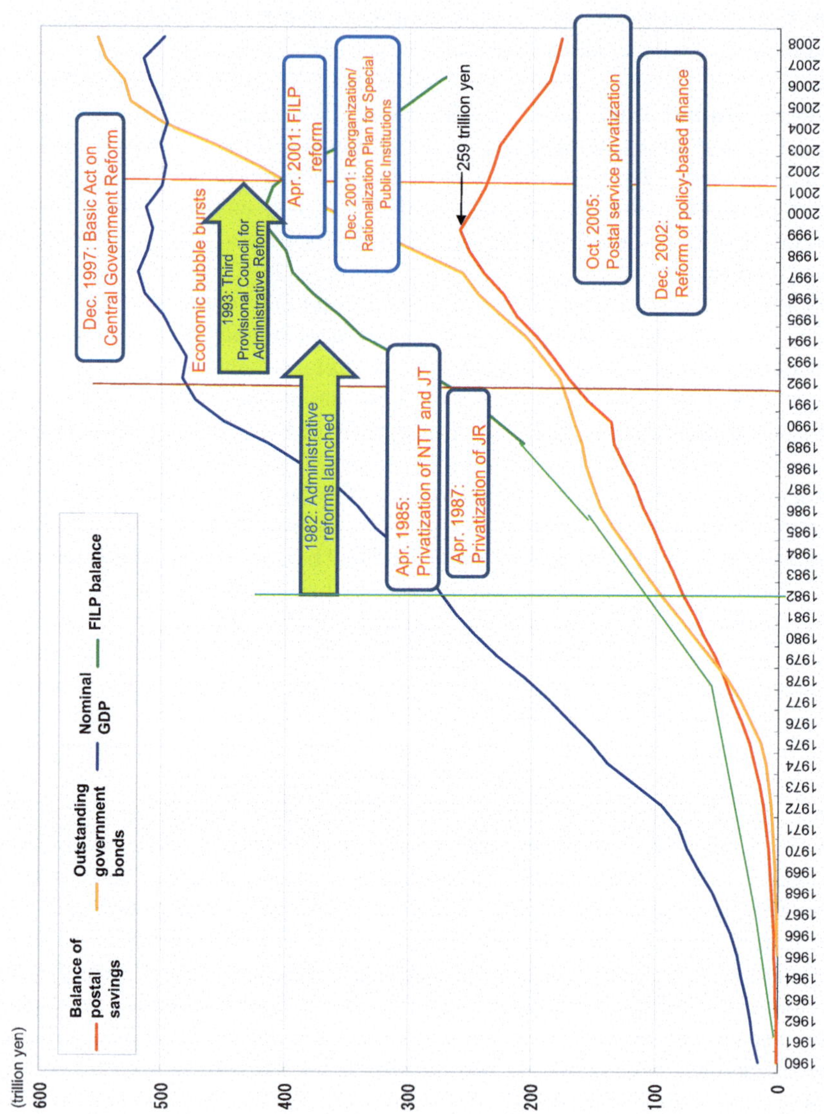

Fig. 1.10 History of administrative and financial reforms

an important role in helping private financial institutions overcome their crisis during the lost decade, it was not the revenue and internal reserve from the public financial system that supported them but its debts (i.e., funds from postal savings deposited with the government and government bonds). In the end, a decline in loans to policy-based financial institutions meant that, as a result of the termination of mandatory deposits of postal savings with the government, outstanding government bonds increased as much as the fund deposits decreased.

To make things worse, Japan's nominal GDP hovered around 500 trillion yen during the lost decade. Unable to increase tax revenue, Japan was left with a huge national debt. On top of insufficient tax revenue, the government faced uncontrollably mounting expenditures, such as costs related to the declining birthrate and aging population, social security costs, tax allocations to local governments, and public debt services, which kept the prospect for economic growth at bay. The government debt was financed by individual financial assets totaling 1500 trillion yen.

Despite stagnant GDP growth, in the absence of a growth strategy, Japan saw individual financial assets stagnate at the same level due partly to deflation. Having almost given up hope in the face of the prolonged zero-interest-rate policy, people opted for increasing low-risk savings and deposits. Since private financial institutions did not have any particular purpose for investing aggregate savings and deposits, they started investing in government bonds, to which a zero-risk weighting was assigned under Bank for International Settlements regulations (on capital adequacy) and increased their holdings of government bonds, primarily short-term bonds. On the other hand, postal savings as well as pension and insurance funds were invested in long-term government bonds. Although the finances of the federal and local governments were supported by deficit-covering bonds, they avoided relying on foreign investors as they managed to finance them solely with domestic sources.

Some similarities can be found between Japan's fiscal condition after the bubble's bursting until today and the fiscal condition of wartime/postwar Japan described earlier. I incorporated general expenditures drawn from the earlier study found in Bank of Japan (1982–1986) *Nihon ginko hyakunenshi* [A one-hundred-year history of the Bank of Japan] into the time axis in Table 1.6 and analyzed how the ratio between general expenditures and nominal GDP changed over the years.

Table 1.10 compares the fiscal condition during the period from the bursting of the economic bubble to financial deregulation on the same time axis as was used in Table 1.6. The ratio of the outstanding balance of government bonds to nominal GDP is about 150% for both periods, the ratio of general expenditure to nominal GDP about 20%, and the ratio of the balance of postal savings to nominal GDP about 40%. They are all very similar for both periods. The table indicates that the deteriorating fiscal health was indirectly caused by the fact that postal savings were primarily invested in government bonds. Looking at the similarities in financial deterioration for both periods, one sees how financial health was restored later on [Table 1.10 (1)]. Table 1.10 (2) shows that, under its medium-term economic and fiscal management plan, the government tried to turn the primary balance around

Table 1.10 Similarities between current and wartime/postwar financial conditions

As of end of year (interval)	1930	1936 (6 years)	1944 (8 years)	1949 (5 years)	1959 (years)	1964 (5 years)
(1) Wartime/postwar financial condition (100 million yen)						
Long-term domestic bonds, A	44	92	1067	2908	4598	4332
Nominal GNP, B	138	178	745	33,752	133,772	282,360
A/B ratio (%)	31.9	51.7	143.2	8.6	3.4	1.5
General spending, C	15.5	22.8	198.7	6994	14,953	33,109
C/B ratio (%)	11.5	12.8	26.6	20.7	11.1	11.7
Balance of postal savings, D	23.4	34.8	303.7	1220	9866	22,000
D/B ratio (%)	16.9	19.6	40.6	3.6	7.3	7.8

Source: The data on the *left* (1930–1944) are taken from Bank of Japan and Toshihiko Yoshino (1966) *Waga kuni no kinyu seido* [The Japanese financial system], p.67; data for general expenditures and balance of postal savings added by author

(Interval)	1990	1997	2003 (6 years)	2011 (8 years)	2016 (5 years)	2026 (10 years)
(2) Financial condition during lost decade following collapse of economic bubble (trillion yen)						
Outstanding government bonds, A	166	257	456	669	845	1178[a]
Nominal GNP, B	451	521	501	470	539	732
A/B ratio (%)	36.8	49.3	91	142.3	156.7	160.9
General spending, C	66.9	80.8	85.1	100.7	97.5	126.1[b]
C/B ratio (%)	14.8	15.5	16.9	21.4	18.1	17.2
Balance of postal savings, D	136	240	227	175	179	179[c]
D/B ratio (%)	29.5	46	45.3	37.2	33.2	24.4

[a]*Source*: Jan. 2018 data published by Abe cabinet
[b]Nominal GDP in 2026: 732 trillion yen (*Source*: Medium- and long-term economic and fiscal management plan, Council on Economic and Fiscal Policy, Cabinet Office)
13.6% of GDP if general expenditure remains 100 trillion yen
[c]No change
Data on *left* (1997–2011) created by author based on same time intervals as used in table shown previously

ASAP to reduce public debt but had to work on repaying it over a long term. The restoration of financial health is the third notable lesson we can learn from the history leading up to the privatization of public financial services described in Sect. 1.3.

As discussed so far, the relationship between public and private financial services went through three phases from the Meiji period until financial deregulation. The first phase took place between the early Meiji period and the end of WWII when public and private financial services were in a *complementary* relationship under government control. The second phase started immediately after the war when both public and private financial services had to start over from scratch and were in a relationship of *coexistence and coprosperity* as they were supported by economic growth and government guarantees until the era of the bubble economy. In the third phase, which took place during the lost decade following the collapse of the economic bubble, private-sector financial institutions were too busy writing off bad loans to function normally, so public financial services had to cover the losses they incurred. Public financial services benefited from this situation and later increased their assets but failed to find any outlet and needed the support of the private financial institutions that had nursed their balance sheets back to health. Compared with the figures for 2002, the balance sheets of JBA-affiliated private banks for 2012 shows their deposit balance up 93 trillion yen and their holdings of government bonds up 103 trillion yen. Their loan balance increased by a mere two trillion yen. That is a clear indication that JBA-affiliated private banks were unable to increase loans to companies and had to depend on zero-risk government bonds. This period can be described as the age of *interdependence* when both public and private financial services increased their deposit and loan balances thanks to government guarantees. Despite a series of financial reforms, including the zero-interest-rate policy and FILP reform implemented in 2000, the 2003 reform of special public institutions, privatization of the postal service in 2007, and privatization of policy-based financial institutions in 2008, private financial services, which automatically come with a guarantee by the government, are still "privately operated but government owned" and are not fully privatized yet. The next section will discuss ways to solve problems through financial reforms by drawing on the three lessons learned in this section.

1.3.1 An Age of Uncertainty, Sinking Together, or Win-Win?

Figure 1.11 provides an overview of the three phases. Since public and private financial services are mutually dependent now, if both fiscal reconstruction and economic growth are not achieved, what lies ahead may be the age of uncertainty or the age of sinking together. The next section will analyze obstacles to realizing a win-win relationship between public and private financial services and examine solutions.

2 Challenges Ahead and Solutions in Light of Japan's Pre-Public Financial Services Privatization Years

2.1 Ways to Improve Fiscal Health Via Financial Reforms Based on Similarities in Financial Conditions Today and Wartime/Postwar Japan in Terms of Increasing Public Debt in the Face of Growing Postal Savings as Well as Financial Deterioration in the Face of Growing Postal Savings

I have analyzed how postal savings have affected Japanese present-day financial system since the Meiji period by dividing the preprivatization era into three periods. A number of extensive studies have been done in regard to how FILP and policy-

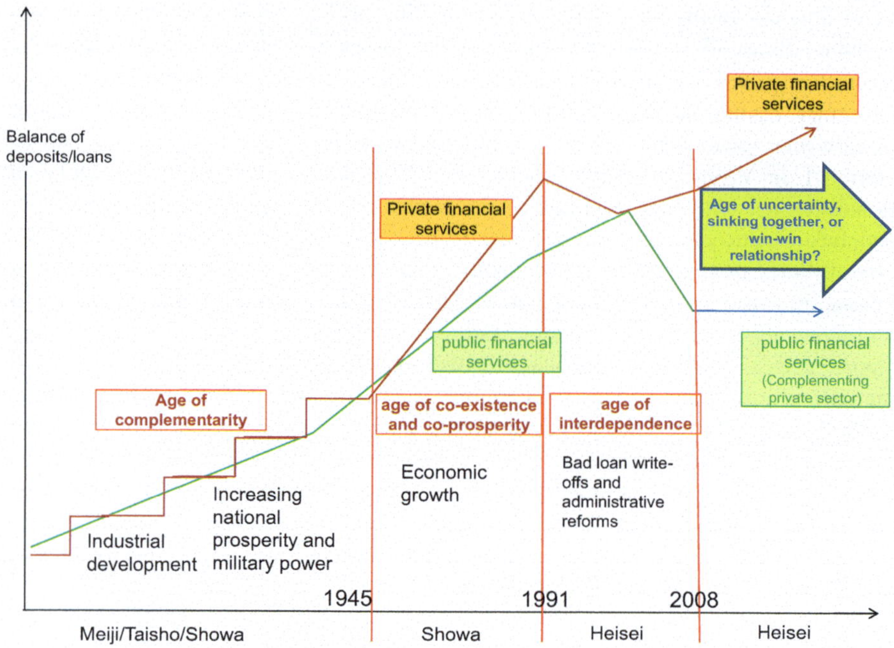

Fig. 1.11 History of public and private financial services

based financial institutions, which function as an asset management department of public financial services, affected Japan's economic development. At the same time, these studies fully recognize the importance of the postal savings apparatus, which historically served as the fund-raising arm that sourced the cash needed to finance Japan's industrial development.

In this section I will analyze how postal savings, which are individual assets that are indirectly used to buy government bonds, are closely linked to Japan's finances. I then propose ways to restore Japan's financial health and look at designing a financial system through financial reforms in Chap. 4.

Professor Makoto Saito at Hitotsubashi University refers to the consequences of wartime and postwar government policies as a "helicopter money extravaganza" and notes that the drastic decrease in the real value of the national debt is evidenced by the fact that it dropped to less than a thirtieth of what it was (going from 199.5 billion yen in 1945 to 6.4 billion yen in 1951), even though its nominal value increased from 199.5 billion yen to 645.5 billion yen (Saito 2016). He notes that during that time, the public was forced to repay government debt via a deposit blockade that lasted for 2.5 years (from February 1946 to July 1948), high property taxes, which was tantamount to asset forfeiture, and hyperinflation.

Using data for the ratio of government debt to nominal GDP as well as the ratio of personal savings to nominal GDP covering 20 years after the economic bubble burst, Saito also points out that the Bank of Japan's current quantitative and qualitative monetary easing measures use a scheme in which the Bank of Japan directly underwrites government bonds by replacing long-term government bonds it purchased from private banks with long-dated perpetual bonds, which are linked to floating rates. He further describes Japan's current social security burden and economic measures as a "war" for its people. Unlike what the government did after WWII, the debt Japan owes as a result of this "war" should not be increased beyond the amount of money its people have put away for the future.

I drew the same conclusion in my study. As noted in the previous section, I created data (Table 1.10) for a class I conducted at Kyoto University in 2013 based on Schedule 5, "Ratio between Outstanding Government Bonds and Gross National Product," on page 67 of *Waga kuni no kinyu seido* [The Japanese financial system] published by the Bank of Japan's Research Bureau in 1966. Using this table, which shows general expenditures in relation to the postal savings balance as well as the national debt in relation to postal savings, I identified some similarities.

The results of analysis can be seen in the changes in the ratio of government debt to nominal GDP and the ratio of postal savings to nominal GDP over the 85 years from 1930 to 2016, as shown in Fig. 1.12. Here you can see after the 1931 Mukden Incident government bonds underwritten by the Bank of Japan to raise funds for the war sharply increase under financial measures taken by Finance Minister Takahashi Korekiyo and keep rising for the next 15 years until war spending peaks immediately before the end of WWII. At its peak, the ratio of government debt to GDP was 200%,

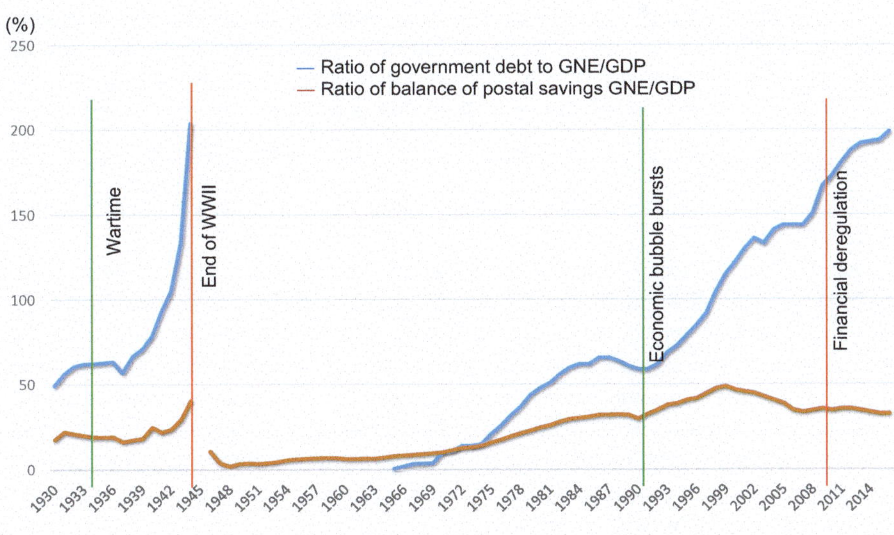

Fig. 1.12 Overview of similarities between wartime/postwar period and postbubble financial deregulation period in terms of national debt and balance of postal savings

and the ratio of postal savings to GDP was 40%. National finances and postal savings did not collapse as the war came to an end in 1945, and the value of debts and credit dropped as a result of the enactment of the Bank of Japan Notes Deposit Ordinance and the Property Tax Act and other postwar measures as well as high inflation and skyrocketing GDP. Both postal savings and personal savings lost value. People's financial assets all lost value, and they ended up paying off the national debt.

Personal savings continued to increase after the war as Japan's economy grew at a rapid pace. Once GDP growth stopped after the economic bubble burst, economic growth slowed down as social security costs increased in step with the declining birth rate and graying population. Public investments and other antirecession measures were wasted, just like the wartime military spending of the previous era. The ratio of government debt to nominal GDP hit nearly 200% while the ratio of postal savings to nominal GDP topped 40%, which were the same levels as what they were toward the end of the war. Although the ratio of postal savings to nominal GDP dropped to 30% + as a result of the FILP reform, special public institution reform, and others, it has remained at that same level. Even in the wake of the privatization of the postal service in 2007 and the privatization of policy-based financial institutions in 2008, little progress has been made, and funds that are automatically guaranteed by the government remain in the financial market. To change this situation, fiscal health must be improved to reduce government debt. Looking at the similarities between the fiscal condition of wartime/postwar Japan [Table 1.10 (1)] and the fiscal condition of postbubble Japan [Table 1.10 (2)] that were highlighted in the previous section, I'd like to offer my view of where Japan should be headed.

As Professor Makoto Saito pointed out (Saito 2018), new issues of government bonds increased as a result of the antirecession measures taken after the collapse of the bubble economy and increasing social security burdens that led to the erosion of fiscal discipline. On top of that they led to an increase of general expenditures, creating a fiscal condition very similar to that of wartime Japan. New government bonds issued to finance fiscal deficits have been covered by the postal savings system. This hard-to-break cycle is the chain that is holding privatization back. It's what exposed the Japan Post Group's failed investment and illegal loans made by Shoko Chukin Bank.

To resolve the current general expenditure problem, the primary balance must be turned around.

One way to do this would be to stabilize the economy under low-growth, low-inflation, and low-interest-rate policies, increase tax revenue over the long term, cut spending, and get general expenditure out of the red in order to repay debts. Another way would be to repay debts over the short term while reducing asset values under high-growth, galloping-inflation, and high-interest-rate policies. Retaining approximately 1800 trillion yen in personal financial assets and 350 trillion yen in net external assets, Japan is eminently capable of absorbing risk. There is also room for increasing consumption tax and other taxes to give Japan the ability to repay the national debt over a long term.

The best and most realistic solution would be to take public financial services public to realize full privatization and implement financial reforms needed to build a solid foundation that will withstand the low-growth, low-interest-rate, and low-inflation domestic environment of the free financial market while implementing overseas market strategies to boost profitability and increase not only GDP but also GNI.

References

Bank of Japan (1982–1986) *Nihon ginko hyakunenshi* [A one-hundred-year history of the Bank of Japan]. Vols. 1–6. https://www.boj.or.jp/about/outline/history/hyakunen/hyakus.htm/

Bank of Japan and Toshihiko Yoshino (1966) *Waga kuni no kinyu seido* [The Japanese financial system]. Bank of Japan's Research Bureau, Tokyo

Cyokin-kyoku (1935) *Rokuju nenkan ni okeru yubin chokin keizai shikan* [A look back at the last 60 years of postal savings]. Bureau of Posts, Tokyo

Cyokin-kyoku (1942) *Zoku yubin chokin keizai shikan* [A look back at the last 60 years of postal savings, Vol. 2]. Bureau of Posts, Tokyo

Gordon, Andrew, ed. (1993) Postwar Japan as history. University of California Press, Berkeley

Kobayashi, Masayoshi (2009) *Shirarezaru Maejima Hisoka* [Who was Maejima Hisoka?]. Yukensha, Tokyo

Ministry of Posts and Telecommunications ed (1968) *Rokuju nenkan ni okeru yubin chokin keizai shikan* [A look back at the last 60 years of postal savings]. In: *Yusei hyakunenshi shiryo* [Centenary history of the postal service], vol.15. Yoshikawa Kobunkan, Tokyo

Saito, Makoto (2016) *Herikoputa mane to ijigen kinyu kanwa no hikaku ko* [Comparative study on helicopter money and new quantitative and qualitative monetary easing measures]. Chuo Koron, August

Saito, Makoto (2018) *Kiki no ryoiki* [Crisis zone]. Keiso Shobo, Tokyo

Yucho Shikin Kenkyu Kyokai (2006). *Yubin chokin no keiei doko* [Postal savings operation trends]. Yu-cho Foundation, Tokyo

Chapter 2
Privatization of Public Financial Services and Financial Reforms

1 Factors and Reasons Behind the FILP Reform, Postal Privatization, and Reform of Policy-Based Finance—Public Financial Services and a Financial Market Under Interest-Rate Deregulation

1.1 Position of Public Financial Services in Japanese Financial Market

In this book, public financial services refer to the Japan Post Bank, which is affiliated with the Japan Post Group, in which the government has an equity stake, as well as policy-based financial institutions and special public institutions such as the Development Bank of Japan (DBJ). These are two different types of financial institution. Japan Post Bank, which raises capital, is where money flows in, whereas policy-based financial institutions and special public institutions, which use that capital for lending, are where money flows out, and they offer two different types of accounts, i.e., one is for savings and the other loans (Fig. 2.1). Specifically, as at the end of fiscal year 2016 the government held a stake in 23 special corporations worth 24.4 trillion yen. The government owns 56.9% of all shares in Japan Post Holdings Co., worth 5.06 trillion yen (after its share sale in September 2017). It also owns a 100% stake in the DBJ worth 2939.3 billion yen. In addition, it owns a 46.5% stake in Shoko Chukin Bank worth 179.8 billion yen and a 100% stake in Japan Finance Corporation worth 5130.8 billion yen, as well as a 100% stake in the Japan Bank for International Cooperation worth 2507.6 billion yen. This government-guaranteed financial system, where the government owns stock in Japan Post Holdings Co. (holding an 89% stake in Japan Post Bank Co.), which serves a fund-raising function, as well as policy-based financial institutions, which serve a funds management function, is referred to as the public financial system. Private financial services, on the other hand, are financial institutions where the money comes in and goes out

A. Uno, *Japan Post Bank*, https://doi.org/10.1007/978-981-15-1408-1_2

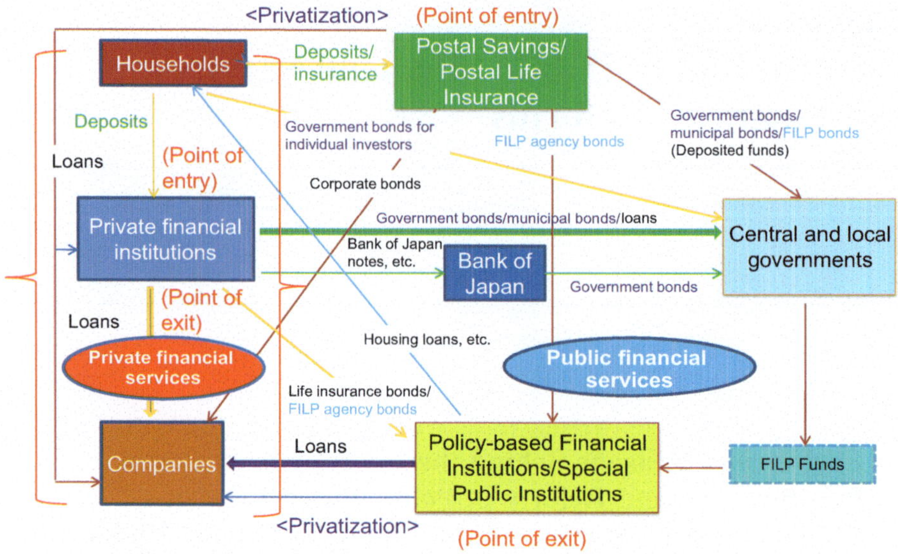

Fig. 2.1 Public vs. private financial services. Points of entry and exit and flow of funds

the same door. The money that is deposited with them is lent, for example, depending on the risks involved.

According to the chart of financial assets and liabilities by sector provided in the Bank of Japan's Flow of Funds Accounts Statistics, deposits in the domestic household sector amounted to 982 trillion yen out of total assets amounting to 1803 trillion yen as of late March 2017. The balance of postal savings was 179 trillion yen, with the remaining 753 trillion yen deposited with private financial institutions. The flow of deposits, shown in Fig. 2.1, has not changed since the Meiji period. Postal savings were guaranteed by the government from 1875 until postal services were privatized in October 2007, and the deposit balance peaked after the economic bubble burst. Even after privatization, postal savings are still automatically guaranteed by the government, keeping the mechanism of public financial services alive. Under public financial services the government guarantees funds at the points of both entry and exit, ultimately assuming the risk of financial collapse, a financial burden that would in the end fall on the public's shoulders.

In December 2002, the Council on Economic and Fiscal Policy charted a new course for the reform of policy-based finance based on the Reorganization and Rationalization Plan for Special Public Institutions, which was approved by the Cabinet in December 2001. The council claimed that Japan's policy-based finance system was a behemoth when stacked up against the systems of other countries and that the increasing scale of it had caused the financial and capital markets' resource allocation mechanism to break down. Emphasizing that enhancing the efficiency of the financial and capital markets is a top priority for Japan, the council urged that a drastic reform of policy-based finance was crucial to maximize the free and voluntary activities of the private sector. In June 2006, the government finalized an institutional design for policy-based finance reform based on this proposal.

The government decided that policy-based financial institutions would focus on complementing private financial institutions in order to make the shift from public to private. The objectives of the reform were to limit functions to those that were only absolutely necessary for policy-based finance and cut the ratio of outstanding loans to GDP by half through the restructuring of policy-based financial institutions, develop a crisis management system that incorporates private financial institutions, and achieve efficient operation of policy-based financial institutions. Under the new system, these financial institutions were positioned as special corporations and stock companies (as defined in the Companies Act) to be established under a special law and operated in accordance with the Companies Act. The DBJ and Shoko Chukin Bank were to be fully privatized.

The objectives of full privatization were to make the DBJ a private financial institution that could meet a broad range of increasingly sophisticated and diverse financial service needs and Shoko Chukin Bank a private financial institution that could provide extensive financial services to small- and medium-sized enterprise (SME) cooperatives and their affiliated members by leveraging its relationship of trust with these organizations.

Postal savings, on the other hand, had provided the Ministry of Finance with deposits to be injected into policy-based financial institutions and special public institutions as Fiscal Investment and Loan Program (FILP) funds through a special account (also known as the government's spare wallet) since the Meiji period. In January 2001, the Ministry of Posts, Ministry of Home Affairs, and the Management and Coordination Agency were reorganized into the Ministry of Internal Affairs and Communications and the Postal Services Agency as a result of central government reforms. In April 2003, the three postal service operations were transferred to Japan Post, a public corporation wholly owned by the government, under the Japan Post Act. Following the enactment of the Postal Service Privatization Act in 2005, Japan Post operations were split into Japan Post Holdings and four separate companies established under its umbrella in October 2007. This process, which occurred concurrently with the policy-based finance reform and FILP reform, was aimed at circulating Japan's huge postal bank savings in private-sector markets through full privatization of the postal savings bank, thereby stimulating the stagnant economy by providing loans to private companies. It also aimed to reduce the ratios of outstanding government bonds, outstanding loans made by policy-based financial institutions, and the FILP balance to GDP in order to improve fiscal health. With the implementation of the policy-based finance reform in October 2008, Prime Minister Koizumi's structural reform reached the point where Japan was able to see a bright future for its financial markets. Public financial services were divided into financial institutions that were eventually to be fully privatized and those that remained state-owned organizations, and their positioning was clearly defined. This positioning has not changed to date although, rocky government transitions that have resulted in detours have pushed deadlines back.

As shown in Table 2.1 for assets held by public and private financial institutions prior to privatization, as of the fiscal year ending March 31, 2005, the private financial sector accounted for 73.9% of total assets while the public financial sector accounted for 26.1%, or about a quarter. This shows just how bloated the public financial sector was. The privatization of policy-based financial institutions and the postal savings bank reform would now pave the way from public to private for all the reasons stated earlier. Maintaining the right asset ratio between the public and private sectors in allocating resources in the financial and capital markets was the biggest problem prior to privatization.

Table 2.1 shows the aggregated financial assets of public and private financial institutions before privatization based on their balance sheets for the fiscal year ending March 31, 2005.

1.2 Causes of Public Financial Services' Systemic Fatigue

As stated earlier, deposits and savings sourced from the postal savings system were used to complement private financial services in promoting industrial development from its beginning in the Meiji period until the bursting of the economic bubble. Before the end of WWII, in particular, they were used to finance Japan's war effort under a national government policy of increasing national prosperity and military power. During the postwar economic growth period when private financial institutions were major players, policy-based finances and FILP provided loans for infrastructure development, national projects, and other long-term projects, with banks and finance corporations established accordingly.

In 1965, when Japan was in the midst of its high economic growth period, the deposit balance at private banks affiliated with the Japan Bankers Association (JBA) totaled 20.6 trillion yen, and their loan balance amounted to 19.2 trillion yen, which helped emerging companies grow. Outstanding loans made by policy-based financial institutions amounted to 3.3 trillion yen, the FILP balance 5.1 trillion yen, the balance of postal savings deposits 2.7 trillion yen, and the nominal GDP 33 trillion yen. Deposit and loan balances are shown, in chronological order, in Table 2.2 for the high growth period (1965), the bubble economy period (1989), the bad-loan-write-off period (1996), and the FILP reform/zero interest rate period (2000). These figures show how imbalanced the changes in the deposit and loan balances of public financial services were.

The systemic fatigue of public financial services can be treated as the flipside of the following basic principles underlying the institutional design of policy-based finance reform:

1. Cut the ratio of outstanding loans to GDP by half.
2. Carefully implement policy-based finance as a government function.
3. Ensure efficient operation with clear management responsibilities.
4. Ensure transparency, evaluation, and monitoring.
5. Maintain and enhance convenience for users.

Table 2.1 Total assets of financial institutions for March 2005 (trillion yen). Nonconsolidated balance sheets of public and private financial institutions

	Private sector						Public sector								
							Before privatization[a]				Policy-based financial institutions[b]				
	Commercial banks	Regional banks	Trust banks	Credit unions	Agricultural cooperatives	Total	Japan Post Bank	Development Bank of Japan	Shoko Chukin Bank	Total (A)	Japan Finance Corporation [c]	Japan Bank for International Cooperation	Total (B)	Total (A + B)	Total
Deposits	28	12	3	26	54	123	6	0	0	6	2	0	2	8	131
Marketable securities	110	70	18	32	4	234	133	1	2	136	0	0	0	136	370
(Government bonds)	64	28	7	9	2	110	113	1	1	114	0	–	0	114	224
Loans	200	177	30	71	21	499	4	13	10	27	24	20	44	71	570
Other	67	14	6	4	16	107	122	0	0	122	2	1	3	125	232
Total assets	405	273	57	133	95	963	265	14	12	291	28	21	49	340	1303
Deposits	260	242	34	122	77	735	211	0	8	219	0	0	0	219	954
Borrowings							38	10	1	49	16	10	26	75	75
Other liabilities	131	17	20	4	2	174	11	2	2	15	9	2	11	26	200
Total liabilities	391	259	54	126	79	909	260	12	11	283	25	12	37	320	1229
Total net assets	14	14	3	7	16	54	5	2	1	8	3	9	12	20	74
Total liabilities and net assets (%)	405 (31.1)	273 (20.9)	57 (4.4)	133 (10.2)	95 (7.3)	963 (73.9)	265 (20.3)	14 (1.1)	12 (0.9)	291 (22.3)	28 (2.2)	21 (1.6)	49 (3.8)	340 (26.1)	1303 (100)

JBA-affiliated private banks: Total for commercial banks, regional banks, and trust banks

Sources:

[a]Ministry of Finance's statistical data and government-affiliated financial institutions' financial statements

[b]Japanese Bankers Association (2001), National Association of Shinkin Banks, Shinkumi Federation Bank, and National Federation of Agricultural Cooperative Associations (ZEN-NOH) statistics

[c]Based on data for the fiscal year ending March 31, 2009 (merged in October 2008)

Table 2.2 Balances at JBA-affiliated private banks and public financial institutions (trillion yen)

	Balances at JBA-affiliated private banks		Balances at public financial institutions					
			Deposit	Loan				
	Deposits	Loans	Postal savings	Policy-based financial institutions	FILP	Total (a)	Nominal GDP (b)	a/b (%)
1965	20.6	19.2	2.7	3.3	5.1	8.4	33	25.4
1989	429	412	134	83	207	290	414	70.0
1996	469	513	224	137	377	514	513	100
2000	476	475	249	162	417	579	504	114
2013	631	447	176	72	172	244	492	49.6

Sources: Yu-cho Foundation, Ministry of Finance, Cabinet Office, and Japanese Bankers Association (2001)

First of all, although public financial services were meant to complement private financial services, the combined balance of loans by policy-based financial institutions and FILP reached 290 trillion yen in 1989, accounting for 41% of the loan balance at JBA-affiliated private banks totaling 412 trillion yen. In 1996, the loan balance of public financial services reached 514 trillion yen, which was almost on a par with the loan balance of JBA-affiliated private banks totaling 513 trillion yen and 100% of GDP, making the public financial sector a major player in the financial market. The biggest factor feeding the bloated public sector was the declined financial intermediary function of private financial institutions due to the problem of bad loans, which was the primary cause that led to the systemic fatigue of public financial services.

Second, at the same time, the government compiled a large supplementary budget for stimulating the economy and implemented pump-priming measures in several phases. However, these measures were focused on public works and construction projects that did not lead to sustained economic growth. The fact that public financial services were never intended to fund these kinds of projects also contributed to the systemic fatigue. As shown in Table 2.3, the government spent a total of 118 trillion yen from 1992 to 1999 on public works projects, tax cuts, and other economic measures.

Third, the government created a number of special public institutions via *amakudari* (a practice whereby government bureaucrats are rewarded with plum jobs upon retirement). The inefficient operation of these entities where the responsibilities of management were not clearly defined also caused the systemic fatigue of public financial services.

Fourth, the government failed to follow the principle of transparency and neither shared the outcomes of the investments and loans with the public nor evaluated them on the basis of a reasonable assessment system. This was another aspect of the systemic fatigue resulting from the bloated public financial services.

Table 2.3 Government spending for public works, tax cuts, and other economic measures (trillion yen)

Date/Cabinet	Spending	Amount	Description
August 1992/ Miyazawa	Economic stimulus package	10.7	Public works Measures for SMEs
April 1993/Miyazawa	New economic stimulus package	13.2	New infrastructure development Public works
September 1993/ Hosokawa	Emergency economic stimulus package	6.1	Public works, deregulation
February 1994/ Hosokawa	Economic stimulus package	15.2	Public works, income tax cuts
September 1995/ Murayama	Economic policy	14.2	Public works, special tax cuts
April 1998/ Hashimoto	Economic stimulus package	16.6	Public works
November 1998/ Obuchi	Emergency economic stimulus package	23.9	Infrastructure development Income tax cuts
November 1999/ Obuchi	Economic revival measures	18.0	Public works, startup support

Sources: Ministry of Finance, Ministry of Economy, Trade and Industry, and the Cabinet Office

Fifth, the declining credibility of private financial institutions facing bad loans gave a boost to the postal savings system. Backed by a government guarantee, postal savings deposits soared and provided a source of loans to public financial institutions. This is a typical pattern of ever-expanding government interference in the financial system.

The government then faced mounting social security costs as Japan saw its birth rate fall against the backdrop of a graying population. Coming together like a perfect storm in the wake of the collapse of the bubble economy, these phenomena quickly worsened the systemic fatigue affecting public financial services.

In Sect. 2 of Chap. 1 we looked at the fiscal similarities between this postbubble period and the wartime/postwar period. It was during these periods that systemic fatigue of public financial services worsened. Table 2.4 shows social security expenditures in relation to the declining birth rate and graying population. As shown in the table, the elderly population had increased significantly by 2012 compared with 1990. During the same period the number of people aged 65 or older rose by 15,940,000, the number of people aged 19 or younger fell by 9,970,000, while the overall population grew by 5,120,000. Social security expenditures jumped 2.3-fold, or 62.3 trillion yen, during the same period.

This increase was largely responsible for the ratio of outstanding government bonds to GDP hitting 144% in 2012 as the ratio of the postal savings balance to GDP climbed to 36.5%. This remains a challenge that Japan has yet to overcome.

Table 2.4 Social security expenditures in relation to declining and graying population, ratio of government debt to GDP, and ratio of postal savings balance to GDP

	Population (ten thousand) (%)				Social security expenditure (trillion yen)	Outstanding government bonds (trillion yen), A	Nominal GDP (trillion yen), B	A/B (%)	Balance of postal savings, C	C/B (%)
	Total	65 years and older	20–64	19 and under						
1990	12,238	1489 (12.1)	7500 (61.3)	3249 (26.6)	47.2	116	451	36.8	136	29.5
2012	12,750	3083 (24.2)	7415 (58.1)	2252 (17.7)	109.5	691	470	144.2	175	36.5
Difference	+512	+1594 (+12.1)	−85 (−3.2)	−997 (−8.9)	+62.3	+525	+19	+107.4	+39	+7.0

Sources: National Institute of Population and Social Security Research, Ministry of Finance, and Japan Post Holdings (2007)

1.3 Financial Liberalization

In 1980 the British government under Margaret Thatcher (1979–1990) implemented economic policies focused on "deregulation," "privatization," and a "smaller state." This was dubbed "Thatcherism." Thatcher also worked on reducing inflation and paying off public debt in order to reverse the stagflation the country was experiencing. To implement its policies, Thatcher's government excluded labor unions from the decision-making process. Meanwhile, the United States government, led by President Ronald Reagan (1981–1989), implemented economic policies, known as "Reaganomics," that introduced tax cuts for the wealthy to increase consumption as well as corporate tax cuts and deregulation to boost investments and supply. These policies helped revive America as an economic power. The Japanese government under Prime Minister Yasuhiro Nakasone (1982–1987) implemented administrative and financial reforms with a focus on privatizing the state-owned Japanese National Railways (JNR), Nippon Telegraph and Telephone Public Corp. (NTT), and the Japan Tobacco & Salt Public Corporation. The series of measures taken in developed countries, all focused on deregulation, free markets, tax reforms, and spending cuts, promoted financial liberalization and privatization of state-owned corporations.

Financial liberalization in free market economies such as the United States and Britain was a significant factor contributing to the systemic fatigue of Japan's public financial services after the bursting of the bubble economy that led to FILP reform and postal privatization.

Financial liberalization was about easing fund-raising regulations, and the first step was deregulation of interest rates. The second step was easing or abolishing regulations on interindustry activities (banking, securities, and insurance), and the third was deregulation of mergers.

Table 2.5 shows the timelines of financial liberalization in the U.S., Britain, and Japan. Interest-rate deregulation in the U.S. began in the 1970s and was completed in 1982. Interindustry activity was first deregulated in 1987 with modification of the Glass-Steagall Act (regulations aimed at the banking and securities industries) and fully deregulated with its repeal in 1999. After the McFadden Act (interstate branching restrictions), which had been a barrier to mergers on a national scale,

Table 2.5 Financial deregulation and mergers in US., UK, and Japan

	USA	UK	Japan
1970s	70. Large time deposits of $100,000 or more deregulated		
		71. Competition and credit control policy (interbank rates become standard)	
		72. Interest rates deregulated	
			78. Short-term interest rates deregulated
			79. Negotiable certificates of deposit introduced
1980s	80. Regulation Q phased out over 6 years		
	80. Money market certificates become available due to deregulation		
	82. Deposit interest rates fully deregulated		
	82. Money market deposit accounts become available due to deregulation		
			85. Large time deposits of 10 million yen or more deregulated uncollateralized call market introduced
		86. Big bang/financial services act passed (over-the-counter sale of pension insurance products begin)	
	87. Glass-Steagall act partially amended (transactions between banks and securities firms deregulated)		
			89. Small time deposits of less than 10 million yen deregulated
1990s		92. [HSBC acquires Midland]	
			93. Interest rates on time deposits fully deregulated
	94. McFadden Act repealed (interstate banking deregulated)		94. Interest rates on liquid fund accounts, except for current deposits, deregulated
			96. Japanese big bang

(continued)

Table 2.5 (continued)

	USA	UK	Japan
	97. Interstate mergers between banks permitted	97. [Barclays NatWest sells its investment banking arm]	97. [Hokkaido Takushoku Bank goes bankrupt]
	98. [NationsBank acquires BankAmerica]		98. Over-the-counter investment trust sales begin
	99. Glass-Steagall act repealed		
2000s	00. [Chase Manhattan acquires JP Morgan]	00. [RBS acquires NatWest]	00. Dai-Ichi Kangyo Bank, Fuji Bank, and Industrial Bank of Japan merge
	01. [First Union acquires Wachovia]		01. [Sakura and Sumitomo merges]
			01. Credit card issuance begins
			02. Over-the-counter sales of pension and insurance products begin
			04. Securities brokerage business deregulated
			06. [Tokyo-Mitsubishi UFJ formed via merger]
			07. Financial instruments and exchange act...Over-the-counter insurance sales fully begin
	08. Collapse of Lehman Brothers...Subprime loan crisis	08. Collapse of Lehman brothers	08. Collapse of Lehman brothers

was repealed in 1994, banks were allowed to acquire or merge with a bank in another state beginning in 1997.

In the UK, deregulation of interest rates was completed in 1972. Accompanying the Big Bang, the Financial Services Act was passed in 1986, enabling banks to sell pension insurance products over the counter. In the 1990s banks stepped up their acquisitions and sales in a bid for survival and were consolidated into three major banks: HSBC, Barclays, and RBS.

In 1985, 10 years behind the U.S. and UK, interest-rate deregulation started in Japan with large time deposits. Interest rates were fully deregulated in 1994 when the cap on liquid fund account interest rates, with the exception of current deposits, was lifted. The government under Prime Minister Ryutaro Hashimoto initiated Japan's Big Bang financial regulatory reforms in 1996. The Financial System Reform Act went into effect in December 1998, enabling banks to sell investment trusts over the counter, and the sale of insurance products was permitted in phases starting in 2001. Commercial banks, which shifted their focus from corporate finance to personal finance after the bursting of the bubble economy, worked to expand their operations through mergers in order to avoid bankruptcy. In the end banks were consolidated into mega bank groups, including the Sumitomo Mitsui Financial Group (2002), Mizuho Financial Group (2003), and Mitsubishi UFJ Financial Group (2005).

On the other hand, there were virtually no regional bank mergers. As interest rates were deregulated, the base rate dropped, and the zero-interest-rate policy was introduced in 2000. The short-term prime rate fell to 1.5% and the 1-year time deposit rate dropped to 0.15%, forcing banks to operate on a low profit margin. The majority of mergers between regional banks that took place after the bursting of the economic bubble were bailout takeovers, and there were a number of mergers of small regional banks until around 2012. Struggling under the zero-interest-rate policy, regional banks merged beyond prefectural borders to form a large bank in pursuit of economies of scale.

While we will look at the reorganization of regional banks in greater depth in Chap. 4, one example of this initiative was the 2014 merger of Higo Bank and Kagoshima Bank to form a joint holding company.

Financial liberalization brought about the easing of financial restrictions and triggered financial reforms. Working in the sales planning division of a bank in my 30s and 40s gave me a front-row seat on financial liberalization in the U.S., UK, and Japan. In studying the workings of mega banks in the U.S. and UK, I was fortunate to be given an up-close look at their operations and have incorporated insights gained in the field into my current research on public financial services.

1.4 Postal Privatization in UK, Germany, and France

This section will look at the privatization of state-owned corporations and postal services in foreign countries and compare them with the Japanese postal privatization model.

1.4.1 Privatization in UK

During her first term (1979–1984) in office Margaret Thatcher worked to privatize about 50 state-owned corporations with the aim of downsizing the public sector, diversifying stocks by taking them public, and weakening labor unions. She privatized British Aerospace in 1981, then Enterprise Oil, Cable & Wireless, and more in 1984. During her second term (1985–1990) Thatcher privatized public corporations such as British Gas, British Telecommunications, and British Airways. As a result of these privatization efforts, the number of state-owned corporations was cut in half, thereby knocking 800,000 workers off the government payroll and reducing the number of public service employees to 1,000,000.

As a precursor to postal privatization, the Post Office (now the Royal Mail), a government department that had been providing postal, telecommunications, and postal savings services since 1880, was turned into a public corporation in 1969, and incidentally the Post Office Savings Bank was transferred to the Department for National Savings, an agency under the Treasury, and renamed the National Savings Bank. In 1981 the postal and telecommunications services were split off into a separate public corporation, and in 2001 the Post Office became a public limited company wholly owned by the government. The Post Office Savings Bank was established by the Post Office Savings Bank Act of 1861 (the postal savings system in Japan was introduced in 1875) and became the National Savings Bank in 1969. In 1996 it became an executive agency, which later became known as National Savings and Investments (NS&I).

All funds from NS&I are deposited with the government, which makes NS&I similar to the Japanese public financial system. The difference is that NS&I, with its assets accounting for only 2–3% of personal savings, does not compete with private financial institutions. The Post Office serves as a retail company that sells financial products and services provided by NS&I and private financial institutions.

The British postal market was opened up to competition in 2006. Upon the enactment of the Postal Services Act in 2011, Royal Mail Group underwent a reorganization. The act allowed private investors to own up to 90% of Royal Mail while allowing the Post Office to remain wholly owned by the government. As of March 2012 the number of Post Office branches totaled 11,818, with 373 of them operated directly by the Post Office. The remaining 11,445 Post Office branches were operated by individual agents. Among these branches 9818 are called sub-post offices, and are run by independent business operators who sign a contract with the Post Office. The postal sector is legally bound to provide a universal service, delivering mail at a uniform price anywhere in the UK. The financial sector, on the other hand, is not bound by any such obligation.

While the postal service in the UK, once originally operated by the government, was transferred to a public limited corporation wholly owned by the government, it remains a state-run business. The small-scale postal savings business, on the other hand, remained a state-owned financial institution operating partially in the investment sector and today has no business operating as a private financial institution.

1.4.2 Privatization in Germany

Privatization in Germany dates back to October 1990 when East and West Germany reunited. After the antitrust law was revised, the government's stake in Lufthansa was reduced, and Deutsche Bahn AG was created following the passage of a law to privatize the German national railway in 1993. Deutschen Bundespost (the federal post office) was split into three public corporations (the postal service, postal savings, and telecommunications). Under the Post and Telecommunications Reorganization Act of 1994, these public corporations were to be turned into stock companies wholly owned by the government.

Deutsche Post, Deutsche Postbank, and Deutsche Telekom were created in 1995. In 1999 the government sold all shares in Deutsche Postbank to Deutsche Post, making it a subsidiary of Deutsche Post. Deutsche Post went public in 2000, and Deutsche Postbank went public in 2004. Deutsche Bank started acquiring a stake in Deutsche Postbank in 2008.

Deutsche Bank continued to buy shares through a tender offer until December 2010. It eventually gained a majority stake (51.98%) in the company. By February 2012 Deutsche Bank acquired a 93.7% stake. You could say that the German postal savings business was fully privatized through Deutsche Bank's acquisition of its shares. Deutsche Postbank does not have a legal obligation to provide a universal service. As of the end of September 2011 Deutsche Postbank was Germany's tenth biggest asset holder, but its net assets, totaling 203.3 billion euros, are small.

In April 2015 Deutsche Bank planned to reduce its stake in Deutsche Postbank from 96% to less than 50% to exclude it from its scope of consolidation and eventually sell shares in the market. In March 2017, however, it decided not to sell Deutsche Postbank but absorb it with an eye toward enhancing its personal banking business.

1.4.3 Privatization in France

The National Savings Bank was established in 1881 following the enactment of a law to make the post office a savings bank.

In 1991 the government transferred its postal savings, postal service, and telecommunications operations to public corporations, La Poste and France Telecom. La Poste created La Banque Postale as a wholly owned subsidiary in 2006. In 2010, it became a public limited company. The government liberalized the postal market the following year. Following market liberalization, La Banque Postale obtained the authorization to operate financial services and started dealing in the same products and services handled by private banks. The French government owns a 77.1% stake in La Poste, which owns a 100% stake in La Banque Postale. This is similar to Japan's postal privatization model in which the postal service is simply the operations of a public limited company.

La Banque Postale is required by law to provide a universal financial service, just as La Poste is required by law to provide a universal postal service. At the end of 2010, La Banque Postale had the seventh largest assets total in France, amounting to 171.2 billion euros, which is relatively small.

The governments of all these countries were historically responsible for their postal services and postal savings systems, whether big or small. In recent years they have been working to fully privatize these services while enhancing logistics and financial operations in order to break free from the tough operating environment of the postal sector.

Additionally, the United States Postal Service is operated by the federal government, but it has been streamlining and downsizing its services. The U.S. postal savings system was abolished in 1966.

1.5 *Postal Privatization in China*

1.5.1 Postal Reform

China's postal savings system began in 1919 when the government of the Republic of China established a postal savings bureau. Three decades later the People's Republic of China's Ministry of Posts and Telecommunications took over the postal savings bureau's operations and placed them under the People's Bank of China in 1949. The postal savings business was eventually abolished in September 1953. Thirty-three years later the People's Bank of China resumed the postal savings business after the Ministry of Posts and Telecommunications decided to resume the business in April 1986.

In May 1995 the Chinese government initiated financial reforms and introduced the Commercial Banking Law, which applied to the postal savings business as well.

In 1983 the People's Bank of China, which was under the Ministry of Finance, was designated the central bank, and its commercial banking operations were spun off.

This led to the establishment of four state-owned banks, including the Industrial and Commercial Bank of China, the Agricultural Bank of China, the Bank of China, and the China Construction Bank. Today these state-owned commercial banks are still in operation under the Commercial Banking Law of 1995.

In March 1994, Sumitomo Bank sent me to China at the request of the Chinese government (headed by Jiang Zemin/Zhu Rongji) to participate in the commercial banking reform conference in Beijing as the head instructor. About 70 people from the People's Bank of China, four state-owned commercial banks, the State Administration of Foreign Exchange, and the China Investment Corporation received training at the conference and traveled to Japan 6 months later to get hands-on experience with Japanese banking operations. While China was experiencing rapid economic growth in the 1990s, its financial system had never been modernized, causing delays in payment and lending operations. The Chinese government probably believed that Japan's financial system would serve as a good model, even though Japan was facing a bad loan problem that came on the heels of the bubble economy's collapse.

In 1998, aiming to improve the fiscal health of its state-owned commercial banks, China separated policy-based financial operations from state-owned commercial banks and created three policy-based banks: the China Development Bank, the Export-Import Bank of China, and the Agricultural Development Bank of China.

The Export-Import Bank of China plays the same role as the Japan Bank for International Cooperation and the Japan International Cooperation Agency. The Agricultural Development Bank of China is responsible for supporting the agricultural sector through developing infrastructure in farming villages and developing agricultural projects. It stands in stark contrast to Japan's Norinchukin Bank, which, while specializing in managing the savings of agricultural cooperatives, provides virtually no support to the agricultural sector. After 2000 China started working on financial reforms with policies focused on stock exchange listings and an eye toward entering the global financial market, enhancing the transparency of corporate information, and increasing its capital adequacy ratio. All of the state-owned commercial banks made an initial public offering beginning in 2005, with the China Construction Bank going public first and raising 132.6 billion yuan. The Bank of China and the Industrial and Commercial Bank of China then went public in 2006, raising 110 billion yuan and 173.2 billion yuan, respectively. This was followed by the Agricultural Bank of China, which went public in 2010 and raised 148.7 billion yuan.

1.5.2 Listing (Privatization) of Postal Savings Bank of China

The Postal Savings Bank of China's deposit balance rose sharply in step with China's rapid economic growth in the 1990s. The total deposit amount topped a trillion yuan in 2004, and the bank became China's fifth largest bank in deposits behind the four major commercial banks. In the same year the number of post office branches that handled postal savings numbered 32,000, with 11,000 branches located in urban areas and 21,000 in rural areas. The postal savings deposit balance was growing at a faster rate than the bank deposit balance. The factors behind this rapid increase were similar to those seen in Japan. First, the interest rates for postal savings were higher than bank interest rates. Second, the postal savings system had a strong branch network. Third, the postal giro provided migrant workers from rural areas with a convenient way to transfer money. When interest rates were deregulated across the globe, China stopped depositing postal savings with the government in response to deregulation trends. At the same time the government set up the China Post Group in March 2007 as part of its postal reforms. Then the Postal Savings Bank of China was created as a wholly owned subsidiary of the China Post Group and was privatized (Table 2.6).

In 2009 the Postal Savings Bank of China started lending operations to diversify its asset management channels and in January 2012 changed its corporate status from a limited company to a stock company with the aim of going public. The bank became listed on the Hong Kong Stock Exchange in September 2016. The Postal Savings Bank of China went public on the Hong Kong Stock Exchange on September 28, 2016. In taking the bank public, the government tried to highlight that it was a private organization and a sound financial institution. The bank sold 13.9 billion shares at an initial public offering price of 4.76 Hong Kong dollars per share (HK$1 = approx. ¥61). This raised 56.6 billion Hong Kong dollars (approx. 730 billion yen). Prior to the initial public offering, the Postal Savings Bank of China raised 45.1 billion yuan by selling shares to strategic investors through a private offering in December 2015. Through this private offering the bank sold a 17% stake to 10 firms. Among them were global financial institutions such as UBS and JP Morgan, each of which got a 4.99% stake, as well as China Life Insurance (a similar institution to Japan Post Insurance) and China Telecom, who respectively acquired a 4.87% and 1.6% stake. As a result, the stake held by the China Post Group, the bank's holding company, dropped to 83%. Since China Post Group is under control of China's State Post Bureau, this 83% stake is practically held by the State Post

Table 2.6 Overview of Postal Savings Bank of China and Japan Post Bank

	Postal Savings Bank of China	Japan Post Bank
Established	1919 (abolished 1953) 1986 operation resumed 2007 privatized (as a private limited company) 2011 (becomes a stock company)	1875 2007 privatized (as a stock company)
Stock listing	September 2016 Hong Kong stock exchange	November 2015 first section of the Tokyo stock exchange
Service network	39,000 outlets (all agencies)	24,000 outlets (233 directly-managed)
ATM	56,000 locations	26,000 locations
Governing law	Commercial Banking Law (1995)	Postal Service Privatization Act (2005)
Total assets	5.5 trillion yuan (December 2013)	202 trillion yen (March 2014)
Deposit balance	5.2 trillion yuan	176 trillion yen
Revenue	145 billion yuan	2070.4 billion yen
Net profit	29.7 billion yuan	354.7 billion yen
Ratio of postal savings subsidizing cost to revenue	48%	55%

Source: Author

Bureau. It means that China still has a long way to go toward fully privatizing its postal service—although it is advanced than Japan.

Comparison of Japan Post Bank with the Postal Savings Bank of China in light of its public listing as noted previously reveals that they are similar in terms of the amount of capital raised and the percentage of the stake held by the government as well as how they are both fumbling around in the dark toward privatization. It will be interesting to see their next move and who takes the lead.

China's financial system helped the nation's economy grow because the People's Bank of China had postal savings deposited with it and used those funds to lend money to state-owned commercial banks, which made loans to companies. After the 2003 financial reform, the Postal Savings Bank of China was able to use new postal savings deposits at its discretion and started underwriting financing bonds to policy-based banks as well as commercial banks.

The problem with Japan's postal savings system is that deposits worth 170 trillion yen made mainly by local individuals are collected centrally by the government and used mostly for government bonds that become FILP funds for special public institutions. This flow of funds has not really changed from the old system that was based on mandatory deposits.

Furthermore, since postal privatization has not been fully completed, the Japan Post Bank remains unable to exert its financial intermediary function of helping private-sector corporate activities.

The problem with China's postal savings system is that, since the government has not separated fiscal and monetary policies for the People's Bank of China, it may become an obstacle to freeing financial activities in the private sector. While China's political system does not seem to be a perfect match with capitalism and democracy, consideration of the progress made with postal reforms in China and Japan reveals that the Postal Savings Bank of China is ahead of Japan Post Bank because it is a listed company that is moving toward full privatization based on commercial banking law while providing financial intermediary services to small and medium-sized companies. Japan Post Bank, which is still on its way to privatization, is operating under a special law that does not allow it to use postal savings to create credit through financial intermediary services, which is why it cannot catch up with the Postal Savings Bank of China. Operating under these circumstances, Japan Post Bank is moving toward privatization by going public, just as the Postal Savings Bank of China did, but the role it plays will be completely different until it achieves full privatization.

In *Kansei kinyu kaikaku to chigin saihen* [Public financial reform and regional bank reorganization] published in March 2015, I proposed the kind of institutional design Japan Post Bank needs to fully privatize so it can solve the problem of not being able to serve a financial intermediary function, which is the key to diversifying its asset management channels. That book was added to the collection of the National Library of China in June 2016. Table 2.7 compares the financial standing of the Postal Savings Bank of China and Japan Post Bank.

Table 2.7 Balance sheets of Postal Savings Bank of China (December 2013) and Japan Post Bank (March 2014)

Postal Savings Bank of China (trillion yuan)				Japan Post Bank (trillion yen)			
Assets		Liability		Assets		Liability	
Deposits[a]	1.2	Deposits	5.2	Cash and deposits	19.5	Deposits	(176.6)
Deposits at financial institutions	1.0	Allowances	0.1	Marketable securities	166.1	Allowances	(0.1)
		Other	0.1	(Domestic bonds)	(126.4)	Other	(14.3)
		Total liability	5.4			Total liability	191
Loans	2.6	(Capital)	(0.05)	Loans	3.1	(capital)	(3.5)
Fixed assets	0.1	Total net assets	0.1	Fixed assets	0.2	Total net assets	11.5
Other assets	0.6			Other assets	13.6		
Assets total	5.5	Total liabilities and net assets	5.5	Assets total	202.5	Total liabilities and net assets	202.5

Loans to individuals and SMEs: Postal Savings Bank of China 2.6 trillion yuan, Japan Post Bank 209.7 billion yen (6.8%)
Number of credit cards issued: Postal Savings Bank of China 5.1 million, Japan Post Bank 1.97 million
Sources: Japan Post Bank's balance sheet (via annual report) and Postal Savings Bank of China's balance sheet
[a]People's Bank of China

1.6 Privatization of Three Public Corporations

The rising tide of deregulation in the 1980s engulfed advanced economies, causing governments to liberalize financial markets and privatize public corporations. The Japanese government under Prime Minister Yasuhiro Nakasone (1982–1987) implemented administrative reforms with a focus on privatizing the state-owned NTT, Japan Tobacco & Salt Public Corporation, and JNR. NTT was privatized following the passage of three laws to reform telephone and telegraph operations in July 1984. The Act on Special Measures for Promoting the Rehabilitation of JNR (National Railways Rehabilitation Act) went into effect in 1980. Then eight JNR reform laws were passed in November 1986, under which Japan's state-run railway operations were privatized and divided into separate companies.

1.6.1 Privatization of Nippon Telegraph and Telephone Public Corporation

After three telephone and telegraph reform laws were passed, NTT was established in April 1985. The government aimed to enhance the efficiency of business operations through privatization, which would allow for more flexible management, as well as to stimulate competition in the telecommunications industry by harnessing the power of the private sector. Injecting 780 billion yen as initial capital, the government owned a 100% stake in the company and took it public in February the following year. The opening price reached 1.6 million yen per share and the share price hit a record high of 3.18 million yen on April 22, 1987. The government sold a total of 5.4 million shares through two public offerings, raising 10.2 trillion yen, which went directly into state coffers.

Upon privatization, the NTT Group launched a subsidiary, NTT Lease Corp., as part of its business strategy to facilitate operations in the deregulated telecommunications market and diversify business operations.

To circumvent arguments that NTT should split its bloated operations into different regional companies, the company spun off its systems department into NTT Data Corp. in 1988. Then it separated its cell phone operations with the establishment of NTT DoCoMo, Inc. in 1992. Pressure to downsize NTT's operations remained strong, and the Information and Communications Council proposed reorganizing NTT into a long-distance telecommunications company and two regional telecommunications companies by 1998. In June 1997 the law to partially revise the NTT law went into effect, and NTT was reorganized. NTT became the holding company, under which two regional companies (NTT East and NTT West) were established as special public institutions along with a fully privatized long-distance telecommunications company (NTT Communications).

This business and regional split implemented under group strategies resulted in the overhaul of a huge organization and enabled NTT to not only conduct its operations more efficiently but also introduce free competition into the telecommunications industry. The split and privatization of NTT produced the following five outcomes:

(a) Lower charges for telecommunication and dedicated line services;
(b) An open network;
(c) More streamlined, labor-saving operations;
(d) Profits from stock sales, dividends, taxes, and fees;
(e) Stable group financial performance.

1.6.2 Privatization of Japanese National Railways

After eight laws aimed at reforming JNR were passed, the national railway was divided into individual private companies that took over operations of the former public entity on April 12, 1987. JNR, a public corporation carrying a cumulative deficit of a whopping 37 trillion yen, was divided into six regional passenger rail companies and a freight rail company, collectively known as the Japan Railways Group (JR Group), as well as five related firms. As shown in Fig. 2.2, some of JNR's successor companies have been fully privatized, and some have been dissolved or merged.

Privatization of JNR solved its huge debt problem and rehabilitated railway operations through private-sector operations. Out of the huge debt totaling 37 trillion yen, 12 trillion yen was steadily repaid with profits from the fully privatized JR East, JR Tokai, JR West, and JR Freight, as well as Shinkansen Holding Corp. The Japanese National Railways Settlement Corporation took over the remaining debt totaling 25 trillion yen, which was later transferred to the government's general account. Out of that amount, 4 trillion yen was paid by the Railway Construction Public Corporation's JNR Settlement Headquarters, and 8 trillion yen was waived.

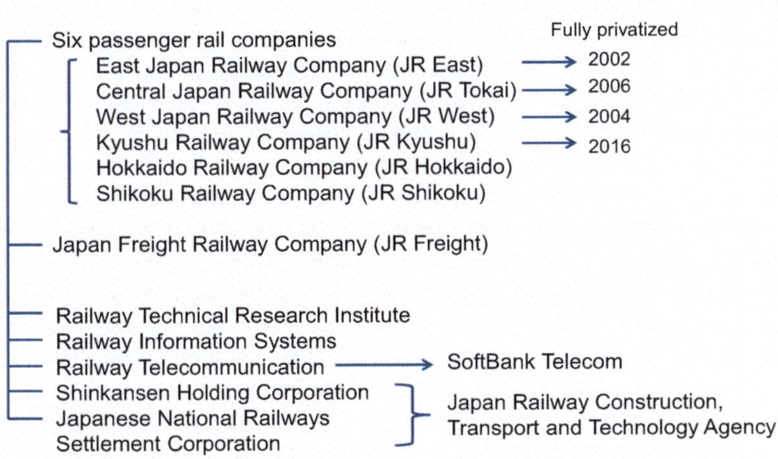

Fig. 2.2 List of Japanese National Railways' twelve successors. (*Sources*: Kasai (2001) *Mikan no kokutetsu kaikaku* [Unfinished national railway reform], etc)

Privatization of JNR brought about the following seven outcomes:

(a) Fewer rail accidents after privatization,
(b) Enhanced customer service,
(c) A better bottom line despite no fare hikes,
(d) Reduced labor conflicts,
(e) Expansion of related businesses,
(f) Improved efficiency via automation (Suica Card),
(g) Significant increase in passenger transport.

As a result of these improvements, four passenger rail companies, JR East (2002), JR West (2004), JR Tokai (2006), and JR Kyushu (2016), went public and were fully privatized.

While the number of employees hovered around 400,000 before the breakup and privatization, streamlining enabled the JR Group to pare that number down to 270,000, while 200,000 of those were transferred to the 12 successor companies. The breakup and privatization enabled the JR Group to build a more efficient and flexible organization while cutting personnel, a feat that its predecessor's powerful labor unions would have surely blocked. Privatization and reorganization of JNR by way of dividing operations by business and geographical area was lauded as an outstanding way to revive railway operations and provided a model for German and British railway reforms.

2 Integrated Institutional Design for FILP Reform, Postal Privatization, and Policy-Based Finance Reform

History has proven that using postal savings as a source of funding for industrial development works as a government policy. However, Japan has seen many problems arise from such a policy. For example, depending on the level of government involvement, bloated public financial services backed by government guarantees can put pressure on the private financial sector and cause the erosion of fiscal discipline, resulting in the deterioration of fiscal health. Private-sector businesses and financial institutions were faced with large amounts of bad loans after the bubble economy burst, which caused them to lose credibility. In turn, postal savings backed by government guarantees started increasing sharply. This resulted in an imbalance between the fund-raising arms of the public and private financial sectors and gave public financial services a leg up. Public financial services aggressively took over the financial intermediary operations of private financial institutions, which lost momentum due to a growing lack of trust, and expanded lending.

Just as we saw during and after the Pacific War, the government-guaranteed postal savings system, which served as a government fund raising function, became bloated and the balance between the public and private financial sectors was disrupted. At the same time, FILP and policy-based financial institutions, which served as the government's fund management function, grew as well. The public financial system's pressure on the private financial sector caused the economy to stagnate and tax revenue to decline, resulting in the deterioration of fiscal health.

This section will examine how the government fixed the imbalance between public and private financial sectors by privatizing public financial services with a focus on complementing the private sector or by reducing the ratio of total assets of public financial institutions or government debt to the economic scale (i.e., GDP) to adequate levels.

2.1 *Drastic FILP Reform – Challenges in Restoring Fiscal Health*

As discussed in the previous section, deregulation in the UK, Germany, and France resulted in free competition and financial liberalization. On the other hand, Japan's postal savings system and FILP made special public institutions extremely bloated after the economic bubble burst while state-owned companies distorted markets, causing stress on Japan's economic system. To change this situation, the government initiated a drastic FILP reform.

According to the Ministry of Finance, FILP

1. is a system for using public funds collected through national systems and credit, such as postal savings and pension premiums, to achieve policy objectives aligned with socioeconomic development and public welfare; and
2. uses FILP funds sourced from deposits made by the public rather than taxes, which are the government's primary source of funds, for making loans that are to be repaid with interest. FILP is different from government bonds in that it uses profits from FILP-funded projects to make repayments rather than future tax revenues.

The structure of FILP prior to its 2001 reform was as shown in Fig. 2.3.

First, individual postal savings as well as employee and national pension premiums are deposited with the Ministry of Finance's Trust Fund Bureau. Postal life insurance premiums and funds collected from financial institutions through the issuance of government bonds are used as funding sources for the FILP plan. The plan dictates that a budget must be allocated to public finance corporations, public corporations, special public institutions, and so forth, based on the funds' purpose. Under this mechanism, money invested in projects is paid back out of the profits they generate. According to 1996 data, a total of 328 trillion yen out of 356 trillion yen earmarked under the FILP plan came from postal savings (212 trillion yen) and pension premiums (116 trillion yen), while the rest was sourced from postal life insurance premiums. This means that a huge amount of funds were sourced from individuals. Attention must be given here to whether or not operators of projects in which FILP funds are injected are making a profit. Deficits produced by a number of

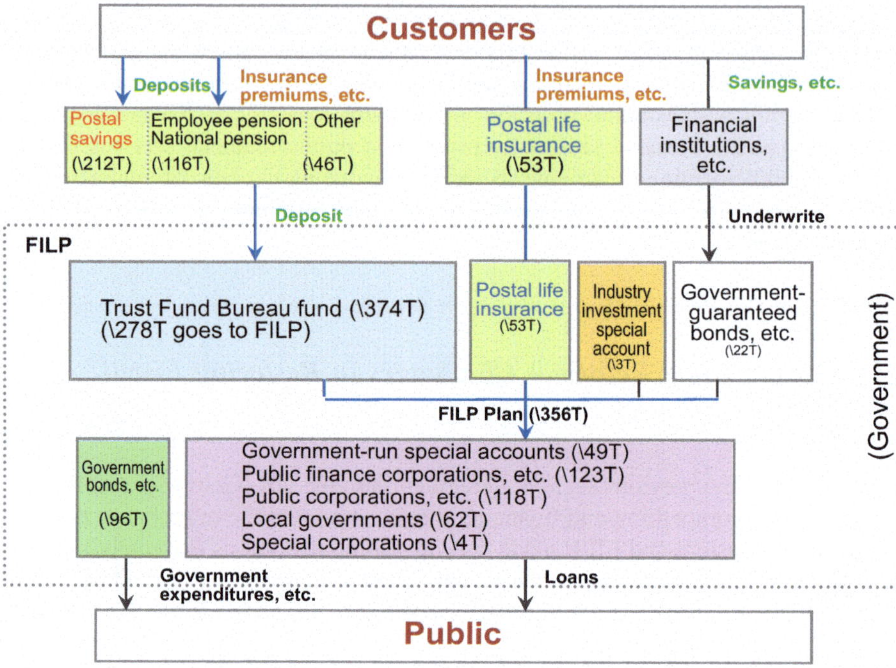

Fig. 2.3 Fiscal Investment and Loan Program (FILP) system, as of fiscal year 1996. (*Source*: Ministry of Finance Financial Bureau)

public corporations and special public institutions were a problem in the past. We have seen many bloated FILP group organizations survive like amoebae, merging a money-losing company with a profit-making one to make up for the deficit. We have also frequently seen FILP group organizations routinely employing the practice of *amakudari* (where retired bureaucrats are rewarded with cushy jobs upon retirement), and a lack of real governance is seen in the deficits. FILP, into which a huge amount of money went after the bursting of the economic bubble, was the birth child of the bloated postal savings system.

Faced with an urgent need to restore fiscal health, the government started looking into reorganizing and streamlining special public institutions in 1994, and later the Ministry of Finance looked for ways to drastically reform FILP.

In December 1999, the Ministry of Finance announced a proposal to drastically reform FILP. It decided to end mandatory deposits of postal savings and pension funds with the government and complement the private sector with FILP. In 2001 the ministry decided to shift to full discretionary use of postal savings and introduce FILP bonds and FILP agency bonds.

The Reorganization and Rationalization Plan for Special Public Institutions, which was approved by the Koizumi Cabinet in December 2001, specified 163 special public institutions and government-authorized corporations that were subject to reorganization as well as reform measures needed for each corporation. Under the plan some special public institutions and government-authorized corporations were abolished or privatized (turned into special corporations or private companies, or fully privatized), and others were turned into independent administrative agencies or other types of organizations. While the total amounts of funds under the initial FILP plan accounted for 38.7% of the initial general account budget in 1960, the percentage kept on increasing to 45.0% in 1970, 42.7% in 1980, 52.2% in 1990, and 67.9% in 1995. It gradually declined afterwards and dropped to 39.4% in 2001 and 17.9% in 2009 (Fig.2.4, Table 2.8).

A series of structural reforms brought a change to the way funds from postal savings and other sources were used, including mandatory deposits of these funds with the Ministry of Finance, which had been the norm for 115 years since 1885. In 2001 mandatory deposits were abolished, allowing for full discretionary use of these funds. This put a chip in the wall surrounding the public financial system under control of the Ministry of Finance.

When it comes to changing the fund-raising and fund-management mechanisms of public financial services that use postal savings for FILP and policy-based finance, there is no sense arguing which one to change first. Here's why. If you were to overhaul private financial services, you would change both the fund-raising and fund-management mechanisms at the same time (or together as one). Public financial services, however, have separate organizations for fund-raising and fund management.

To establish a small and efficient government, the government implemented administrative reforms with a focus on improving fiscal health while making a shift from public to private and from the central government to local governments in accordance with the General Principle of Administrative Reform adopted in December 2000.

The focus of the December 2001 Reorganization and Rationalization Plan for Special Public Institutions was reforming FILP and policy-based finance. In light of the public consensus, the primary reason for implementing the FILP reform was to ban *amakudari*, i.e., the postretirement appointment of senior officials to special public institutions. The second reason was to put an end to the sloppy management of special public institutions, and the third reason was to deregulate interest rates through regulatory reforms. Unfortunately, the public did not see the flipside of FILP. This includes such as aspects as higher interest rates on deposits and subsidized interest payments for FILP agencies.

In September 2003 Prime Minister Koizumi claimed that postal privatization constituted the very core of the structural reform and decided to implement postal service, FILP, and special public institution (including policy-based finance) reforms in an integrated manner. He vowed to shift postal savings from the public to private sector. However, he failed to map out a clear path to privatization at that point and did not indicate whether he would break up and privatize postal services, as was done with JR and NTT, or downsize its operations.

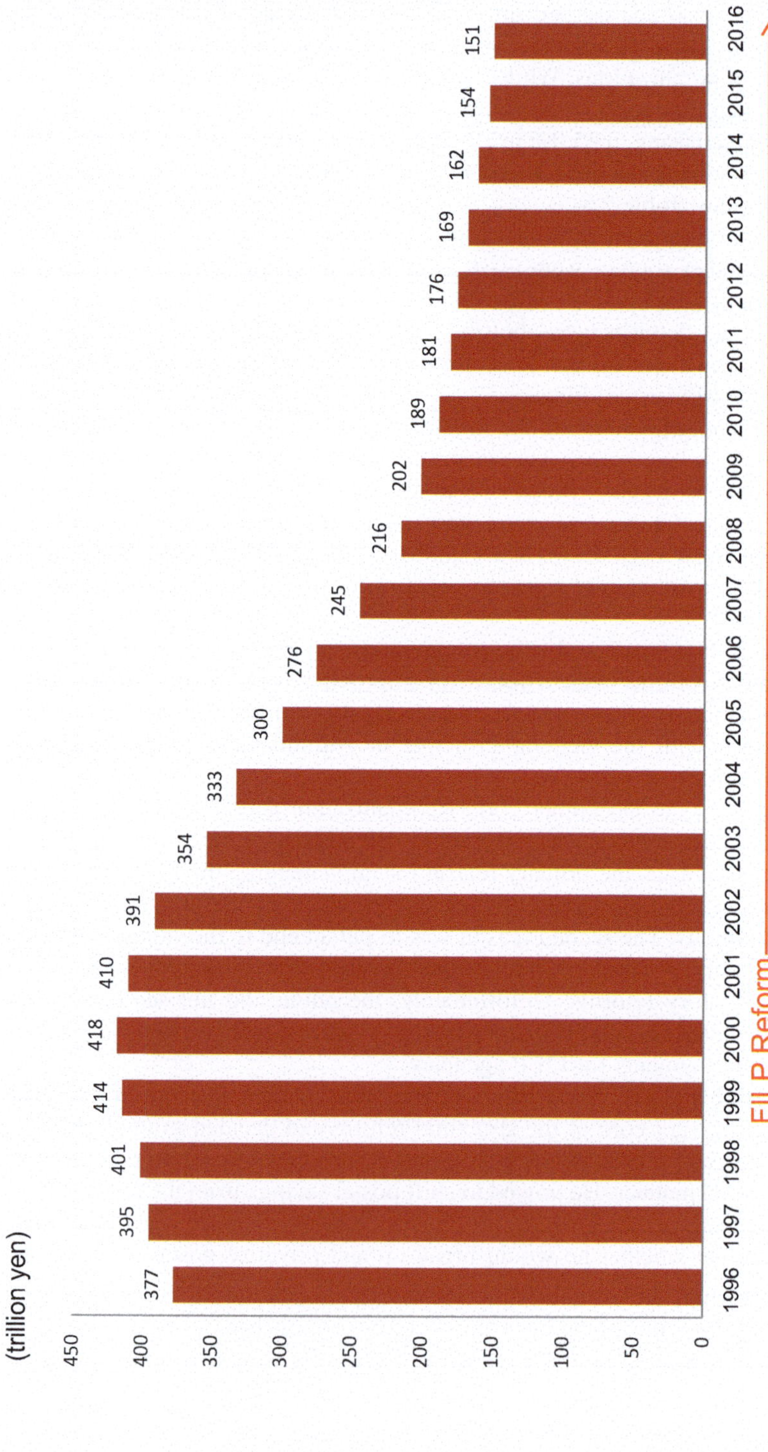

Fig. 2.4 FILP balance after FILP reform. (*Source: Nihon no zaisei* [Finances of Japan])

Table 2.8 Financing plan for policy-based financial institutions under FILP plan (100 million yen)

	1953	1973	1987	1996	2001	2008
Government housing Loan Corporation	158	5842	48,589	101,205	23,543	–
Japan Housing Finance Agency	–					6
Agriculture Forestry and Fisheries Finance Corporation	256	2488	3775	2350	1950	956
Japan Finance Corporation for Small and Medium Enterprise	130	6016	17,370	14,519	12,900	5684
Hokkaido Tohoku Development Corporation	–	680	983	1027	–	–
Japan Finance Corporation for Municipal Enterprises	–	1082	10,110	17,379	16,667	2949
Environmental Sanitation Business Financing Corporation	–	999	1799	3048	–	–
Okinawa Development Finance Corporation	–	550	1060	1912	1452	695
People's Finance Corporation	96	6149	18,838	28,800	–	–
National Life Finance Corporation	–				33,828	9512
Japan Development Bank	557	3857	8330	12,040	–	–
Development Bank of Japan	–				10,130	3700
Export-Import Bank of Japan	–	5360	3300	6500		JICA (loans)
Japan Bank for International Cooperation	–				4226	1430
Shoko Chukin Bank	–	1040	1235	762	350	–
Total						24,932

Source: Ministry of Finance data
Underline: peaks

2.2 *Postal Privatization and the Postal Savings Bank – Problems of the Fund-Raising Function*

The postal privatization policy for reforming postal services was first examined in 1982 by the government under Prime Minister Nakasone. At that time the government decided to privatize three public corporations based on a report authored by the Provisional Commission for Administrative Reform, which was headed by Keidanren (Japan Business Federation) chairman, Toshio Doko. In 1985 the Japan Tobacco & Salt Public Corp. and NTT became private companies and were renamed Japan Tobacco Inc. and Nippon Telegraph and Telephone Corp., respectively. JNR was broken up into seven regional JR companies in 1987. The government under Prime Minister Ryutaro Hashimoto (January 1996–July 1998) voted against postal privatization at the July 1997 Administrative Reform Council meeting but stipulated the abolishment of mandatory deposits of postal savings with the government and discretionary fund management in the Basic Act on Central Government Reform in

December of the same year. In December 1999 the Ministry of Finance announced its plan for a drastic FILP reform, which was implemented in 2000 following the passage of the FILP Reform Act.

In June 1998 the Basic Act on Central Government Reform went into effect, under which a central government reform was implemented beginning in January 2001, paring down the central government organization consisting of a cabinet office and 21 ministries and agencies to a cabinet office and 12 ministries and agencies. The Ministry of Posts and Telecommunications became the Postal Services Agency, an independent organ affiliated with the Ministry of Internal Affairs and Communications.

The government's structural reform policy gathered pace with deregulation, privatization, and so forth after the formation of the Koizumi Cabinet in April 2001.

In December 2001 the Headquarters for Promoting Administrative Reform formulated the Reorganization and Rationalization Plan for Special Public Institutions, specifying reform measures for 163 special public institutions and government-authorized corporations, including the Japan Highway Public Corporation (and 10 other public corporations), NTT (and 12 other special corporations), the National Space Development Agency of Japan (and 11 other agencies), the People's Finance Corporation (and 5 other finance corporations), the Japan Bank for International Cooperation, the DBJ, Shoko Chukin Bank, and Teito Rapid Transit Authority. The government decided to look into a policy-based finance reform based on this plan, and in December 2002 the Council on Economic and Fiscal Policy took reform of policy-based finance in a new direction.

At the same time the government also looked into creating a public corporation for postal services under its postal reform policy, and the Postal Services Agency became Japan Post in April 2003.

2.2.1 Discussions on Postal Privatization

In his general policy speech delivered at the 157th session of the Diet held on September 26, 2003, Prime Minister Koizumi spotlighted what he saw as three guideposts on the path to privatizing postal services.

- "Leave to the private sector what it can do." "Postal privatization is at the very core of structural reform."
- Carry out simple, efficient, and high-quality reforms for the postal service, FILP, and special public institutions in an integrated manner.
- Hold a nationwide discussion and introduce a postal reform bill to the Diet in 2005 with an eye to privatizing postal services beginning in 2007.

He also spoke at the 20th meeting of the Council on Economic and Fiscal Policy held on the same day and said the following:

> I've finally brought privatization of three postal service operations, which lies at the very core of structural reform, to the Cabinet's discussion table. This is the most important issue of all. Reforming FILP and special public institutions has not been possible due to political

> opposition. Neither the Liberal Democratic Party nor the Social Democratic Party have been willing to take it on because it could mean losing the public employee union vote. Political parties just don't seem to have what it takes to implement structural reforms. The unions have made it a taboo topic for both the Liberal Democratic and Social Democratic Parties. However, privatization is the policy foundation upon which the Koizumi Cabinet stands.

Postal savings, which constituted the core of Koizumi's structural reform policy and served as a fund-raising function for public financial services, surged, posing a huge problem. After the bubble burst, the balance of postal savings reached 170 trillion yen in 1992 and peaked in 1999 at 259 trillion yen. That's an increase of 89 trillion yen. The factors behind this jump included an influx of customers who switched from private financial institutions as well as an increase in fixed-amount postal savings because of the interest accrued once the interest rate peaked. While fixed-amount postal savings decreased due to the low interest rate policy implemented in 1995, the balance increased after a new fixed-amount postal savings account was introduced, bringing the ratio of postal savings balance to JBA-affiliated private bank deposit balance up to 54%. The postal savings special account turned into the red in 1998, and a fiscal deficit problem also surfaced, requiring the government to take action.

During the 21st-meeting of the Council on Economic and Fiscal Policy held in October 2003 Naoki Tanaka, head of the advisory panel on postal reform, pointed out that the postal reform was at the heart of structural reforms aimed at restoring fiscal health, maintaining financial order, and reforming local and central governments. Heizo Takenaka, Minister of State for Economic and Fiscal Policy, then proposed the following five principles for postal privatization.

- Revitalization: Make the shift from public to private. Absorb and integrate the three postal services into the private market system both in terms of the real economy and fund flow in order to revitalize the economy.
- Consistency: Align postal privatization with financial system, regulatory, and fiscal reforms.
- Convenience: Give full attention to convenience while emphasizing the roles postal services have played and should play for the public and local economies.
- Use of resources: Make sure that the post office network and other resources are fully utilized.
- Consideration: Give special consideration to hiring Japan Post employees.

These principles, aimed at countering opposition to postal privatization, were designed to deliver results while giving consideration to the opposing side's arguments on maintaining universal service and the post office network, cutting costs, streamlining operations by saving labor and enhancing efficiency, for example, and preserving jobs.

Substantial discussions on postal privatization took place at the 18th meeting of the Council on Economic and Fiscal Policy held in August 2004. Specific areas discussed included giving management more freedom and competing with the private sector on an equal footing, problems with the current postal system, limiting universal service to the postal service, ensuring transparency through company split-ups, and ensuring that the Postal Privatization Committee reviewed corporate organizations every 3 years.

At the end of the meeting Prime Minister Koizumi made the following remarks (excerpt).

> If you were to ask people if special post offices are necessary, most would say yes. That's why the number of special post offices have kept on growing. The Postal Life Insurance Welfare Corporation and Pension Welfare Service Public Corporation are building inns and member hotels in places where there is simply no demand but just say they are for "the welfare of people" and nobody would dare balk about it. The top priority of my Cabinet is administrative reforms. When it comes to fiscal and administrative reforms, everyone agrees. They tell me to take more drastic measures to restore fiscal health. When I actually do it, however, there are those who oppose what I do. I believe postal reform is really important. How can we revitalize the economy by effectively using the people's assets and money? Postal services can grow more if you let the public sector handle them rather than putting the public sector in charge. Everyone including postal tribe politicians should stop debating about whether postal privatization is necessary in the first place and just move on.

The minutes of the meeting reveal how the government was trying to develop a concrete institutional design based on policy proposals. The prime minister's remarks sent a clear message that struck a chord with the public and reflected general sentiment.

In September 2004 the basic policy for postal privatization was adopted at the 24th meeting of the Council on Economic and Fiscal Policy.

[Basic perspective]

It is vital that privatization lead each of the four functions of Japan Post to be absorbed and integrated into each of their respective markets, becoming independent under market principles. To this end, it is necessary that greater operational freedom and an equal footing with the private sector be ensured. At the same time profits and losses from each of the four Japan Post businesses must be made clear, and measures should be taken to ensure that the burdens of one Japan Post business do not weigh down the others.

[Framework of the organizational structure at time of final privatization]

<u>Separate stock companies will be established for each of the four Japan Post functions, and the decision to divide operations other than the postal service by geographical area will be left up to the new companies' management</u>. A holding company under which the four businesses will operate as subsidiaries will be established to ensure the integrity of management.

A corporate body to maintain old postal savings and postal life insurance contracts together with corresponding asset accounts will be established as the Japan Post's succeeding company.

[Modality of each operating company at the time of final privatization]

- Over-the-counter service network company.
- Postal service company.
- Postal savings company.

- Postal life insurance company.
- Corporate body succeeding the public company.

The modality of each operating company listed above will be incorporated into the Bill on the Privatization of the Japan Post.

[Transitional and preparatory periods]

- The period subsequent to initial privatization and up to final privatization (end of March 2017 at the latest) shall be designated as the transitional period (which will be detailed in the Postal Service Privatization Act).
- The period until privatization in April 2007 shall be designated as the preparatory period.

During the preparatory period, the government shall set up an executive committee, sort accounts into the four functions, and make arrangements for separating new contracts from old. The government shall also make arrangements to enter new business fields, such as international logistics services and over-the-counter sale of investment trusts. The government shall examine how facilities related to postal savings and postal life insurance should be operated after separation of the services among the four companies.

[Employment]

- Japan Post employees will lose the status of civil servants upon establishment of the new companies and will instead become employees of the new companies.
- Terms of employment will be developed in the process of designing new systems.
- Consideration will be given to employee morale and stability in industrial relations.

[Setting up an organization for promoting privatization]

A Headquarters for the Promotion of Privatization of the Postal Services will be established.

[Submission of bills, etc.]

The government will immediately start formulating bills on postal privatization in line with the basic policy. Additionally, it will work on detailed institutional design. The basic bill and related bills shall be submitted to the next regular session of the Diet, and efforts shall be made to achieve their enactment.

As described above, following the discussions that took place over the year after Prime Minister Koizumi's general policy speech in September 2003, the government set to formulate postal privatization bills and work on institutional design for the reforms.

2.2.2 Postal Privatization Bills

In 2005 postal privatization bills were passed by the House of Representatives but voted down by the House of Councilors in July due to some opposition from the ruling Liberal Democratic Party. In August, Prime Minister Koizumi decided to dissolve the House of Representatives in a strategic maneuver dubbed the "postal dissolution" and called for a snap general election in September. This election was virtually a referendum on postal privatization, and Liberal Democratic Party candidates who were split over the pros and cons of privatization contested one another for seats in single-seat constituencies. Voters, however, were not fully convinced about why postal privatization was necessary or how significant it was to improve fiscal health and reform FILP and special public institutions. They had to decide whether to vote yes or no on the basis of Koizumi's catchy slogans, such as "no reform, no growth" and "postal privatization is the heart of reform" (which were pretty much straight to the point).

Six postal privatization bills passed the Diet on October 14, 2005, and were enacted on October 21.

The six bills included (1) the Postal Service Privatization Act (Act No. 97), (2) the Act on Japan Post Holdings Co. (Act No. 98), (3) the Act on Japan Post Service Co. (Act No. 99), (4) the Act on Japan Post Network Co. (Act No. 100), (5) the Act on the Management Organization for Postal Savings and Postal Life Insurance, Independent Administrative Agency (Act No. 101), and (6) the Act on the Arrangement of Relevant Acts Associated with the Postal Service Privatization Act (Act No. 102).

All six postal privatization bills were designed in line with the basic policy adopted by the Council on Economic and Fiscal Policy and covered most of the proposals outlined in the policy.

Full privatization (i.e., becoming privately owned and operated), which is the main subject of this book, was stipulated in Chapter 2, Article 7–2 of the Postal Service Privatization Act (Act No. 97).

[Article 7. Shares of New Companies]

1. The ratio of shares in Japan Post Holdings Co. held by the government to the number of shares outstanding shall be reduced as soon as possible. However, the said ratio shall be more than one to three at all times.
2. Japan Post Holdings Co. shall dispose of all shares in the postal savings bank and postal life insurance company during the transitional period (October 1, 2007, to September 30, 2017, and the same shall apply hereafter).

In accordance with the six postal privatization laws, the government established a transitional company for postal privatization and developed an implementation plan for changing the status of the Japan Post from a public entity to a stock company.

2.2.3 Setting Up a Transitional Company and Developing an Implementation Plan

In November 2005 the government decided that a former mega bank executive with experience running a private company should be appointed president (and CEO) of Japan Post Holdings Co., rather than a bureaucrat or someone with only a background in politics. The fact that Japan Post public corporation's top two executives were appointed from the private sector logistics and manufacturing industries speaks volumes about how the government gave greater weight to Japan Post's financial operations, namely postal savings and postal life insurance.

In January 2006 Japan Post Holdings Co. was launched with an initial capital investment of 300 billion yen. A former top official of the Financial Services Agency and the Ministry of Posts and Telecommunications was appointed second in command of the transitional company. Other officers were appointed from both the public and private sectors as well as the Bank of Japan. Now privatization was ready to roll. What had to be done in the run-up to privatization was to develop an implementation plan for postal privatization and transfer Japan Post operations to Japan Post Holdings with government authorization. This involved breaking up the postal services into four separate companies under integrated management. In June 2006 the government set up four companies that would take over Japan Post operations upon privatization and appointed CEOs and COOs for these companies.

In light of the Council on Economic and Fiscal Policy's basic policy that aimed at shifting public financial services to private financial services and eventually fully privatizing them as well as the objectives of the fiscal and special public institutions reforms, the government used a personnel placement strategy (known as *tasukigake jinji*) under which the top positions at the four companies were periodically rotated between people from the public and private sectors. The government also used the same strategy when appointing top management positions under the policy-based finance reform. While the institutional design for full privatization was completed, some changes were made in top management during the implementation phase and more former government officials were appointed, undermining the vision the government initially had for the private initiative.

The laws for full privatization were proposed by Diet members but formulated by the bureaucrats. They wrote laws that embodied the intent of the government and designed relevant systems, but when completed, the laws may not have fully reflected the government's intentions because they were written from the bureaucrats' perspective.

I was involved in developing an institutional design for postal privatization and during the preparatory process had several opportunities to ask one of the bureaucrats (who was on loan) that wrote the postal privatization bills about the purpose of making the laws. When I found some discrepancies in the drafted laws, vis-à-vis private financial services, I asked him to make some changes. As I had expected, he flatly refused my request saying, "It's in the hands of the Diet." He then made reference to questions and answers from past Diet sessions, ministerial orders issued in the past, and so forth, leaving me no choice but to give up.

I found statements indicating that postal services would be exempt from the current Commercial Code, Companies Act, and Banking Act here and there in the postal privatization bills, granting an extraterritorial sanctuary to the postal services. This would make it impossible for the private sector to compete on an equal footing with the public sector. Furthermore, in developing a long-term plan for public financial services, i.e., the postal savings bank, the officials had a hard time coming up with an economic outlook upon which the plan would be based. They were simply unable to complete it. The former bureaucrats could talk about ultra-long-term issues but were hesitant to make plans for something that had to be materialized over the short run. They were unable to draft even a single-year's budget, let alone a budget for 2 or 3 years out.

To make things worse, the Postal Privatization Committee was formed in April 2006 to oversee the transitional company. Since the committee was mainly made up of scholars and researchers, preparation for postal privatization became a joint industry-academic-government endeavor. The unique characteristics of each sector shone through during the decision-making process. In the private sector, decisions are made by top management. In the public sector, nobody makes decisions. Instead, everything is done according to the law. In the academic sector, decisions are hardly made at all unless everyone unanimously agrees, which seldom happens because everybody is an expert on the particular issue and has their own opinion on it. While the opinions of the Postal Privatization Committee were finally put in writing, they were interpreted in different ways depending on the reader.

Preparation for privatization kicked into gear in February 2006. July of the same year was the deadline for submitting an implementation plan for transferring old Japan Post operations. The biggest job was to develop a long-term operational plan with the objectives of taking Japan Post public as soon as possible and fully privatizing it no later than 10 years after initial privatization, as prescribed by the Postal Service Privatization Act. To achieve these goals, the new Japan Post's two financial companies, in particular, had to obtain official authorization and expand their business operations. The Postal Privatization Committee would conduct public hearings to decide whether or not to give the green light to a new business proposed by any of the four Japan Post companies in light of their long-term operational plans. These public hearings enabled the committee to examine whether the new business proposal would put pressure on the private sector. This is stipulated in Article 110 of the Postal Service Privatization Act.

[Article 110–6-4. Restricting Postal Savings Bank Operations]

In cases where a request for authorization (for a new business) is filed as described in paragraph (1), the prime minister and the minister for internal affairs and communications must grant authorization if the said business is deemed unlikely to affect neither the appropriate competitive relationship between the postal savings bank and other financial institutions nor their appropriate provision of services to users, in light of the following matters.

1. The ratio of Japan Post Holdings Co.'s voting rights in the postal savings bank to voting rights of all its shareholders and circumstances that affect its competitive relationships with other financial institutions, for example;
2. The postal savings bank's financial condition;
3. In cases where a request for authorization is filed as described in paragraph (1), opinions of the Postal Privatization Committee must be taken into account.

Today Japan Post Bank is still at the mercy of this law when starting a new business, especially when it comes to housing loans and small loans. This is because the Act for Partial Revision of the Postal Service Privatization Act that replaced the Postal Service Privatization Act obscured the deadline for full privatization of the two Japan Post financial companies.

2.2.4 Implementation Plan for Transferring Japan Post Operations

[Privatization schedule]

Formulation of an implementation plan began in February 2006, and its outline was submitted to the government at the end of July of that year. While there had been a concern over possible delays in developing systems necessary for transferring Japan Post's operations to Japan Post Holdings, it became a reality on March 1 the following year, and the deadline for privatization, which was originally scheduled for April 1, was postponed for 6 months to October 1 due to a delay in systems development. The implementation plan was submitted at the end of April 2007 to meet the deadline for requesting authorization and was scheduled to be authorized by the end of July. As a result, Japan Post was dissolved at the end of September 2007, and its operations were taken over by the four companies, which were privatized on October 1, 2007, as well as an independent administrative agency.

[Outline of implementation plan]

(a) Long-term strategic vision
Under the plan, Japan Post Bank and Japan Post Insurance aimed to transform themselves into independent financial institutions while complying with strict rules and regulatory requirements for financial institutions, such as protecting customers and investors as well as ensuring fair competition while enhancing their expertise in risk management, investment management, and financial product development. The plan also presented a road map to full privatization, including the listing of Japan Post Bank and Japan Post Insurance on the stock exchange. The first phase of the plan entails taking the two companies public no later than 4 years into privatization. The second phase entails fully privatizing both companies and achieving sustained growth with diversified and enhanced revenue sources. The plan describes the third phase merely as one in which both companies would aim for a new growth trajectory after the transitional period for privatization.

(b) Financial condition (assets and liabilities transferred from the public corporation)
As shown in Table 2.9 Japan Post Holdings projected it would, on a nonconsolidated basis, take over assets totaling 9460 billion yen from the Japan Post public corporation. This figure included shares in subsidiaries totaling 9069 billion yen, with 200 billion yen for Post Service Co., 200 billion yen for Japan Post Network Co., 7669 billion yen for Japan Post Bank Co., and 1000 billion yen for Japan Post Insurance Co. Japan Post Holdings also took over assets related to facilities designed for publicizing the postal savings system (such as its string of hotels, branded Mielparque) and facilities for postal life insurance policyholders (such as their inns known as *Kanpo no Yado*), as well as the main office building of the Japan Post public corporation. Japan Post Holdings was set to take over liabilities totaling 1520 billion yen, the bulk of which was accrued retirement benefits totaling 1415 billion yen. Net assets were estimated at 7940 billion yen. Japan Post Holdings planned to issue 150 million shares, all of which were to be owned by the government at the time of privatization.
(c) Financial outlook
The combined net profit for the Japan Post Group was projected at 507 billion yen for fiscal year 2008 and 584 billion yen for fiscal year 2011. As shown in Table 2.10, Japan Post Bank's financial performance was based on a flat-interest-rate estimate (i.e., interest rates would remain the same as they were at the end of December 2006) as well as the government's outlook scenario where the interest rate of long-term government bonds with a maturity of 10 years would increase to 4% in 5 years after privatization. Under the government's scenario where the interest rate would rise, net profit for fiscal 2011 was projected to total 79 billion yen, 226 billion yen less compared with the flat-interest-rate scenario.

Japan Post Bank will be exposed to an interest rate risk when the interest rate rises because there is a greater likelihood of a negative spread due to a mismatch between long-term investments primarily in 10-year government bonds and short-term fund procurement primarily from fixed-amount postal savings maturing every 6 months. If the interest rate rises 3% as projected in the government's outlook scenario, net profit will be less than a third of what it would be if there were no interest rate fluctuations.

The implementation plan for postal privatization aimed at structural reform outlined above has some problems.

[Japan Post Group organization (relationship with four operating companies)]

The implementation plan defined the relationship between Japan Post Holdings and the four operating companies, as shown in Fig. 2.5, and provided a road map that they could follow. The plan describes the third phase, which begins after the transitional period ends on September 30, 2017, only as a phase for seeking a new growth trajectory. While in its basic policy the Council on Economic and Fiscal

Table 2.9 Financial conditions of Japan Post Holdings and Japan Post Bank, at time of privatization (100 million yen)

JP Holdings Co.				JP Bank			
Assets		Liabilities and net assets		Assets		Liabilities and net assets	
Current assets	1300	Liabilities	15,200	Current assets	2,219,640	Total liabilities	2,145,580
Fixed assets	93,300	Current liabilities	(1000)	Property, plant, and equipment	2140		
Property, plant, and equipment	(2240)	Fixed liabilities	(14,200)	Intangible fixed assets	610		
Intangible fixed assets	(370)	Reserve for employees' retirement benefits	(14,150)	Allowance for doubtful accounts	−120		
Investments (shares)	(90,690)					Net assets	76,690
Postal Service Co.	(2000)	Net assets	79,400			Capital	(35,000)
Japan Post Network Co., Ltd.	(2000)	Capital	(35,000)			Capital surplus	(41,690)
Japan Post Bank	(76,690)	Capital surplus	(44,400)			Total net assets	
Japan Post Life Insurance	(10,000)						
Total assets	94,600	Total liabilities and net assets	94,600	Total assets	2,222,270	Total liabilities and net assets	2,222,270

Source: Implementation Plan for transferring Japan Post Operations (Japan Post Holdings 2007)

Table 2.10 Financial outlook (2007–2011) for Japan Post Bank published in implementation plan upon privatization (100 million yen)

(1) Flat scenario: Based on assumption that interest rates would remain the same as they were at the end of December 2006					
	2007	2008	2009	2010	2011
Ordinary revenue	12,920	24,480	23,520	23,010	22,090
Ordinary expenses	10,750	19,130	17,510	16,920	17,020
Ordinary profit	2170	5350	6010	6080	5080
Profit after tax	1300	3210	3610	3650	3050
Balance of deposits (trillion yen)	186.9	185.0	183.4	171.8	163.8
(2) Government's outlook scenario: Based on assumption that interest rate of long-term government bonds with a maturity of 10 years would increase to 4% in 5 years after privatization					
	2007	2008	2009	2010	2011
Ordinary revenue	13,560	26,940	28,580	32,420	36,600
Ordinary expenses	11,400	22,800	25,300	29,940	35,290
Ordinary profit	2130	4140	3280	2480	1310
Profit after tax	1280	2480	1970	1490	790
Balance of deposits (trillion yen)	184.6	178.3	174.4	170.0	167.3

Sources: Implementation plan for transferring Japan Post operations (September 2007) and Japan Post Holdings (2007)

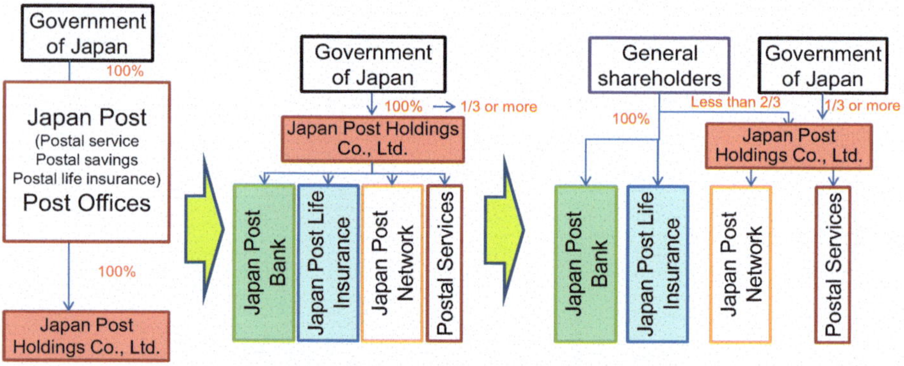

Fig. 2.5 Japan Post Group organizational evolution

Policy left the decision to divide operations by geographical area up to the new companies' management, it should follow the example of NTT Group and JR Group and spend the third phase looking into drastically overhauling public financial services by breaking up operations based on geographical area and other measures.

In light of my hands-on experience with this institutional design process at the transitional company for postal privatization, I'd like to review the important points of postal privatization and offer my insights:

- While postal privatization is mixed up with the privatization of three postal services, according to the postal privatization bill, only two financial companies were subjected to full privatization, and the postal service company was to become a special public institution under government control. Therefore, only the postal service company would be required to provide universal service under the policy. However, since it was discovered later that maintaining a universal service would cost too much and be too great a financial burden for the postal service, the government changed course and decided to require the two financial companies to maintain a universal service until they are fully privatized so that the postal service company could rely on their profits to keep its business up and running. Universal service was originally introduced by Maejima Hisoka, who set the flat postal rates for all domestic service (modeled after the British system). It should not be applied to the two financial companies (universal service is not a requirement for the privatized British and German postal banks, but it is mandatory for the French postal bank since it is state-owned).
- Postal reform was positioned at the heart of structural reforms aimed at restoring fiscal health, maintaining financial order, and reforming local and central governments. The goal of postal reform is to make the special public institution more like a private company to reduce the number of national government employees and enhance operational efficiency of the postal service. Privatization of the postal savings service could facilitate restoring Japan's fiscal health and normalizing financial order through FILP and policy-based finance reforms.
- While the basic policy left the decision to divide operations other than the postal service by geographical area up to the new companies' management, postal privatization aimed at decentralization and local government reform fails to heed the lesson the successful break-up and privatization of JR and NTT taught us. If the postal savings service were to be broken up into different regional companies, the Japan Post Bank, which serves a fund-raising function, and policy-based financial institutions, which serve a fund management function, should be integrated first so both functions work together as one. Once the service is split into separate companies by geographical area, each company should operate on an equal footing with private financial institutions; otherwise financial order cannot be maintained. I will discuss this in more detail in Chap. 4.

For now, let us look at some studies that were done in connection with how Japan Post Bank should operate after privatization, i.e., the third phase of privatization.

- **Previous studies on postal privatization**

Heizo Takenaka, a former member of the House of Councilors who was appointed Minister of State for Economic and Fiscal Policy and Minister of State for Privatization of the Postal Services for the reshuffled second Koizumi Cabinet in September 2004, published a book entitled *Yusei mineika* [Postal privatization] from PHP Institute in January 2005. At the beginning of the book he writes, "Postal privatization has been the focal point of Japan's economic policies and political issues. Surprisingly, however, there are virtually no books that look closely into postal privatization and discuss it straightforwardly as a real issue. I know this to be a fact from my own experience. I started attending the Council on Economic and Fiscal Policy meetings in early 2003, where I attempted to immerse myself in the discussion on postal privatization by listening to experts' opinions and reading a wide range of literature, but I rarely found written material that would be useful for Japan's postal privatization efforts."

Hiroshi Kato (1926–2013), who was a Keio University professor and the brains behind the Koizumi Cabinet, published a book entitled *Yusei wa hokai suru* [The postal system will fall] in January 1984 (Diamond). In this book, which he co-authored with Yoichi Sando, he describes the ideal form of postal privatization as follows. "The postal issue is not just about enhancing operational efficiency. Solving the postal issue will help the government turn its finances around and lead to administrative reform." In the epilogue, offering prospects for the national bank and a proposed solution, Dr. Kato writes, "After analyzing how our national bank operates without a president as well as the adverse effects of its operations, I came up with a possible solution, i.e., breaking up and privatizing the postal services, consequently downsizing the fiscal plan, and subsidizing interest payments for FILP agencies using taxes from broken up and privatized companies as well as increased tax revenue as a result of socioeconomic revitalization." This epilogue points in the same direction as the solution for restoring public financial health through privatization of public financial services, which I will discuss in Chap. 4 of this book.

Three years after the postal services were privatized (in December 2010), Dr. Kato provided a critique of Japan's postal privatization on his blog, Salumera, writing:

> When it comes to postal privatization, those who oppose breaking up postal services by geographical area will invariably say, 'If postal services were divided into regional companies, postal savings and postal life insurance businesses would wither away in the already battered local economies.' They were wrong. Postal services should have been divided into regional companies as a way to revitalize local economies. If operations were divided by geographical area, each regional company would do their best to raise funds in the region in which they operate and beat their brains out to come up with ways to best use those funds for their local communities. (snip) This would ultimately lead to decentralization, such as the *doshusei* proposal to divide Japan into regional administration blocs. The biggest problem in decentralization is money, but if Japan Post Bank was divided into regional companies, it would provide a source of revenue to each region. It's also important to note that most people living in rural areas, such as farmers, deposit money in Japan Post Bank, meaning rural areas have financial resources too. If Japan Post Bank were to be divided into regional companies, they could serve as equalizers to end the current regional disparity. Breaking up Japan Post Bank into regional companies would have given a big boost to the decentralization trend.

I agree with his conclusion. At the time he wrote that, the government was under the rule of the Democratic Party and no one could see where we were headed with privatization. In my talks about ways financial institutions should function in Japan in my special lecture course, "Introduction to Public and Private Financial Services," the studies done by Dr. Kato provide the foundation upon which the discussion is built. That's because Dr. Kato was the very man behind the privatization and regional breakup of NTT and JNR.

Next, we will look at research done by the JBA that provides a clear path for the third phase. When the postal service was transferred from the Ministry of Posts and Telecommunications to the Postal Services Agency in January 2001, JBA published a report entitled "JBA's View on the Future of Postal Savings" and presented its outlook based on extensive data.

– **JBA's study on postal privatization**

JBA's View on the Future of Postal Savings: Toward Privatization

Following the government's decision on postal reform in 2001, JBA published a report in which it shared its stance on postal savings, claiming that reducing postal savings was imperative and that operations should be divided into reasonably smaller units.

<Summary of the Report>

I. Introduction
Japan's postal savings system has deviated from its original purpose and become bloated both quantitatively and qualitatively. It simultaneously imposes a substantial burden on the public through "hidden subsidies," such as tax exemptions, and benefits from a government guarantee and other advantages it enjoys as a public service, distorting the flow of funds in the market and significantly interfering with the creation of an efficient financial market. (snip).

II. Basic View on Current Postal Savings System

1. Current Postal Savings System (Fig. 2.6)
The balance of Japan's postal savings reached approximately 255 trillion yen as of the end of December 2000 (accounting for 36.5% of the balance of personal savings in 1999). (snip) The postal savings system is increasingly expanding into areas of business that private financial institutions can fully cover.
2. Outline of Postal Reform
The current situation, where the bloated postal savings system deviates from the market principle and continues to grow through the provision of products and services that go beyond the scope of its role of complementing the private sector while an overt or hidden public financial burden constantly increases, poses a serious problem.

III. Evaluation of Vision for Future of Postal Savings
The government report claims that the postal savings system will play an increasingly vital role in ensuring a profit for small personal accounts. However, without specifying the scope of its role, it recommends the expansion of the postal savings service into new areas of business with the assumption that they fall within that scope. (snip) Implementing such measures while keeping

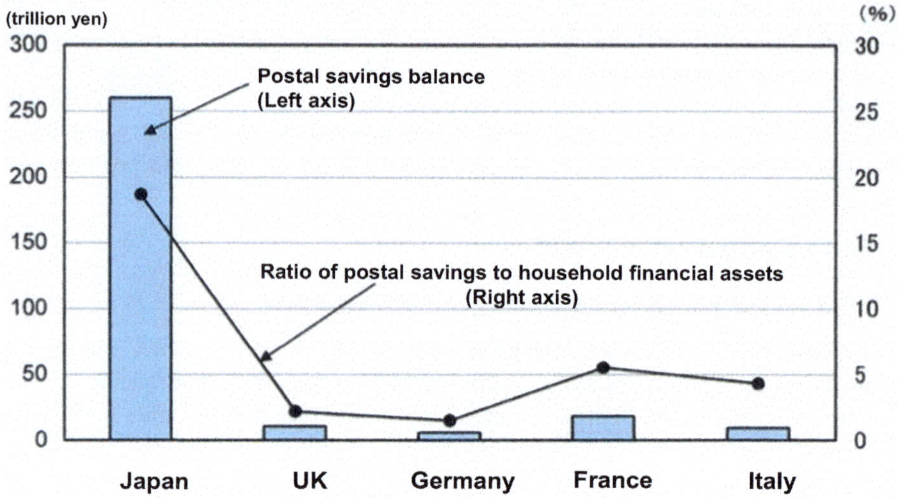

Fig. 2.6 Balances of postal savings in major Western countries
Notes:
1. Figures are current as of end of fiscal year 1999 for Japan, end of 1999 for UK, Germany, and France, and end of 1997 for Italy
2. Household financial assets in UK and Germany include those for nonprofit organizations
Sources: Bank of Japan's international comparison data, annual reports of relevant organizations, Office for National Statistics' Financial Statistics, and others

the postal savings system under government control violates the fundamental rule of "leaving the private sector in charge of the jobs it can handle." The vision for the future of postal savings can be achieved only by privatization of the postal savings system.

IV. JBA's Vision for Postal Savings

1. Basic Vision
   There are generally two paths to take: either keep the postal savings system under government control or privatize it. In light of (1) the national economy, (2) facilitating the Japanese Big Bang, (3) fiscal reform, and (4) global trends, JBA believes that the government should take the latter path, i.e., privatize the postal savings system.
2. Concrete Vision
   There are two specific steps to privatizing the postal savings system to choose from: (1) separating postal savings from other postal services or (2) keeping the scope of postal savings on par with private services after privatization.

(a) In Japan it would be ideal to separate the postal savings system from the postal and postal life insurance services and privatize to ensure fair competition.
(b) Keeping the scope of the postal savings system on an even keel with the private sector after privatization should enhance convenience for users as the postal savings system experiences revitalization (Fig. 2.7).

1. Preliminary privatization phase (snip)
2. Privatization phase
   The postal savings system is privatized once the balance of postal savings is substantially reduced. The following options are possible.

   (i) Conventional private bank model

      (a) Regional operation model
      The postal savings system is privatized after it is split into smaller units to ensure fair competition with existing private financial institutions.
      (b) Central operation model
      The scale of the postal savings system must be reduced to a level where fair competition with existing private financial institutions can be ensured. This is prior to privatizing it as a centrally operated bank.

   (ii) Upper fund management organization model (financial institution with a fund management organization)

      (a) Operational know-how building phase
      Post office banks are created in different municipalities by grouping a certain number of post offices, and the upper organization manages the funds raised.
      (b) Full-scale break-up and privatization phase
      To ensure fair competition with private financial institutions, the upper organization is divided into smaller block units and postal savings banks operating under its umbrella are reorganized.
      Each bank manages funds and deposits surplus funds with the upper organization in its block.
      (Source: Japanese Bankers Association)

Here's my take on the JBA report outlined above.

JBA's basic view is still valid in the context of today's financial markets because the postal savings system has deviated from its original purpose and become extremely bloated and needs to be downsized as much as possible so the huge amount of money tied up in the system can be fed back into the market to make it more efficient.

The Vision for the Future of Postal Savings, the final report of the Postal Services Council published in June 1997, proposed enhancing services and streamlining operations while maintaining or expanding the existing system and concluded that privatization of the three postal services was impossible. The report also pointed out

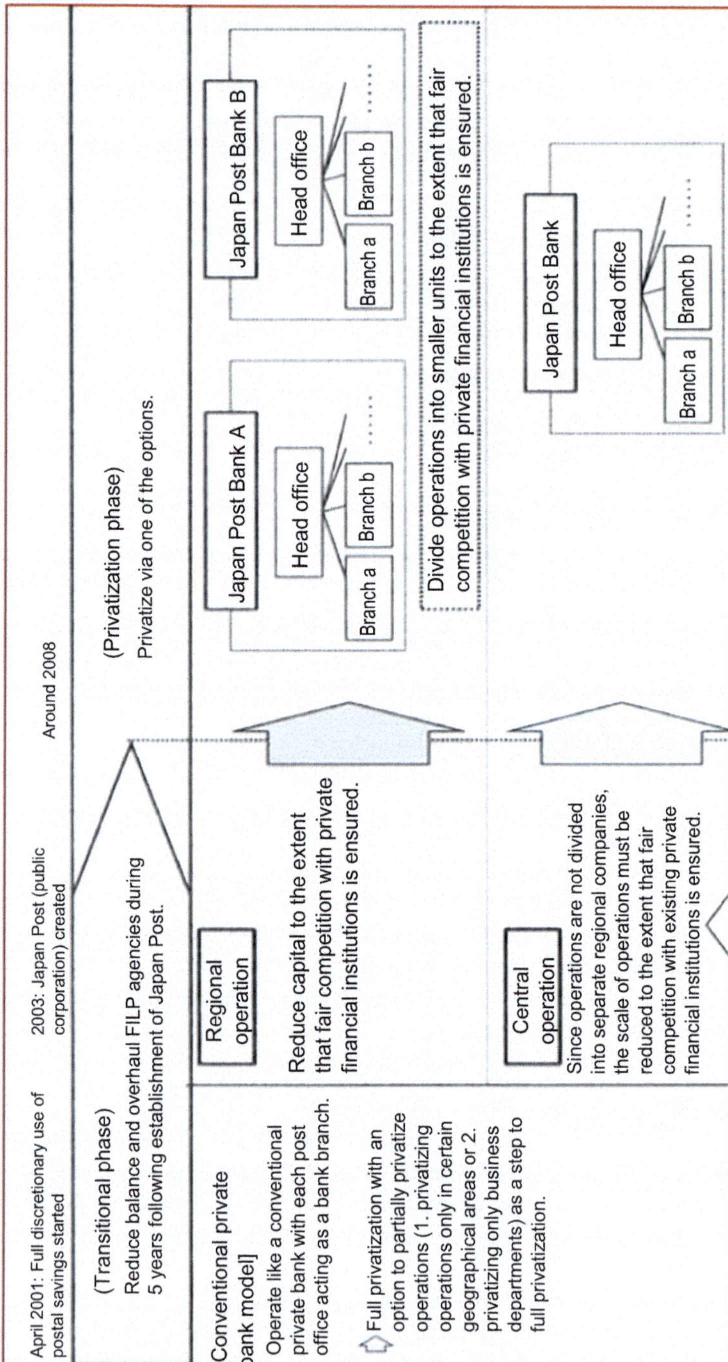

Fig. 2.7 Big picture of postal savings privatization options

that there were 554 municipalities where no private financial institutions were in operation and that 80% of post offices were running in the red and could not be sustained by the private sector, representing drawbacks for privatization. In response to this report, JBA claimed that various roadblocks to privatization could be surmounted. Naturally another reasonable prerequisite for privatization is allowing the private sector to compete on an equal footing. Today's Japan Post Bank cannot have a clear vision for new businesses and services as long as its privatization remains a mere illusion. Full privatization is the only solution.

In response to the Vision for the Future of Postal Savings, JBA proposed a phased shift to a private company in its 2001 report, and now the phase of turning the postal service into a public company has been completed. Let us take a look at the full privatization scenario.

Specifically, JBA proposed that the postal savings system be broken up into regional companies and privatized as a private banking service after having been divided into smaller units or downsized so that fair competition with existing private financial institutions could be ensured. This proposal sounds just like one of the possible solutions I have come up with, namely, the super-regional bank model, which I will discuss later in this book along with its institutional design.

Next, the central operation model, which seeks to create a national bank and downsize operations as much as possible, corresponds to my narrow bank model. This is transaction banking via a national network with separate services for ordinary savings and time deposit accounts (e.g., Britain's postal privatization).

Although it may not have been so back then, the upper fund management organization model is similar to the Norinchukin Bank–credit federation (Shinnoren)–Japan Agricultural Cooperative (JA) model. The so-called Norinchukin model has a lot of drawbacks since it makes the bank like a political organization, where former *zoku-giin* (party faction Diet members) are appointed to executive positions via the *amakudari* practice. This model would neither make full privatization possible nor create an efficient and fair private financial market.

The best choice in my opinion would be the JBA-recommended regionally operated private bank model.

Back in the preprivatization era, Dr. Hiroshi Kato urged then-Minister of State Heizo Takenaka to break up and privatize the postal savings system. Dr. Kato said that if the primary goal of privatization was giving postal savings back to the public, both the postal savings system and labor unions had to be split into regional units.

Many Japanese researchers of postal services have contributed to research journals published by the Yu-cho Foundation, but unfortunately no studies have proposed either how Japan Post Bank should be operated after its full privatization or an institutional design.

2.3 Reforming Policy-Based Financial Institutions – Problems with Fund Management Function

Having completed the drastic reform of the postal savings system, which is the money's point of entry, and the FILP, which is one of the points of exit, the Council on Economic and Fiscal Policy set out to reform policy-based finance in December 2002.

The policy proposal for this reform was made via the Basic Policy on the Reform of Policy-based Finance at the November 2005 meeting of the Council on Economic and Fiscal Policy and was approved by the Cabinet the following month as part of the Important Policy of Administrative Reform. In May 2006 the Act on Promotion of Administrative Reform for Realization of Small and Efficient Government (Administrative Reform Promotion Act) went into effect, and institutional designs for new policy-based financial institutions were ready to be put on the drawing board. In the following month institutional designs were developed for the DBJ and other policy-based financial institutions based on the Institutional Design for Policy-Based Finance Reform. As a result, in October 2008, the DBJ and Shoko Chukin Bank became stock companies as a step toward full privatization, and Japan Finance Corporation was created by integrating a number of policy-based financial institutions.

– **Institutional design for reform of special public institutions**

After emerging from the postbubble lost decade, the Japanese government embarked, in December 2000, on the task of reforming 163 bloated special public institutions and other related organizations. Following the passage of the General Principle of Administrative Reform and the Basic Law on Special Public Institutions Reform, the Special Public Institutions Reform Promotion Headquarters formulated the Reorganization and Rationalization Plan for Special Public Institutions in December 2001. Approved by the Cabinet, the plan specified revisions to be made to the operations and organizational structure of each of the 163 special public institutions and government-authorized corporations as well as overall reform measures to be implemented.

For example, the following five reform measures were specified for the DBJ:

1. Leave the areas the private sector can handle to the private sector whenever possible.
2. Increase the liquidity of loan claims and reduce the outstanding balance.
3. Manage risks associated with, for example, loan assets, and disclose information about reserves.
4. Specify who is responsible for determining interest rates.
5. Examine methodologies for evaluating policy-based finance and the mechanism for addressing evaluation findings in operations. Also, clarify policy costs.

The Council on Economic and Fiscal Policy started looking into specifics with a focus on complementing the private sector, minimizing policy costs, and integrating and streamlining organizations and operations. A draft proposal for policy-based finance reform was compiled by the Council on Economic and Fiscal Policy on December 13, 2002. The purpose of the reform is stated in the foreword as follows.

Japan's policy-based finance is a behemoth when stacked up against the systems of other countries and the increasing scale of it has caused the financial and capital markets' resource allocation mechanism to break down. Enhancing the efficiency of the financial and capital markets is a top priority for Japan, and a drastic reform of policy-based finance is crucial if we are to fully untie the hands of the private sector.

The council proposed the path to completing the reform in three phases. The first phase focuses on writing off bad loans (until the end of fiscal 2004). The second phase is a transitional period (fiscal 2005–2007) where wrinkles in policy-based finance can be ironed out. The third and final phase entails an immediate shift to the new system (fiscal 2008 and onward). The council focused on four steps to realizing ideal policy-based finance (as outlined below).

1. Carefully select focus areas: Carefully select organizations the government should r operate under the policy-based finance scheme. Sort them out according to operations and decide which ones to abolish or privatize in light of other policy instruments and functions that have similar purposes.
2. Downsize: Reduce the ratio of outstanding loan balance to GDP by half for eight policy-based financial institutions (National Life Finance Corporation, Agriculture Forestry and Fisheries Finance Corporation, Japan Finance Corporation for Small and Medium Enterprise, Okinawa Development Finance Corporation, Japan Bank for International Cooperation, DBJ, Shoko Chukin Bank, and the Japan Finance Corporation for Municipal Enterprises) with an eye toward normalizing the function of private financial institutions.
3. Reorganize: Review the organizational structures of the eight policy-based financial institutions with abolishment or privatization in mind. Next, dismantle the organizational structure currently known as the special public institution by the end of 2007. Then boldly integrate and consolidate any such institutions into new organizations that will take their place. Develop an institutional design that meets given requirements, such as making management responsibilities clear, enhancing operational efficiency, hiring people who are reform-oriented (both from the public and private sectors), ensuring financial transparency, developing a system for ex-ante as well as ex-post assessment and monitoring, and adhering to corporate accounting principles, to ensure strict governance.
4. Innovate new techniques for policy-based finance, ensure appropriate loan terms and conditions, and implement other possible measures as soon as possible.

The government made a bold step toward reforming bloated policy-based finance. It identified the problems facing the DBJ and Shoko Chukin Bank, which were set to be fully privatized, and provided a direction for the reforms needed to reduce bloated policy-based finance and restore the balance between the public and private sectors.

The DBJ (formerly Japan Development Bank) was established in April 1951 as a public financial institution wholly owned by the government. It was designed to complement private financial services by providing long-term loans needed to help get the economy back on its feet. During the high-growth period, the bank focused on boosting Japan's energy and transport capability while narrowing the economic gaps among regions through regional development. As a result, the bank's loan balance exceeded 1 trillion yen at the end of fiscal 1965. In the late 1960s and early 1970s the bank zeroed in on technological development, urban development, modernization of physical distribution, and preventing pollution, all with an eye toward enhancing Japan's ability to compete in the global arena. While Japan's economic growth slowed down in the wake of the 1971 Nixon Shock, the bank focused its operations on enhancing the quality of people's lives, ensuring a stable energy supply, developing a basic social infrastructure, and facilitating a change in the industrial structure right up until the bubble period. During the bubble years, as trade frictions with other countries increased as a result of the Plaza Accord, Japan faced an urgent need to increase domestic demand and revamp its industrial economic structure. Working against this backdrop, the bank focused on the area of energy and environment. The bank's outstanding loan balance topped 10 trillion yen at the end of fiscal 1991.

After the bubble burst, private financial institutions witnessed an upsurge in lending regulations and mounting bad loans against a backdrop of declining loans. At the same time, working in line with the government's large-scale economic policy, the bank continued to increase its loan balance by providing loans for social capital improvement as well as reconstruction efforts in the wake of the Great Hanshin earthquake and serving as a safety net by providing loans in response to changes in the financial environment to stabilize the financial system. Its loan balance peaked at 18,751.9 billion yen at the end of fiscal 1999.

In October 1999, following the merger with the Hokkaido-Tohoku Development Finance Public Corp., the bank was renamed the DBJ. The bank sustained investment and lending operations with a focus on support for regional revitalization, the environment and infrastructure, and creation of technologies and industries. As the bank became extremely bloated, competing with private financial institutions, it was selected as one of the organizations to be privatized under the Basic Law on Special Public Institutions Reform of 2000.

In June 2007 the Act on DBJ Inc. (New DBJ Act) went into effect as part of the drastic reform of policy-based finance. On October 1, 2008, DBJ Inc. was established as a privately operated but government-owned organization. The new DBJ born out of the New DBJ Act is different from the old one in that it does not rely on FILP funds but raises funds by (1) issuing bonds, including finance bonds, to institutional investors, (2) borrowing additional funds from private financial institutions, and (3) issuing negotiable certificates of deposit.

The Shoko Chukin Bank, like the aforementioned DBJ, became subject to privatization as specified in the Reorganization and Rationalization Plan for Special Public Institutions released in December 2001. In accordance with the privatization policy spelled out in the plan, while providing comprehensive financial services to small and medium-sized enterprise (SME) cooperatives and their members, the bank was required to review whether they were truly necessary in light of the circumstances at the time and establish maturity periods for future as well as existing loan programs along with guidelines for those to be abolished. The bank also had to (1) take responsibility for risk management of loan assets and disclosure of information about reserves, (2) specify who was responsible for determining interest rates in light of policy necessity, and (3) examine methodologies for evaluating policy-based finance and the mechanism for addressing evaluation findings in operations.

Following the December 2002 meeting of the Council on Economic and Fiscal Policy where full privatization of the Shoko Chukin Bank was proposed, the Shoko Chukin Bank Limited Act went into effect in May 2007, stipulating the operation and management of the new Shoko Chukin Bank during the transitional period until its full privatization.

On October 1, 2008, while maintaining the purpose and function of facilitating financing for SME cooperatives and their members, the Shoko Chukin Bank changed its status from a jointly owned financial institution to a special corporation (stock company) pursuant to the Shoko Chukin Bank Limited Act.

Leveraging its new status as a stock company, the bank expanded its full banking services, including deposits, currency exchange, loans, and guarantees, for example. In its efforts to maintain the core of the Shoko Chukin Bank's SME financing functions, the bank continued to issue bank debentures as it limited borrowers primarily to SME cooperatives and their members. It also allowed SME cooperatives to conduct business as a proxy for the bank. To provide more diverse services to SMEs, for example, the bank expanded the scope of eligible borrowers and eliminated relevant limitations on guaranty operations. The bank also lifted depositor eligibility restrictions so its products would be covered by the deposit insurance system. It was further tasked with the responsibility of implementing crisis response measures in the event of a disaster, economic or financial crisis, and others.

As described earlier, various restrictions were eliminated to transform the Shoko Chukin Bank into a private financial institution. These policy-based financial institutions served as an engine driving Japan's economic growth forward as they complemented private financial services during the high-growth period. Although they served as a safety net in postbubble Japan, they also became extremely bloated during the lost decade and continued to squeeze out the private financial services sector. In 2006 the government formulated the administrative reform bill in an attempt to shift gears and downsize policy-based financial institutions (Fig. 2.8).

The government created the Japan Finance Corporation in October 2008 as a wholly owned special public institution to take over operations of the National Life Finance Corporation, Agriculture Forestry and Fisheries Finance Corporation, Japan Finance Corporation for Small and Medium Enterprise, and the Japan Bank for International Cooperation. It was then decided that the International Financial

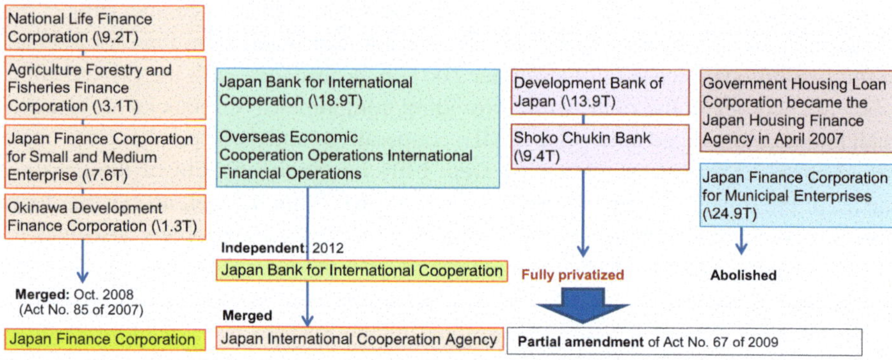

Fig. 2.8 Organizational reform of government-affiliated financial institutions: full privatization. Implemented in October 2008. 8 organizations totaling 87.5 trillion yen in FY 2005. (*Source*: Ministry of Finance data)

Operations of the Japan Bank for International Cooperation would be separated and established as an independent entity under the same name in 2012. The international trust and independence of international finance operations is maintained by the new Japan Bank for International Cooperation as it works to complement private financial services overseas.

The Japan Finance Corporation, whose mission is to provide focused policy-based financing as a government function, has steadily provided funds for business operators who were affected by the March 2011 Great East Japan Earthquake and flexibly responded to the needs for safety net services.

The institutional designs under the policy-based finance reform that focused on complementing the private sector and realize a shift from public to private pointed to two different paths. One was to fully privatize policy-based financial institutions and the other was to enable them to flexibly provide policy-based financing based on government policies with a focus on complementing private financial institutions. The former emphasized more transparent operations with a focus on risk management and profit. The latter focused on providing safety net loans as well as credit enhancement loans and responding to crisis situations by providing various services such as special earthquake recovery loans, requiring policy-based financial institutions to operate so swiftly and smoothly that they ended up carrying huge risk assets.

The Export Bank of Japan was created back in 1950 and renamed the Export-Import Bank of Japan in 1952. In 1961 the Overseas Economic Cooperation Fund was established and integrated with the Export-Import Bank of Japan in 1999, creating the Japan Bank for International Cooperation. It played a vital role in Japan's policy-based finance by providing loans to fund trade transactions that supported the economic growth of postwar Japan. Following the passage of the Act on Promotion of Administrative Reform for Realization of Small and Efficient Government in May 2006 and the Japan Finance Corporation Act in May 2007, the international financial operations of the Japan Bank for International Cooperation were merged with the Japan Finance Corporation on October 1, 2008, while its

Overseas Economic Cooperation Operations were integrated into the Japan International Cooperation Agency.

As initially planned, on April 1, 2012, the Japan Bank for International Cooperation was separated from the Japan Finance Corporation and was established as an independent entity under the Japan Bank for International Cooperation Act. Capitalized at 1.36 trillion yen, the bank is wholly owned by the Japanese government, but its governor was appointed from the private sector ranks. The bank is a stock company employing 536 people and operating 17 offices overseas, but it is considered a special public institution based on the Act on Japan Bank for International Cooperation.

The bank's mission is to complement private financial services and contribute to the sound development of Japan and the international society at large by providing financial services for the following purposes:

- Facilitating overseas development and securement of resources which are important for Japan;
- Maintaining and improving the international competitiveness of Japanese industries;
- Promoting overseas operations aimed at preserving the global environment, such as preventing global warming;
- Preventing disruptions to international financial order or taking appropriate measures with respect to damage caused by such disruptions.

The Japan Bank for International Cooperation gives priority to complementing private financial institutions through international finance operations that serve as a reliable source of funds for private companies looking to enter overseas growth markets. It serves one of the three functions specified under the policy-based finance reform, i.e., providing financial services crucial to securing resources abroad, which are vital to Japan's national policies and international competitiveness. I expect the bank to step up to bat and take risks that will contribute to Japan's growth strategy in overseas markets.

University of Tokyo Professor Yasushi Iwamoto conducted studies on the privatization of policy-based financial institutions in *Seisaku kinyu kikan kaikaku no ronten, mingyo appaku o kaihishi jikanjiku ni ojita kaikaku o* [Discussion on the reform of policy-based financial institutions: Eliminate pressure on the private sector and implement reform measures needed today], published in June 2002, and *Koteki bumon no kaikaku, kinyu 'chusho' igai mineika hayaku* [Public sector reform: Expedite privatization of financial services other than SME finance], published in September 2003. In summing up his findings on the future of policy-based financial institutions, Dr. Iwamoto writes as follows, indicating a clear path they should follow:

> When it comes to reforming special public institutions, we have several options, including abolishing or privatizing them, or turning them into independent administrative agencies. If a special public institution is privatized, the government can completely withdraw from the relevant operations and use accumulated resources for other purposes. That's why the reform should focus on privatizing organizations that no longer serve policy objectives. Public

> financial institutions that are based on industrial policies have already served their roles, so the DBJ should be privatized. Export and import financing should also be shifted to the private sector, so the operations of the former Export-Import Bank of Japan, which was taken over by the Japan Bank for International Cooperation, should be privatized. The Shoko Chukin Bank should easily be privatized since it has an organizational structure similar to that of a private financial institution and does not depend on government subsidies. Therefore it should be first on the privatization list since the need for sound private financial services is high in SME finance. We should leave crisis response to the National Life Finance Corporation and the Japan Finance Corporation for Small and Medium Enterprise for the time being.

While his view on the privatization of the Japan Bank for International Cooperation was different from the government's reform policy, Dr. Iwamoto urged the government to privatize the DBJ and the Shoko Chukin Bank for clear reasons.

After the bubble economy collapsed, the source of funds shifted from the public to private sector as private financial institutions lost credibility, resulting in a sharp increase in postal savings. The loss of credibility triggered an economic recession, and public spending was increased to stimulate the economy, resulting in an increase in the FILP balance due to public investments, tax cuts, and so forth. While private financial institutions lost their financial intermediary function, policy-based financial institutions increased non-policy-based loans, putting pressure on the private sector, and became more and more bloated.

As a result of these events, the balance between the public and private sectors was lost, and the ratio of policy-based financial institutions' loan balance to the economic scale (i.e., GDP) also became significantly lopsided. This growth was driven by the corporate sector's bad loans and write-offs by private financial institutions. As the fund-raising arm of the public financial sector continued to do well, policy-based financial institutions kept on financing the deficits in the central government's special account, local governments, and special public institutions. In other words, funds were not allocated for FILP and economic measures through private-sector financing but instead invested in public institutions, and that was a problem. If Japan was to break free of the vicious cycle that caused its financial markets' capital allocation mechanism to break down, the government would have to implement drastic policy-based finance reforms.

3 Goals of Financial Structural Reform via Privatization of Public Financial Services

3.1 Complementing the Private Sector with Public Financial Services and Reducing Their Assets

Public financial services exist to complement private financial institutions' intermediary function in the financial markets. In principle, private financial institutions should play the leading role while public financial institutions take a backseat. If public financial institutions deviated from their role of complementing the private sector, became bloated, and invaded the private sector's business realm during the financial turmoil of the postbubble years, they must be put back on track. If financial markets have changed over the years, however, or if the purpose of a policy-based financial institution that was created during the postwar reconstruction period was changed to remain in step with the sound development of private financial services, it could be privatized rather than operated as a public entity, even if the capital allocation was appropriate when it was established. The purpose of implementing the FILP reform, postal privatization, and policy-based finance reform in an integrated manner was to restore the balance between public and private financial institutions and reduce the total number of assets owned by public financial institutions to an amount small enough that they would be complementary to private-sector services. At the same time, it aimed to privatize public financial institutions that had been protected by special laws so that private financial institutions could compete with them on an equal footing under the same terms and conditions of the Banking Act.

As shown in Figs. 2.9 and 2.10, after the bubble economy burst, the balances of postal savings, policy-based financial institutions, and FILP kept rising sharply until the zero-interest-rate policy was implemented in 2000. Later the FILP reform was carried out along with the deregulation of interest rates, and the balances returned to what they were before the bubble economy of 2018. Since the nominal GDP remained at 500 trillion yen during this period, its ratio to each of the aforementioned balances changed in the same way they did. Figure 2.9 shows the ideal asset size of financial institutions in Japan. Combined assets of the public and private sector in the fiscal year ending March 31, 2005, prior to the privatization of special public institutions, totaled 1303 trillion yen, with the public sector (excluding agricultural cooperatives) accounting for 66.6%. Total assets for the fiscal year ending March 31, 2015, after the FILP reform and privatization, were 1570 trillion yen, with the public sector (excluding agricultural cooperatives) accounting for 74.4%. The factor behind this increase was a 7% decrease in Japan Post Bank's share due to the decrease in postal savings. Once full privatization is realized, they will all be governed by the Banking Act, and private financial institutions will have a 95% share of the pie, as shown in the figure, leaving the public-sector financial institutions (policy-based financial institutions) to focus on complementing the private sector. I will discuss steps to attaining this in Chap. 4.

3.2 *Improving Public Financial Services Revenue and Return on Assets*

Public financial institutions exist so that the government can assume the risk when loans are not available from private financial institutions or are only available at a low interest rate, and that means that they may end up as a public financial burden. In

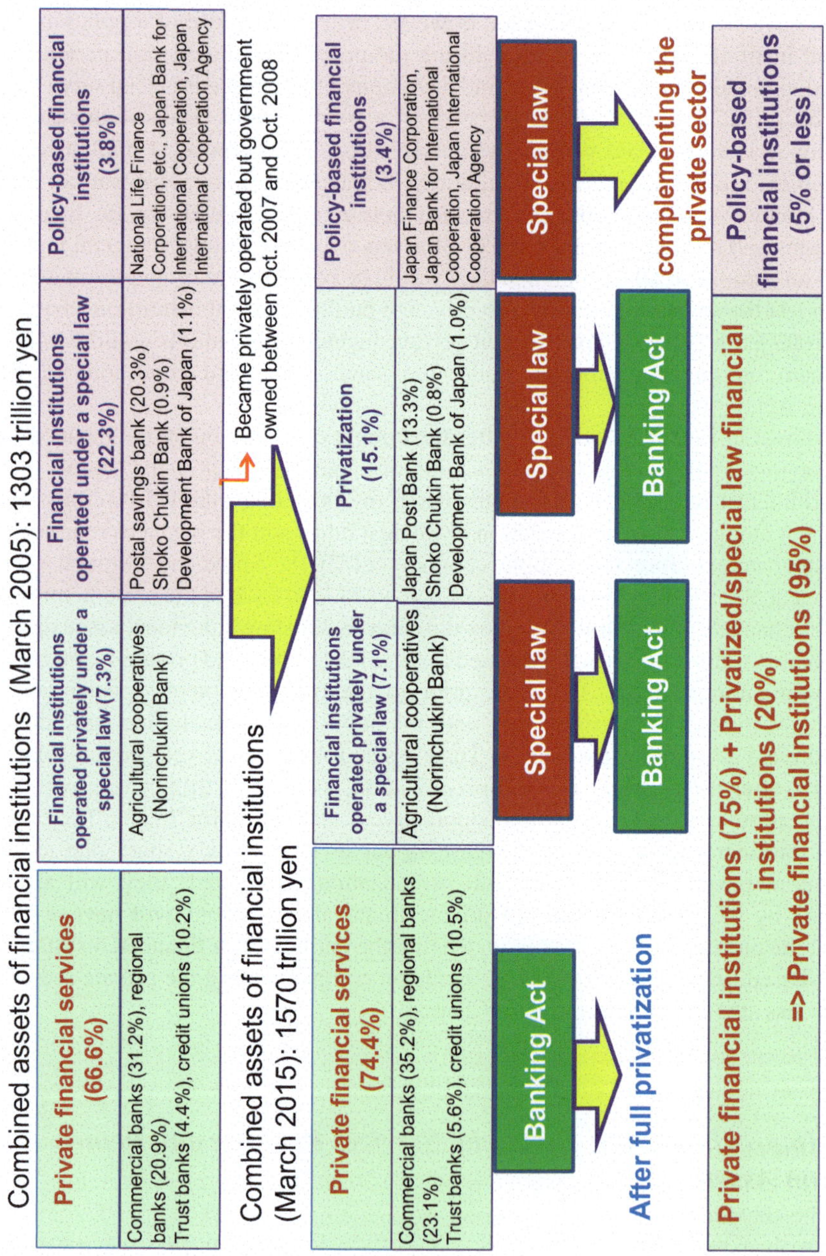

Fig. 2.9 Asset sizes and governing laws of financial institutions in Japan

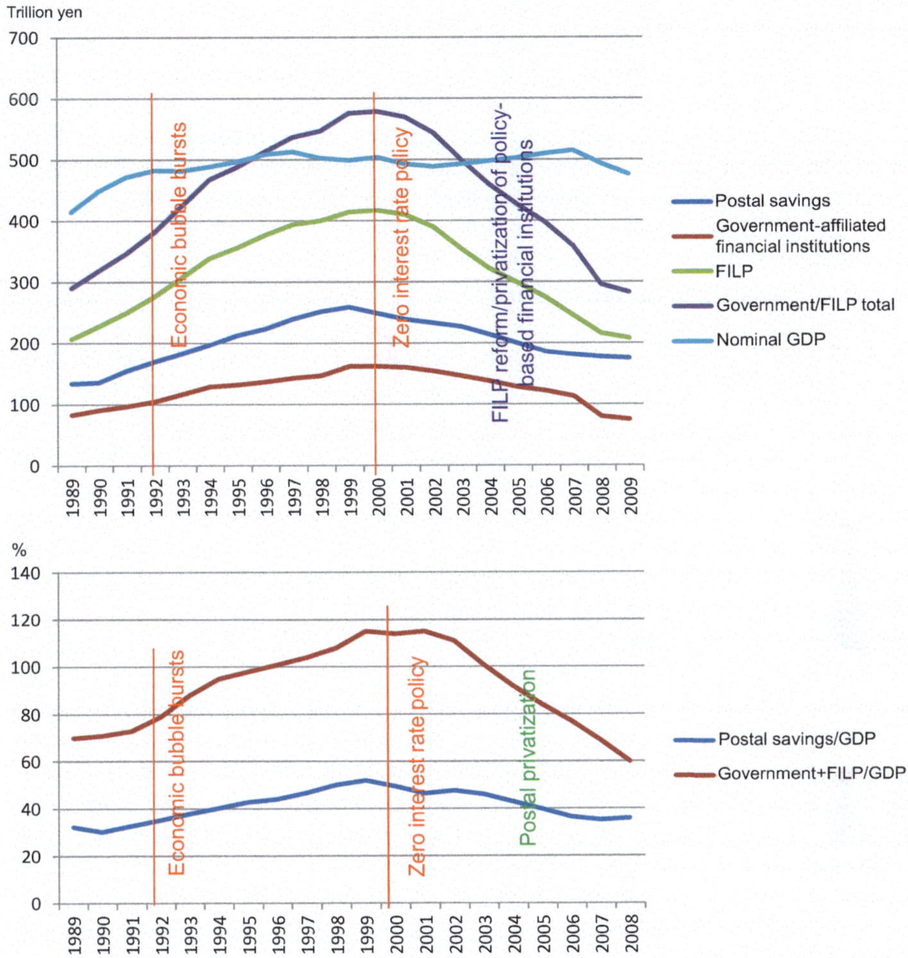

Fig. 2.10 *Top*: Postal savings balance, policy-based financial institutions + FILP balance total, and nominal GDP (1989–2009); *Bottom*: ratio of postal savings to GDP and ratio of policy-based financial institutions + FILP to GDP (1989–2008)

providing private financial institutions with subsidies that make up for the loss on low-interest-rate loans, or if they should run into the red, public financial institutions just have to take it on the chin.

In reforming the assets of Japan's public and private financial institutions altogether, we should look at ways to maximize Japan's financial revenue if we are to give priority to the national interest in a free and fair global financial market. To this end, public financial institutions should be privatized so that they can maximize revenue while competing with private financial institutions and increase return on assets (ROA). Safety net loans and crisis response loans for which the government assumes the risk of covering a deficit should be incorporated into the government budget to the extent that they are fiscally sound.

As shown in Table 2.11, the ROA of different types of public and private financial institutions significantly deteriorated after public financial institutions were privatized as well as between 2009 and 2011, when Japan was hit by two economic crises. If you look at the ROA for different types of financial institution before privatization, however, you can see that the ROA for the three privatized banks was low, at 12.2%, in the fiscal year ending March 31, 2008, compared with 38.7% for all private financial institutions that same year. Ten years later (in the fiscal year ending March 31, 2017), the ROA for the private sector was 33.7% while the ROA for three privatized banks rose to 25.3%, which was still low. Looking at ROAs for the fiscal year ending March 31, 2017, the ROA of all private financial institutions, from commercial banks to agricultural cooperatives, declined, while the ROAs for the three privatized banks are all different. Japan Post Bank's ROA is as low as that of the credit unions and agricultural cooperatives. That is why the bank should be fully privatized as soon as possible so it can diversify its fund management options, streamline operations, and improve revenue. The Shoko Chukin Bank's ROA is similar to commercial banks' but should be regarded as an abnormal value because of the illicit loans the bank made using the emergency financing system (which will be detailed in Chap. 3). The DBJ's ROA remained high after it was privatized. This is because, backed by government guarantees, the bank has efficiently provided loans mainly to large companies without taking any risk, often squeezing private-sector players out of the market. The bank should be fully privatized as soon as possible and compete with private financial institutions on an equal footing. As noted earlier, the amount of assets held by Japan's public and private financial institutions should be recalibrated in an integrated manner to create a free financial market where all types of financial institutions can compete on an equal footing to maximize their financial performance. Improved revenues of financial institutions in Japan will revitalize its economy and society as a whole, which will lead to increased tax revenue and better fiscal health (Table 2.11). I will discuss ways to improve the bottom lines of public financial services in Chap. 4.

Table 2.11 Analysis of ROAs of private financial institutions, 3 privatized banks, and public financial institutions. Total assets, ordinary profit, and ROA (consolidated basis) by type of financial institution (March, 2008–2012, 2017) (trillion yen)

		Private financial institutions						Privatization three banks						
Year (March)		Commercial banks	Regional banks	Trust banks	Credit unions	Agricultural cooperatives	Total	Japan Post Bank	Development Bank of Japan	Shoko Chukin Bank	Total	Policy-based financial institutions three banks total	Public financial services six banks total	Public and private total
2008 Before privatization	Total assets	409	385	61	140	99	1094	222	12.8	10.8	245.6	–	–	–
	Ordinary profit	1.9	1.1	0.50	0.13	0.22	3.85	0.26	0.02	0.02	0.30	–	–	–
	ROA (%)	45.7	38.6	82.0	9.3	22.2	38.7	11.7	15.6	18.5	12.2	–	–	–
2009 Collapse of Lehman Brothers	Total assets	427	288	63	141	101	1020	204	13.3	10.8	228.1	49	270	1302
	Ordinary profit	−0.6	−0.6	−0.02	−0.22	0.2	−1.3	0.39	−0.12	−0.01	0.26	−0.53	−0.27	−1.5
	ROA (%)	−14.1	−20.7	−3.2	−15.6	19.8	−12.7	19.1	−90.2	−9.3	13.2	−108.8	−10	−11.9
2010 After privatization	Total assets	438	294	63	143	102	1040	195	14.8	11.5	221.3	53.8	276	1315
	Ordinary profit	1.3	0.81	0.29	0.24	0.21	2.85	0.49	0.05	0.01	0.55	−0.90	−0.35	2.50
	ROA (%)	29.7	27.6	46.0	16.8	20.6	27.4	25.1	33.8	8.7	24.8	−167	−12.7	19.0
2011 Great East Japan earthquake	Total assets	447	302	65	146	103	1063	194	15.2	12.0	221.2	60	281	1359
	Ordinary profit	1.9	1	0.28	0.22	0.2	3.6	0.53	0.09	0.03	0.65	−0.66	−0.01	3.6
	ROA (%)	42.3	33.1	43.1	15.1	19.4	33.9	27.3	59.2	25.0	27.0	−110	−3.6	26.8
2012	Total assets	463	313	67	149	105	1097	195	15.2	12.2	222.4	62	284	1380
	Ordinary profit	2.2	1.2	0.31	0.26	0.17	4.14	0.58	0.10	0.03	0.71	−0.14	0.57	4.71
	ROA (%)	47.5	38.3	46.3	17.4	16.2	37.7	29.7	65.8	24.6	32.0	−22.5	20.1	34.1
2017	Total assets	554	367	98	172	115	1306	209	16.1	12.6	237.7	52	289	1594
	Ordinary profit	2.2	1.4	0.35	0.43	0.16	4.5	0.44	0.11	0.05	0.6	0.01	0.62	5.1
	ROA (%)	39.7	38.1	35.7	25.0	13.9	33.7	21.1	68.3	39.7	25.3	19.2	21.5	32.0

Sources: Financial statements of Japanese Bankers Association (2001), credit union associations, National Federation of Agricultural Cooperative Associations (ZEN-NOH), and government-affiliated financial institutions

References

Japanese Bankers Association (2001) *Wareware ga kangaeru yubin chokin no shoraizo* [Our vision for the future of postal savings]. https://www.zenginkyo.or.jp/fileadmin/res/news/yuchoshouraizou.pdf

Japan Post Holdings (2007) *Nippon yusei kosha no gyomu tou no shokei ni kansuru jisshi keikaku* [Implementation plan for transferring Japan post operations]. https://www.yuseimineika.go.jp/iinkai/dai26/siryou1_2.pdf

Kasai, Yoshiyuki (2001) *Mikan no kokutetsu kaikaku* [Unfinished national railway reform]. Toyo Keizai Inc., Tokyo

Chapter 3
Progress After the Privatization of Public Financial Services and Trends by Type of Financial Institution: Listing of Japan Post Bank and Reorganization of Regional Banks

In October 2007, five companies affiliated with the Japan Post Group became stock companies wholly owned by the government, i.e., privately operated but government owned companies. In October of the following year, policy-based financial institutions (Development Bank of Japan, Shoko Chukin Bank, and Japan Finance Corporation) also became privately operated but government-owned stock companies.

I was in New York in early September 2008. Serving as the Japan Post Bank director in charge of new businesses, I visited the headquarters of Mastercard to sign a licensing agreement and the headquarters of AIG and MetLife to make deals for handling variable-annuity contracts. While everything seemed calm while I was in New York, as soon as I returned to Japan Lehman Brothers filed for bankruptcy on September 15 in the wake of the subprime mortgage crisis.

1 Postprivatization Economic Trends in Japan (2008–2017)

The Japanese economy was hit hard by the global recession triggered by the collapse of Lehman Brothers, and the nominal GDP for fiscal 2008 fell 4.6% year on year and by 3.7% in real terms. Nominal GDP declined again in fiscal 2009. Although it picked up slightly in fiscal 2010 with an increase of 1.4%, it dropped 1.3% year on year the following year due to the March 2011 Great East Japan Earthquake. Nominal GDP climbed back to the previous year's level in 2012 as public investments increased due to tax hikes to fund reconstruction efforts in areas affected by the Great East Japan Earthquake.

Electronic supplementary material The online version of this chapter (https://doi.org/10.1007/978-981-15-1408-1_3) contains supplementary material, which is available to authorized users.

A. Uno, *Japan Post Bank*, https://doi.org/10.1007/978-981-15-1408-1_3

The nuclear plant accident in Fukushima that was caused by the earthquake raised alarm over Japan's energy policy, and voters were left with the task of electing leaders who would implement a comprehensive reform of social security and taxes. The Liberal Democratic Party then came back to power in December 2012. The government led by Prime Minister Abe worked on reviving the economy via his Abenomics monetary and fiscal policies.

Beginning in November 2012 the yen depreciated about 17% against the dollar, and stock prices rose 45% in fiscal 2013. This resulted in improved bottom lines primarily for big companies. The increase in stock prices drove consumer spending up about 1%, mainly among the elderly. Under the September 2013 monetary policy, the Bank of Japan introduced quantitative and qualitative monetary easing and implemented drastic monetary easing measures with an eye toward substantially expanding the monetary base. Manufacturers increased overseas production and stepped up efforts to expand into overseas markets with the aim of capturing local demand. The Bank of Japan's monetary easing measures helped Japanese companies expand their overseas operations and gain vitality in the global market. They also boosted direct investment balances of financial and insurance companies as well as wholesalers, retailers, and others. As a result, nominal GDP for fiscal 2013 was up 2.6% both on a year-on-year basis and in real terms. Nominal gross national income (GNI) also rose 3.2% year on year, indicating that the success of the growth strategy lay overseas.

While nominal GDP for fiscal 2014 rose 2.0% year on year, the consumption tax hike implemented in April 2014, which saw the tax rate jump from 5% to 8%, put a damper on consumer spending, causing it to decline significantly. Corporate earnings, however, remained upbeat as companies enjoyed growing revenue and profits due to the last-minute uptick in demand prior to the consumption tax hike as well as the weak yen. The Bank of Japan's policy to buy a large amount of government bonds helped interest rates, especially long-term interest rates, stay low. After the quantitative and qualitative monetary easing policy was introduced, the percentage of the Bank of Japan's current deposits climbed while the percentage of government bonds fell significantly.

Nominal GDP rose 2.7% year over year in fiscal 2015 for the largest increase in 24 years. The drop in oil prices started to benefit trade terms in late 2014, buoying the nominal GNI a substantial 2.8%. On top of that robust corporate earnings led to higher wages that put the economy on an upward trajectory. Financial institutions other than the Bank of Japan shifted from government bonds to other assets, and domestic banks rebalanced their portfolios. While the ratio of government debt to GDP had continued to increase due to deflation, growth started to slow down in fiscal 2011. Japan needed integrated measures to revive its economy and fiscal health.

The growth of nominal GDP and nominal GNI slowed down in fiscal 2016, with the former increasing by a mere 1.1% and the latter by just 0.5% year on year. Then Britain's vote for Brexit cast a shadow of uncertainty over the entire global economy. Private companies cut their capital expenditures, delaying measures designed to cultivate future growth, and experienced stagnant financial performance. In January 2016 the Bank of Japan introduced quantitative and qualitative monetary easing coupled with a negative interest rate, causing domestic banks to see their net interest margins drop and their financial intermediary functions deteriorate. In the end, both their fund management revenues and net business profit declined. Finally, in the second half of 2016, the corporate sector started to see corporate performance improve as the global economy recovered.

The structure of consumer spending began to change in Japan. The household structure was altered as a result of an increase in single-person households, the graying of the population, and other factors, driving service consumption up and causing distribution channels to shift to convenience stores and drug stores. The percentage of households using online shopping reached 30%, indicating a shift from brick-and-mortar to online retailing. Companies turned their attention to technological innovations, such as Internet of Things, big data, artificial intelligence, robotics, and 3D printing. By leveraging these new technologies, they developed new products and expanded their customer base. The impact of quantitative and qualitative monetary easing with a negative interest rate could be seen in a decline in interest rates on corporate loans and personal mortgages. While the outstanding balance of bank loans increased, banks' profit margins for the long-term investment of funds raised on a short-term basis diminished.

As noted earlier, the collapse of Lehman Brothers happened on the heels of Japan's privatizing of public financial services in 2008 and sent the Japanese economy on a roller coaster ride. A decade has passed since then, and the Japanese economy today remains on a long-term recovery track as it sustains low growth, low inflation, and low interest rates.

In this chapter we will look into developments at different types of privatized financial institutions, with a focus on three privatized banks, in the 10 years since privatization. We will also examine and analyze trends in different types of Japanese banking businesses, with a focus on regional banks. The chapter will then propose ideal modalities of Japan's financial institutions, which will be discussed in Chap. 4, based on the analysis findings and provide institutional designs for proposed modalities.

2 Structural Analysis and Challenges Based on Total Assets and Return on Assets

2.1 Assets of Financial Institutions (2009–2017)

Here financial institutions are divided into 11 different types. Five of them are private financial services that include commercial banks, trust banks, regional banks, shinkin banks (regional financial cooperatives) and credit unions, and the Japan Agricultural Cooperatives (JA). The rest are public financial services that include three privatized banks, i.e., JP Bank, Shoko Chukin Bank, and the Development Bank of Japan (DBJ), and three state-owned financial institutions, i.e., Japan Finance Corporation (JFC), Japan Bank for International Cooperation (JBIC), and the Japan International Cooperation Agency (JICA).

Table 3.1 shows changes in the share of total assets by type of financial institution from the fiscal year ending March 31, 2009, immediately after the collapse of

Table 3.1 Share of total assets of private financial institutions and public financial services (March, 2009–2017) (%)

		Private financial institutions						Public financial services									
								Three privatized banks				State-owned financial institutions					
Year	Events	Commercial banks	Regional banks	Trust banks	Shinkin banks/ credit unions	JA	Total	Japan Post Bank	Development Bank of Japan	Shoko Chukin Bank	Total	Japan Finance Corporation	Japan Bank for International Cooperation	Japan International Cooperation Agency (JICA)	Total	Total	Public and private sector total
2017	Declining profit margin	35.0	23.3	6.2	10.6	7.1	82.2	12.8	1.0	0.8	14.6	1.4	1.1	0.7	3.2	17.8	100
2016	Negative interest rate	34.9	22.9	5.8	10.8	7.3	81.5	13.3	1.0	0.8	15.1	1.5	1.2	0.7	3.4	18.5	100
2015	BOJ's buying of govern-ment bonds	34.5	22.9	5.3	10.7	7.4	80.8	13.7	1.1	0.9	15.7	1.6	1.2	0.7	3.5	19.2	100
2014	8% consump-tion tax	34.3	23.1	5.1	10.7	7.5	80.8	13.8	1.1	0.8	15.7	1.7	1.1	0.8	3.5	19.2	100
2013	Weak yen	34.0	22.9	4.9	10.7	7.6	80.1	13.9	1.1	0.9	15.9	2.2	1.0	0.8	4.0	19.9	100
2012	Tax hike for reconstruction	33.6	22.7	4.8	10.8	7.6	79.5	14.1	1.1	0.9	16.1	2.7	0.9	0.8	4.4	20.5	100
2011	Great East Japan Earthquake	33.2	22.5	4.8	10.9	7.7	79.1	14.5	1.1	0.9	16.5	2.7	0.9	0.8	4.4	20.9	100
2010		33.3	22.4	4.8	10.7	7.8	79	14.8	1.2	0.9	16.9	2.4	0.8	0.9	4.1	21.0	100
2009	Collapse of Lehman Brothers	32.9	22.2	4.8	10.9	7.8	78.6	15.7	1.0	0.9	17.6	2.2	0.8	0.8	3.8	21.4	100

Sources: Financial statements of Japanese Bankers Association (2001), shinkin banks/credit union associations, National Federation of Agricultural Cooperative Associations (ZEN-NOH), and government-affiliated financial institutions

Lehman Brothers until the fiscal year ending March 31, 2017. First of all, as the table shows, private financial services' share gradually increased from 7% to 80%, while public financial services' share decreased. However, it remains high at nearly 20% because public financial services have not been fully privatized and are automatically guaranteed by the government. Second, looking at the figures by type of financial institution, one can see that the commercial banks' share increased as the Japanese economy recovered while JP Bank's share decreased. The factors behind the drop in JP Bank's share include a decline in the balance of deposits, which account for the bulk of its total assets, owing to the declining and aging population. Third, if you look at the table chronologically, you will see that the private financial services' share, especially commercial banks and trust banks, increased over the years while local banks, such as regional banks, shinkin banks, and credit unions, as well as the JA, saw their share remain flat. The share held by public financial institutions other than JP Bank, whose share dropped, also remained flat due to the allocation of the FILP budget.

Overall total assets by type of financial institution did not change that much after privatization, and Japan's financial market is far from being free and open as public financial institutions continue to enjoy automatic government guarantees. Although we can take the listing of JP Bank and the restructuring of regional banks as signs of change in the financial structure, we still cannot see the light at the end of the tunnel. What we can foresee, however, is that expediting full privatization of the three privatized banks as prescribed by law will drastically change the share of total assets by type of financial institution and that state-owned financial institutions designed to complement private financial services will be the only public financial services available.

2.2 *Optimizing Total Assets of Financial Institutions*

While the combined total assets of public and private financial services were 1639 trillion yen in the fiscal year ending March 31, 2017, there were disparities among the different types of financial institutions. Table 3.2 shows total assets per institution by type of financial institution for March 2017 in comparison with those 10 years prior (March 2007). The total asset figure per institution for the fiscal year ending March 31, 2017, is 100 trillion yen for commercial banks, which is comparable to the asset size of megabanks. When it comes to the regional banking system, which is oversupplied by banks, with 105 institutions, however, the assets figure is quite small at 3.7 trillion yen. About a third of these regional banks have increased their total assets through mergers to form holding companies. They will all eventually have to opt for mergers to maximize revenue.

Locally based shinkin banks and credit unions and the JA must increase their assets to stabilize their operational foundation; otherwise they will find themselves unable to stay afloat in a low-growth economy along with a shrinking and aging population.

Boasting a grand total of assets that no financial institution in the world can rival, JP Bank has to bear a high cost of funds and risks associated with the revenue earned

Table 3.2 Assets of private financial institutions and public financial services, 2007 and 2017. Asset balance as of end of each fiscal year (trillion yen)

		Private financial institutions						Public financial services									Public and private sector total
								3 privatized banks				State-owned financial institutions					
Fiscal year (March)		Commercial banks	Regional banks	Trust banks	Shinkin banks/ credit unions	JA	Total	Japan Post Bank	Development Bank of Japan	Shoko Chukin Bank	Total	Japan Finance Corporation	Japan Bank for International Cooperation	Japan International Cooperation Agency (JICA)	Total	Total	
2017	Total assets	573	386	100	174	115	1348	210	16.4	12.7	239	21.9	18.5	11.8	52	291	1639
	Number of banks	5	105	4	417	667	1198	1	1	1	3	1	1	1	3	6	1204
	Assets per bank	114	3.7	25	0.42	0.17	1.13	210	16.4	12.7	80	21.9	18.5	11.8	17.3	48.5	1.36
2007	Total assets	402	283	60	138	98	982	232	13	10.9	256	28	20.9		49	304	1286
	Number of banks	6	110	7	455	835	1413	1	1	1	3	1	2		3	6	1419
	Assets per bank	67	2.6	8.6	0.31	0.12	0.69	232	13	10.9	85	28	10.4		16.3	50.6	0.91
Difference	Changes	+47	+1.1	+16.4	+0.11	+0.05	+0.44	−22	+3.4	+1.8	−5	−6	+4.7		+1.0	−2.1	+0.45

Sources: Financial statements of Japanese Bankers Association (2001), shinkin banks/credit union associations, National Federation of Agricultural Cooperative Associations (ZEN-NOH), and government-affiliated financial institutions from investing in marketable securities. It must diversify asset management channels, such as lending, to make a profit from new fee revenues in order to stay afloat. Its operational efficiency is poor and its return on assets (ROA) also remains low because of its bloated operations. Nippon Telegraph and Telephone Public Corp. (NTT) was once a large corporation with considerable assets when it went public, but it was split into independent businesses and regional companies, which were put under the control of a holding company. Downsizing its asset size enabled NTT to get a better handle on its operations while making each business more competitive as it revitalized business and regional operations, enabling NTT to achieve sustainable growth as a whole. When NTT was broken up and privatized, its president at the time, Norio Wada, famously noted, "We can't see the trees for the forest." Now that JP Bank has gone public, it seems to be in the same boat that NTT was in when it went public. We'll discuss JP Bank's ideal asset size in Chap. 4.

As is evident from the analysis of working-age population trends, Japan's regional financial market is unlikely to expand, which is why regional banks must optimize their asset sizes through mergers and break-ups. Reorganizing regional banks' assets totaling 386 trillion yen and addressing the three privatized banks' assets totaling 240 trillion yen are especially pressing issues that need to be resolved.

2.3 *Optimizing the ROA of Financial Institutions*

Table 3.3 shows changes in the ROA by type of financial institution over 10 years from the fiscal year ending March 31, 2007, to the fiscal year ending March 31, 2017. The first thing one notices when looking at the table is that private financial institutions have the highest ROA, followed by the three privatized banks and state-owned banks. Second, based on ROA by type of financial institution, commercial banks and trust banks have higher ROAs than other private financial institutions, followed by regional banks, shinkin banks and credit unions, and the JA.

Among the three privatized banks, DBJ was the most efficient at generating a profit, unlike JP Bank and Shoko Chukin Bank, whose profitability is as low as that of shinkin banks and credit unions. If these three banks were to merge, their ROA would be on par with shinkin banks and credit unions, but if they divided their assets to maximize profits, their ROA would be as high as regional banks'. In terms of the national interest, breaking them up into regional private companies makes sense if they want to improve their bottom line.

Third, considering the chronology in the table, ROA by type of financial institution increased or decreased depending on Japan's economic conditions or monetary policies. Among private financial institutions, the ROAs of commercial banks operating in urban areas are higher than those of locally operated banks, and this tendency is evident over the entire 10-year span. While this basically applies to the three privatized banks, some abnormal ROA figures stand out because their operations are affected by government policy. Between the fiscal year ending March 31, 2014, and the fiscal year ending March 31, 2017, DBJ and Shoko Chukin Bank made loans under the Ministry of Economy, Trade and Industry's crisis response and

Table 3.3 ROA (= Ordinary profit/Total assets) of private financial institutions, three privatized banks, and state-owned financial institutions 2007–2017 (nonconsolidated basis) (%)

Fiscal year (March)	Event	Commercial banks	Regional banks	Trust banks	Shinkin banks/credit unions	JA	Private financial institutions, Average	Japan Post Bank	Development Bank of Japan	Shoko Chukin Bank	Three privatized banks, Average	Japan Finance Corporation	Japan Bank for International Cooperation	Japan International Cooperation Agency (JICA)	State-owned financial institutions, Average	Public financial services, Average	Public and private sector, Average
2017	Declining profit margin	0.389	0.370	0.350	0.250	0.139	0.330	0.211	0.683	0.397	0.253	−0.452	0.221	0.598	0.192	0.215	0.315
2016	Jan 2016 Negative interest rate	0.460	0.476	0.538	0.292	0.140	0.420	0.231	1.063	0.240	0.288	0.217	0.221	0.869	0.363	0.301	0.397
2015	BOJ's buying of government bonds	0.542	0.466	0.637	0.315	0.135	0.462	0.277	0.926	0.317	0.340	−0.165	0.689	0.973	0.380	0.268	0.420
2014	8% consumption tax introduced	0.578	0.443	0.613	0.318	0.182	0.472	0.282	0.926	0.242	0.326	−0.119	0.584	1.161	0.375	0.335	0.445
2013	Weak yen Dec 2012 LDP returns to power	0.475	0.368	0.514	0.226	0.148	0.386	0.298	0.692	0.244	0.310	−0.912	0.417	0.811	−0.230	0.212	0.352
2012	Tax hike for reconstruction	0.475	0.383	0.463	0.174	0.194	0.377	0.297	0.658	0.246	0.320	−0.773	0.472	0.811	−0.225	0.201	0.341
2011	Great East Japan Earthquake	0.425	0.331	0.431	0.151	0.194	0.339	0.273	0.592	0.250	0.270	−2.431	0.406	1.518	−0.110	−0.036	0.268
2010	Sept 2009 DPJ becomes the ruling party	0.297	0.276	0.460	0.168	0.206	0.274	0.251	0.338	0.870	0.248	−3.522	0.278	1.711	−1.673	−0.127	0.190
2009	Collapse of Lehman Brothers	−0.141	−0.207	−0.320	−0.156	0.198	−0.127	0.191	−0.902[b]	−0.930[b]	0.132	−2.357	0.422	0.844	−1.081	−0.10	−0.115
2008		0.457	0.386	0.820	0.930	0.222	0.387	0.117[a]	0.156	0.185	0.122	–	–	–	–	–	–
2007		0.559	0.454	1.108	0.273	0.237	0.490	0.423	0.168	0.258	0.402	–	–	–	–	–	–

Sources: Financial statements of Japanese Bankers Association (2001), shinkin banks/credit union associations, National Federation of Agricultural Cooperative Associations (ZEN-NOH), and government-affiliated financial institutions

[a]Privatized in October 2017

[b]Privatized in October 2018

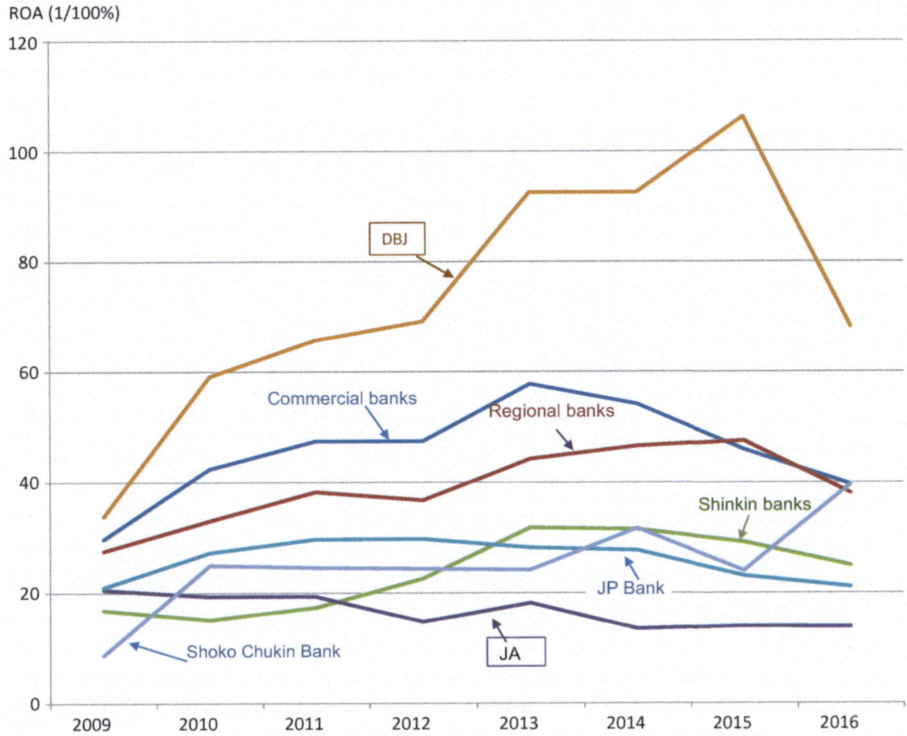

Fig. 3.1 Changes in ROA of four private and three privatized financial institutions

emergency financing systems, some of which were found to be illicit loans that capitalized on such systems. They effectively squeezed private financial institutions out of the market and reaped unusually high ROAs as a result. Overall ROAs of state-owned banks are at a level where they can play their role of complementing the private sector (Fig. 3.1).

While the overall ROA of both public and private financial institutions in Japan is lower than the regional banks' ROA, it is about time that financial institutions accounting for 96% of total assets, other than the state-owned financial institutions that serve to complement the private sector, started looking into ways to optimize their ROAs. The first issue that needs to be addressed is completing the privatization of the three semiprivatized banks as soon as possible. The second issue is reorganizing regional banks with an eye toward shoring up their operating foundations. Specific tasks to be done include scheduling a second public offering of shares in JP Bank and creating a road map for listing Shoko Chukin Bank and DBJ. The process of reorganizing regional banks, which will be covered in detail later, must incorporate the building of sustainable operating foundations. JA and Norinchukin Bank need to reform the Norinchukin model, which is the basis for their organizational structures and fund management operations, in addition to implementing agricultural reforms.

Financial institutions should work to maximize GDP in the domestic market and GNI in overseas markets. This is key to optimizing their ROAs.

While I have so far discussed the profit structures of different types of financial institutions using ROA as an indicator, I should note that ROE also serves as an important performance indicator, so in what follows I will analyze their performance using ROE and other indicators. Before going into that analysis, some additional points need to be made concerning the analysis of total assets.

Combined total assets of public and private financial institutions in Japan amounted to 1640 trillion yen in the fiscal year ending March 31, 2017, with the private sector having 1347 trillion yen and the public sector 293 trillion yen. Public financial institutions are the six banks that include four institutions that use FILP funds to operate, i.e., JFC, the JBIC, JICA (official development assistance [ODA] loan operations), and DBJ, along with the JP Bank and Shoko Chukin Bank, which are virtually under government control. In May 2006, policy-based financial reform was implemented under the Administrative Reform Promotion Act, turning DBJ and Shoko Chukin Bank into stock companies. The Postal Service Privatization Act also went into force at the same time, to make JP Bank a stock company, meaning all three banks had been privatized. If these three banks were to be fully privatized, private-sector financial institutions would hold approximately 95% of Japan's total assets, with public-sector institutions holding the remaining 5%.

This research focuses on an analysis of ROA because of the unique nature of public financial institutions when it comes to both lending and raising capital. Total assets consist of both equity and borrowed capital. Deposits in the JP Bank, which raises funds for public financial services, accounted for 90.4% of its borrowed capital in the fiscal year ending March 31, 2017. Its equity capital comes from the wholly state-owned Japan Post Holdings, which is sourced from taxes paid by the public. This means that almost all of JP Bank's total assets are funded by the public. Likewise, the total assets of other government-affiliated institutions are mostly provided by taxpayers. As shown in the Ministry of Finance's FILP fund balance sheet for the fiscal year ending March 31, 2019, out of 92 trillion yen in outstanding government bonds, a total of 21.6 trillion yen was lent to government-affiliated institutions, with 4.3 trillion yen going to DBJ and 17.3 trillion yen to other public institutions. Now that mandatory deposits of postal savings are no longer required, postal savings are not necessarily tied to lending, but mandatory deposits still virtually exist, as discussed in this book. In that sense, postal savings are used to issue government bonds, which are then used to raise funds for making loans to government-affiliated institutions.

Table 3.4 shows the combined balance sheets of six public financial institutions for the fiscal year ending March 31, 2017. Total liabilities and net assets of the six financial institutions amount to 293 trillion yen. Out of borrowed capital totaling 260 trillion yen, JP Bank's deposits totaling 179 trillion yen and FILP funds totaling 35 trillion yen account for the bulk of it, and 30 trillion yen out of combined net assets totaling 33 trillion yen is equity capital. On the asset side, funds are used for deposits due from banks (Bank of Japan) totaling 60 trillion yen (accounting for 20% of total assets), securities totaling 142 trillion yen (48%), of which 70 trillion yen

Table 3.4 Total assets of private and public financial institutions (trillion yen). Nonconsolidated balance sheets for fiscal year ending March 31, 2017

	Public financial services									Private sector									
	To be fully privatized				State-owned financial institutions						Regional banks								Total for public and private sectors
	Japan Post Bank	Development Bank of Japan	Shoko Chukin Bank	Total	Japan Finance Corporation	Japan Bank for International Cooperation	Japan International Cooperation Agency (JICA)	Total	Total	Five commercial banks	64 regional banks	41 secondary regional banks	105 regional banks (subtotal)	Four trust banks	Shinkin banks	Credit unions	JA	Total	
Assets																			
Cash and due from banks	51	1	2	54	4	2	0.2	6	60	141	33	6	39	27	36	7	71	321	381
Securities	139	2	1	142	0.1	0.3	0	0.4	142	102	76	16	92	21	43	4	4	266	408
(Government bonds)	(69)	(0)	(1)	(70)	(0)	(–)	–	(0)	(70)	(44)	(25)	(5)	(30)	(5)	(7)	(1)	(2)	(89)	(159)
Loans	4	13	9	26	18	14	11	43	69	254	193	51	244	46	69	11	22	646	715
Other	16	1	1	18	0	3	0.2	4	22	76	9	2	11	6	3	0	18	114	136
Total	210	17	13	240	22	19	12	53	293	573	311	75	386	100	151	22	115	1347	1640
Liabilities																			
Deposits	179	0	5	184	0	0	0	0	184	390	255	66	321	49	138	20	96	1014	1198
Borrowings	0	8	1	9	14	10	2	26	35										35
Other	19	6	6	31	3	6	0.5	10	41	156	38	5	43	46	4	1	1	251	292
Total	198	14	12	224	17	16	2	36	260	546	293	71	364	95	142	21	97	1265	1525
Total net assets	12	3	1	16	5	3	10	17	33	27	18	4	22	5	9	1	18	82	115
Total liabilities and net assets	210	17	13	240	22	19	12	53	293	573	311	75	386	100	151	22	115	1347	1640
	14.6%				3.2%				17.8%	34.9%	23.5%			6.1%	10.6%		7.1%	82.2%	100%

Sources: Ministry of Finance's statistical data and government-affiliated financial institutions' financial statements
Japanese Bankers Association, National Association of Shinkin Banks, Shinkumi Federation Bank, National Federation of Agricultural Cooperative Associations (ZEN-NOH) statistics (ZEN-NOH data are for fiscal year ending March 31, 2016)

(24%) is invested in government bonds, as well as loans totaling 69 trillion yen (22%). Because public financial institutions' equity capital and borrowed capital are both sourced from the public, it would be more appropriate to compare them with other types of financial institutions in term of ROA, which is an indicator for overall asset performance, based on whether they are benefitting the public (i.e., if they are in the national interest).

Despite this unique nature of public financial institutions' equity capital, analyzing ROE still makes sense, so in what follows we will look at the ROE of different types of financial institutions and compare them with the ROA analysis. Table 3.5 and Fig. 3.2 show changes in ROE by type of financial institution from the fiscal year ending March 31, 2010, to the fiscal year ending March 31, 2017.

Private financial institutions' ROE remained somewhere between 5 and 7%, while the three privatized banks' ROE was in the 3% range. The overall ROE of public financial institutions, including government-affiliated (i.e., state-owned) financial institutions, is low at 1–2%, about a third of private financial institutions' ROE. The same gap can be found between private and public financial institutions in the ROA analysis (Table 3.3 and Fig. 3.1). Both analyses indicate that the private sector enjoys higher profitability.

Looking at the ROA and ROE of private financial institutions by type reveals that commercial banks have the highest profitability, followed by trust banks, regional banks, shinkin banks/credit unions, and JA. Among the three privatized banks, JP Bank has a slightly higher ROE than ROA because of the higher ratio of its borrowed capital as well as its portfolio strategy that puts more weight on foreign bonds and investment trusts to generate a higher profit. Public financial institutions other than JP Bank have a large sum of government-funded capital and capital reserves. Due to the high ratio of equity capital, its ROE is lower than that of other types of financial institutions. What makes public financial institutions' capital policy unique is that their finances are sourced from taxpayer money, making their capital cost low. They tend to rely on operational stability and zero-interest-rate policy to generate profits and increase capital as much as possible. State-owned financial institutions tend to offset deficits by increasing their capital.

Due to the uniqueness of the assets, liabilities, and equity capital of public financial institutions, which are heavily influenced by government policy, as noted earlier, it would be better to use ROA rather than ROE as an indicator for analyzing overall financial institutions if one wishes to focus on the soundness of their portfolios. The ROE analysis also revealed some issues concerning the nature of JP Bank's operations, as noted below.

JP Bank was listed on the First Section of the Tokyo Stock Exchange in November 2015. The three Japan Post Holdings companies went public in order to use the proceeds from the sale of their stocks to fund reconstruction efforts in areas affected by the Great East Japan Earthquake in addition to tax hikes. The Reconstruction Funding Act went into effect on November 30, 2011, and Article 14 of the law's supplementary provisions stipulated that reconstruction funds would be sourced from the sale of Japan Post shares. The Ministry of Finance decided to sell Japan Post shares through three public offerings between February 2013 and March 2022, selling 1.3 trillion yen each time, to raise 4 trillion yen in total to repay

Table 3.5 Return on equity (ROE, %) of private financial institutions, three privatized banks, and state-owned financial institutions (March, 2010–2017)

Year	Commercial banks	Regional banks	Trust banks	Shinkin banks/ credit unions	JA	Private financial institutions, Average	Japan Post Bank	Development Bank of Japan	Shoko Chukin Bank	3 privatized banks, Average	Japan Finance Corporation	Japan Bank for International Cooperation	Japan International Cooperation Agency (JICA)	State-owned financial institutions, Average	Public financial services, Average	Public and private sector, Average
2010	6.25	4.23	4.95	2.29	3.72	4.68	3.43	0.71	1.71	2.94	−25.10	1.79	2.27	−6.12	−2.11	2.24
2011	8.63	4.48	6.14	2.84	3.44	5.84	3.56	1.76	4.21	3.61	−20.94	3.12	1.9	−4.52	−0.88	3.47
2012	7.95	4.82	4.38	1.54	2.99	5.29	3.69	1.17	3.01	3.34	−4.95	2.46	1.08	−0.89	0.9	3.7
2013	9.23	5.18	7.06	2.85	2.57	6.25	4.01	1.62	2.85	3.59	−6.84	2.85	1.06	−0.86	1.15	4.51
2014	9.36	6.69	8.22	4.28	3.35	7.08	3.68	1.49	4.72	3.72	−0.8	2.85	1.38	1.14	1.04	5.01
2015	8.54	6.36	8.42	4.17	2.45	6.54	4.37	1.82	3.46	4.02	−2.92	5.29	1.22	0.64	1.33	4.8
2016	8.36	6.67	8.75	3.82	2.56	6.52	3.72	1.25	4.34	3.67	1.06	1.82	1.09	1.19	2.25	5.12
2017	7.66	5.48	5.85	3.24	2.19	5.57	3.55	3.4	2.79	3.36	1.98	1.67	0.77	1.27	2.15	4.43

Sources: Financial statements of the Japanese Bankers Association, Shinkin Central Bank, Shinkumi Federation Bank, National Federation of Agricultural Cooperative Associations, and government-affiliated financial institutions

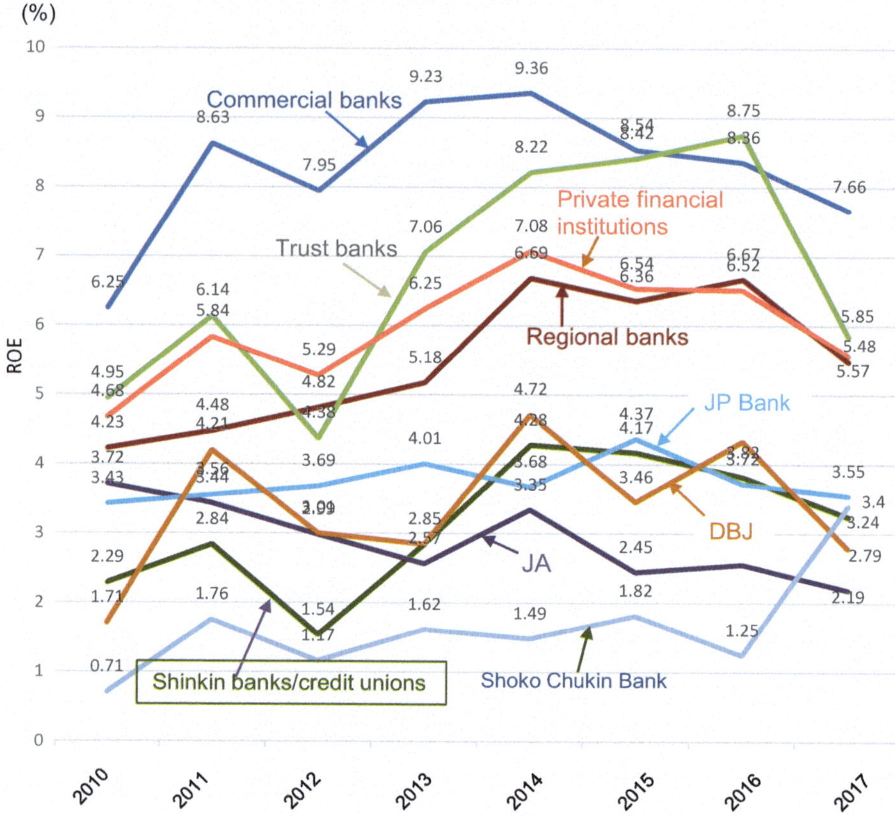

Fig. 3.2 Return on equity (ROE) of private and privatized financial institutions. Privatized (JP, DBJ, Shoko Chukin) banks' ROE is lower than private banks' ROE, just like the case of ROA
Sources: Financial statements of the Japanese Bankers Association, Shinkin Central Bank, Shinkumi Federation Bank, National Federation of Agricultural Cooperative Associations, and government-affiliated financial institutions

reconstruction bonds. The government has already raised 2.6 trillion yen through two public offerings and still needs to sell the remaining shares worth 1.3 trillion yen. At the root of recent revelations about improper sales practices at Japan Post Life Insurance and JP Bank, where unreasonable sales quotas for insurance products and investment trusts were imposed on their employees, is likely a struggle to increase the profits needed to sustain their listed status.

Since its listing, JP Bank has suffered a gradual decline in revenue due to a low yield on interest-earning assets amid the low-interest-rate policy. As shown in Table 3.6, the bank is investing less and less in government bonds but more and more in foreign bonds and investment trusts.

Its yield on interest-earning assets and the interest rate on interest-bearing liabilities for domestic and overseas operations are declining every year, and its net interest margin is also gradually falling, as shown in Table 3.7. The bank is staying in the black as revenues from its overseas operations offset declining profitability of

Table 3.6 Japan Post Bank portfolio (March, 2010–2019) (trillion yen)

	2010	2011	2012	2013	2014	2015	2016	2017	2018	2019
Japanese government bonds	155.8	146.4	144.9	138.1	126.3	106.7	82.2	68.8	62.7	58.3
Corporate bonds	12.2	12.9	12.7	11.8	11.3	10.9	10.5	10.7	10.5	9.7
Foreign bonds	3.7	7.3	9.4	11.6	14.5	18.8	19.8	20.1	20.2	22.0
Investment trusts	1.0	2.6	3.0	4.1	8.2	13.9	25.5	32.7	39	40.4
Loans	4.0	4.2	4.1	3.9	3.0	2.7	2.5	4.1	6.1	5.3
Risk assets	9.1	11.5	12.9	13.8	16.5	21.5	32.2	38.8	50.3	56.0
Home mortgages (intermediary) (one hundred million yen)										
New mortgages	740	618	315	240	244	348	363	399	356	–[a]
Cumulative total of new mortgages	1302	1921	2236	2477	2721	3669	3433	3832	4189	–

Source: Japan Post Bank financial statements
[a]Discontinued intermediary operations

Table 3.7 Japan Post Bank's yield on interest-earning assets and interest rate on interest-bearing liabilities (March, 2010–2019) (%)

	2010	2011	2012	2013	2014	2015	2016	2017	2018	2019
Yield on interest-earning assets, A	1.09	1.11	1.10	1.02	0.93	0.95	0.86	0.78	0.74	0.67
Interest rate on interest-bearing liabilities, B	0.24	0.20	0.19	0.19	0.19	0.18	0.19	0.18	0.17	0.17
Net interest margin, A – B	0.84	0.91	0.91	0.83	0.73	0.77	0.67	0.60	0.57	0.50
Expense-to-deposit ratio	0.68	0.68	0.66	0.63	0.61	0.62	0.59	0.58	0.57	0.57
Overhead ratio	71.4	70.4	70.33	68.42	69.86	68.19	73.42	74.89	71.46	78.18

Yield on interest-earning assets and interest rate on interest-bearing liabilities for domestic and overseas operations (March, 2010–2019) (%)

		2010	2011	2012	2013	2014	2015	2016	2017	2018	2019
Domestic	Yield on interest-earning assets	1.07	1.05	1.01	0.90	0.82	0.74	0.64	0.53	0.43	0.38
	Interest rate on interest-bearing liabilities	0.24	0.20	0.18	0.17	0.16	0.15	0.15	0.13	0.09	0.06
Overseas	Yield on interest-earning assets	1.29	1.56	1.67	1.90	1.31	1.81	1.33	1.23	1.34	1.18
	Interest rate on interest-bearing liabilities	0.24	0.26	0.33	0.46	0.48	0.41	0.40	0.37	0.41	0.55
Total	Yield on interest-earning assets	1.09	1.11	1.10	1.02	0.93	0.95	0.86	0.78	0.74	0.67
	Interest rate on interest-bearing liabilities	0.24	0.20	0.19	0.19	0.19	0.18	0.19	0.18	0.17	0.17

Source: Japan Post Bank financial statements

Table 3.8 Japan Post Bank's net profit, annual dividend payment, and dividend payout ratio

FY ending, March		2015	2016	2017	2018	2019
Net profit (100 million yen)		3694	3250	3122	3527	2661
Total dividend amount (100 million yen)		1847	937	1874	1874	1874
Dividend payout ratio (%)		54.9	28.8	60	53.1	70.4
Annual dividend (yen)		50	25	50	50	50
Net profit per share (yen)		89.58	86.69	83.28	94.09	71
ROE (%)		4.37	3.72	3.55	3.94	3.01
Dividend to general shareholders (11%) 100 million yen		0	103	206	206	206
Dividend to Japan Post Holdings (89%) 100 million yen		1847	834	1668	1668	1668
Comparison with other banks						
SMBC	Dividend payout ratio (%)	26.2	32.7	29.9	32.7	34.6
	Annual dividend (yen)	140	150	150	170	180
	ROE (%)	11.2	8.9	9.1	8.8	8.2
MUFG	Dividend payout ratio (%)	24.8	28.3	26.4	25.5	32.9
	Annual dividend (yen)	18	18	18	19	22
	ROE (%)	8.74	7.63	7.25	7.53	6.45
Chiba	Dividend payout ratio (%)	23.6	21.9	24.7	23.7	25.6
	Annual dividend (yen)	13	14	15	15	16
	ROE (%)			6.86	6.76	6.15
Shizuoka	Dividend payout ratio (%)	23.37	27.91	49.83	28.74	30.38
	Annual dividend (yen)	20	20	20	21	22
	ROE (%)	5.06	5.18	3.15	5.21	4.67

Source: Financial statements of Japan Post Bank, SMBC, MUFG, Chiba Bank, and Shizuoka Bank

its domestic operations. An analysis of this drastic change in JP Bank's asset structure has revealed that the cause of the change lies in the bank's dividend policy.

Table 3.8 shows changes in JP Bank's net profit, annual dividend amount, and payout ratio. With the exception of the fiscal year ending March 31, 2016, when Japan Post Holdings posted a deficit due to impairment accounting, the bank paid an annual dividend of 50 yen per share every year, maintaining a payout ratio of 50% or more, in line with its dividend policy. In the fiscal year ending March 31, 2019, its payout ratio climbed to 70.4%, about three times higher than other banks' payout ratio. JP Bank's policy of paying an annual dividend of 50 yen per share and maintaining a 3% dividend yield, which the bank announced when it went public, has prevented it from generating a profit and keeping the stock price from falling. This dividend policy poses a new challenge to the bank's operations. Additionally, the fact that the bank has maintained the same ROE level indicates that it opts for a high-risk, high-return portfolio due to its investment and dividend policies.

3 Listing of JP Bank and Path to Full Privatization

While postal privatization seemed to have gotten off to a good start, the thrust that moved it forward lost steam in 2009 in the face of the economic crisis that surfaced on the heels of Lehman Brothers' collapse and also because Liberal Democratic Party members who had opposed postal privatization returned to the fold after Prime Minister Koizumi stepped down. To add insult to injury, the Democratic Party of Japan defeated the Liberal Democratic Party in the September 2009 election to replace them as the ruling party.

The People's New Party that formed a ruling coalition with the Democratic Party of Japan had been opposed to postal privatization and demanded that postal services be overhauled prior to agreeing to become its ally. It made passing a bill to freeze the government's sale of Japan Post shares the cornerstone of that agreement. This bill was approved by the Diet and passed in December of the same year under the government led by Prime Minister Hatoyama. After going public, Japan Post was slated to be fully privatized by 2017, but the enactment of the law slammed the brakes on full privatization.

Following the March 2011 Great East Japan Earthquake, the government left no stone unturned in its quest to secure reconstruction funds, but the effort went nowhere since the huge amount of money could not be sourced solely from tax increases.

On July 15, 2011, I published an article on Nikkei Business Online entitled "*Fukko e no michi: yucho ni nemuru fukko maizokin 6-cho en* [Path to reconstruction: Treasure worth 6 trillion yen hidden in Japan Post]." In the article I argued that, out of the Japan Post shares whose sale had been suspended, capital and capital reserves worth up to 6.1 trillion yen should be returned to the government and used as a source of reconstruction funds in addition to tax increases.

On September 8, 2011, the *Asahi Shimbun* published an article with the headline "*Yusei kabu fukko zaigen ni fujo* [Japan Post shares emerge as a source of reconstruction funds]." According to this piece, the People's New Party would give in to selling Japan Post shares on the condition that the postal reform bill would be passed, indicating the possibility of raising up to 6.4 trillion yen using two thirds of the Japan Post shares held by the government worth 9.6 trillion yen.

As a follow-up, I published an article entitled "*Shinsai fukko ni taishite yucho ginko ga hatasubeki yakuwari* [The role JP Bank should play in postearthquake reconstruction]" in *Kinyu Zaisei Jijo*, a weekly financial magazine, on October 3, 2011. In the article I maintained that since the sale of Japan Post shares was suspended, JP Bank's capital reserve worth 4 trillion yen should be returned to the government and used to fund reconstruction. On top of that, I suggested that the postal savings totaling 10 trillion yen that had been collected in the Tohoku region should be invested locally. I then urged that JP Bank, DBJ, and Shoko Chukin Bank be merged once they were fully privatized and then broken up into regional banks. This article was used by government officials as a reference.

In an October 22, 2011, article with the headline "*Fukko zaigen Komei ni shudoken* [Komei takes initiative in financing reconstruction]" the Nikkei reported that the Komeito, Democratic Party of Japan, and the Liberal Democratic Party had reached an agreement, giving the greenlight to passing laws to create funds for recovery and reconstruction.

The Reconstruction Funding Act went into effect on November 30, 2011, and Article 14 of the law's supplementary provisions stipulated that reconstruction funds would be sourced from the sale of Japan Post shares. This marked the beginning of the revival of postal privatization. As a result, under the framework for funding reconstruction efforts, which were estimated to cost 23 trillion yen, the government decided to raise 10.5 trillion yen through tax hikes for reconstruction, 8.5 trillion yen from expenditure cuts and nontax revenues, and 4 trillion yen from the sale of Japan Post shares, which were to be used to repay reconstruction bonds.

On April 27, 2012, the Act for Partial Revision of the Postal Service Privatization Act was enacted, putting postal privatization back on track. (The bill to freeze the government's sale of Japan Post shares was repealed on May 8.)

In December 2012 the Liberal Democratic Party came back to power for the first time in 3 years after defeating the Democratic Party of Japan. Soon after making its comeback, the ruling party swiftly set the date for taking the three Japan Post companies public, and they all went public on November 4, 2015.

JP Bank had come a long way to becoming a listed company, and fiscal year 2017 marked the tenth year since its privatization. While looking below at the events that occurred during those 10 years, we will explore the path to full privatization as we gain an understanding of how the bank sold its shares before it went public in light of the findings of a chronological analysis of total assets and ROA by type of financial institution. We will assess the optimal ratio of JP Bank's total assets to the combined total assets of public and private financial institutions and examine the optimal ROA for the bank in light of the national interest (Table 3.9).

The collapse of Lehman Brothers shook the world just a year after JP Bank was privatized in October 2007. While other financial institutions fell into the red for the fiscal year ending March 31, 2009, only JP Bank and the JA remained in the black. JP Bank's share of the combined total assets of public and private financial institutions dropped from 15% to 12%. Its total assets, amounting to 200 trillion yen, dwarf the assets of every postal savings bank in the world. The asset size and share have been addressed in the special public institutions reform. Although downsizing its assets has been the biggest issue, the government has not come up with any specific solutions yet.

Table 3.9 Total assets (trillion yen) and ROA: Japan Post Bank

March	2009	2010	2011	2012	2013	2014	2015	2016	2017
Total assets	204	195	194	195	198	202	206	207	209
Share (%)[a]	15.7	14.8	14.5	14.1	13.9	13.8	13.7	13.3	12.8
ROA (%)	0.191	0.251	0.273	0.297	0.298	0.282	0.277	0.231	0.211

[a]Percentage of Japan Post Bank's total assets to combined total assets of public and private financial institutions

The bank's profitability has not changed over the last 10 years, with its ROA remaining low. Since its ROA is less than half the average ROA of other types of private financial institutions, it cannot be overlooked in light of the national interest and given its hefty total assets. Most of these assets come from the personal savings of local citizens. If the government were to sell its shares in the bank, the bank would be free to utilize its total assets and generate a profit from the assets of individual account holders. There is a lot of room for optimizing the ROA for each type of financial institution.

JP Bank should change its status from a privately operated but government-owned entity to a fully privatized company so it can generate a profit and give back to the public.

This analysis of JP Bank's total assets has shed light on the problems that exist. In Chap. 4 we will look at solutions to these problems and discuss institutional designs.

3.1 Postal Privatization Began on October 1, 2007, but...

The Japan Post Group began operating under a new organizational structure. Japan Post Holdings Co. became a holding company, overseeing the management of four business companies operating under its umbrella. There was not much change in the workforce from the time it was a public corporation. About 100 employees from the private sector were added to the ranks of 220,000 public corporation employees. Operations were taken over as they were without any change. However, due to the company split-up, there were changes in administrative procedures, and sales operations were broken into smaller tasks, which made work more complex, requiring the company to spend more time on training employees. Although media reports, much-talked-about TV advertisements, and other kinds of publicity gave the impression that Japan Post had become a whole new entity, the mechanisms it had maintained since the Meiji period hadn't really changed at all.

Yet, with new signs and uniforms, Japan Post had a brand new look on the surface. Directly managed branches were being renovated one after another, and the Shibuya branch was given a whole new makeover. Japan Post Network started selling stationery and postal related products. Above all, workers were no longer civil servants but now private company employees. The Postal Privatization Committee gave permission to JP Bank to sell variable-annuity contracts, issue credit cards, mediate home mortgages for other companies, and offer syndicated loans, interest-rate swaps, and other financial instruments in phases. Employees of Japan Post's two financial companies who were assigned to work in directly managed branches as well as employees of Japan Post Network's agencies spent their days learning all the ins and outs of a vast array of products along with new work procedures. They had to grope around in the dark to find the right sales techniques and rely on personal relationships JP Bank had built because it lacked a database of customer info. However, retail banking where sales reps provide customized services incurs huge costs. Sooner or later JP Bank will lose out in the competition with private banks.

While the bank started home mortgage intermediation, this required all employees to have screening skills. Considering that private banks spend 5 years on training their employees in lending operations, it was impossible for JP Bank to put their employees to work in the field right away. Today JP Bank is still not authorized to make direct home mortgage loans. This is probably because the Financial Services Agency still has doubts about JP Bank's screening capability and not because it is concerned about the pressure it would put on the private sector. The biggest problem is that JP Bank lacks the personnel needed to provide training on lending operations. JP Bank is at the point where it should look into the possibility of a merger with a policy-based financial institution or private bank in order to acquire lending capabilities.

3.2 What Followed after the Democratic Party of Japan Took Power in September 2009 and the Bill to Freeze the Government's Sale of Japan Post Shares

In September 2009 the coalition of the Democratic Party of Japan, People's New Party, and the Social Democratic Party took power from the Liberal Democratic Party-Komeito coalition and agreed to overhaul the postal services. Since the People's New Party made overhauling postal services the primary focus of its manifesto, its intention was strongly reflected in the tripartite agreement. In October of the same year the ruling coalition drastically overhauled postal services under its policy agreement, and the following five measures were approved by the Cabinet.

(a) Drastically overhaul postal services with an eye toward ensuring people's livelihoods and revitalizing local economies.
(b) Immediately enact a law to suspend the sale of shares in Japan Post Holdings, JP Bank, and Japan Post Life Insurance. Scrutinize the services and management of each of the Japan Post Group companies, review the break-up of postal services into four companies, and establish a mechanism for making postal services available equally to everyone across the nation in a simple, user-friendly way.
(c) Make postal, postal savings, and insurance services available at post offices.
(d) Examine the operations of the Japan Post Group, including the ownership of its shares, to enhance convenience for the public.
(e) Discuss specific measures for drastically overhauling postal services in light of the preceding points and immediately draft and pass basic postal reform legislation.

In the August 2009 election for the House of Representatives, which turned out to be the flipside of the previous election that focused on postal privatization, many of the candidates who had been elected as a member of the House of Representatives for the first time in the previous election were defeated, causing the postal reform to fall through the cracks. As demanded by the People's New Party, whose primary goal set in its party platform was re-examining postal privatization, the Democratic Party of Japan embarked on a drastic overhaul of postal services in a coalition agreement. Given Japan's fiscal condition, however, it was reluctant to reverse course and make the postal services state-owned again or do any costly overhaul. After taking over the reins of power, the new government brought together skilled bureaucrats from across the ministries and agencies to draft a postal reform bill, most of whom were those who drafted the Postal Service Privatization Act. Between the lines of the postal reform bill one can see the Postal Service Privatization Act as clear as day. In other words, it was deliberately written to be ambiguous and open to different interpretations. The bill neither specified whether the government would continue to own 100% of Japan Post shares nor required Japan Post to provide fully universal service. In December 2009, the Hatoyama Cabinet approved and passed the People's New Party bill to freeze the government's sale of Japan Post shares. In May 2010 a proposal to drastically overhaul postal services in accordance with the coalition agreement was submitted by the government as part of the postal reform bill but was shelved and repealed in July of the same year.

3.3 Changes after the March 2011 Great East Japan Earthquake—Law to Freeze the Government's Sale of Japan Post Shares Repealed, Enabling Use of Japan Post Shares to Fund Reconstruction

The prime minister and leader of the Democratic Party of Japan, Naoto Kan, agreed to step down after the passage of a reconstruction budget following the Great East Japan Earthquake and a deficit-financing bond bill for fiscal 2011. While the government planned a third extra budget amounting to 10 trillion yen for full disaster recovery, it had to rely on reconstruction-related tax hikes. In a July 15, 2011, op-ed I contributed to Nikkei Business Online entitled "*Fukko eno michi: Yucho ni nemuru fukko maizokin 6-cho en* [Path to reconstruction: Treasure worth 6 trillion yen hidden in Japan Post]," I proposed solutions for minimizing the tax burden on the public.

In the piece, I argued that, since the government still had a long way to go until it could take JP Bank public, it could not expect to make a profit from selling its shares in the bank for a while. That being the case, JP Bank's shareholder equity should be returned to the government and used toward funding reconstruction. I proposed cutting JP Bank's equity capital totaling 7.8 trillion yen (capital surplus of 4.3 trillion yen and capital of 3.5 trillion yen) down to 1.7 trillion yen and returning the remaining total of 6.1 trillion yen to the government to curb reconstruction-related tax hikes. I made this proposal because the postal savings system, a monetary entry point, was frozen without being fully utilized by the private financial sector with all its untapped growth potential, and because JP Bank would not be violating the capital adequacy requirements if its enormous equity capital was reduced by 6 trillion yen as long as the money was used to finance government bonds.

I also made four other proposals. What follows is the English translation of the original Japanese text:

(a) The money collected from the people really ought to be returned to the region where they live, but it doesn't work that way. In the wake of the earthquake Japan finds itself in a state of emergency. It would make more sense for JP Bank to contribute up to 6 trillion yen to finance postdisaster reconstruction and maintain fiscal discipline rather than issuing additional government bonds only to lose the confidence of the market, see interest rates and credit risks spiral upward, and eventually witness the decline of its financial health.
(b) The postal service was operated by the Ministry of Posts and Telecommunications and the Ministry of Finance using taxes collected from the public. The ministries would use tax revenue from the general account to cover deficits.
(c) Even if there were a legal problem in reducing JP Bank's capital, postal savings have been used to finance reconstruction whenever Japan faced a crisis since the Meiji period.
(d) In the fallout from the double disaster of an earthquake and nuclear accident, Japan finds itself short on funds needed to fuel any kind of recovery.

This essay published in Nikkei Business Online generated a lot of interest, garnering about 70,000 page views in just a week.

The Noda Cabinet that was formed on August 30, 2011, sat down to seriously look into a third extra budget for reconstruction to be financed with tax increases. The headlines in the *Asahi Shimbun* and the Nikkei on September 8 of the same year read, "*Yusei kabu fukko zaigen ni fujo* [Japan Post shares emerge as a source of reconstruction funds]," "*Baikyaku shunyu 6.4 cho en* [6.4 trillion yen from sale]," and "*Fukko zozei asshuku o kento* [Government to look into curbing reconstruction-related tax hikes]." According to the *Asahi Shimbun*, passing the postal reform bill to revamp the postal privatization policy had been a long-sought goal of the People's New Party. However, the Democratic Party of Japan decided to throw its lot in with the Liberal Democratic Party-Komeito coalition and tabled the bill. Claiming that funds needed for reconstruction could be raised by selling shares in Japan Post, the People's New Party set its sights on getting the postal reform bill passed. Soon some members of the Democratic Party of Japan that strongly opposed special tax hikes started hopping aboard the bandwagon. Even the Liberal Democratic Party's own president, Tanigaki, despite the party's opposition to the postal reform bill, was reported to have said that the government should devise different ways to secure funds from various sources. The People's New Party took this opportunity and ran with it.

Later I published an article entitled "*Shinsai fukko de yucho ginko ga hatasubeki yakuwari* [The role JP Bank should play in postearthquake reconstruction]" in the October 3 issue of *Kinyu Zaisei Jijo*, a weekly financial magazine, proposing steps to achieve full privatization and the listing of JP Bank, which was the original goal of postal privatization.

I made two proposals. Japan was facing the huge challenge of restoring fiscal health while achieving economic growth. To overcome this challenge, I proposed possible roles JP Bank could play in postdisaster recovery. First, I suggested that out of JP Bank's equity capital, the government should use capital reserves amounting to about 4 trillion yen, paid by taxpayers, to finance reconstruction. Second, JP Bank should focus on local finance and use deposits collected in Tohoku to cultivate economic growth in the region.

<Proposal 1, key points>

- The government declared that it would sell government assets and revive the post of Minister of State for Government Revitalization to thoroughly review and prioritize its operations prior to increasing taxes. Government screening of JP Bank operations would reveal a "hidden treasure" that would be immediately available for use, i.e., JP Bank's huge equity capital. Since the government still has a long way to go until it can take JP Bank public now that the selling of shares in the Japan Post Group is blocked, it cannot expect to make a profit from selling its shares for a while. That is why the government should return JP Bank's capital reserves to its coffers and use it to fund a chunk of postdisaster reconstruction while curbing tax hikes.
- While the initial objective of creating JP Bank was to channel money from public financial institutions to private financial institutions with a higher growth potential, in reality nothing has changed, and JP Bank merely serves as an underwriter of government bonds that is digging the Japanese economy deeper and deeper into a hole. It would make more sense if JP Bank contributed funds for reconstruction rather than issuing a large amount of government bonds that would only cause long-term interest rates to rise and the bank's financial health to deteriorate.
- Even if JP Bank's capital reserves worth 4296.2 billion yen were returned to the government, it would still have a balance of 3500 billion yen left over in addition to retained earnings worth 894.8 billion yen, for a total of 4394.8 billion yen in equity capital. The capital adequacy ratio in this case would be 38.17%. This should be good enough for a bank that has no international operations. Therefore, 4296.2 billion yen out of the capital reserves could be earmarked for reconstruction, offsetting 40% of the slated tax increase. If JP Bank's risk assets were to increase in the event the bank launches a new business in the future, such as corporate lending, the government could increase its capital just as megabanks increase their capital, or it could seek help from the private sector. (This is the same scheme JP Bank used when it repurchased its shares worth 1.3 trillion yen on September 30, 2014.)
- Laws can be changed via Diet deliberations. Some say that nothing can be done about Japan Post shares because of the legal issues associated with the Postal Service Privatization Act, the law to freeze the government's sale of Japan Post shares, and the postal reform bill currently under discussion, but if the government pulls together and works in the interest of the public, the problem can be solved immediately.

<Proposal 2>

- "Use deposits collected in Tohoku to revitalize the local economy." Specifically, the Postal Privatization Committee as well as relevant ministries and government agencies should allow JP Bank's branches and Japan Post Network's major distributors in the Tohoku region to make loans to SMEs, for example. For instance, they could be financed with ultra-low-interest-rate, ultra-long-term municipal bonds, or reconstruction bonds issued by disaster-affected prefectures.
- JP Bank should be able to start lending operations exclusively at its branches in Morioka, Sendai, and Fukushima located in the disaster areas with government authorization. Naturally, local private banks would strongly oppose JP Bank's expansion into the loan market. However, they should not be so self-serving in the face of a national crisis. If 10 trillion yen in postal savings collected in Tohoku cannot be put to work for the people and companies of Tohoku, then what is the point of JP Bank's existence in the first place?
- Breaking up JP Bank into regional banks in the future: Elaborating on the idea of using deposits collected in Tohoku for the local economy, it all boils down to the idea of splitting up JP Bank, which is the entry point of money used for public financial services, as well as the DBJ, Shoko Chukin Bank, and the JFC's SME Unit and Agriculture, Forestry, Fisheries and Food Business Unit, the Japan Housing Finance Agency, and other public financial institutions operating in Tohoku, all of which are the money's point of exit, and merging them into a new regional bank covering the entire Tohoku region. In other words, JP Bank and government-affiliated financial institutions that have evolved into centralized financial giants no longer play a role in the low-growth economy and should shift their focus to regional banking in step with decentralization. We'll have to wait until a policy to divide Japan into regional administration blocs, such as *doshusei*, is introduced before we can come up with a specific scheme for dividing them into regional operations. I emphasize here that the idea of using deposits collected in Tohoku to fuel the local economy is the role JP Bank should play in postdisaster reconstruction and expect the bank to become a real private financial institution for the recovery of Tohoku that can handle everything from fund procurement to management.

The key points I make in this article are as follows:

JP Bank should return capital reserves worth 4 trillion yen to minimize tax hikes.
Its capital adequacy ratio would be 38% after returning 4 trillion yen, and the bank could increase capital later.
Laws could be quickly changed if the government pulls together in the interest of the public good.
Deposits collected in Tohoku should be used to revitalize the local economy.
Finally, JP Bank should be turned into a privately owned and operated financial institution in the future, perhaps by being split up into regional companies.

I received feedback as soon as the issue of *Kinyu Zaisei Jijo* was hot off the press. An acquaintance in Tokyo's halls of government (a.k.a. Kasumigaseki) informed me that the Ministry of Finance asked him to identify the author.

On October 22, 2011, the Nikkei published an article with the headline "*Fukko zaigen Komei ni shudoken: yusei shingi iri yonin jimin nimo unagasu* [Komei takes initiative in financing reconstruction: Urges the Liberal Democratic Party to greenlight Diet deliberations on postal reform]." According to the article, once Komeito started looking into introducing the postal reform bill in the current Diet session, which would pave the way to selling shares in Japan Post and expand nontax revenue avenues while curbing tax hikes, the Liberal Democratic Party started taking a softer line toward the bill.

Since the deadline for enacting the following year's budget that would finalize tax hikes for reconstruction was drawing near, all parties began singing the same tune, with the refrain being that Japan Post shares should be used to fund reconstruction work.

While deliberating on the plan to sell Japan Post shares to secure funds was time-consuming, as they rushed to pass the third extra budget to fund reconstruction work, the ruling and opposition parties decided on raising funds for reconstruction through tax hikes totaling 10,670 billion yen, with a 7.5-trillion-yen increase in income taxes, a 2.4-trillion-yen increase in corporate taxes, and a 770-billion-yen increase in inhabitant taxes, while keeping the passing of the plan in mind.

Finally, the Act on Special Measures for Securing Financial Resources Necessary to Implement Measures for Reconstruction following the Great East Japan Earthquake (the Reconstruction Funding Act) was passed on November 30, 2011. Article 14 of the supplementary provisions of the Reconstruction Funding Act stipulated that approximately 4 trillion yen from the sale of Japan Post shares were to be spent on reconstruction efforts.

[Article 14 of the Supplementary Provisions].

In addition to the measures specified in each subparagraph of Paragraph 1 of the preceding article, to secure funds for paying redemption costs through nontax revenues, the government shall look into disposing of its shares in Japan Post Holdings Co. [with the exception of the shares the government is required to hold pursuant to Article 2 of the Act on Japan Post Holdings Co. (Act No. 98 of 2005)] in light of the financial standing and outlook of Japan Post Holdings Co. and other relevant circumstances and dispose of said shares as soon as possible based on its findings.

I believe that my two timely articles moved the Diet to take a positive step forward. The government was at the point where it was ready to put the theory of disposing of the shares it held in Japan Post into practice with the realization that it was vital to making the privatization of public financial services happen. No other studies were conducted during this period on the law to freeze the government's sale of Japan Post shares and the postal reform bill.

3.4 *Plan to Take Three Japan Post Group Companies Public Gets off the Ground*

3.4.1 Passage of the Act for Partial Revision of Postal Service Privatization Act

The discussion on selling Japan Post shares to fund reconstruction work led to reversing the course of privatization, and the government looked into not only revising the law to freeze the government's sale of Japan Post shares but also its ownership of shares in Japan Post group companies. After deliberating on revising the Postal Service Privatization Act, the government passed a bill partially amending the law (Act for Partial Revision of the Postal Service Privatization Act) on April 27, 2012.

[Outline of Act for Partial Revision of Postal Service Privatization Act]

- The purpose of postal privatization was changed to implementing reforms that would enable the stock companies to operate with a focus on postal services.
- The conventional five-company system was changed to a four-company system, and Post Service Co., Ltd. was merged into Japan Post Network, which was renamed Japan Post Co., Ltd.
- Japan Post Holding Co. and Japan Post Co. became responsible for providing everything from basic postal to savings and insurance services at its post offices. To this end, the law required that (1) companies set up post offices across Japan and request authorization for over-the-counter banking and insurance sales operations, (2) companies leverage the post office network to serve the public interest and respond to local needs, and (3) the government take measures necessary for postal services.
- The law stipulates that Japan Post Holdings dispose of shares in the postal savings and postal insurance companies (hereinafter "two financial companies") as soon as possible while considering the two financial companies' financial standing, possible impact on ensuring basic postal services, and other relevant factors, with an eye toward disposing of all shares.
- While the two financial companies are still required to obtain the authorization of the prime minister and the internal affairs and communications minister prior to starting any new business, once half of their shares are disposed of, they will be required to merely notify those two bodies. The law also made notification to the Postal Privatization Committee mandatory and made the two financial companies subject to its supervisory orders and regulations while requiring them to ensure fair competition with other financial institutions.
- Japan Post Co. is required to notify the internal affairs and communications minister prior to voluntarily starting an additional business. The law also made notification to the Postal Privatization Committee mandatory while requiring the company to ensure fair competition with other financial institutions as well.

- The Act on Japan Post Service Co. and the Act on the Suspension of the Sale of Shares in Japan Post Holdings Co., JP Bank, and Japan Post Insurance were to be abolished.
- The law was to become effective on the date specified by a government ordinance no later than a year from the day of its promulgation. It excluded the purpose of postal privatization and the lifting of the freeze on the sale of shares in Japan Post Holdings Co. and the others, which became effective on the day of its promulgation (May 8, 2012).

3.4.2 Progress on the Process of Taking Japan Post Holdings Co. Public

(a) In October 2012, Japan Post Holdings Co. announced its plan to go public within 3 years (in the fall of 2015).
(b) On February 14, 2013, the Ministry of Finance announced the estimated revenue figures for the sale of Japan Post Holdings. According to that estimate, the revenue will total approximately 4 trillion yen by 2022 if shares worth 1.3 trillion are sold every 3 years (1.3 trillion yen $\times$ 3 $=$ 3.9 trillion yen $=$ approx. 4 trillion yen).

As a result, under the framework for funding reconstruction efforts, which were estimated to cost 23 trillion yen, 10.5 trillion yen was going to be raised through tax hikes for reconstruction, 8.5 trillion yen from expenditure cuts and nontax revenues, and 4 trillion yen from the sale of Japan Post shares, for a total of 23 trillion yen. The government planned to issue reconstruction bonds to finance intensive rebuilding work, which was scheduled to run up until fiscal 2015, and use the revenue from the sale of Japan Post shares and other sources to repay the bonds.

(c) On April 14, 2014, the finance minister asked the Finance System Council for opinions on the government's selling of Japan Post shares. The council provided the finance minister with the following recommendations on June 5, 2014, based on the discussions of its National Property Committee.

[Basic Principles]

(i) Sell shares at a fair price and in a fair way.
(ii) Sell shares to a wide range of investors instead of targeting only specific individuals and companies.
(iii) Carefully decide on the timing of the sale, amount of shares to be sold, and so forth in light of securities and financial market trends and the amount of shares to be sold.
(iv) Appropriately disclose information about business operations and other necessary information to protect investors.
(v) When selling shares in JP Bank and Japan Post Life Insurance (hereinafter "two financial companies") held by Japan Post Holdings through an initial public offering (IPO), the government and Japan Post Holdings must fulfill their

accountability to the public and ensure transparency in the market so that the selling of shares in these two financial companies will not damage the value of Japan Post Holdings' shares.

Although the council specified neither when shares should be sold nor how many shares should be sold in its recommendations, it provided a detailed institutional design that included, for example, selling methods and prices and the selection of lead managing underwriters.

Although the council touched on the selling of shares of the two financial companies through an IPO in paragraph v, it did not explain why or how it could damage the value of Japan Post Holdings shares.

(d) On September 30, 2014, JP Bank bought back shares held by its parent company, Japan Post Holdings. It is assumed this was done with an eye toward giving back to its shareholders.

The number of shares repurchased totaled 25,017,500, which accounted for 16.67% of the bank's 150 million outstanding shares. The bank spent a total of 1.3 trillion yen on the share buyback, making the price per share 51,963 yen. Instead of retiring the repurchased shares, the bank added them to its treasury stock. Following this move, Japan Post Holdings decided to spend 700 billion yen out of 1.3 trillion yen on disposing of the entire amount of the pension liabilities it had carried over since it was operating as the Ministry of Posts and Telecommunications to improve its financial standing before going public. The company invested the remaining 600 billion yen in Japan Post for the capital increase it needed to acquire a stake in Toll Holdings Limited, an Australian leading logistics company. This was done as part of a group-wide growth strategy.

While Japan Post Holdings' justification for this move was to enhance the group's corporate value prior to going public, Japan Post Holdings could have used that money to repay the reconstruction bonds, using the scheme I had proposed, in which funds are returned to the government from JP Bank's shareholder equity through Japan Post Holdings to finance reconstruction work. (We will look into this issue later.)

(e) On October 1, 2014, the Ministry of Finance selected lead managing underwriters who could handle the sale of Japan Post Holdings shares and authorized 11 companies (including 4 global coordinators).

(f) On December 26, 2014, the Japan Post Group revealed its new plan to sell shares in its three companies. In addition to Japan Post Holdings' IPO, which would generate cash needed to finance a recovery from the devastating impact of the March 2011 earthquake and tsunami, its two financial companies (JP Bank and Japan Post Life Insurance) were going to go public at the same time no later than September 2015. Eight years after the wheels of postal privatization had been set in motion, the two financial companies were finally starting to move toward full privatization.

Explaining the reason for this move, Japan Post Holdings said that the simultaneous IPOs were ideal because the company was required to sell its shares as soon as possible under the Postal Service Privatization Act. However, the real motive behind this play may have been that Japan Post Holdings thought that selling shares in the two financial companies would facilitate expanding into new markets, such as lending, and diversify its operations because once more than 50% of shares were sold, they would no longer be required to obtain authorization for starting a new business but only need to file a notification.

Performance of the two financial companies supporting Japan Post Holdings was declining due to the prevailing low interest rates. If JP Bank was to mitigate this interest rate risk, it had to quickly build a diverse operating structure.

(g) On February 24, 2015, the Tokyo Stock Exchange made a special rule for the IPOs of the three Japan Post Group companies. The special rule exempted them from the listing requirement under which companies must maintain a ratio of tradable shares to listed shares at 35% or more when listing their stock directly on the first section of the stock exchange. The Tokyo Stock Exchange made this exemption in light of the additional resolution of the Diet and also because it feared that the immense scale of the public offerings (i.e., IPOs of state-owned companies) might disrupt the market.
(h) On June 30, 2015, the three Japan Post Group companies filed an application to list their shares.
(i) On July 16, 2015, the three Japan Post Group companies announced the record date for a stock split and implemented a 30-for-1 stock split effective August 1, 2015.
(j) On September 10, 2015, the Tokyo Stock Exchange announced that it would finalize the offering prices for JP Bank and Japan Post Life Insurance on October 9 and for Japan Post Holdings on October 26 before approving their listing on its first section on November 4.

3.4.3 Feedback from Private Financial Institutions on the Listing of JP Bank

On July 29, 2015, the government asked the Postal Privatization Committee to look into and discuss how to proceed with postal privatization (FSA No. 2296). In regard to Japan Post Holdings' December 26, 2014, announcement of the three Japan Post Group companies' plan to go public in mid-2015, the committee noted that, 7 years since its initial phase of privatization in October 2017, the IPOs would usher in a new phase as the Japan Post Group companies gained new shareholders and as market discipline took root in their operations. The committee concluded that the Japan Post Group should increase its corporate value to ensure the success of the IPOs and urged the government to closely examine ways to proceed with postal privatization via innovative administrative management.

Upon the government's request, on July 14, 2015, the Postal Privatization Committee recommended that the government solicit opinions widely from the public on how to proceed with postal privatization. Public opinions were solicited until August 4, 2015.

In response, the Japanese Bankers Association and the Regional Banks Association of Japan submitted their opinions on August 4, 2015. The gist of their opinions are summarized in what follows.

(a) Basic Vision for Postal Privatization

As specified in Articles 1 and 2 of the Postal Service Privatization Act, the basic vision is to leave as much as possible up to private financial institutions with an eye toward cultivating a freer and more vibrant economy. The law also requires that the postal service take measures necessary for ensuring an equal footing with competing businesses while paying attention to the impact it may have on the sound development of local economies as well as the market.

To this end, fair and free competition must be promoted along with market discipline, enabling private financial institutions and the Japan Post Group to provide diverse, high-quality services.

(b) Changes after IPO

The planned IPO is an important step that is indispensable for steadily privatizing postal services, and the financial sector should work toward its success.

(c) JP Bank's Role in Making a Successful IPO

i. Steadily implementing growth strategies to enhance JP Bank's corporate value

Under the Japan Post Group Medium-term Management Plan announced in April 2015, the group plans to leverage its post office network to sell investment products in the authorized areas of operation in line with the shifting trend from savings to investments with an eye toward increasing service revenues. As one of the largest institutional investors in Japan, the group also plans to work on diversified and sophisticated asset management through appropriate risk management to ensure stable profits. These initiatives of JP Bank are desirable for making its stock listing a success.

ii. Cooperation and coordination with private financial institutions on an even playing field

If postal privatization is to boost the standard of living and pave the way to a sound national economy, it is important that JP Bank and private financial institutions work together and coordinate with one another while leveraging their own functions and operating foundations to respond to customer needs.

Further alliances and partnerships (e.g., offering funds that will help revitalize local economies, use of post office network by private financial institutions) will enhance the corporate value of JP Bank and the Japan Post Group and will eventually help promote Japan's growth strategies and vitalize local economies.

iii. Building a risk management system through downsizing

Operating on an enormous scale, JP Bank is exposed to an equally huge interest-rate risk due to an operational structure in which it uses funds raised via fixed-amount postal savings to invest in government bonds. The activities of a behemoth like JP Bank can significantly affect the market, which can make asset management difficult or cause any number of other problems. To increase corporate value as a listed company, the bank needs to be downsized enough to ensure appropriate risk management.

iv. Ensuring transparency of transactions with Japan Post

While the Banking Act prohibits banks from operating nonbanking businesses, Japan Post Holdings with its stake in JP Bank has been given special permission to own Japan Post, which is a nonbanking company, as a subsidiary under the Postal Service Privatization Act.

It is necessary to protect JP Bank from risks associated with nonbanking operations, ensure stability of the financial system, and justify the outsourcing fees paid to Japan Post. To do this, the transparency of transactions between JP Bank and Japan Post should be ensured.

(d) Future Direction of Postal Privatization

In addition to working on the aforementioned four areas, JP Bank should establish its own business model as soon as possible to enhance its corporate value and make its stock listing a success.

The vision for postal privatization should be one where JP Bank and private financial institutions can compete on an equal footing in the development of Japan's financial market and economy as well as regional revitalization.

After the initial privatization of postal services in October 2007, JP Bank and other private financial institutions repeatedly made similar claims. Although the stock listing did not necessarily point the way to their full privatization, their tone changed as privatization became a reality.

They became more cooperative, showing support for the successful listing of JP Bank's stock. While requiring the bank to compete with private financial institutions on an equal footing under the Banking Act, they also listed challenges the bank needed to overcome to carry out the kind of operation required for a listed company rather than just emphasizing the automatic guarantee they get from the government and concerns that the bank may squeeze private financial institutions out of the market.

However, neither of the associations addressed a schedule for full privatization or a deadline for the sale of all shares, which remains an important outstanding issue. I believe that both associations should have suggested a methodology and deadline for full privatization (which will be discussed later).

3.4.4 Studies on the Listing of Three Japan Post Group Companies

So far I have discussed in detail a series of events that led to the listing of three Japan Post Group companies. Due to the unique nature of the sale of Japan Post shares as a way to finance postdisaster reconstruction, virtually no research had been conducted into the listing of the three privately operated, government-owned companies following postal privatization (and the vision for the future).

However, as preparations for their stock listing took place, various industry journals and books started to highlight the topic, bringing discussion of stock listing and privatization of the Japan Post Group out of the shadows.

These studies primarily looked into the profitability of the Japan Post Group operations based on a share price forecast, as well as ensuring transparency among group companies, and other issues that need to be cleared before their IPOs. They also pointed out the absence of a road map for disposing of all Japan Post Group shares, which blurred any future vision for the Japan Post Group and was thus the biggest hurdle it faced. What follows is a list of studies on the stock listing as well as my own insights.

- Dr. Hideki Fujii, professor of financial accounting at Kyoto University, has published a number of research papers on the Japan Post Group. Between March 2012 and March 2017 his analysis of Japan Post Group operations and its corporate value was published annually by Tsushin Kenkyukai, for example. He discussed the listing of Japan Post Group and its estimated corporate value in a peer-reviewed paper on public service published in July 2014. Dr. Fujii served as a member of the committee for studying new postal service business models for the government in 2010 when the Democratic Party of Japan was the ruling party. He was a promoter of the postal reform bill (which was submitted by the People's New Party and later repealed). He has been supported by Teishin Kenkyukai (headed by Hisaoki Kamei and renamed Tsushin Kenkyukai after the postal service was privatized) for many years. His political stance on postal privatization differs from mine and his feelings came to the fore in the peer review process.

With this in mind, I will offer my views on Dr. Fujii's March 2015 study on Japan Post Group operations and corporate value noted subsequently. In the preface of his paper, Dr. Fujii writes: "Japan Post's stock market debut is finally in the countdown stage. In light of the current circumstances and trends, my study for this year placed special emphasis on analyzing the operating environment of the Japan Post Group. When it comes to privatization of state-owned businesses, while they follow the fundamental market mechanism, they are inevitably affected by politics. In writing this year's report, I was reminded of the fact that the listing of Japan Post shares is no exception. This year marks the fourth year since I started working on this annual research commissioned by Kenkyu Tsushinkai. I would like to thank everyone at Kenkyu Tsushinkai, especially Chairman Hisaoki Kamei and Secretary-General Tadahiro Shimazaki, for their support of our research over the years."

In his study, Dr. Fujii uses the residual income model to estimate JP Bank's corporate value under the assumption that the bank would go public. He then calculates the price of its shares via an analysis of the model in comparison with three megabanks. His study focuses only on the analysis of the residual income model without discussing a road map to full privatization, the most important issue for JP Bank, or a vision for the bank. He also fails to clarify his stance on postal privatization (i.e., keeping it state-owned). The study is based on an unsubstantiated theory that does not conform to reality. His thesis is lacking in logic and any institutional context.

- Dr. Yoshiaki Shikano, economics professor at Doshisha University, published *Nihon no kinyu seido* [The financial system of Japan] (second edition) from Toyo Keizai in August 2006 (in the run-up to postal privatization). In Chap. 19 of the book he discusses policies for postal privatization and government-affiliated financial institutions.

He writes, "After breaking up Japan Post into four companies, the government decided to sell all shares in the company in the market over the following ten years to fully privatize it by the end of September 2017. Privatizing the postal savings and postal life insurance systems is vital to ensuring an equal footing with private financial institutions and, as has already been said, is urgently needed in light of the Japanese Big Bang. This is why postal privatization has a huge role to play in the reform of Japan's financial system.

"How will things change after postal privatization? First, the postal savings system will be placed under supervision and regulation of the Financial Services Agency, as are the banks, and incorporated into Japan's financial framework in both name and reality. Second, postal savings will no longer be government-guaranteed, and postal savings bank operations will become subject to monitoring and the discipline of the market. Third, the status of employees will be changed to nonpublic employees to increase their motivation to work. At the same time the privatization of the postal savings system, which serves as a point of entry for public financial services, is expected to push the government to give a second look at how public financial services should be operated."

With regard to the privatization of government-affiliated financial institutions, Dr. Shikano touches on the fact that the government immediately started working on reforming eight government-affiliated financial institutions following the privatization of postal services. Then he briefly describes the government's January 2006 plan to reduce its stake in DBJ and Shoko Chukin Bank to zero between fiscal 2013 and 2015 in order to fully privatize them.

In his book Dr. Shikano neither discusses a process of full privatization and problems that may arise in that process nor offers specific solutions to these problems, partly because it was written immediately after the implementation plan for postal privatization was approved.

His article "*Yusei jojo no kadai: Shuekiryoku no kojo ga kyumu* [Challenge to listing of Japan Post stock: Enhancing profitability is imperative]," published in the July 27, 2015, Nikkei column *Keizai kyoshitsu* [Economics class], states the following: "About five years ago I wrote in this column (dated April 27, 2010) that taking JP Bank public was difficult due to its low profitability. Back then after the Democratic Party of Japan was in power and the movement toward postal privatization had suffered a setback, I criticized the situation with an aim toward keeping it in check. Later the postal privatization ball started rolling again out of a necessity to secure funds for recovery work from the Great East Japan Earthquake, and the stocks of three Japan Post Group companies are slated to be listed on the Tokyo Stock Exchange this fall. The listing of Japan Post Group stocks is the second step toward privatization, following Japan Post's transformation into a stock company in October 2007, and it's heading into a crucial stage. Below are my views on what's needed to make postal privatization a success." Dr. Shikano then goes on to list the keys to successful postal privatization as follows: (1) JP Bank must take some risks because its profitability is half of regional banks' profitability. (2) Raising the deposit cap is not necessary because it does not improve profitability. (3) Change ownership of former special post offices and put them under direct ownership of Japan Post to increase profits. My take on this article is that the problem with JP Bank's profit structure lies in its inefficient fund procurement method and the low profit margin due to the kind of investments that yield a low return. Listing JP Bank stock and charting a course for its full privatization will solve this structural problem. Dr. Shikano simply fails to see the big picture.

3.4.5 Japan Post Holdings' Capital Policy and Listing of JP Bank Stock

A sum of 1420.9 billion yen, consisting of 730.9 billion yen generated from Japan Post Holdings' buyback of government-owned shares on December 3, 2015, and 690 billion yen from the sale of Japan Post shares on November 4, 2015, was allotted for the first fund to pay back reconstruction bonds.

This scheme was explained at the 127th meeting of the Postal Privatization Committee held on January 16, 2015 (Fig. 3.3).

Under this scheme, the government would first sell shares in Japan Post Holdings on the stock exchange and use the revenue from the sales to fund reconstruction work.

> Then Japan Post Holdings would sell stock in its two financial companies on the stock exchange and use the revenue from the sales to buy back its own shares from the government, which would use the proceeds to fund reconstruction work.

This scheme is almost the same as the one I discussed in my article published in the October 3, 2011, issue of *Kinyu Zaisei Jijo*, which I noted in the previous section. Next I would like to analyze the capital policy Japan Post Holdings seeks to have

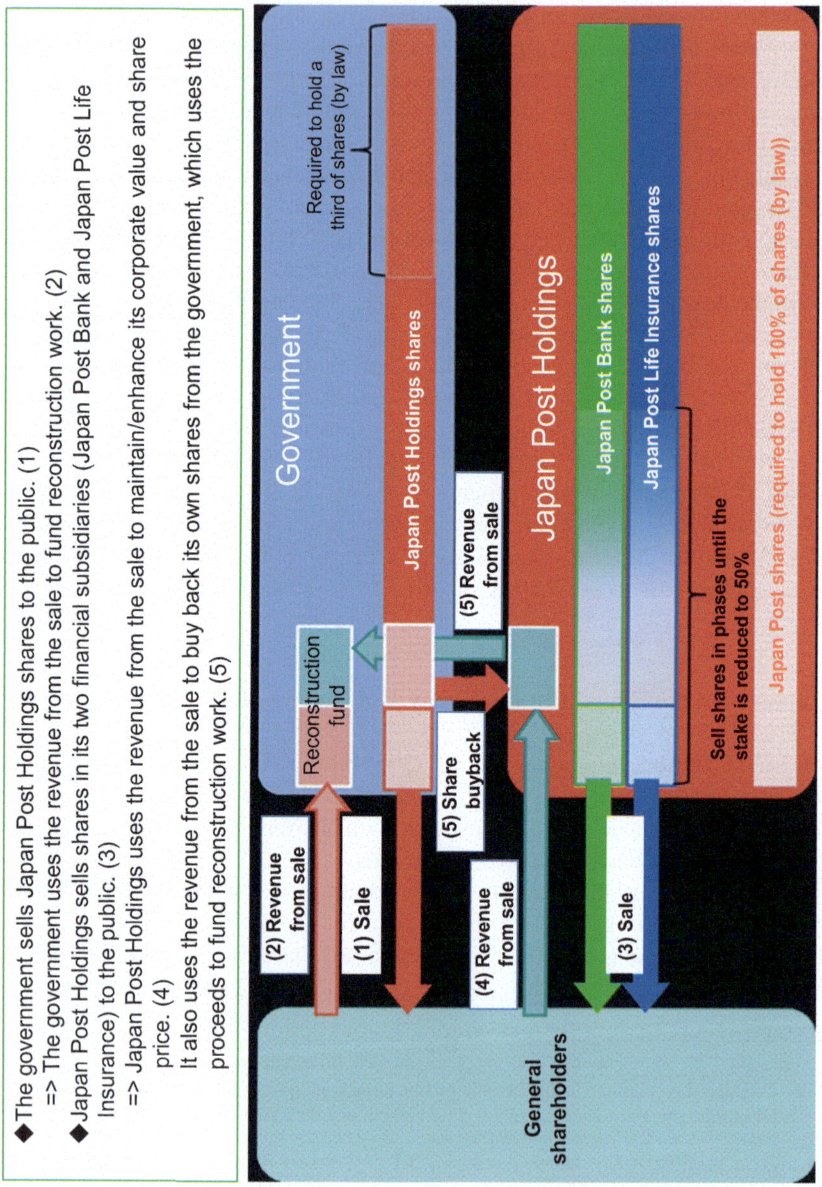

Fig. 3.3 Listing of three Japan Post Group companies
Source: Postal Privatization Committee (2007)

upon going public and estimate decreases in shares of Japan Post Co. owned by the government and shares of JP Bank owned by Japan Post Holdings.

- Views on Japan Post Holding's Reconstruction Fund Scheme and My Reconstruction Fund Scheme ("Financial Scheme")

The government proclaimed that it would sell government assets and revive the post of the Minister of State for Government Revitalization to thoroughly review and prioritize its operations prior to increasing taxes. Government screening of JP Bank operations would reveal a "hidden treasure" that is immediately available for use, i.e., JP Bank's huge equity capital. Since the government still has a long way to go before it can take JP Bank public now that the selling of shares in the Japan Post Group is blocked, it cannot expect to make a profit from selling its shares in the bank for a while. That is why the government should return JP Bank's capital reserves totaling approximately 4 trillion yen to its coffers and use it to fund a chunk of postdisaster reconstruction while curbing tax hikes. This is the financial scheme I proposed.

On September 30, 2014 JP Bank bought back shares held by its parent company, Japan Post Holdings, to give back to its shareholders. Following this move, Japan Post Holdings decided to spend 700 billion yen out of 1.3 trillion yen it raised from disposing of the entire amount of the pension liabilities it had carried over since it was operating as the Ministry of Posts and Telecommunications to improve its financial standing before going public. The company invested the remaining 600 billion yen in Japan Post for the capital increase it needed to acquire a stake in Toll Holdings Limited, an Australian leading logistics company, as part of its growth strategy. This growth strategy, however, ended up as an impairment loss of 400 billion yen for the fiscal year ending March 31, 2017, making Japan Post Holding fall into the red.

If this scheme had been possible before JP Bank went public, the government could have made JP Bank buy back its own shares worth 4 trillion yen from Japan Post Holdings and then have Japan Post Holdings use that 4 trillion yen to buy back its own shares worth 4 trillion yen from the government. The government used this scheme before and after selling Japan Post shares on the stock exchange to secure funds for postdisaster reconstruction.

Under the financial scheme, capital reserves totaling 4 trillion yen were supposed to be returned to the government to fund reconstruction efforts, even though listing of Japan Post stocks was not possible, unless it was approved by the Diet in the event of a national crisis. In the first place, JP Bank's capital reserves worth 4 trillion yen came from assets worth 9460 billion yen, which Japan Post Holdings took over from the Japan Post public company when it was established, which included shares in subsidiaries worth 9069 billion yen. The 4 trillion yen is part of the 7669 billion yen worth of JP Bank shares it holds. It would have been okay if people's assets had been used directly to fund reconstruction work.

The money generated from JP Bank's buyback of its own shares on September 30, 2014, should have been used for reconstruction work.

Offering stock to the public weakens the government's control through sale of shares and allows for fair and transparent operations under market oversight. The public offering moves the privatization of JP Bank forward as market discipline is maintained by new shareholders. I believe my paper helped the government to chip away at the law that froze its sale of Japan Post shares and add Article 14 to the supplementary provisions of the Reconstruction Funding Act.

- **Japan Post Holdings' Capital Policy and JP Bank's Majority Shareholders**
- **Capital Relationship between Japan Post Holdings and JP Bank and Their Share Holdings**
- On September 30, 2014, JP Bank decided to buy back its own shares from Japan Post Holdings as part of a Japan Post Holdings group-wide capital policy. I incorporated this scheme into each company's balance sheet to show their relationship in a chart. Figure 3.4 (This information was submitted to the Postal Privatization Committee at its 122nd meeting held on November 10, 2014)

- Since a 30-for-1 stock split was implemented on August 1, 2015, for the three Japan Post Group companies to go public, the number of outstanding shares of JP Bank hit 4.5 billion, and the repurchased shares that were added to the treasury stock rose to 750,525,000. The remaining balance of shares held by Japan Post Holdings totaled 3,749,475,000.
- JP Bank put up 412,442,300 shares (11.00% held by general shareholders) in its November 4, 2015, public offering, and Japan Post Holdings' stake dropped to 89% (Table 3.10).
- **Capital Relationship between Government and Japan Post Holdings and Their Holdings**
- Japan Post Holdings went public on November 4, 2015, selling 447,636,400 shares to general shareholders and 47,363,600 shares to the Japan Post Holdings Employee Shareholding Association, for a total of 495 million shares. As a result, the stake held by the government ended up at 89%, with the remaining 9.95% of the shares in the hands of general shareholders.
- On December 3, 2015, Japan Post Holdings bought back its own shares by selling government-owned shares to help finance disaster area reconstruction efforts and promote postal privatization.
- It acquired a total of 383,306,000 shares for 730.9 billion yen. The government's stake dropped to 87.97%, while the stake held by general shareholders rose to 10.87% as a result of an increase in treasury shares.

In September 2017, the government implemented its second reconstruction fund scheme. Japan Post Holdings revealed its failed strategic investment in Toll Holdings Limited when it announced the financial results for the fiscal year ending March 31, 2017. Looking to offer its shares to the public for the second time, the company came up with a new mergers and acquisitions (M&A) strategy in a bid to achieve a V-shaped turnaround but ended up backing down.

- Outline of second offering

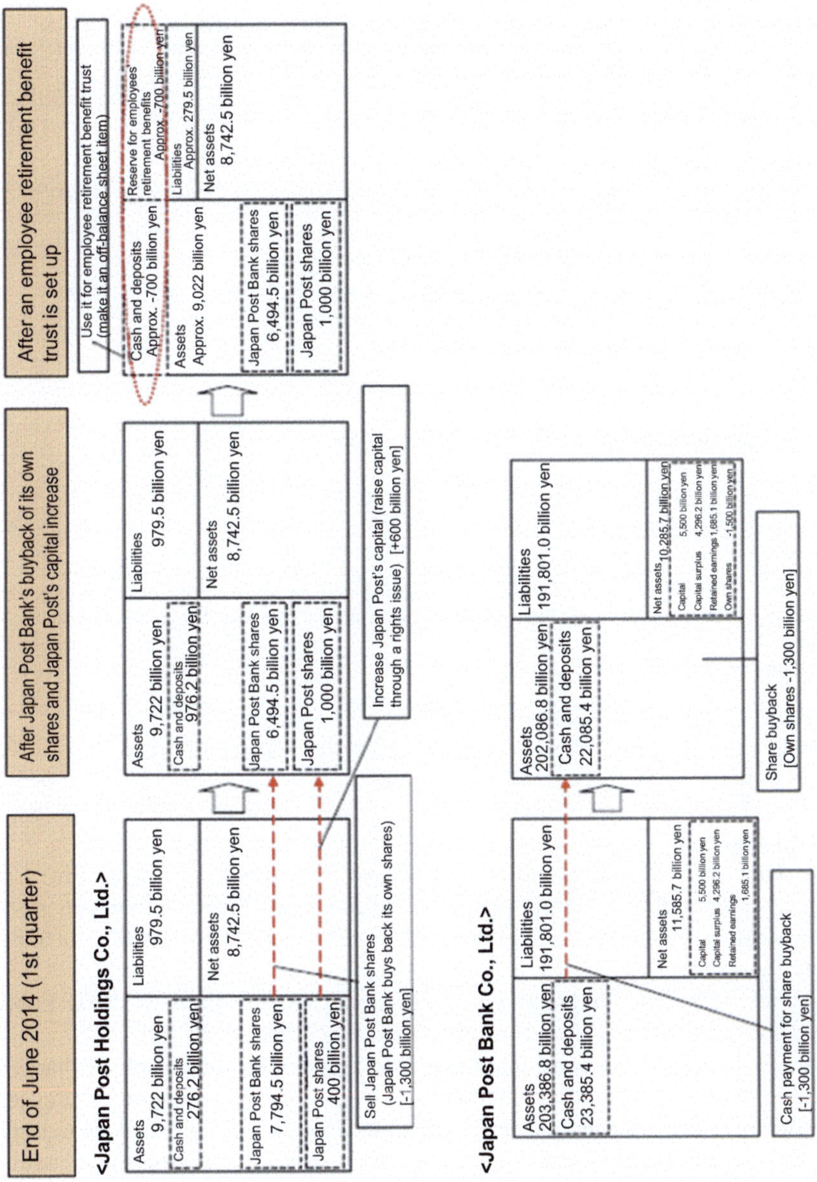

Fig. 3.4 Transition of Japan Post Group's shares

– Number of shares to be acquired by JP Bank	25,017,500 shares
– Number of JP Bank's outstanding shares	150 million shares (16.67% of outstanding shares)
– Total acquisition cost of shares	1,299,999,363,000 yen (approximately 1.3 trillion yen), resulting in Japan Post Holdings' possessing 83.33% of voting shares in JP Bank

Table 3.10 Approval for listing of three Japan Post Group companies (September 10, 2015)

	Japan Post Holdings Co.	Japan Post Bank Co.	Japan Post Life Insurance Co.
Estimated offering price (yen)	1350 => 1400[a]	1400 => 1450	2150 => 2200
Number of shares sold (million)	495	412.44	66
Value of shares sold (billion yen)	668.2	577.4	142.9
Number of shares outstanding (million)	4500	4500	600
Total market value (billion yen)	6075	6300	1290
Government's stake after sale	89%	89%	89%

Timeline: October 9 offering price finalized for JP Bank and Japan Post Life Insurance; October 26 offering price finalized for Japan Post Holdings; November 4 listed on Tokyo Stock Exchange's first section

[a]Final offering price

Although the government's stake drops after the second offering, Japan Post continues benefitting from government guarantees.

The Postal Service Privatization Act requires the government to hold more than a third of all shares.

Since Japan Post Holdings did not sell shares in JP Bank and Japan Post Life Insurance via this public offering, operations of these two financial companies will not be expanded. (Japan Post Holdings' stake: 74.2% in JP Bank and 89% in Japan Post Life Insurance) (Table 3.11).

The stock price and dividend yield will remain stable until the next public offering (due to the government-controlled market) (Table 3.12).

Although there were concerns that Japan Post may not be able to sell all shares in its second public offering, individual investors seemed to opt for owning shares just as they did in the first offering rather than earning interest on their postal savings at a rate of 0.01% when they could expect the stock price to remain stable with a dividend yield of 3% thanks to the automatic government guarantee. As before, even if postal savings amounting to 1.3 trillion yen were invested in stocks, the postal savings balance of over 170 trillion yen would remain unaffected.

	Japan Post Holdings Co.			Japan Post Bank Co.			Japan Post Life Insurance Co.		
March	Net assets (trillion yen)	Ordinary profit (trillion yen)	Net profit (100 million yen)	Net assets (trillion yen)	Ordinary profit (100 million yen)	Net profit (100 million yen)	Net assets (trillion yen)	Ordinary profit (100 million yen)	Net profit (100 million yen)
2013	12.5	1.2	5627	11.0	5935	3739	1.5	5293	910
2014	13.4	1.1	4790	11.5	5650	3546	1.5	4635	634
2015	15.3	1.1	4826	11.6	5694	3694	2.0	4931	817
2016	—	0.86	3700	—	4600	3200	—	3500	840
Dividend yield (%)	3.40			3.57			5.20		

Revenue from sales (combined total for three companies) totaling 1388.6 billion yen is used to fund reconstruction work
Total market value (combined total for three companies): 13,665 billion yen

Shares sold to general shareholders on September 25, 2017			
	910 million shares	1.2 trillion yen (at 1320 yen)	
Additional shares sold to general shareholders on September 29, 2017			
	76 million shares	0.1 trillion yen	
Share buyback	76 million shares	0.1 trillion yen	Total 1.4 trillion yen
End of March 2017	Number of shares outstanding	4.5 billion shares	
	Number of shares held by government		
	3.62 billion shares (80.4% stake)		
End of September 2017	Number of shares held by government		
	2.63 billion shares (58.5% stake)		
If shares worth 1.4 trillion yen are sold by 2020 via the same scheme			
	Number of shares held by government		
	1.64 billion shares (36.5% stake)		
(41.4% stake in voting shares because treasury shares do not carry voting rights)			

Table 3.11 Stock price and dividend yield (yen)

	Offering price	Opening price	29 Sept. 2017	Highest price	Dividend	Dividend yield (%)
Japan Post Holdings	1400	1631	1329	1999	50	3.83
Japan Post Bank	1450	1689	1390	1823	50	3.7
Japan Post Life Insurance	2200	2929	2411	4120	64	2.81

As the next step toward full privatization, Japan Post Holdings' stake in JP Bank must be reduced to less than 50% to enhance JP Bank's operational freedom and transparency, which is the purpose of going public.

While the Act for Partial Revision of the Postal Service Privatization Act requires JP Bank to obtain authorization of the prime minister and the internal affairs and communications minister prior to starting any new business, once half of its shares are disposed of, the bank is required to merely notify them but must ensure fair competition with other financial institutions, notify the Postal Privatization Committee, and become subject to its supervisory orders and regulations.

This means that, once Japan Post Holdings' stake in JP Bank is reduced to less than 50%, it will be easier for JP Bank to diversify its operations because new

Table 3.12 Government's stake in Japan Post Holdings

November 4, 2015
Number of shares held by government: 4,500,000,000 after IPO
– Government: 4,005,000,000 (89.00%)
– Japan Post Holdings Employee Shareholding Association: 47,363,600 (1.05%)
– General shareholders: 447,636,400 (9.95%)
December 3, 2015 Buyback of 383,306,000 shares [no voting rights]
Number of shares held by government: 3,621,694,000 after share buyback
– Government: 3,621,694,000 (87.97%)
– JPH Employee Shareholding Association: 47,363,600 (1.15%)
– General shareholders: 447,636,400 (10.87%)
– Number of shares with voting rights: 4,116,694,000 (100%)
– Number of shares repurchased 383,306,000 (–)
September 25–29, 2017 second public offering
Number of Japan Post Holdings shares sold: 986,000,000
– Share buyback: 76,000,000 shares
– Government: 2,559,694,400 (63.35%)
– JPH Employee Shareholding Association: 47,363,600 (1.17%)
– General shareholders: 1,433,636,400 (35.48%)
– Number of shares with voting rights: 4,040,694,000 (100%)
– Number of shares repurchased 459,306,000 (–)
If shares are sold for third time via same scheme by 2022
Number of Japan Post Holdings shares sold: 986,000,000
– Share buyback: 76,000,000 shares
– Government: 1,497,694,000 (37.78%)
– JPH Employee Shareholding Association: 47,363,600 (1.19%)
– General shareholders: 2,419,636,400 (61.03%)
– Number of shares with voting rights: 3,964,694,000 (100%)
– Number of shares repurchased 535,306,000 (–)

businesses will be authorized on a notification basis. Once the bank reaches this point, the remaining problem for JP Bank will be its bloated assets, and the bank will have to build up its lending capability as it diversifies its asset management channels. The key to solving the problem will be training personnel and hiring people with the right lending operations skills.

4 Problems in Stock Listing and Path to Full Privatization

As a result of the public offerings, the status of the three Japan Post Group companies changed from privately operated but government-owned entities to privately owned and (partially) privately operated entities. This is a positive development following the privatization of postal services, which turned them into stock companies.

With many individual investors holding its shares, the Japan Post Group now has the system in place where these shareholders, who are more interested in its operations than ever, can keep a check on corporate governance by the government, which has a controlling stake in the company, while ensuring that market discipline is maintained. These individual investors seemed to have used their postal savings to buy shares (based on the fact that postal savings decreased by about 1 trillion yen when payments for shares were made). While the Ministry of Finance and Japan Post Holdings initially had concerns about whether shares would sell smoothly, that concern proved unfounded.

In the monthly magazine *Wedge*, I wrote the following, published on October 20, 2015. "Investing in [Japan Post] shares is much more advantageous than depositing money in postal savings at an interest rate of 0.025% because these shares are automatically guaranteed by the government and come with a 3% dividend yield. Since the balance of postal savings is 177 trillion yen, it's no surprise 1 to 3 trillion yen in savings were spent on investing in shares."

In other words, investors' savings became the reconstruction fund through the public offering.

Now the problem is that, under the current scheme, the government's stake in Japan Post Holdings is still over 50%, making the government its major shareholder. This slows down the privatization of its two financial subsidiaries and hinders giving them greater freedom to operate. Another problem is that JP Bank's profitability will decline when interest rates drop. When interest rates go up, on the other hand, since the bank will be exposed to interest-rate risk, its profitability may also decline depending on financial conditions, resulting in lagging share prices and dividend yields. While the bank is automatically covered by a government guarantee, this high risk poses the biggest problem.

As a way to solve these two problems, Japan Post should work on enhancing its corporate value, just like real private companies do, in going public and implement growth strategies aimed at increasing its share price, regardless of how it will affect the dynamics of the Reconstruction Funding Act, all with an eye toward reducing the percentage of government-owned shares to less than 50% as soon as possible to take it down to a third. The government should also sell shares in JP Bank to reduce national debt in order to achieve the goal of restoring its fiscal health by 2025.

JP Bank ought to buy back its own shares in order to reduce Japan Post Holdings' stake and implement measures to give back to shareholders such as increasing its ROE. Actually, reducing the government's stake in controlling shares to less than a third will enable JP Bank to compete with private companies on an equal footing. Diversifying operations is a sure way to increase sources of revenue and bolster the profit structure, building a solid operating foundation that can weather risks.

On page 85 of *Kansei kinyu kaikaku to chigin saihen* [Public financial reform and regional bank reorganization] published on March 26, 2015, I discussed the initial public offering of Japan Post's two financial companies announced on December 26, 2014.

In the book I maintain that JP Bank cannot be equal to banks that are governed by the Banking Act as long as it is operating under the Postal Service Privatization Act. Whatever the reason may be, selling government-owned shares through a public offering is a step toward full privatization and a clear sign the bank is headed in the right direction.

Since public companies, which are protected by special laws, are managed by the Diet, i.e., legislation, their freedom of operation is restricted by cabinet orders, ministerial ordinances, and administrative directives, for example. That is why public companies send people from their bloated organization to serve as members of the Diet in a bid to change laws. These politicians are known as the postal tribe and are supported by the National Association of Special Post Office Masters (*Zentoku*) as well as the Japan Postal Group Union (JPGU). A total of nearly 1,000,000 people, including 220,000 members of these organizations plus their families, provide these politicians with the organized support they need to bring in votes. Japanese National Railways and NTT also once had their own tribe of politicians, but their organizational power has diminished since they were privatized and split up. Once public corporations have greater management transparency and are freed from legal restrictions on their operations by going public, they are able to compete with private companies on an equal footing. They can then become fully privatized.

The fact that public corporations are managed by bureaucrats means that they are managed by the Diet and the laws they write. When they are financially troubled, taxpayers' money is used to increase their capital or cover any deficit. In other words, their managers never have to make any real effort to solve their problems.

In the ongoing process of fully privatizing JP Bank as well as DBJ and Shoko Chukin Bank, based on the opinions of the academic sector such as the Postal Privatization Committee, the government has used a personnel placement strategy (known as *tasukigake jinji*) under which the top positions at these companies are periodically rotated between people from the public and private sectors. Although they were transformed into private stock companies, the typical decision-making function found in private industry has been undermined, turning privatization into a mere illusion. When a select few corporate managers use private industry decision-making practices, they often find it difficult to coordinate with the public business sector (including the political world) that is governed by laws and end up hitting a dead end.

Turning public financial services into private financial services takes changing the shareholder of a public financial institution from the government to general shareholders through a public offering. In other words, it means changing the decision-making process, which constitutes the backbone of corporate management, from public to private as noted earlier. The government should repeal the Postal Service Privatization Act, the Act on DBJ Inc., and the Shoko Chukin Bank Limited Act so JP Bank, DBJ, and Shoko Chukin Bank can operate on an equal footing with private financial institutions under the Banking Act.

It makes sense that the JFC and the JBIC should take risks in their operations by providing emergency loans in the event of a global financial crisis or in response to a catastrophe like the Great East Japan Earthquake when directed to do so by the government. When it comes to JP Bank, DBJ, and Shoko Chukin Bank, however, every time the government makes them put off selling all of their government-owned shares whenever the opportunity arises, it seems that they want to enjoy the benefits of being government-run even though they are aiming to become fully privatized at the same time.

JP Bank faces major hurdles to realizing its future institutional design. By the time it sells all its shares, the bank must build a framework that will enable it to compete with private financial institutions on an equal footing and wean itself off its government guarantees under the Postal Service Privatization Act so it can operate under the Banking Act.

4.1 Shoko Chukin Bank Loan Fraud and Full Privatization

The special public institutions reform law was enacted in 2005, about the same time the Postal Service Privatization Act and the Shoko Chukin Bank Limited Act also went into effect. These laws were designed to reclaim the free and fair financial market and rein in the out-of-control public financial services. The reform of special public institutions, however, only turned them into privately operated yet government-owned stock companies and failed to really privatize them. Although it has been 10 years since they first set out on the road to privatization, they have lost their way over the years as Japan has experienced a change in ruling parties, the Great East Japan Earthquake, and other events, and their operating policies have become muddied. Shoko Chukin Bank had been engaging in lending operations over the entire 10 years, but then a look at its fiscal 2016 financial results revealed that it had committed fraud.

More specifically, the bank took advantage of the government's crisis loan program for companies that had suffered damage in the Great East Japan Earthquake and falsified customers' sales data and other financial figures in order to boost lending. The bank's management turned a blind eye to 760 cases of illicit loans at 35 branches. As a result, Shoko Chukin Bank was ordered by the Ministry of Economy, Trade and Industry to submit a business improvement plan on June 9, 2017.

In the wake of the scandal, on June 10, 2017, the Nikkei published an article addressing what the bank should do to solve its problems. The article proposed that Shoko Chukin Bank revamp the crisis loan program, stop evaluating employee performance based on sales quota and numerical targets, which were the breeding ground for fraud, and step up efforts on compliance training.

These improvement measures proposed by the Nikkei, however, are not the best. Shoko Chukin Bank's scandal was destined to happen because of the way public financial services are operated and never reformed.

Mishandling of the crisis response loan program by the bank led to illegal loans because of the government's strong-arm intervention in the bank's personnel affairs

<Past and present presidents>

Before privatization	1993–2001	Yukiharu Kodama (Vice-Minister of International Trade and Industry)
	2001–2008	Tadashi Ezaki (Director-General, Industrial Policy Bureau, Ministry of International Trade and Industry)
After privatization	2008–2013	Tetsuo Seki (Representative Director and Executive Vice President, Nippon Steel Corporation)
	2013–2016	Hideji Sugiyama (Vice-Minister of Economy, Trade and Industry)
	2016–March 2018	Kenyu Adachi (Vice-Minister of Economy, Trade and Industry)
	April 2018–present	Masahiro Sekine (Managing Executive Officer, Prince Hotels, previously Mizuho Financial Group employee)

as well as repeated partial amendments of a special law, the Shoko Chukin Bank Limited Act, which closed the doors on the bank's full privatization (stock listing). We will look into how the government's intervention and legal revisions led to the bank's misconduct.

4.1.1 Why Shoko Chukin's Crisis Response Loan Program and Privatization Policy was Doomed—Problems with Repeated Amendments of the Shoko Chukin Bank Limited Act

Let us first take a look at the repeated amendments made to the Shoko Chukin Bank Limited Act in chronological order.

- In May 2007, the Shoko Chukin Bank Limited Act went into effect, stipulating that Shoko Chukin Bank would dispose of all its government-owned shares (46.6%) in 5 to 7 years with the establishment of the Shoko Chukin Bank special corporation. The special rules that were applicable during the transitional period were abolished, and the bank was privatized on October 1, 2008, with a plan for full privatization.
- In June 2009, following on the heels of the collapse of Lehman Brothers, the law was partially amended in order to enhance the bank's operations for lending to crisis-hit companies. The revised law enabled the government to take a stake in the bank until the end of March 2012 and stipulated that the bank would be fully privatized in 5 to 7 years from April 2012.
- Following the Great East Japan Earthquake, a special fiscal-measures law was enacted in May 2013 to provide financial assistance to cope with its aftermath. The law allowed a 3-year extension to the period during which the government could take a stake in the bank (until late March 2015) and extended the deadline for full privatization until 5 to 7 years from April 2015. The government decided

to overhaul the bank's organization, including its shareholding, by the end of fiscal 2014.

- After implementing an overhaul at the end of fiscal 2014, the government partially revised the Shoko Chukin Bank Limited Act in May 2015. The revision focused on leveraging the bank's investing and lending function to provide funds for financing crisis management and growth while maintaining the policy to fully privatize the bank. Specifically, the revision allowed the government to invest in Shoko Chukin Bank for an unspecified period in order for the bank to make emergency loans. Under the revised law, Shoko Chukin Bank was required to work on intensively lending growth funds through special investment operations until the end of fiscal 2020 and make efforts to dispose of all investment assets in the said operations to complete the operations by the end of fiscal 2025. The government was allowed to invest in Shoko Chukin Bank to finance special investment operations. It was also required to reduce shares in the bank in light of the impact its shareholding may have on achieving the bank's objectives as well as market trends and dispose of all shares as soon as possible. The revised law also required the government to hold more than a third of all outstanding shares while measures on the emergency lending operations were taken and more than half of all outstanding shares while the measures concerning the special investment operations were taken.

As noted previously, the law was frequently revised to impede the path to full privatization, all the while using emergency lending and special investment operations as excuses. Furthermore, while appointing top executives from the private sector was a basic premise of privatization, the bank's president, who had a private-sector background, was replaced by a former bureaucrat (the vice-minister of economy, trade and industry) on the pretext of conducting the emergency lending operations with subsequent presidents recruited from the public sector as well.

Top executives of other privatized policy-based financial institutions, DBJ, and four Japan Post Group companies have been appointed from the private sector.

As stated earlier, the government and the Ministry of Economy, Trade and Industry have been deeply involved in the management of Shoko Chukin Bank by leveraging the crisis response loan program and using local-economy vitalization and growth of SMEs as justification for it, turning the bank back into a public financial institution.

This resulted in setting back its full privatization.

While government-led management may have worked while the crisis response loan program was still functioning, demand for emergency loans subsided once some progress was made in postdisaster reconstruction. Low-risk crisis response loans that came with an interest subsidy and guarantee had advantages for both customers and Shoko Chukin Bank, providing the perfect breeding ground for illicit loans. On top of that, the bank set crisis loan targets and tasked its branches with making them, which is why they made illicit loans for the sake of achieving the targets and got away with it. The fact that illegal loans were made at branches across Japan simply underscores the fact that it is a problem rooted in its management.

A third-party committee gave a detailed report on the illegal lending problem in April 2017.

Since the report was based on a random sampling survey and was considered insufficient, the bank investigated all accounts. In October 2017 it submitted a report to the Small and Medium Enterprise Agency with the finding that it made 4609 illegal loans at 97 branches.

Subsequently an expert panel was established under the Ministry of Economy, Trade and Industry to look into measures for reforming Shoko Chukin Bank.

The primary factor in the illicit loans was the overallocation of the government budget to the Small and Medium Enterprise Agency for the crisis response loan program. On top of that, continuous demand for allocating funds to the program resulted in excessive allocation of funds to branches and pressuring branches to fulfill their quota.

Another factor was that when Shoko Chukin Bank was privatized in 2008, the government incorporated government-led strategies that were not aligned with the initial purpose of the crisis response loan program into the bank's capital policy upon its launch. Under this capital policy a government contribution totaling 303.8 billion yen was transferred to a special reserve for SMEs, and a crisis response reserve totaling 150 billion yen was incorporated into equity capital. On the face of it, owning shares worth 101.6 billion yen out of a total capital amount of 218.6 billion yen, the government owned a 46.5% stake in the bank. However, according to the bank's annual report, the bank regarded these reserves totaling 550.8 billion yen as a special Tier 1 Capital (e.g., common stock) reserve that constitutes a primary part of its equity capital, and in light of that, the government virtually owned a 72% stake as of late March 2017.

Revising this capital policy is an urgent issue that should be addressed in order to get the bank on the privatization track.

On October 25, 2017, the Ministry of Economy, Trade and Industry, the Ministry of Finance, Financial Services Agency, and the Ministry of Agriculture, Forestry and Fisheries took administrative disciplinary action against Shoko Chukin Bank. The root causes of the illicit lending practice were as follows:

- Positioning emergency lending operations as the bank's primary business, management at Shoko Chukin Bank and its headquarters set crisis loan targets for each branch and applied intense sales pressure on their staff to achieve those targets. They also aimed to maintain these operations even after the need for crisis loans had subsided.
- Even though the role of government-affiliated financial institutions is to complement the private sector, management and headquarters saw the crisis response loan program as a competitive weapon and used it to maintain and expand profits as well as their operating foundation.
- Management at Shoko Chukin Bank and its headquarters encouraged employees to make crisis loans, even if customers were not eligible, by doctoring the loans to make it look like they were. Employees were under immense pressure to meet quotas and management turned a blind eye to their malfeasance. Management's

attitude lowered any psychological barriers employees had about committing fraud, resulting in plummeting concern for compliance.

- The bank lacked internal controls and governance needed to prevent illicit loans. In particular, since the executive vice president and other inside directors made all the important business decisions, the board of directors meetings were a mere formality where decisions were rubber-stamped without any check by outside directors.

In light of these findings, the bank was ordered to drastically overhaul its legal compliance, management, internal control, and other systems as soon as possible under the supervision of a competent authority.

An expert panel was established under the Ministry of Economy, Trade and Industry to look into reform measures for Shoko Chukin Bank.

The panel, consisting of Yusuke Kawamura (deputy chairman of Daiwa Institute of Research) and five other individuals from the private sector as well as Hisayoshi Ando (head of the Small and Medium Enterprise Agency) along with officials from the Financial Services Agency and the Ministry of Finance, met seven times beginning in November 2017.

On January 11, 2018, the panel made proposals on the direction in which Shoko Chukin Bank should head. The panel recommended that the bank reorganize its board of directors so that outside directors made up the majority and have a third-party committee supervise its management in order to enhance governance. It proposed that the bank redefine crisis loans, substantially downsize such lending by limiting the scope to large-scale disasters, and enable other financial institutions to pick up any slack.

The panel also proposed that the bank look into a future business model and focus on helping SMEs turn around or sustain their businesses while nurturing companies with low creditworthiness but good growth potential. The panel clearly stated that the bank should decide on making the move to full privatization in light of the outcome of its reform efforts over the next 4 years. At the same time the economy, trade, and industry minister approved the appointment of new Shoko Chukin president from the private sector, putting a stop to the practice of *amakudari*.

4.1.2 Shoko Chukin's Path to Full Privatization

Instead of merely requiring Shoko Chukin Bank to improve its business practices, the government should take this opportunity to revisit the original purpose of the special public institutions reform, change the governing law from a special law to the Banking Act, enhance management transparency by offering its stock to the public, and show a clear path to full privatization that would give the bank greater operational freedom.

To make this happen, the government should reverse the May 2015 partial revision to the Shoko Chukin Bank Limited Act, just as the Democratic Party of Japan reversed the flow of postal privatization by enacting a law to freeze the government's selling of Japan Post shares, and indicate when it plans to sell shares

Table 3.13 Changes in ROA: Shoko Chukin Bank

Year (March)	2010	2011	2012	2013	2014	2015	2016	2017	2018
ROA (%)	0.087	0.250	0.240	0.244	0.242	0.317	0.240	0.397	0.471

in the bank following a 4-year reform period in which it would improve bank operation.

Since its privatization, Shoko Chukin Bank has carried water for the Ministry of Economy, Trade and Industry in materializing its policy as a result of frequent revision to the Shoko Chukin Bank Limited Act (Table 3.13).

Shoko Chukin Bank got a leg up over regional banks in interest rates and enjoyed a boost in sales growth about the same time it started engaging in illicit lending. As a result, its ROA started to rise. Ironically the bank generated record profits in the fiscal year ending March 31, 2018.

I will discuss an institutional design (e.g., organizational structure) for Shoko Chukin Bank after its full privatization in Chap. 4 based on my proposal for optimizing ROA and profitability for different types of financial institutions in Japan.

4.2 *Progress and Challenges in the Reorganization of Regional Banks*

4.2.1 Reorganization: An Alien Concept to Regional Banks

Due to the decline in population and industries, the profitability of regional banks, which have hit the saturation point, is expected to drop at an accelerating pace. In May 2014 the government and the Liberal Democratic Party came out with a plan to reorganize regional financial institutions as part of its Japan Revitalization Strategy and Japan Revival Vision.

In 1990 just before the economic bubble burst, Japan had 13 commercial banks, 10 trust banks and others (seven trust banks and three others), 64 regional banks, 68 secondary regional banks (i.e., banks affiliated with the Second Association of Regional Banks), 451 shinkin banks, and 408 credit unions. To write off bad loans and respond to the Japanese Big Bang that followed, commercial banks and trust banks had to expand operations and increase efficiency through restructuring and consolidation that would boost profitability. As a result, the total number of banks fell by half during the lost two decades, with commercial banks consolidated into four and trust banks and others into six. Of the three long-term-credit banks, the Industrial Bank of Japan was merged into Mizuho, while the Nippon Credit Bank and the Long-Term Credit Bank of Japan were turned into general banks after being placed under special public management.

After getting capital injections from the government, megabanks worked on expanding operations to boost revenue and stay afloat. The major reason for doing this was to enhance efficiency by eliminating overlapping corporate transactions,

Table 3.14 Changes in number of regional financial institutions

	Regional banks	Secondary regional banks	Shinkin banks	Credit unions
1990	64	68	451	408
2000	64	60	386	291
2005	64	48	298	175
2010	63	42	272	158
2017	64	41	264	151
Difference (2017–1990)	0	−27	−187	−257

Table 3.15 Total assets (trillion yen) and ROA: regional banks

Year (March)	2009	2010	2011	2012	2013	2014	2015	2016	2017
Total assets	288	294	302	313	326	338	343	357	378
Share (%)	22.2	22.4	22.5	22.7	22.9	23.1	22.9	22.9	23.3
ROA (%)	−0.207	0.276	0.331	0.383	0.368	0.443	0.466	0.476	0.381

branch locations, and so forth. They also expanded their base of individual customers through mergers to build up a stable flow of revenue. On the other hand, faced with bad loans after the collapse of the economic bubble, small secondary regional banks, shinkin banks, and credit unions went bankrupt and were merged into larger banks.

After the bubble burst regional banks had to adjust their balance sheets and worked on bringing their profitability and capital adequacy ratio up to help stabilize their financial systems and credit offerings. Ashikaga Bank was temporarily nationalized, while many failed secondary regional banks in Japan's three major urban areas had no choice but to be merged into other banks as a bailout measure, resulting in a drop in the number of secondary regional banks.

Sticking to the one-bank-per-prefecture policy, regional banks have worked closely with politicians and bureaucrats to protect regional financial services. Their defensive stance, however, did not lead to investments and loans that would stimulate local economies or actively promote industries but instead drove them to invest in government bonds and contributed to the decline of local economies today. As indicated in Table 3.14, which shows changes in the number of regional financial institutions, while the number of regional banks went through some ups and downs after the bubble burst, there were no mergers among regional banks. Once secondary regional banks began struggling, and their total fell to 27, regional banks either took over secondary regional banks in bailouts or consolidated operations with them to form holding companies.

The number of secondary regional banks decreased by 26 over the two decades between 1990 and 2010 as a result of mergers and consolidations. As shown in Table 3.15, there were a staggering 12 cases of regional bank reorganizations aimed at increasing total assets after the collapse of Lehman Brothers. These include five consolidations of banks across a wide area to operate under a holding company, four mergers between banks operating in neighboring prefectures, and three mergers between banks operating in the same prefecture.

After the privatization of postal services, regional banks took the initiative in restructuring the regional banking system due to the growing rivalry with JP Bank and a sense of crisis. Looking at changes in total assets and ROA by type of financial institution, one can see that the regional banks' share of total assets of public and private financial institutions hovered around 23% after the collapse of Lehman Brothers. Overall private financial institutions' share increased while public financial institutions' share decreased. Regional banks did well in terms of ROA, which remained almost twice the ROA of shinkin banks/credit unions, JA, or JP Bank. However, the ROA data, taken in chronological order, reveal that their ROA took a hit from the low-interest-rate policy and spiraled downward despite the positive effects of the reorganization.

I will analyze Table 3.16 in "[3] Reorganization of Regional Banks" by looking closely into specific cases, as well as in "[4] Theoretical Values Based on the Outcomes of Regional Bank Reorganizations."

Bolstering local financial services is crucial to the development of local economies. The regional banks' one-bank-per-prefecture policy has its roots in the abolition of Japan's han system in 1871. In July 1871, the Meiji government abolished the *han* system as part of its reform aimed at creating a centralized government. Back then there were 277 hans, which were replaced with three urban prefectures (*fu*) and 302 prefectures (*ken*), a figure almost equal to the number of today's single-member constituencies in the House of Representatives. Since the number of prefectures presented a stumbling block to unification, they were consolidated into 3 urban prefectures (*fu*) and 72 prefectures (*ken*) in November of the same year. The number of prefectures was further reduced through consolidation every year, totaling 59 prefectures by 1875 and 38 prefectures (including 3 urban prefectures) by 1876. Some prefectures were later split due partly to increasing administrative work involved in the broader-based local government system, and in 1889 the number totaled 46 prefectures (including 3 urban prefectures). This is similar to today's administrative divisions consisting of 1 metropolis (*to*), a circuit (*do*), 2 urban prefectures (*fu*), and 43 larger prefectures (*ken*).

Modeled after the national banking system in the U.S., Japan's national banks were established as privately operated banks governed by national law as part of the fiscal and financial reform under the Meiji Restoration. They were authorized to issue convertible paper money (bank notes) that had to be exchanged with gold. Following the amendment of the National Banking Act in 1876, the banks were authorized to issue nonconvertible paper money as well. The number of national banks, which stood at 26 in 1877, surged to 153 by 1879. The banks were numbered in the order of establishment, and the number of banks that are categorized today as regional banks peaked at 2358. This number later dropped to 1200 in the early Showa era.

Under the Banking Act, which went into effect during the Showa Financial Crisis, the Ministry of Finance upheld the one-bank-per-prefecture policy in order to raise funds for selling government bonds and promote industry, but banks were consolidated after the outbreak of the Sino-Japanese war, leaving Japan with 8 commercial banks and 53 regional banks by the time the war ended. Due to this historical

Table 3.16 Regional bank mergers and reorganizations (1991–2017)

Date merged	Bank	Merger or Holding company	Types of banks merged			Location
			Regional bank	Secondary regional bank	Financial group	
Apr-1991	San-in Godo (Fuso)	M	○	○		Shimane, Tottori
Apr-1992	Iyo (Toho Sogo)	M	○	○		Ehime
	Kumamoto Family (Higo Family)	M		○		Kumamoto
Apr-1993	Hokuto (Akita Akebono)	M	○	○		Akita
Oct-1998	Kansai (Kansai Sawayaka)	M		○		Osaka, Shiga
Apr-1999	Minato (Hyogo)	M		○		Hyogo
Aug-2000	Yachiyo (Kokumin)	M		○		Tokyo
Apr-2001	North Pacific (Sapporo)	H		○		Hokkaido
Sep-2001	Momiji HD (Hiroshima Sogo, Setouchi)	H		○		Hiroshima
Apr-2002	Shinwa (Kyushu)	H	○	○		Nagasaki
Apr-2003	Kanto Tsukuba (Kanto, Tsukuba)	M	○	○		Ibaraki
Feb-2004	Kansai Urban (Kansai, Kofuku)	M		○		Osaka
Aug-2004	Hokuhoku FG (Hokuriku, Hokkaido)	H	○			Toyama, Hokkaido
Oct-2004	Nishi-Nippon City (Nishi-Nippon, Fukuoka City)	M	○	○		Fukuoka
Oct-2005	Kirayaka (Shokusan, Yamagata Shiawase)	H		○		Yamagata
Feb-2006	Kiyo (Wakayama)	H	○	○		Wakayama
Oct-2006	Yamaguchi FG (Momiji)	H	○	○		Yamaguchi, Hiroshima
Apr-2007	Fukuoka FG (Fukuoka, Kumamoto Family)	H	○	○		Fukuoka, Kumamoto
Oct-2007	Fukuoka FG (Fukuoka FG, Shinwa)	H	○		○	Fukuoka, Nagasaki

(continued)

Table 3.16 (continued)

Date merged	Bank	Merger or Holding company	Types of banks merged: Regional bank	Secondary regional bank	Financial group	Location
Oct-2009[a]	FIDEA HD (Hokuto, Shonai)	H	○			Akita, Yamagata
	Senshu Ikeda (Senshu, Ikeda)	M	○			Osaka
Mar-2010	Tsukuba (Kanto Tsukuba, Ibaraki)	M	○	○		Ibaraki
	Kansai Urban (Kansai, Biwako)	M		○		Osaka, Shiga
Apr-2010	TOMONY HD (Tokushima, Kagawa, Taisho)	H		○		Tokushima, Kagawa, Osaka
Sep-2012	Juroku (Gifu)	M	○	○		Gifu
Oct-2012	Jimoto HD (Kirayaka, Sendai)	H		○		Yamagata, Miyagi
	Kiraboshi (Yachiyo, Tokyo Tomin, ShinGinko)	H	○	○		Tokyo
Nov-2014	Concordia (Yokohama, Higashi-Nippon)	H	○	○		Kanagawa, Tokyo
	Kyushu FG (Kagoshima, Higo)	H	○			Kagoshima, Kumamoto
Nov-2015	Mebuki FG (Joyo, Ashikaga)	H	○			Ibaraki, Tochigi
Feb-2017	San ju San (Mie, Daisan)	H	○	○		Mie
Mar-2017	Kansai Mirai FG (Kinki Osaka, Kansai Urban, Minato)	H		○		Osaka, Hyogo
Apr-2017	Daishi, Hokuetsu	H	○			Niigata

[a]After Lehman Brothers' collapse

development, regional banks have maintained the one-bank-per-prefecture policy, and that is why there were no mergers or consolidations even when the financial markets were deregulated. The tendency to put weight on administrative divisions is even reflected in their names. This is why people often say they are a bunch of amateurs.

If the administrative division system dating back to the Meiji period were reformed through decentralization or the *doshusei* proposal to divide Japan into regional administration blocs that would quickly change regional banks, which have been immune to any kind of reform aimed at private banks. Secondary regional banks also find themselves in the same boat. The regional banking sector has remained virtually unchanged over the last 20 years. That is because regional banks have secured a firm footing in their respective region as financial institutions designated by local municipal governments. Not even the Financial Services Agency has dared disturb the local "financial order" that was created back in the old convoy system days, even though its primary focus is on restoring the stability of the financial system.

4.2.2 Regional Banks Moving toward Reorganization

The long-term prime rate dropped to 1.20% in 2012 and since then has hovered around 1%. At the same time a shift in demographics in rural areas due to the shrinking and graying population has taken a toll on local economies. As the balance of deposits at regional financial institutions declined, regional finances seemed to be on a downward trajectory (Fig. 3.4).

In the Comprehensive Guidelines for Supervision of Regional Financial Institutions released in September 2013, the Financial Services Agency stated that, now that the lending market across Japan is expected to diminish with the graying of the population and a decline in the number of working-age adults, regional financial institutions should develop not only short-term plans but also medium- to long-term sustainable plans for the next 5 to 10 years with an eye to medium- to long-term economic and industrial outlooks for the local areas in which their operations are based. It suggested regional financial institutions identify problems as well as the roles and functions they should play in revitalizing the local economy over the medium to long term while reviewing the goals spelled out by management and in business plans, for example. Unfortunately, however, the Financial Services Agency failed to provide any specific measures they should implement.

Against this backdrop, Masaaki Tani, then-chairman of the Regional Banks Association of Japan (and president of Bank of Fukuoka), stated in a January 6, 2014, Nikkei column, "*Kinyu 2014 koko o semeru* [Key issues in finance 2014]," that restructuring the regional banking system was his mission. In sum, Tani emphasized that he would keep his sights set on restructuring in light of a shrinking market. This is because it was management's responsibility to look at reorganizing the bank while its operations were running smoothly. He said regional banks, most of which are listed, should fulfill their role as key components of the local infrastructure as well as their responsibilities to their shareholders, employees, and customers by reorganizing operations while they are financially sound. According to Tani, Bank of Fukuoka spent more than 6 years on building a business model in which three banks are operated under a holding company. He expressed his desire to move ahead with reorganization but stressed that expanding the bank's operating area to cover a wider geographical area would weaken governance and synergy.

As discussed in total asset analysis, financial institutions are recurring revenue businesses and are unlikely to run into sudden financial difficulty unless they are saddled with a huge amount of bad debt. When the local economy in the area where they operate declines, however, their financial health will fail and could cause problems in their respective financial systems.

Japan's diminishing population, which stood at 128 million in 2010, is projected to fall sharply to 107 million in 2040. Thirty-eight prefectures, which account for 80% of all prefectures in Japan, are expected to see their populations shrink and their economies decline. On top of that, the declining birth rate and graying population will intensify the regional economic slowdown. A decline in the working-age population (people aged 15 to 64), in particular, will cause both prefectural gross production and consumption to stagnate. Without anyone to carry the torch, local economies today are seeing SMEs going out of business left and right. As large-scale shopping centers expand into rural areas and more and more major corporations move their manufacturing operations overseas, the number of companies and business establishments is decreasing, resulting in a shortage of jobs. It is a vicious cycle where young people, unable to find jobs, are compelled to move to urban centers in search of employment. Over the long run, when parents living in rural areas die, their children living in urban centers inherit their assets, which means those assets deposited in the regional banks are migrating to the city as well. This phenomenon is in full swing and is widening the gap between rural and urban areas.

The downward spiral of local economies triggered by a shrinking population and the decreasing number of business establishments is shaking the foundation of regional banks. On top of that, the Bank of Japan's prolonged low-interest-rate policy coupled with, for example, low growth and low inflation, has caused regional banks' loan yield to decline. This, as well as declining capital needs, has forced regional banks to face an annual decrease in fund management revenues, their primary source of income (Fig. 3.5, Table 3.17).

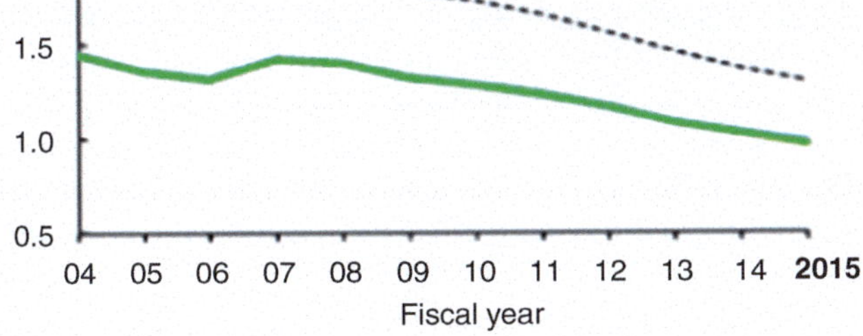

Fig. 3.5 Declining net interest margin

Table 3.17 Declining fund management revenues (10 billion yen)

March	2017	2016	2015	2014	2013	2012	2011	2010	2009	2008
Revenues of 64 regional banks										
Ordinary revenue	465	472	457	456	454	465	467	482	525	554
Fund management revenues, A	317	327	327	329	325	350	360	376	410	420
Ordinary expenses	352	333	323	331	349	362	381	401	539	465
Funding costs, B	26	26	23	24	26	31	37	50	75	88
Profit margin, A − B	291	301	304	305	299	319	323	328	335	332
Ordinary profit	113	139	134	134	104	105	86	81	−13	89
Net profit	79	94	82	78	65	58	54	55	−7	65
Revenues of 41 secondary regional banks										
Ordinary revenue	121	125	127	134	127	131	135	140	149	159
Fund management revenues, A	88	92	94	101	98	101	107	111	121	125
Ordinary expenses	98	96	96	99	107	144	119	131	195	140
Funding costs, B	5	6	7	8	8	10	12	16	21	21
Profit margin, A − B	83	86	87	93	90	91	95	95	100	104
Ordinary profit	23	29	31	31	19	20	16	8	−45	19
Net profit	17	19	21	25	12	11	8	6	−37	9

Source: Financial statements by type of financial institution, Japanese Bankers Association

Working against this economic backdrop, regional banks started moving toward consolidating and reorganizing operations with the approval of the Financial Services Agency.

4.2.3 Reorganization of Regional Banks

Figure 3.6 shows an analysis of the reorganization of regional banks that took place after the collapse of the bubble economy in 1991 up to 2017. During the early years of reorganization, banks that went bankrupt due to bad loan problems were taken over by other banks. Then small regional banks merged for the purpose of enhancing operational efficiency and profitability in order to survive. As regional banks plodded away at getting their balance sheets back on track, they merged with secondary regional banks operating in the same prefecture in an effort to solve the problem of excessive numbers of banks.

The Financial Services Agency released reorganization guidelines in 2013, accelerating regional banks' move toward reorganization. The reorganization of regional banks went into high gear after the Bank of Yokohama and Higashi-Nippon Bank as

Classifications based on past mergers (33 banks)

I. Wide area/asset increase type:
(5) 1. Fukuoka FG (Fukuoka + Kumamoto) 2. Fukuoka FG (Fukuoka + Shinwa + Kumamoto)
3. Yamaguchi FG (Yamaguchi + Momiji + Kitakyushu) 4. TOMONY HD (Tokushima + Kagawa + Taisho)
5. Hokuhoku FG (Hokkaido + Hokuriku)

II. Adjacent prefectures/asset increase type:
(4) 1. Kyushu FG (Kagoshima + Higo) 2. Concordia FG (Yokohama + Higashi-Nippon)
3. Mebuki FG (Joyo + Ashikaga) 4. Kansai Mirai FG (Kinki Osaka + Kansai Urban + Minato)

III. Adjacent prefectures/bailout type:
(4) 1. San-in Godo (San-in Godo + Fuso) 2. FIDEA (Hokuto + Shonai)
3. Kansai Urban (Kansai + Biwako) 4. Jimoto HD (Sendai + Kirayaka)

IV. Same prefecture/asset increase type:
(6) 1. Senshu Ikeda (Senshu + Ikeda) 2. Nishi-Nippon City (Nishi-Nippon + Fukuoka City)
3. Kansai Urban (Kansai + Kofuku) 4. San ju San FG (Mie + Daisan) 5. Daishi + Hokuetsu
6. Kiraboshi FG (Yachiyo + Tokyo Tomin + ShinGinko Tokyo)

V. Same prefecture/bailout type:
(14) 1. Iyo (Iyo + Toho Sogo) 2. Kansai Sawayaka (Kansai + Shiga Sogo)
3. Kumamoto Family (Higo Family + Kumamoto) 4. Hokuto (Hokuto + Akita Akebono)
5. Minato (Minato + Hyogo) 6. Yachiyo (Yachiyo + Kokumin)
7. North Pacific (North Pacific + Sapporo) 8. Momiji (Hiroshima Sogo + Setouchi)
9. Shinwa (Shinwa + Kyushu) 10. Kanto Tsukuba (Kanto + Tsukuba)
11. Tsukuba (Tsukuba + Ibaraki) 12. Kiyo (Kiyo + Wakayama)
13. Kirayaka (Shokusan + Yamagata Shiawase) 14. Juroku (Juroku + Gifu)

Fig. 3.6 Analysis of mergers and reorganizations

well as Higo Bank and Kagoshima Bank announced their plans for interprefectural mergers in November 2014. On October 1, 2015, Higo Bank and Kagoshima Bank established Kyushu Financial Group, a name indicating a wider area of coverage.

The Bank of Japan introduced a negative-interest policy in January 2016. As a result, regional banks suffered a decline in profitability as their net interest margins dropped further.

On April 1, 2016, the Bank of Yokohama and Higashi-Nippon Bank launched Concordia Financial Group, the largest regional banking group in Japan with consolidated assets worth 20 trillion yen. In October 2016 Joyo Bank and Ashikaga Bank (Ashikaga Holdings) announced a merger to create a holding company (Mebuki Financial Group), sparking a change in the entire banking landscape in the northern Kanto region.

In February 2017, Mie Bank and Daisan Bank inked a deal to consolidate operations and set up a holding company, San ju San Financial Group, effective April 2018. In March of the same year Kinki Osaka Bank, Kansai Urban Banking Corporation, and Minato Bank announced a plan to integrate operations under a holding company (Kansai Mirai Financial Group) in April 2018. Kinki Osaka Bank and Kansai Urban Banking also agreed to merge their operations in Osaka in April 2019. I wrote about this large-scale interprefectural (Osaka and Hyogo) merger of banks covering a wide urban area in a paper on the reorganization of regional banks in the Kinki region that was published in 2012. To stay in business, small-scale secondary regional banks operating in urban areas had to enhance efficiency of their infrastructure, such as their branch networks, and boost profitability by expanding their operations. They also had to keep their loan yield high in order to survive the cutthroat interest-rate competition in urban areas.

(1) Wide area/asset increase type: 5 cases	(2) Adjacent prefectures/asset increase type: 4 cases
(3) Adjacent prefectures/bailout type: 4 cases	(4) Same prefecture/asset increase type: 6 cases
(5) Same prefecture/bailout type: 14 cases	33 cases in total

Working against this backdrop, the three banks made the decision to integrate their operations. The biggest factor behind this decision was the agreement on management strategies reached between their major shareholders, Sumitomo Mitsui Financial Group and Resona Holdings. Because this was a merger involving city-based banks, they were able to implement corporate governance without worrying about local needs, which is similar to the reorganization of regional banks that occurred in the U.S. In April of the same year, Niigata Prefecture's Daishi Bank and Hokuetsu Bank signed a basic agreement to consolidate their operations under a holding company from October.

The reorganization of 33 regional banks shown in Fig. 3.6 can be classified as follows.

Five classifications:

Of these, 15 involved an asset increase, while 18 were bailouts.

Of the 16 that took place over the approximately 10 years following April 2007, 12 are categorized as asset increase types and only 4 as bailouts, and 20 involved banks whose operations were integrated under a holding company while 13 were mergers. There were five bailouts where banks initially integrated their operations under a holding company and soon merged.

Of the mergers, 21 were among banks operating in the same prefecture. Another 12 involved mergers of banks that would cover a wider area or two adjoining prefectures, of which 9 were aimed at increasing total assets.

4.2.4 Theoretical Values Based on Outcomes of Regional Bank Reorganizations

When banks choose a merger partner, they normally look at the total assets of a candidate bank to determine how sound its operational foundation is as well as its ordinary profit to assess its profitability. What they really do is assess the overall financial health of a candidate bank based on its rating. They then estimate its potential for growth and stability, for example, based on its total assets. If they are listed companies, they must respect the desire of their stakeholders to get their approval for a consolidation.

In light of the preceding paragraph, the correlation between the ratings of 91 listed regional banks for the fiscal year ending March 31, 2016, and their total assets has been summarized in Fig. 3.7.

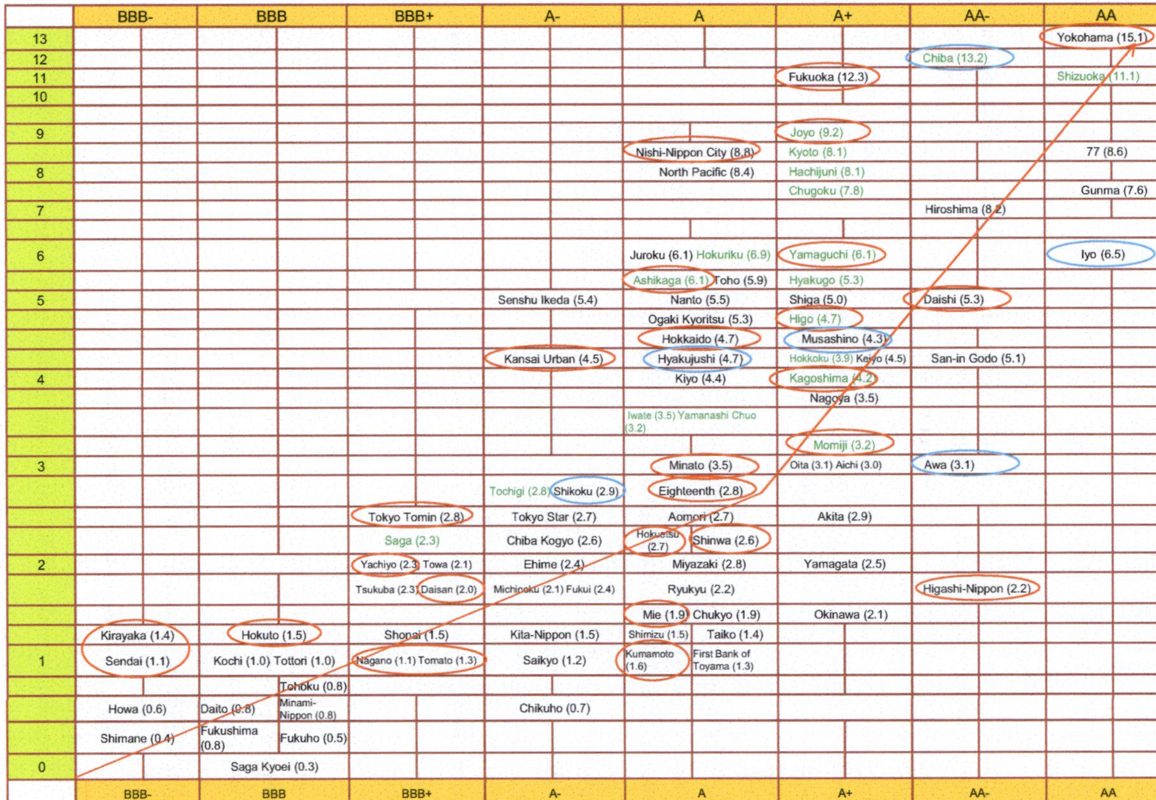

Fig. 3.7 Correlation between regional banks' assets (trillion yen) as of late March 2016 and long-term rating as of April 2017. *Black*, 73 banks rated by Japan Credit Rating Agency; *Green*, 18 banks rated by Rating and Investment Information; *Blue circle*, banks that formed alliances; *Red circle*, banks that were merged
[this can be downloaded from the electronic supplementary material]

Table 3.18 Relation between total assets and net profit of regional banks

	Average performance of regional banks (FY 2013)	Average performance of regional banks (with total assets worth over 10 trillion yen)
Total assets (trillion yen)	3.3	11.6
Net profit (billion yen)	9.8	46.3
Capital adequacy ratio (%)	11	14

Source: Ministry of Economy, Trade and Industry (2014) Rokaru keizaiken no "kasegu chikara" sōshutsu [Building earning power in local economies]
https://www.meti.go.jp/committee/kenkyukai/sansei/kaseguchikara/pdf/006_03_00.pdf

According to "*Rokaru keizaiken no kasegu chikara soshutsu* [Building earning power in local economies]" released by the Ministry of Economy, Trade and Industry, an analysis found a correlation between the total assets held by regional banks and their net profit.

Table 3.18 compares average financial results for fiscal 2013 between regional banks whose total assets exceed 10 trillion yen and all regional banks. Total assets for the former amounted to 11.6 trillion yen on average, with a net profit of 46.3 billion yen and a capital adequacy ratio of 14%. Total assets for the latter amounted to 3.3 trillion yen on average, with a net profit of 9.8 billion yen and a capital adequacy ratio of 11%. Total assets and net profit of regional banks with total assets worth more than 10 trillion yen were respectively 3.5 times and 4.7 times higher compared with the average of all regional banks.

It is clear from Fig. 3.7 that banks with a higher total asset figure have a higher rating and more stable operations. This provides a rationale for large-scale mergers and consolidations. Of the 91 listed regional banks shown in this table, 27 have already carried out mergers.

As shown in Fig. 3.8, the number of regional banks that play a leading role in a merger is declining. There are 18 banks that have total assets worth over 5 trillion yen and are rated A or higher. The 15 banks rated B or lower with total assets worth less than 3 trillion yen are more likely to be absorbed into another bank. The 27 banks that have already merged with other banks as well as 18 leading large-scale banks with solid financial standings may see the remaining 31 middle-standing A-rated banks, with total assets worth over 3 trillion yen but below 5 trillion yen, as potential merger candidates.

Most importantly, even if that left 45 regional banks, the total assets of each bank would come to approximately 8.5 trillion yen when calculated on the basis of total assets held by regional banks. With so many banks with assets worth less than 10 trillion yen still out there, reorganization of the regional banking system cannot be considered complete. Theoretically the wide-area (interprefectural) reorganization already happening in the Kyushu and Kinki regions should pick up pace.

Assets (as of March 2016)	Bank			Total
6 trillion yen or more	0 banks	3 banks Nishi-Nippon City (8.8), Hokuriku (6.9), Ashikaga (6.1)	4 banks Yokohama (15.1), Fukuoka (12.3), Joyo (9.2), Yamaguchi (6.1)	7 banks
1 trillion yen or more but less than 5 trillion yen	7 banks Tokyo Tomin (2.8), Yachiyo (2.3), Daisan (2.0), Shonai (1.5), Hokuto (1.5), Kirayaka (1.4), Sendai (1.1)	8 banks Hokkaido (4.7), Minato (3.5), Eighteenth (2.8), Hokuetsu (2.7), Shinwa (2.6), Mie (1.9), Kumamoto (1.6), Kansai Urban (4.5)	5 banks Daishi (5.3), Higashi-Nippon (2.2), Higo (4.7), Kagoshima (4.2), Momiji (3.2)	20 banks
Rating	BBB- – BBB+: 7 banks	A- – A: 11 banks	A+ – AA: 9 banks	27 banks

reorganize

Assets	Banks			Total
6 trillion yen or more	0 banks	2 banks North Pacific (8.4), Juroku (6.1)	9 banks Shizuoka (11.1), 77 (8.6), Gunma (7.6), Iyo (6.5), Chiba (13.2), Hiroshima (8.2), Kyoto (8.1), Hachijuni (8.1), Chugoku (7.8)	11 banks
5 trillion yen or less	15 banks Saga (2.3), Towa (2.1), Tsukuba (2.3), Kochi (1.0), Tottori (1.0), Nagano (1.1), Tomato (1.3), Tohoku (0.8), Howa (0.6), Daito (0.8), Minami-Nippon (0.8), Fukushima (0.8), Fukuho (0.5), Shimane (0.4), Saga Kyoei (0.3)	25 banks (8 banks) Senshu Ikeda (5.4), Nanto (5.5), Toho (5.9), Ogaki Kyoritsu (5.3), Hyakujushi (4.7), Kiyo (4.4), Iwate (3.5), Yamanashi Chuo (3.2) (17 banks) Tochigi (2.8), Shikoku (2.9), Tokyo Star (2.7), Aomori (2.7), Chiba Kogyo (2.6), Miyazaki (2.8), Ehime (2.4), Michinoku (2.1), Fukui (2.4), Ryukyu (2.2), Chukyo (1.9), Kita-Nippon (1.5), Shimizu (1.5), Taiko (1.4), Saikyo (1.2), First Bank of Toyama (1.3), Chikuho (0.7)	13 banks San-in Godo (5.1), Awa (3.1), Hyakugo (5.3), Shiga (5.0), Musashino (4.3), Hokkoku (3.9), Keiyo (4.5), Nagoya (3.5), Oita (3.1), Aichi (3.0), Akita (2.9), Yamagata (2.5), Okinawa (2.1)	53 banks *
Rating	BBB- – BBB+: 15 banks	A- – A: 27 banks	A+ – AA: 22 banks	64 banks

* 42 of them have assets under 3 trillion yen

Data current as of December 2017

Fig. 3.8 (**a**) Banks that implemented mergers (**b**) Banks that did not reorganize

4.2.5 Regional Banking Trends in U.S. and China

In July 2006, when I was working on the privatization of the postal savings bank at Japan Post Holdings' Office for Privatization of Japan Post, I had the opportunity to visit the United States and observe how regional banks expanded their operations through M&A. A team at McKinsey, which was doing consulting work on the future of the postal savings bank, arranged for me to visit the new kinds of banks in the U.S. that were expanding operations through M&A. I visited the headquarters of Bank of America (NationsBank) and Wachovia in Charlotte, North Carolina, Wells Fargo in San Francisco, and Washington Mutual in Seattle during my week-long stay. The trip gave me the opportunity to learn how regional banks were transformed through M&A.

Having seen changes in the U.S. banking system during the 1970s through 2000 when I worked for Sumitomo Bank, I was able to witness how regional banks in the U.S., freed from the McFadden Act (interstate banking regulations) and the Glass-Steagall Act (regulations on transactions between banks and securities firms), were changing the financial structure by leveraging M&A.

Major Regional Banks in the U.S. in 2003 [Deposit Balance]. Source: American Banker:

1. Wells Fargo (California): $247.5 billion (remains a megabank)
2. Wachovia (North Carolina): $224.4 billion (acquired by Wells Fargo in a bailout takeover in 2008)
3. Bank One (Ohio): $164.6 billion (merged with JPMorgan Chase in 2004)
4. FleetBoston (Massachusetts): $137.7 billion (merged with Bank of America in 2004)

4.2.6 Washington Mutual (Washington): $119.5 billion (acquired by JPMorgan Chase in a bailout takeover in 2008)

In 1998, NationsBank, a regional bank headquartered in Charlotte, North Carolina, with total assets worth $284 billion, acquired San Francisco-based BankAmerica, with total assets worth $570 billion. It then formed Bank of America, headquartered in Charlotte. In 2004, Bank of America purchased Massachusetts-based FleetBoston for $47 billion, becoming the largest megabank in the U.S.

In 1988, Wells Fargo acquired Barclays Bank of California from Britain's Barclays PLC, expanding its operations beyond the regional banking sector and making its debut in the international financial market. Norwest, a Minneapolis-based regional bank, acquired Wells Fargo in the same year while taking over both the trade name and headquarters of Wells Fargo. In 2008, following the collapse of Lehman Brothers, the bank acquired Wachovia (with total assets worth $520.7 billion) for $15.1 billion via a bailout takeover. Starting out as a regional bank, Wells Fargo turned itself into a megabank.

Washington Mutual, a regional bank headquartered in Seattle, Washington, achieved quick growth by expanding operations with a focus on housing mortgage loans, but went bankrupt due to the subprime mortgage crisis in 2008, not long after the collapse of Lehman Brothers, and was acquired by JPMorgan Chase.

In September 2008, while employed by JP Bank, I visited AIG, MetLife, and Mastercard while working on new product development. Lehman Brothers collapsed right after I returned to Japan, and I was surprised by the acquisition of the aforementioned regional banks, which were sound and growing when I visited the U.S. just 2 years earlier. Financially strong leading regional banks in the U.S. are biding their time until there is a sign of some structural change in the financial market before expanding into prospective markets. They will move beyond regional boundaries only as long as it makes economic sense to transform themselves from regional into national banks.

In the U.S., where corporate governance and stakeholders are valued, banks are expanding the scope of their M&A to nonbanking sectors, such as securities and insurance, in order to sustain their operations, outpace the competition, or counter the low interest rate policy there.

Even though the regulations on locations and business operations have already been lifted, managers of Japanese regional banks have their attention riveted solely on regional finances. These banks lack the kind of corporate governance that enables management to act in accordance with good economic sense with both overseas and domestic markets in mind.

As one can see from the analysis of total assets by type of financial institution, regional banks in Japan must first reduce the number of excess banks in the market and focus on optimizing their business scale and corporate value. Optimal reorganizations will be tailored to market conditions and done with an eye toward making economically sensible decisions that may transcend regional boundaries. Regional banks in Japan have something to learn from the reorganization process of regional banks in the U.S.

In 1.5 of Chap. 2, I discussed the privatization of China's postal service. Here we will look at trends in China's regional banking sector in comparison with those in the regional banking sector in the U.S.

In March 1994, Sumitomo Bank sent me to China at the request of the Chinese government (then headed by Jiang Zemin/Zhu Rongji) to participate in a conference on commercial banking reform in Beijing. About 70 people from the People's Bank of China, 4 state-owned commercial banks, the State Administration of Foreign Exchange, and the China Investment Corporation received training at the conference. The conference was devoted to the adoption of Japan's financial system in an attempt to modernize China's financial system.

China implemented financial reforms based on the Commercial Banking Law in May 1995. I won't go into this reform here since it is discussed at length in Chap. 2. What follows is an overview of China's financial institutions and a discussion of regional banks in China. Table 3.19 compares total assets of financial institutions in China and Japan by type of business.

Given China's political system, all financial institutions may be deemed public entities, but many of them, including the four major commercial banks, are listed and can be treated as privately operated but government owned. If we can separate economics from politics for a moment and assume that China's economic legislation

Table 3.19 Comparison of total assets of financial institutions in Japan and China by type of operation

Japan: 1569 trillion yen			China: 172 trillion yuan[a]		
Type of operation	Number of banks	Share (%)[b]	Type of operation	Number of banks	Share (%)[b]
State-owned banks	3	3.4	Policy-based banks	3	9.1
Privatized policy-based financial institutions	2	1.8	Privatized Postal Savings Bank of China	1	3.3
Privatized Japan Post Bank	1	13.3	Foreign banks	41	1.6
Commercial bank/trust bank	13	40.8	Large-scale commercial banks	5	41.2
Regional banks	105	23.1	Joint-stock commercial banks	145	28.7
Shinkin banks/credit unions	429	10.5	Rural commercial banks	665	6.7
Agricultural/forestry/fisheries cooperatives (Norinchukin Bank)	2448	7.1	Rural cooperative banks, etc.	2901	9.4

Source: Kyoto University class material (Japanese financial institution data) and Yu-cho Foundation's country survey (Chinese financial institution data)
[a]3182 trillion yen when converted at exchange rate of 18.5 yen to yuan
[b]Share = percentage of total assets of each type of financial institution to combined total assets of financial institutions in each country

is the same as it is in the capitalist world, we would see that total assets of public financial institutions account for 12.4% of total assets of both the public and private sectors, with three policy-based financial institutions (China Development Bank, Export-Import Bank of China, and Agricultural Development Bank of China) accounting for 9.1% and the partially privatized Postal Savings Bank of China accounting for 3.3%. In contrast, total assets of public financial institutions in Japan, including those that are not fully privatized, account for 18.5%, which is higher than in China.

There are 145 joint-stock commercial banks, which are regional commercial banks, in China. This number, as well as their share of total assets at 28.7%, is low given China's vast land mass and staggering population. Their share is expected to increase in step with the development of regional cities. When it comes to regional banks in Japan, solving the problem of an excessive number of banks should be a priority issue given its small geographic size and shrinking population.

Another notable point in China's banking sector is that many foreign banks are expanding their operations and setting up shop in rural areas. As regulations for foreign banks are eased in phases, China is becoming more like an internationalized capitalist market economy. China is seeking new banking systems for personal account transactions and payment processing as its cyber-social systems quickly take shape.

In *Kansei kinyu kaikaku to chigin saihen* [Public financial reform and regional bank reorganization], published in March 2015, I examined ideal paths for Japan's financial institutions based on the reorganization of regional banks in the U.S. and China's commercial banking reform.

The reasoning behind my analysis of total assets by type of financial institution and optimal reorganization is simple. All you need is key theoretical values that are calculated from the overall data. In 2016 this book was added to the collections of the Library of Congress in the U.S., the National Library of China, and the libraries of universities across the U.S., including Harvard University, Stanford University, Columbia University, Cornell University, Dartmouth College, and University of California, San Diego.

I submitted a summary of this book for the Kyoto University Economic Society's *Keizai-ronso* [The economic review] in October 2016, but my paper was rejected. The journal's editor-in-chief, Mun Se-il, sent me an evaluation by finance division referees along with the rejection letter. In the evaluation the referees wrote, "First of all there are uncertainties involved in not only the break-up of the postal savings bank but also the realization of its full privatization. Mergers and consolidations of regional banks, as assumed by the author, will never happen unless they are mandated by law. The situation assumed in this paper is nothing but a 'fantasy' and will never become reality unless Japan becomes a centralized socialist state like China." The evaluation also stated that "the author's analysis seems to be merely a tally of numbers. If the scenario proposed by the author, in which it is necessary to break up the postal savings bank and merge regional banks, occurs, the assets they have built up will stand for nothing."

In reality, however, the Postal Service Privatization Act clearly stipulates the government's selling of all shares in JP Bank, thereby guaranteeing its full privatization. When it comes to the consolidation of regional banks, the Financial Services Agency released an official document outlining the guidelines for reorganizing regional banks in 2013. Unfortunately, no researchers at Kyoto University's Economics Department are versed in public financial services or the regional banking systems of China and Japan. In talking with Tetsuro Shimamoto, a Kyoto University professor serving as a finance division referee there, with whom I don't see eye to eye with regard to the politics of postal privatization, I learned that he expressed a dissenting view of the theses of my book and paper during the peer review process.

Kazuhito Ikeo, Keio University professor, published a review of my book in *Kinyu Zaisei Jijo* in February 2017. In the review, he writes, "This book provides a useful guide to rethinking the roles of public financial institutions and how they could rival private financial institutions. The author was involved in postal privatization after working for a commercial bank. His opinion backed by practical experience in the field rests on solid ground. The author points out among the major issues facing Japan's finances the biggest issue is getting public financial services back on track after it was derailed by an upset victory over the ruling party, etc. The book proposes specific institutional designs for public financial services in light of their historical development to provide a clear direction. While the book takes a close look at several possible scenarios, it discusses in great detail and most highly recommends the scenario in which JP Bank is broken up into regional companies after it is merged with DBJ, etc. The author argues that regional banks should also work on reorganizing to build up the strength needed to compete with the regionally divided JP Bank companies. It's a grand vision but the author examines its feasibility by drawing on his own experience to substantiate his theory, which makes this book an outstanding study."

It would seem that Kazuhito Ikeo, who served as the chairman of Japan Post public company from April 2003 through September 2007 and as a member of the Financial System Council and other government councils, shares my view on postal privatization.

In Chap. 4, I will discuss institutional designs for the reorganization of regional banks in light of the problems identified in the ongoing cases of reorganization of regional banks in Japan, lessons learned through comparison with the banking systems in the U.S. and China, and issues addressed by researchers, for example.

4.3 *Profit Structure and Challenges of Japan Agricultural Cooperative and Norinchukin Bank*

4.3.1 Inconsistency between Agricultural Cooperative Savings and the Trans-Pacific Partnership

Agricultural cooperatives have been a resisting force against agricultural reforms since the end of WWII. Solving problems surrounding the long protected agricultural sector has not been an easy job. In the pursuit of finding a solution, there was some question about whether or not to join the Trans-Pacific Partnership (TPP). In what follows we will look at problems concerning fund management at the JA Group and discuss in concrete terms the direction in which it should be taken as we seek ways to address its inconsistencies.

Let me explain the JA Group's strong opposition to joining the TPP in terms of economics. Aiming to maintain the status quo, the JA Group, the key player in Japan's primary sector, is strongly opposed to a shift from agriculture, forestry, and fisheries (i.e., the primary sector) to manufacturing and industry (i.e., the secondary sector) and further to the service industry (i.e., the tertiary sector) as well as Japan's accession to the international framework for a free trade agreement, which are both the exact tickets needed to modernize and fuel the economy of Japan's industrial structure. Tolerating this dissent will in the end weaken the protected primary sector.

In the face of globalization, protecting this weak domestic industry (i.e., agriculture) that is virtually impossible to grow or transplant overseas will make it even more resistant and result in driving out foreign players.

This becomes obvious when one considers how Japan's industrial structure has changed. While agriculture, forestry, and fisheries-related financial institutions are driving foreign players out of commodity markets, they have a totally different attitude when it comes to money (i.e., payments for products and financial instruments) and focus on investing in foreign bonds and foreign currency investment trusts. This flow of bond investing becomes clear when you look at how the cooperative system's money is deposited from JA into the Prefectural Banking Federations of Agricultural Cooperatives (JA Shinnoren) and then the Norinchukin Bank.

During the lost decade that followed the collapse of the economic bubble, the Norinchukin Bank downsized its industrial loan business, restructured marginal agricultural cooperatives, and moved quickly to close inefficient branches before the privatization of postal services. The number of branches totaled 7963 in March 2017, 3787 less than what the figure was in March 2005. The bank also withdrew from the retail banking business after selling its credit card division to a megabank-affiliated credit card company and shifted to a new business model of its own focused on investing in marketable securities, known as the Norinchukin model. This turned out to be the wrong move, and the bank's huge investment losses following the collapse of Lehman Brothers remains fresh in people's minds. The bank posted revaluation losses on securitized products totaling 1808.7 billion yen, with a net loss of 572.1 billion yen in its consolidated results for the fiscal year ending March 31, 2009. It boosted capital by 1380.5 billion yen at the end of the same fiscal year to make the total a whopping 3.4 trillion yen. The consolidated capital adequacy ratio, which was 15.56% in the fiscal year ending March 31, 2009, rose to 24.67% 3 years later as the bank turned things around by making a profit from its international business involving high-risk but high-yield investments in foreign securities.

The overall JA organization is supported by the bank's high returns on investment in foreign bonds and foreign investment trusts. There is an underlying reason why the Norinchukin Bank has to maintain this high-risk, high-yield business model. Japan's agriculture, forestry, and fisheries sectors, which are highly profitable, have neglected reforming their operations due to regulations and extremely protective government policies. It would be best if the bank used the money deposited by JA members on these sectors. Simple calculations show that only 40 trillion yen out of the JA Group's core deposits, totaling about 100 trillion yen, was used for lending.

Though investing in foreign firms enables the JA Group to benefit financially from the growth of foreign industries, at the same time the JA Group tries to block foreign produce from reaching these shores while highlighting Japan's declining food self-sufficiency and the need to preserve the country's agriculture, forestry, and fisheries. The fact that all the while it makes no attempt to reform or cultivate these industries just smacks of hypocrisy.

In the Norinchukin Bank's annual report, the top executives describe their business strategies as follows. "As the national-level financial institution for agricultural, fishery and forestry cooperatives in Japan, the mission of The Norinchukin Bank ("the Bank") is to contribute to the development of the agriculture, fishery and forestry industries and to national economic prosperity by facilitating access to financial resources. With the capital provided by JA, Japan Fisheries Cooperatives (JF), Japan Forestry Cooperatives (JForest), etc., as well as the stable funding base through customer deposits at JA Bank and JF Marine Bank, the Bank, to achieve its

Table 3.20 Total assets (trillion yen) and ROA: Japan Agricultural Cooperatives

March	2009	2010	2011	2012	2013	2014	2015	2016	2017
Total assets	101	102	103	105	108	110	111	114	115
Share (%)	7.8	7.8	7.7	7.6	7.6	7.5	7.4	7.3	7.1
ROA (%)	0.198	0.206	0.194	0.194	0.148	0.182	0.135	0.140	0.139

mission, lends funds to its members, agricultural, fishery and forestry workers, and companies related to the agricultural, fisheries and forestry industries. As the ultimate manager of these funds, the Bank also conducts various lending and investment activities in Japan and abroad, efficiently manages funds, and returns steady profits to its members."

However, the outcome of the bank's fund management described in what follows indicates that this strategy is not aimed at contributing to national economic prosperity but solely aimed at returning steady profits to JA members.

4.3.2 Investing JA Savings Locally to Revitalize Local Economies

According to the analysis of ROA by type of financial institution for the fiscal year ending March 31, 2017, JA's total assets came to 115 trillion yen, which accounted for 7.1% of total assets of the public and private sectors combined. While JA's percentage share topped 7% over the last 10 years, it is now on the decline. Standing at 0.139%, its ROA is the lowest among all private financial institutions and is also falling. (Since JA's core deposits are used by JA Shinnoren and the Norinchukin Bank as cooperative deposits, they are regarded as the same financial institution in this book.) I will propose measures for improving its declining performance (Table 3.20).

The quantitative and qualitative monetary easing, along with the negative interest rate that was introduced in January 2016, has shaken the operating foundations of Japan's financial institutions to their core. Commercial banks and regional banks that have focused on financial intermediary operations are facing declining investment revenues due to lower net interest margins. Commercial banks have no choice but to implement cost-cutting measures, such as closing branch locations and reducing personnel, to enhance operational efficiency, while regional banks must merge with one another to expand their operations.

The global trend of low interest rates has also started to affect the financial systems, known as the Norinchukin model, of the JA and the Norinchukin Bank, which had remained stable over the last quarter-century. On April 27, 2016, the headline of the front page of the Nikkei morning edition read, "*Norinchukin yokin kinri sage. Kinri sage nokyo no keiei appaku. 646 nokyo saihen kasoku* [Norinchukin lowers interest rates on deposits, weighing on farm co-ops and accelerating reorganization of 646 co-ops]." While this article simply sees the low-interest-rate trend as a problem, I have previously pointed out that fixing problems

Table 3.21 Movement of funds in Japan Agricultural Group

	Funding		Investment	
Japan Agricultural Cooperatives	Deposits	98.4	Cooperative deposits	73.4
			Loans	20.3
			Securities	4.0
	Total	98.4	Total	97.7
JA Shinnoren	Deposits	63.4	Cooperative deposits	41.2
			Loans	5.2
			Securities	19.3
	Total	63.4	Total	65.7
Norinchukin Bank	Deposits	61.5	Loans	10.9
	Other	39.8	Securities	69.0
	Norinchukin Bank debentures	2.4	Other	23.9
	Total	103.7	Total	103.8

Source: Norinchukin Bank financial statements (FY ending March 2017)

Table 3.22 Changes in Norinchukin Bank revenues by segment and yield for FY 2016 by segment (100 million yen)

	Domestic operations	Fund management revenues	International operations	Fund management revenues	Total gross profit	Fund management revenues
FY 2014	−591	−655	4993	5239	4402	4584
FY 2015	−882	−980	4686	4469	3803	3488
FY 2016	−1386	−1608	4307	4351	2921	2473
Investment yield (%)	–	0.39	–	2.20	–	1.20
Earning yield (%)	–	0.67	–	1.14	–	0.92
Net interest rate spread (%)	–	−0.28	–	1.06	–	0.28

Source: Norinchukin Bank financial statements

in the Norinchukin model will help pave the way to agricultural policy reform. Here are the problems in a nutshell (Tables 3.21 and 3.22).

According to the Norinchukin Bank's financial statements for the fiscal year ending March 31, 2017, the balance of securities held in trust totaled 69 trillion yen, of which international operations accounted for 72%. International operations were in the black, with revenues totaling 435.1 billion yen along with a net interest-rate spread of 1.06%. This is high compared with its domestic operations, which invested 13.2 trillion yen in government bonds at a yield of 0.39%. Domestic operations generated a loss of 138.6 billion yen and had a negative net interest-rate spread of 0.28%. As shown in Table 3.21, the root cause of this loss lies in the fact that 41.2 trillion yen (or 67%) of 61.5 trillion yen deposited at Norinchukin Bank comes from cooperative deposits in the Prefectural Banking Federations of Agricultural Cooperatives (JA Shinnoren) and that the earning yield is an extraordinarily high 0.67% (the interest rate on time deposits is 0.01%). One can assume that the Norinchukin Bank uses JA Shinnoren's cooperative deposits for investing in risk-free high-yield large time deposits and uses returns on the investment to maintain JA Shinnoren's organization. Likewise it uses the same mechanism with agricultural co-ops across Japan that operate under JA Shinnoren to maintain their organizations. This is how Norinchukin Bank has maintained the Norinchukin model for so many years by using returns on investments in foreign securities and foreign investment trusts to prop up agricultural co-ops that operate under the bank.

Of the JA Group's core deposits worth 98 trillion yen, 69 trillion yen is invested in securities at Norinchukin Bank. Roughly 37 trillion yen is used by the group for lending, but the loan-deposit ratio remains a low 37%. The amount that is directly loaned to the agriculture, forestry, and fisheries industries is extremely low. JA Group does not invest domestically with an eye toward reforming and developing Japan's agriculture, forestry, and fisheries industries, but instead invests in foreign firms to financially benefit from the growth of foreign industries.

If changes occur in the investment markets or if interest rates remain low, that will negatively affect JA operations that rely on the high-yield cooperative deposits JA makes with JA Shinnoren and Norinchukin Bank. JA should use its mounting deposits to make more agricultural loans that will contribute to agricultural policies or enhance its financial strength through a reorganization and create a better environment for farmers to make agriculture a growing industry.

The Norinchukin model should be overhauled as soon as possible to build an optimal organizational structure and mechanism. To play a significant role as a financial institution, JA should use deposited funds for lending locally and cultivate an agricultural sector that will continue to grow.

Japan should make farms larger in scale to enhance efficiency. It should also reduce financial burdens by making farming self-sustaining. Japan should then promote agricultural exports and increase production of agricultural products for export. This will help revitalize local economies and increase employment. Implementing a policy designed to make agriculture a "sextiary sector," a key component of the government's national revitalization strategy, will promote the consolidation of farms and encourage young people to take up farming. It will also open the doors to the export industry by combining the primary sector (i.e., agricultural production) with processing and sales, developing new products, and improving quality.

As a specific measure for sustainable regional revitalization, the government proposed promoting renewable energy power generation to boost local economies, industries, and employment. Renewable energy power plants, while requiring advanced industrial capacity, harness the power of nature while existing in harmony with the environment. Since renewable energy includes distributed energy, power generation from renewable sources will involve local companies and public agencies. In pointing to a successful institutional design model for renewable energy power generation, the government cited Denmark where wind power generation helped farmers boost nonagricultural income and make the sustainable development of local economies possible.

While the government is trying to implement a comprehensive reform of social security and taxes, since reform is so urgently needed, it has every right to impose a public consumption tax that will fund social security expenditures. Lowering corporate taxes, which are relatively high by global standards, to make companies more competitive will only drive economic growth. The government should also implement tax reforms to give more power to local governments in order to promote local industries, but Japan, with its large fiscal deficit, cannot afford to do so, which is why the government must create a mechanism for using local people's savings for local people.

4.4 *Reorganization and Challenges of Shinkin Banks and Credit Unions (Table 3.23)*

After dealing with the bad loan problem that followed on the heels of the bubble economy's collapse, shinkin banks and credit unions were then hit by the zero-interest-rate policy and lost financial strength. The number of shinkin banks and credit unions dropped by 88 and 116, respectively, due to mergers and consolidations between 2000 and 2005. In the meantime, the Act on Special Measures for Strengthening Financial Functions was put into effect in 2004 with the aim of putting an end to the financial crisis. As Japan reeled from the economic recession that followed the Lehman Brothers collapse in 2008, financially weak shinkin banks and credit unions merged to survive. Their numbers, however, did not decline that much after the privatization of postal services.

The changes in ROA based on type of financial institution from the fiscal year ending March 31, 2009, to the fiscal year ending March 31, 2017, show why the numbers changed very little. While shinkin banks and credit unions ran up large

Table 3.23 Shinkin banks and credit unions

Number as of March 2000 to 2017				
March	2000	2005	2010	2017 (Difference, 2017–2000)
Shinkin banks	386	298	272	264 (−122)
Credit unions	291	175	158	151 (−140)
Total	677	473	430	415 (−262)

Total assets (trillion yen) and ROA									
March	2009	2010	2011	2012	2013	2014	2015	2016	2017
Total assets	141	143	146	149	153	157	162	168	172
Share (%)	10.9	10.7	10.9	10.8	10.7	10.7	10.7	10.8	10.6
ROA (%)	−0.156	0.168	0.151	0.174	0.226	0.318	0.315	0.292	0.250

deficits after Lehman Brothers collapsed, their ROA picked up as the economy recovered. However, due to quantitative and qualitative monetary easing under the Bank of Japan's low-interest-rate policy, their ROA has fallen in tandem with the shrinking of their net interest margin. The ROA of shinkin banks and credit unions is higher than JA's but about the same as JP Bank's. Even though shinkin banks and credit unions have higher net interest margins and lower expense ratios than other types of financial institutions, if the low interest rate policy remains in effect for a long time, they will need to undergo further reorganization given their current total assets. The total assets of 264 shinkin banks came to 150 trillion yen and 570 billion yen per bank in the fiscal year ending March 31, 2017. Total assets of 151 credit unions amounted to 22 trillion yen and 150 billion yen per bank. Almost zero cost of funds and low interest on loans that cannot go any lower are making their net interest margin infinitely low. Shinkin banks and credit unions have limits on expanding their operations. They need to find a new regional banking model.

4.5 Commercial Banks and Trust Banks Merging to Form Financial Groups

After the asset price bubble burst, commercial banks and trust banks were faced with the bad loan issue, leaving them hard-pressed to write off nonperforming loans. At the same time, the minimum capital adequacy requirements under the Basel Accord went into effect in 1992, imposing an added burden on commercial banks with international operations. Japanese banks maintained their capital adequacy ratio by relying on paper profits on stocks and were not all that transparent about the asset evaluation method they used in writing off bad loans, which caused overseas investors to speculate that Japan's financial sector was on the rocks. In response, banks began disclosing information about their bad loans, and 11 commercial banks announced that their bad loans totaled 10 trillion yen as of the end of March 1994. However, the amount of bad loans continued to mount and reached 20 trillion yen by the end of March 1999. The amount of bad loans written off during these years came to 50 trillion yen.

In 1997 the Hokkaido Takushoku Bank went under, followed by the collapse of the Long-Term Credit Bank of Japan in October 1998 and Nippon Credit Bank in December of the same year. The Act on Emergency Measures for the Revitalization of the Financial Functions and the Act on Emergency Measures for Early Strengthening of Financial Functions were then enacted in October 1998. A framework for the resolution of failed financial institutions was created, and the government injected approximately 60 trillion yen of public money to bail out the banks while preventing any similar failures from occurring in the future. Thirteen major banks posted huge deficits in the fiscal year ending March 31, 2002. To survive, they sought merger and consolidation opportunities, resulting in a rapid transformation of the commercial and trust bank landscape (Table 3.24).

Table 3.24 Number of commercial banks and trust banks, March 1990 and 2012

	March 1990	Merged	March 2012 (after mergers)
Commercial banks	13	Dai-Ichi Kangyo, Sanwa, Tokai, Tokyo, Hokkaido Takushoku, Kobe	Tokyo-Mitsubishi UFJ, Sumitomo Mitsui, Mizuho, Mizuho Corporate, Resona, Saitama Resona
Trust banks	7	Toyo, Chuo	Mitsubishi UFJ, Chuo Mitsui, Sumitomo, Mizuho, Nomura

As a result of reorganizing, total assets per commercial bank increased. In what follows, we will look at the reorganization of the Bank of Tokyo-Mitsubishi UFJ and other banks.

The 1998 revision to the Antimonopoly Act enabled financial institutions to create holding companies. This and the Japanese Big Bang that occurred around the same time triggered the reorganization of a number of commercial banks across different corporate groups in the early 2000s.

- In 2000, Dai-Ichi Kangyo Bank, Fuji Bank, and the Industrial Bank of Japan merged, creating Mizuho Bank and Mizuho Corporate Bank.
- In 2001, Sumitomo Bank and Sakura Bank merged to form Sumitomo Mitsui Banking Corporation.
- In 2002, Sanwa Bank and Tokai Bank merged to form UFJ Bank.
- In 2006, Tokyo Mitsubishi Bank and UFJ Bank merged to form the Bank of Tokyo-Mitsubishi UFJ.

Comparison of the Bank of Tokyo-Mitsubishi UFJ's balance sheets before and after the merger reveals that its assets grew by 1.5 times. The bank's profitability improved as a result of higher operational efficiency (Figs. 3.9, 3.10, and 3.11).

As shown in the figures, here commercial banks merged with commercial banks while trust banks merged with trust banks. Commercial banks and trust banks that merged before the privatization of postal services expanded the scope of their operations with the enactment of the Financial Instruments and Exchange Act of 2007 after postal privatization. Corporate groups' financial holding companies reorganized their securities, insurance, nonbanking, and other operations into financial groups to further expand their assets.

Megabank groups competing in the global financial market completed their reorganizations but are still undergoing restructuring within their groups, as they work to enhance efficiency and promote labor-saving practices with an eye toward bolstering their financial foundation (Table 3.25).

Analysis of total assets and ROA of commercial banks and trust banks by type of financial institution shows that commercial banks steadily increased their share of the total assets of the public and private sectors combined after postal privatization. The reason for this steady increase is the positive effect of the mergers that took place in the early 2000s. Although their total asset figures are on a nonconsolidated basis, absolute amounts are also continuing to grow. Their ROA is relatively high, although it is slightly lower than that of DBJ and trust banks. However, commercial

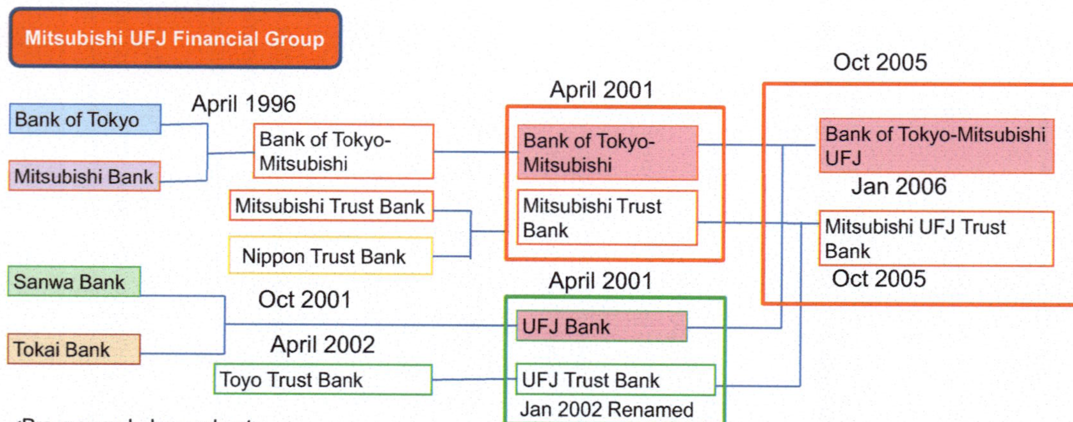

<Pre-merger balance sheet>

FY ending March 2005

	Bank of Tokyo-Mitsubishi	UFJ	Total		Bank of Tokyo-Mitsubishi	UFJ	Total
Cash and dues from banks	7.5	5.6	13.1	Deposits	53.2	46.9	100.1
Trading account assets	3.9	1.1	5.0	Payables under securities lending transactions	6.9	3.4	10.3
Securities	22.8	19.9	42.7	Corporate bonds	2.5	2.0	4.5
Loans	35.1	33.7	68.8	Other liabilities	15.0	14.1	29.1
Other assets	11.8	7.8	19.6	Total liabilities	77.6	66.4	144.0
				Total equity	3.5	1.7	5.2
Total assets	81.1	68.1	149.2	Total liabilities and equity	81.1	68.1	149.2

FY ending March 2017

	Bank of Tokyo-Mitsubis		Bank of Tokyo-Mitsubis
Cash and dues from banks	48.4	Deposits	139.1
Trading account assets	5.4	Payables under securities lending transactions	4.4
Securities	42.2	Corporate bonds	3.3
Loans	81.4	Other liabilities	47.2
Other assets	26.8	Total liabilities	194.0
		Total net assets	10.2
Total assets	204.2	Total liabilities and equity	204.2

Fig. 3.9 Mitsubishi UFJ Financial Group
(1) Structural reform via mergers of commercial banks to form megabanks
(2) Japanese megabanks transformed into universal banks (Banking, Securities, and Credit Cards)

2002	Kokusai Securities, Tokyo-Mitsubishi Personal Securities, and Issei Securities merge to form Mitsubishi Securities.
2002	Million Card and One Financial Card merge to form UFJ Card.
2004	Tokyo-Mitsubishi FG forms a capital alliance with ACOM, and ACOM acquires DC Cash One in 2005.
2005	Nippon Shinpan and UFJ Card merge to form UFJ Card.
2005	Mitsubishi Securities and UFJ Tsubasa Securities merge to form Mitsubishi UFJ Securities.
2007	UFJ NICOS and DC Card merge to form Mitsubishi UFJ NICOS. Mitsubishi UFJ Lease & Finance formed.
2008	Mitsubishi UFJ Financial Group (MUFG) acquires JAL Card. Mitsubishi UFJ NICOS acquires JACCS.
2009	Mitsubishi UFJ Securities and the investment banking operations of Morgan Stanley Japan Securities integrated to form Mitsubishi UFJ Morgan Stanley Securities (focusing on retail brokerage business) and Morgan Stanley MUFG Securities (focusing on wholesale brokerage business)

Fig. 3.9 (continued)

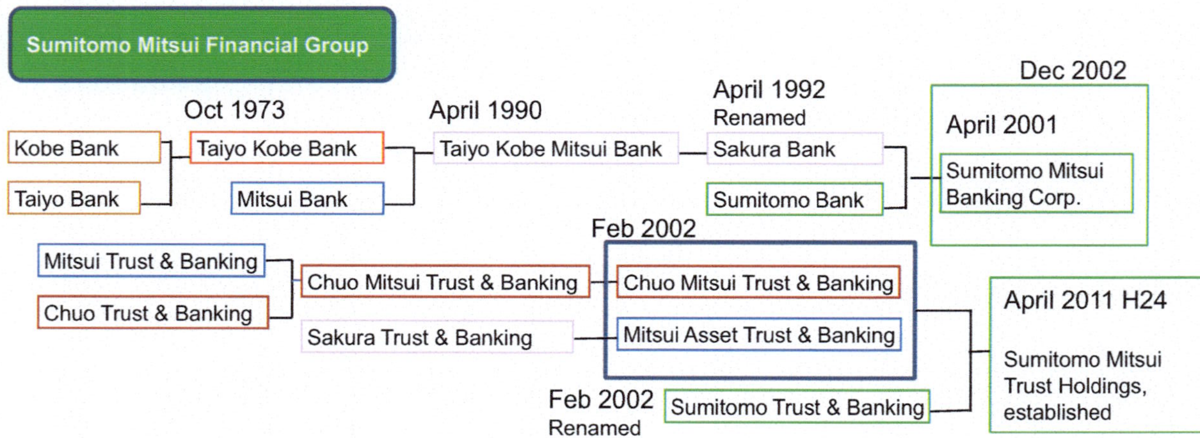

<Pre-merger balance sheet>
FY ending March 2000

	Sumitomo	Sakura	Total		Sumitomo	Sakura	Total
Cash and dues from banks	3.8	2.1	5.9	Deposits	27.4	30.2	57.6
Trading account assets	1.4	1.4	2.8	Negotiable certificates of deposit	6.8	3.5	10.3
Securities	9.0	6.9	15.9	Corporate bonds	0.4	1.0	1.4
Loans	31.3	32.3	63.6	Other liabilities	14.6	11.2	25.8
Other assets	5.6	5.8	11.4	Total liabilities	49.2	45.9	95.1
				Total net assets	1.9	2.2	4.1
Total assets	51.1	48.5	99.6	Total liabilities and equity	51.1	48.5	99.6

FY ending March 2017

	Sumitomo Mitsui		Sumitomo Mitsui
Cash and dues from banks	41.6	Deposits	105.5
Trading account assets	1.9	Negotiable certificates of deposit	12.2
Securities	24.3	Corporate bonds	3.9
Loans	75.6	Other liabilities	33.3
Other assets	18.9	Total liabilities	154.9
		Total net assets	7.4
Total assets	162.3	Total liabilities and equity	162.3

Fig. 3.10 Sumitomo Mitsui Financial Group, structural reform via mergers

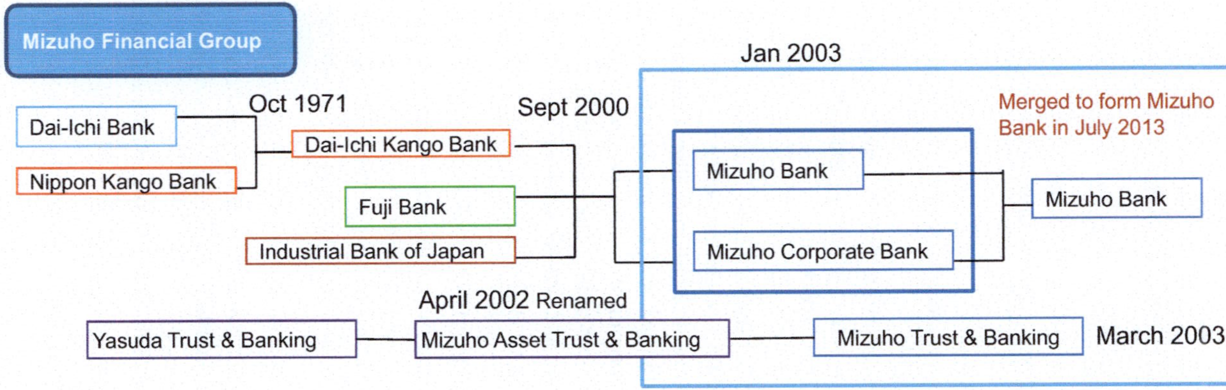

<Pre-merger balance sheet>
FY ending March 2001

	DKB	Fuji	Industrial Bank of Japan	Total		DKB	Fuji	Industrial Bank of Japan	Total
Cash and dues from banks	1.8	2.0	1.0	4.8	Deposits	29.8	28.6	5.8	64.2
Trading account assets	3.9	2.0	2.8	8.7	Negotiable certificates of deposit	4.1	5.1	2.5	11.7
Securities	7.1	10.5	9.6	27.2	Corporate bonds/debentures	0.0	0.3	18.4	18.7
Loans	31.5	31.6	22.5	85.6	Other liabilities	15.4	17.0	15.3	47.7
Other assets	7.5	7.3	7.8	22.6	Total liabilities	49.3	51.0	42.0	142.3
					Total net assets	2.5	2.4	1.7	6.6
Total assets	51.8	53.4	43.7	148.9	Total liabilities and equity	51.8	53.4	43.7	148.9

FY ending March 2017

	Mizuho		Mizuho
Cash and dues from banks	38.9	Deposits	107.7
Trading account assets	4.2	Negotiable certificates of deposit	10.1
Securities	31.2	Corporate bonds	3.7
Loans	71.3	Other liabilities	33.3
Other assets	16.5	Total liabilities	154.8
		Total net assets	7.3
Total assets	162.1	Total liabilities and equity	162.1

Fig. 3.11 Mizuho Financial Group, structural reform via mergers

Table 3.25 Total assets (trillion yen) and ROA: commercial banks and trust banks

Year (March)	2009	2010	2011	2012	2013	2014	2015	2016	2017
Commercial banks									
Total assets	427	438	447	463	484	502	517	543	566
Share (%)	32.9	33.3	33.2	33.6	34	34.3	34.5	34.9	35
ROA (%)	−0.141	0.297	0.425	0.475	0.475	0.578	0.542	0.46	0.397
Trust banks									
Total assets	63	63	65	67	70	75	80	91	100
Share (%)	4.8	4.8	4.8	4.8	4.9	5.1	5.3	5.8	6.2
ROA (%)	−0.32	0.46	0.431	0.463	0.514	0.613	0.637	0.538	0.357

banks experienced a sharp decline in revenue from financial intermediary operations after the negative-interest-rate policy was introduced.

Trust banks steadily increased their share of total assets as they joined commercial banks' financial groups. This is due to the positive impact of mergers, which came later than it did for commercial banks. Their ROA also shows a tendency similar to that of commercial banks.

Commercial banks and trust banks that were subsumed under financial holding companies established their own position within their corporate group and reorganized their securities, insurance, nonbanking, leasing, and other operations. This analysis indicates that commercial banks and trust banks teamed up to expand operations while enhancing efficiency through reorganization and creating synergy.

The issue is what role financial groups of commercial banks and trust banks, which hold more than 40% of total assets of public and private financial institutions in Japan, will play in optimizing the total assets of regional financial institutions (especially JP Bank and regional banks).

In the U.S., when interstate banking was deregulated in the 1990s to enable banks to expand their customer base and enhance profitability, banks of all sizes sought mergers and acquisitions to survive. The center of attention in the banking sector reorganization was super-regional banks with good earning power. What follows is a timeline of the reorganization of commercial banks and regional banks in the U.S. for reference.

In the U.S. the revision of the Glass-Steagall Act in 1987 led to a wave of bank mergers in the 1990s. As shown in Fig. 3.12, another wave of bank mergers occurred in the U.S. following the bursting of the housing bubble that triggered the subprime mortgage crisis and the collapse of Lehman Brothers in 2008.

Later, the banks were consolidated into four major banks, JPMorgan Chase Bank, N.A., Citibank, N.A., Bank of America, N.A., and Wells Fargo & Company.

1988 Norwest, a Minneapolis-based regional bank, acquires Wells Fargo, which later acquires Wachovia in 2008
1998 California-based Bank of America and North Carolina-based regional bank, NationsBank, merge, with NationsBank being the surviving bank (taking the name of Bank of America)
2001 First Union, the largest regional bank in North Carolina, acquires Wachovia, a Georgia-based regional bank, and renamed itself Wachovia
2004 Wachovia acquires SouthTrust, a Florida-based regional bank
2004 Bank of America acquires FleetBoston, a Massachusetts-based regional bank
2005 Bank of America acquires MBNA, the world's largest independent credit card company specializing in affinity cards
2008 Lehman Brothers files for bankruptcy

Fig. 3.12 Shift from era of financial regulation to era of financial deregulation: expanding operations via M&As
Source: Naoki Togashi (2009)

4.6 Full Privatization and Challenges of the Development Bank of Japan

The DBJ was established on October 1, 2008, based on the Act on Promotion of Administrative Reform for Realization of Small and Efficient Government (Administrative Reform Promotion Act), which went into effect in May 2006, and the Act on DBJ Inc., which went into effect in June 2007.

The Act for Partial Amendment of the DBJ Inc. Act was instituted in June 2009 to enable the bank to enhance its emergency lending operations following the collapse of Lehman Brothers.

When it was launched, DBJ was slated to be fully privatized in 5 to 7 years. The revision to the law allowed the government to hold a stake in the bank until the end of March 2012 and extended the deadline for full privatization until 5 to 7 years from April 2012.

Following the Great East Japan Earthquake, a special fiscal-measures law was enacted in May 2011 to provide financial assistance to cope in the aftermath of the disaster. The law allowed a 3-year extension to the period during which the government could take a stake in the bank (until late March 2015) and extended the deadline for full privatization until 5 to 7 years from April 1, 2015. The government also decided to overhaul the bank's organization, including its shareholding policy, by the end of fiscal 2014.

After looking into ways to overhaul the bank at the end of fiscal 2014, the government promulgated the Act for Partial Amendment of DBJ Inc. Act in May 2015. Under the revised law, DBJ is to leverage its investing and lending functions to supply funds for crisis management and growth while upholding the full privatization policy.

The revision allows the government to invest in the bank for an unspecified period so the bank can conduct emergency lending operations. The law requires DBJ to focus on providing growth funds through special investment operations until the end of fiscal 2020 and make efforts to dispose of all investment assets related to the said operations and cap off the operations by the end of fiscal 2025. The government is allowed to invest in DBJ so it can conduct special investment operations. It is also required to reduce its shares in the bank in light of the impact its holdings may have on achieving the bank's objectives as well as market trends and dispose of all shares as soon as possible.

The revised law also requires the government to hold more than a third of all outstanding shares while measures related to the emergency lending operations are put in place and more than half of all outstanding shares while measures related to special investment operations are taken.

The supplementary provision requires the government to take necessary measures concerning emergency lending and special investment operations as well as the government's involvement in DBJ when such measures are deemed necessary.

As noted earlier, while maintaining the policy on disposing of all shares in DBJ, the government fails to specify when it plans to fully privatize it through a public

Table 3.26 Total assets (trillion yen) and ROA: DBJ

Year (March)	2009	2010	2011	2012	2013	2014	2015	2016	2017
Total assets	13.3	14.8	15.2	15.2	15.9	16.2	16.2	16	16.1
Share (%)	1.0	1.2	1.1	1.1	1.1	1.1	1.1	1.0	1.0
ROA (%)	−0.902	0.338	0.592	0.658	0.692	0.926	0.926	1.063	0.683

offering because it may or may not sell its shares depending on economic circumstances. The repeated deferment of the bank's IPO is proof that public financial services are under the government's control. The government always leaves room for its involvement by adding supplementary provisions or making additional resolutions.

While DBJ has been in the state described since it was privatized, an analysis of its ROA during these years reveals the following (Table 3.26).

DBJ represents only 1.0% of the financial sector in terms of total assets, and that figure has decreased over time. However, its ROA is almost double that of commercial banks, with the exception of the immediate aftermath of Lehman Brothers' collapse. The bank earned large profits especially after the Great East Japan Earthquake as a result of intensive lending of growth funds through the emergency lending and special investment operations while benefitting from the special fiscal-measures law. This is because most of the loans were made to government projects and major corporations that incurred minimum operating expenses and cost of risk.

The expense ratio was 20% on average, which is much lower than the 50% at Shoko Chukin Bank or the 60–75% at megabanks. To optimize the ROA of each type of financial institution, the governing law for DBJ should be changed to the Banking Act so that it will not benefit from a special law, and its abnormal cost structure should be changed back to what it was so that it will not squeeze out private financial institutions.

4.6.1 History of Development Bank of Japan and the Path to Reform

We will now turn our attention to the history of DBJ to determine why it was subjected to in-depth review under the Reorganization and Rationalization Plan for Special Public Institutions in December 2011 and the Council on Economic and Fiscal Policy's policy-based finance reform proposals in December 2012.

The Japanese economy boomed as demand soared after the Korean War broke out in June 1950, and Japan faced the need to modernize its core industries, such as steel, coal, sea transportation, and power generation, which constituted the foundation of economic and industrial development.

The Development Bank of Japan (formerly Japan Development Bank) was established in April 1951 as a public financial institution wholly owned by the government. It was designed to complement private financial services by providing long-term loans needed to help get the economy back on its feet. During the high-growth period, the bank focused on boosting Japan's energy and transport capability while narrowing the economic gaps among regions through regional development. As a result, the bank's loan balance exceeded one trillion yen at the end of fiscal 1965. In the late 1960s and early 1970s, the bank zeroed in on technological development, urban development, modernization of physical distribution, and preventing pollution, all with an eye toward enhancing Japan's ability to compete in the global arena.

While Japan's economic growth slowed in the wake of the 1971 Nixon Shock, the bank focused its operations on enhancing the quality of people's lives, ensuring a stable energy supply, developing a basic social infrastructure, and facilitating a change in the industrial structure right up to the bubble period.

During the bubble years, as trade frictions with other countries increased as a result of the Plaza Accord, Japan faced an urgent need to increase domestic demand and revamp its industrial economic structure. Working against this backdrop, the bank focused on the areas of energy and the environment. The bank's outstanding loan balance topped 10 trillion yen at the end of fiscal 1991.

After the bubble burst, private financial institutions witnessed an upsurge in lending regulations and mounting bad loans against a backdrop of declining loans. At the same time, working in line with the government's large-scale economic policy, the bank continued to increase its loan balance by providing loans for social capital improvement, as well as reconstruction efforts in the wake of the Great Hanshin earthquake, and serving as a safety net by providing loans in response to changes in the financial environment to stabilize the financial system. Its loan balance peaked at 18,751.9 billion yen at the end of fiscal 1999.

In October 1999, following the merger with the Hokkaido-Tohoku Development Finance Public Corporation, the bank was renamed DBJ. The bank sustained investment and lending operations with a focus on support for regional revitalization, the environment and infrastructure, and the creation of technologies and industries. As the bank became overbloated, competing with private financial institutions, it was selected as one of the organizations to be privatized under the Basic Law on Special Public Institutions Reform of 2000.

The law limited the functions of policy-based financial institutions to three areas, and they withdrew from other operations. The three functions included assisting SMEs and individuals in procuring funds; (2) providing financial services crucial to securing resources abroad that are vital to Japan's national policies and international competitiveness, and providing ODA loans (having both policy-based finance and assistance functions). To serve these functions, the law stipulated that the government would fully privatize DBJ and Shoko Chukin Bank, abolish the JFC for Municipal Enterprises, and consolidate the National Life Finance Corporation, JFC for SMEs, Agriculture, Forestry and Fisheries Finance Corporation, Okinawa Development Finance Corporation, and JBIC to form a new policy-based financial institution.

In May 2006 the Act on the Promotion of Administrative Reform for the Realization of Small and Efficient Government (Administrative Reform Promotion Act) went into effect, and in June 2007 the Act on DBJ Inc. was passed as part of the drastic reform of policy-based finance reforms. On October 1, 2008, DBJ Inc. was established as a privately operated but government-owned organization. The new

DBJ born out of the New DBJ Act is different from the old one in that it does not rely on FILP funds but raises funds by (1) issuing bonds, including finance bonds, to institutional investors, (2) borrowing additional funds from private financial institutions, and (3) issuing negotiable certificates of deposit. The bank's loan balance hovered around 13,740.9 billion yen at the end of fiscal 2001.

The biggest challenge facing Japan now is how to increase its GDP and gross national income (GNI). DBJ should be used to advance policy-based finance reforms that are a vital part of growth strategies and facilitate active investments and loans for growth industries, whether in Japan or overseas. The bank must also change its organizational structure via full privatization in order to develop capabilities for aggressive project-based sales and customer-oriented proposals. We are witnessing dramatic changes unfold across the global financial spectrum with the rise of emerging economies, fiscal problems in the EU, and political issues.

4.7 *State-owned Financial Institutions Complementing the Private Sector—JBIC, Japan International Cooperation Agency, and the Japan Finance Corporation*

The Basic Law on Special Public Institutions Reform of 2000 divided policy-based financial institutions into those that were slated to be privatized and those that were to remain state-owned financial institutions.

The Basic Policy on the Reform of Policy-based Finance was compiled by the Council on Economic and Fiscal Policy in November 2005. The government decided to limit the functions of policy-based financial institutions to three areas and withdraw them from other operations. The three functions included assisting SMEs and individuals in procuring funds, providing financial services crucial to securing resources abroad that are vital to Japan's national policies and international competitiveness, and providing ODA loans (having both policy-based finance and assistance functions). As a result, the government decided to fully privatize DBJ and Shoko Chukin Bank, abolish the JFC for Municipal Enterprises, and consolidate the National Life Finance Corporation, JFC for SMEs, Agriculture, Forestry and Fisheries Finance Corporation, Okinawa Development Finance Corporation, and the JBIC to form a new state-owned, policy-based financial institution. The outcome was the current JFC, JBIC, and JICA (Table 3.27).

4.7.1 Japan Bank for International Cooperation

- Act (Special Law)

On April 1, 2012, the JBIC was separated from the JFC and established as an independent entity. Capitalized at 1.36 trillion yen, the bank is wholly owned by the Japanese government, although its first governor was appointed from the private sector.

Table 3.27 Nonconsolidated balance sheets of public financial institutions (fiscal year ending March 31, 2017) (trillion yen)

	To be fully privatized[a]				State-owned financial institutions[b]				Total for public financial services, A + B	Total for public and private sectors
	Japan Post Bank	Development Bank of Japan	Shoko Chukin Bank	Total for 3 privatized banks, A	Japan Finance Corporation	Japan Bank for International Cooperation	Japan International Cooperation Agency (JICA)	Total for state-owned financial institutions, B		
Cash and due from banks	51	1	2	54	4	2	0.2	6	60	381
Securities	139	2	1	142	0.1	0.3	0	0.4	142	408
(government bonds)	(69)	(0.2)	(0.9)	(70)	(0.1)	(–)	–	(0.1)	(70)	(159)
Loans	4	13	9	26	18	14	11	43	69	715
Other	16	1	1	18	0	3	0.2	4	22	136
Total assets	210	17	13	240	22	19	12	53	293	1640
Deposits	179	0	5	184	0	0	0	0	184	1198
Borrowings	0	8	1	9	14	10	2	26	35	35
Other liabilities	19	6	6	31	3	6	0.5	10	41	292
Total liabilities	198	14	12	224	17	16	2	36	260	1525
Total net assets	12	3	1	16	5	3	10	17	33	115
Total liabilities and net assets	210	17	13	240	22	19	12	53	293	1640
	14.6%				3.2%				17.8%	100%

Sources:
[a]Ministry of Finance's statistical data and government-affiliated financial institutions' financial statements
[b]Japanese Bankers Association, National Association of Shinkin Banks, Shinkumi Federation Bank, and National Federation of Agricultural Cooperative Associations (ZEN-NOH) statistics (ZEN-NOH data are for fiscal year ending March 31, 2016)

Like other state-owned financial institutions, the JBIC clearly states that its mission is to complement private financial services.

- History and Path to Reform

The Export Bank of Japan was created back in 1950 and in 1952 was renamed the Export-Import Bank of Japan. In 1961 the Overseas Economic Cooperation Fund was established and integrated with the Export-Import Bank of Japan in 1999, creating the JBIC.

It played a vital role in Japan's policy-based finance by providing loans to fund trade transactions that supported the economic growth of postwar Japan. Following the passage of the JFC Act in May 2007, the International Financial Operations of the JBIC were merged with the JFC on October 1, 2008, while its Overseas Economic Cooperation Operations were integrated into JICA.

As initially planned, on April 1, 2012, the JBIC was separated from the JFC and was established as an independent entity under the JBIC Act. Capitalized at 1.36 trillion yen, the bank is wholly owned by the Japanese government, but its first governor was appointed from the private-sector ranks. The bank is a stock company employing 536 people and operating 17 offices overseas but is considered a special public institution based on the Act on JBIC.

The bank's mission is to complement private financial services and contribute to the sound development of Japan and the international society at large by providing financial services for the following purposes.

- Facilitating overseas development and securement of resources that are important for Japan
- Maintaining and improving the international competitiveness of Japanese industries
- Promoting overseas operations aimed at preserving the global environment, such as preventing global warming
- Preventing disruptions to the international financial order or taking appropriate measures with respect to damage caused by such disruptions

The JBIC gives priority to complementing private financial institutions through international finance operations that serve as a reliable source of funds for private companies looking to enter overseas growth markets. It serves one of the three functions specified under policy-based finance reform, i.e., providing financial services crucial to securing resources abroad which are vital to Japan's national policies and international competitiveness. I expect the bank to step up to bat and take risks that will contribute to Japan's growth strategy in overseas markets.

Its balance sheet reveals that the bank uses borrowings from FILP, government-guaranteed bonds, and equity capital for lending. Its financial operations are focused on facilitating overseas development and the securement of resources that are vital to Japan, maintaining and improving the international competitiveness of Japanese industries, promoting overseas operations aimed at preserving the global environment such as preventing global warming, and preventing disruptions to the international financial order or taking appropriate measures with respect to damage caused by such disruptions. It is a bank private companies can count on when they are expanding into growth markets overseas. It should also serve as a good example of coexistence and coprosperity for public and private financial services despite concerns that it could become a big fat government-controlled financial institution.

4.7.2 Japan International Cooperation Agency (Special Law)

The JICA provides developing countries with ODA. It provides financial and personnel assistance needed to build water supply and sewer systems, roads, and other infrastructure vital to people's lives, along with disaster relief and medical assistance. State-owned financial institutions raise funds on government credit and receive subsidies from the government's special account.

JICA uses the money borrowed from FILP and its equity capital to make ODA loans and uses them for investing. Loans to countries in Asia and other parts of the world totaled 11 trillion yen in the fiscal year ending March 31, 2017. These loans were made using 1.7 trillion yen borrowed from FILP and shareholders' equity worth 9 trillion yen. Out of shareholders' equity, 7.7 trillion yen came entirely from the government's general account. This is proof that JICA is simply a state-owned financial institution.

I visited ten countries in the 5 years following 2011 to conduct an automobile industry survey for ASEAN Plus Three. The locations I visited included Japanese automakers' overseas factories, their parts factories, and dealers. I also met with officials from the Japan External Trade Organization (JETRO) and JICA to find out about the political and economic conditions of each country. Serving as advance troops in the field, the Japanese staff in each country had an excellent handle on the local situation and outlook for the future. A mechanism is taking shape that will enable the public and private sectors to work together to make aggressive investments across the globe with an eye toward increasing Japan's GNI. I was surprised, however, to find out that China and Korea were providing ASEAN countries with financial and personnel assistance that was far greater than what was coming from Japan.

4.7.3 Japan Finance Corporation (Special Law)

Following the passage of the JFC Act in May 2007, the National Life Finance Corporation, JFC for SMEs, Agriculture Forestry and Fisheries Finance Corporation, and the JBIC were integrated into the JFC in October 2008. Its objectives, specified in the Institutional Design for Policy-Based Finance Reform in June 2006, focus on policy-based financing as a government function as well as maintaining international trust and the independence of international finance operations. The government decided that the JFC should be a special corporation wholly owned by the government and that its budget would require approval of the Diet since it secures funds on government credit and issues large credit sums. The JFC's basic philosophy is provided in the following statement: "Following the national policy, provide flexible policy-based financing by utilizing a variety of financing programs and schemes to meet the needs of society, while complementing the activities of private financial institutions." Its balance sheet shows that it uses borrowings from FILP, government-guaranteed bonds, and equity capital, which is invested entirely by the government, for lending.

4.7.4 History of Japan Finance Corporation and the Path to Reform

Following the passage of the Act on the Promotion of Administrative Reform for the Realization of Small and Efficient Government in May 2006 as well as the JFC Act in May 2007, which were designed to consolidate the National Life Finance Corporation, Agriculture Forestry and Fisheries Finance Corporation, JFC for SMEs, and the JBIC, the JFC was established on October 1, 2008.

What follows is an outline of the institutional design of these four policy-based financial institutions specified in the Institutional Design for Policy-Based Finance Reform, which was adopted by the Headquarters for the Promotion of the Reform of Policy-Based Finance and the Headquarters for Promoting Administrative Reform in June 2006.

[Overall vision]

1. Carefully implement policy-based finance as a government function
2. Ensure efficient operation with clear management responsibilities
3. Ensure transparency, evaluation, and monitoring
4. Maintain and enhance convenience for users
5. Maintain international trust and independence of international finance operations

[Organizational structure]

(1) Corporate form: Special corporation

A special corporation is a joint stock company stipulated in the Companies Act that is established on the basis of a special law and governed by the Companies Act.

- The corporation focuses on operations in line with government policies. Since policy-based financing is a function necessary for implementing government policies, correct and quick action is required in meeting the challenge of whatever economic and financial conditions arise.
- The government should own all shares in the corporation, and its budget must be approved by the Diet since it secures funds on government credit and issues large credit sums.
- (2) Maintaining strong governance
- The corporation will set medium-term business goals and make them public.
- The corporation will use generally accepted accounting practices.
- The corporation will set up separate accounts for different policies and define responsibilities.
- The corporation will assess and manage risks using an objective risk assessment technique.

- The corporation will be careful not to simply appoint CEOs from the public service ranks.
- The corporation will review money-losing operations so the government only has to provide it with financial assistance when absolutely necessary.

The Institutional Design for Policy-Based Finance Reform also outlined the policies for the corporation's organizational design and operation as well as business operations and specified that the corporation would be created in October 2008.

The roots of the business units that constitute the JFC lie in policy-based financial institutions that were set up by the government for postwar economic recovery purposes and were all established around the same time. The predecessor of the Micro Business and Individual Unit was the People's Finance Corporation launched in June 1949. The Agriculture, Forestry, Fisheries and Food Business Unit was originally the Agriculture Forestry and Fisheries Finance Corporation established in April 1953. The JBIC was originally established as the Export-Import Bank of Japan in December 1950 and renamed the Export Bank of Japan in April 1952. While the predecessors of these business units were established for different purposes, they were all policy-based financial institutions that shared the same mission, which was to "contribute to the sound development of the Japanese and international economies and societies and improvement in the living standards of Japanese people." These policy-based financial institutions served as an engine driving Japan's economic growth forward as they complemented private financial services during the high-growth period. Although they served as a safety net in postbubble Japan, they also became overbloated during the lost decade and continued to squeeze out the private financial services sector. In 2006, the government formulated the administrative reform bill in an attempt to shift gears and downsize policy-based financial institutions.

The Japan Finance Corporation, whose mission is to provide focused policy-based financing as a government function, has steadily provided funds for business operators affected by the March 2011 Great East Japan Earthquake and flexibly responded to the needs for safety net services.

The institutional designs under the policy-based finance reform that focused on complementing the private sector and carry out a shift from public to private pointed to two different paths. One was to fully privatize policy-based financial institutions, while the other was to enable them to flexibly provide policy-based financing based on government policies with a focus on complementing private financial institutions. The former emphasized more transparent operations with a focus on risk management and profit. The latter focused on providing safety net loans as well as credit enhancement loans and responding to crisis situations by providing various services, such as special earthquake recovery loans, requiring policy-based financial institutions to operate so swiftly and smoothly that they ended up carrying huge risk assets.

What is the difference between public and private financial services? The answer is determined by whether or not the government is involved in the fund-raising process of a financial institution. Depositors decide whether or not to trust a private financial institution at their own risk. In other words, private financial services use depositors' money to make loans to private companies or individuals, while public

Table 3.28 Total assets (trillion yen) and ROA: state-owned financial institutions

March	2009	2010	2011	2012	2013	2014	2015	2016	2017
Total assets	49.0	53.8	60.0	62.0	56.5	50.6	52.6	52.3	52.0
Share (%)	3.8	4.1	4.4	4.4	4.0	3.5	3.5	3.4	3.2
ROA (%)	−1.081	−1.673	−0.110	−0.225	−0.230	0.375	0.380	0.363	0.192

financial services use government-guaranteed or automatically government-guaranteed deposits and taxpayer money to make loans to state-owned financial institutions.

In summary, let us look at the balance sheets of financial institutions in Japan for the fiscal year ending March 31, 2017. Table 3.28 compares state-owned financial institutions (public financial services that receive government guarantees) with public financial institutions that aim to become fully privatized and automatically receive government guarantees.

The total of government bonds and loans at the three state-owned financial institutions (JFC, JBIC, and JICA) amounts to 43 trillion yen, which is 4.9% of the total for both public and private financial institutions, standing at 874 trillion yen. The total for the three banks that automatically receive government guarantees (JP Bank, DBJ, and Shoko Chukin Bank) is 96 trillion yen, accounting for 11.0%. These figures indicate that Japan's financial market will become more liberalized once government-guaranteed funds used for government bonds and loans account for only about 5% of the market.

References

Fujii, Hideki (2012–2017) *Nippon yusei no keiei bunseki to kigyo kachi hyoka* [Analysis of Japan Post operations and corporate value]. Tsushin Kenkyukai, Tokyo

Japanese Bankers Association. (2001) *Wareware ga kangaeru yubin chokin no shoraizo* [Our vision for the future of postal savings]. https://www.zenginkyo.or.jp/fileadmin/res/news/yuchoshouraizou.pdf

Ikeo, Kazuhito (2013) *Defure to keizai seisaku* [Deflation and economic policy]. Tokyo: Nikkei Business Publications, Inc.

Ikeo, Kazuhito (2017) Kansei kinyu kaikaku to chigin saihen no shohyo. Review of Kansei kinyu kaikaku to chigin saihen [Public financial reform and regional bank reorganization], by Akira Uno. Kinyu Zaisei Jijo, February 27

Iwamoto, Yasushi (2003) *Koteki bumon no kaikaku, kinyu 'chusho' igai mineika hayaku* [Public sector reform: Expediting privatization of financial services except SME finance]. The Nikkei (Tokyo), September 11

Iwamoto, Yasushi. (2013) *Seifu ruiseki saimu no kiketsu: Kiki ka saiken ka* [Consequences of High Government Debt: Crisis or Adjustment?]. https://iwmtyss.com/Docs/2013/SeifuRuisekiSaimunoKiketsuRevised.pdf

Jinno, Naohiko (2008) *Chiiki saisei no keizaigaku* [Economics for regional revitalization]. Tokyo: Chuokoron-Shinsha, Inc., Tokyo

Kobayashi, Keiichiro (2017) *Saimu mondai to choki keizai teitai* [The debt crisis and our long-term economic slump]. In: Kazuhito Ikeo and Hiroto Koda (ed) *Nihon keizai saisei 25-nen no kei* [25 years of reviving Japan's economy]. Nikkei Publishing Inc., Tokyo, pp. 85–116

Regional Banks Association of Japan (2007) *Yubin chokin ginko oyobi yubin hoken gaisha no shinki gyomu no chosa shingi ni kansuru shoken* [Reactions to the Postal Privatization Committee's views on new business horizons for the postal savings bank and postal life insurance company]. https://www.chiginkyo.or.jp/app/images/pdf_data/11_newsrelease/2007/news_1.pdf.

Shikano, Yoshiaki (2006) *Nihon no kinyu seido* [Japanese financial system]. Toyo Keizai Inc., Tokyo

Shikano, Yoshiaki (2015) Yusei jojo no kadai: Shuekiryoku no kojo ga kyumu [Challenge to listing of Japan Post stock: Enhancing profitability is imperative]. *The Nikkei* (Tokyo), July 27

Uno, Akira (2015) *Kansei kinyu kaikaku to chigin saihen* [Public financial reform and regional bank reorganization]. Kinzai Institute for Financial Affairs, Inc., Tokyo

Chapter 4
Theory and Empirical Analysis for the Restructuring of the Three Privatized Public Financial Institutions and Regional Banks

1 Theory for Creating an Optimal Balance Among and Within Different Types of Financial Institutions Toward a Free, Fair, and Efficient Financial Market

In 2002, following the FILP reform, the government[1] claimed that Japan's policy-based finance system was a behemoth when stacked up against the systems of other countries and that its burgeoning scale had caused the financial and capital markets' resource allocation mechanism to break down. Stressing that enhancing the efficiency of the financial and capital markets was a top priority, the Japanese government insisted that a drastic reform of policy-based finance was crucial in order to unshackle the private sector. The government believed that public funds should be used by private financial services to promote its growth strategy.

The Mitsubishi Research Institute pointed out in its 2005 report[2] on postal privatization (privatization of the postal savings bank) that postal privatization was the Big Bang in public finance because it changed the flow of funds. The report noted that the flow of funds should be changed across Japan by enhancing the efficiency of the economic supply structure in order to channel money to private financial institutions with better growth potential.

However, 10 years after privatization, there was still no change to the flow of funds as local economies remained in the doldrums, and the deposits collected by JP Bank were invested in foreign bonds and Japanese government bonds (JGBs) before reaching the local private financial sector.

Electronic supplementary material The online version of this chapter (https://doi.org/10.1007/978-981-15-1408-1_4) contains supplementary material, which is available to authorized users.

[1]Council on Economic and Fiscal Policy, "Outline of the policy-based finance reform," December 13, 2002.

[2]Mitsubishi Research Institute, "Significance of postal privatization," August 23, 2005.

A. Uno, *Japan Post Bank*, https://doi.org/10.1007/978-981-15-1408-1_4

During a 2010 Postal Privatization Committee meeting, the Japanese Bankers Association (JBA) claimed that this mechanism that funnels a huge amount of money into JP Bank, which operates outside the market, would block the efficient flow of funds and have an adverse effect on the Japanese economy, interfering with the creation of an efficient financial market. The JBA also pointed out that the automatic government guarantee for public financial intermediary operations would prevent private financial institutions from competing with JP Bank on an equal footing. The JBA expressed its concern over this guarantee enjoyed by the government-backed financial institution, saying that it would make competitive conditions unequal for private financial institutions when it came to fund raising or lending operations using that fund. Their concern proved to be well founded with the discovery of illicit lending practices at Shoko Chukin Bank, a privately operated but government-owned financial institution. The uneven playing field is abundantly clear when you look at the DBJ's profit margin, which towers over the profit margins of the megabanks.

The majority of publicly traded companies in Japan close their fiscal year (FY) books in March. Those that announce their financial results in May rush to file their earnings summaries with the stock exchange so they can publish their financial results. The earnings summary[3] provides a huge amount of important information, all on a single A4 size piece of paper. The figures for operating results and financial standing are particularly important. Operating profit and return on assets (ROA) are significant indicators, respectively demonstrating how well a company is doing and how profitable a company is relative to its total assets. While the assets-to-equity ratio is a key indicator of a company's financial standing, total assets are used to measure a company's position in the industry as well as demonstrate how solid a company's operating foundation is.

A company that is looking to merge with another company would focus on how the merger partner's assets would help it shore up its operating foundation after looking at the growth potential of the industry in which that company operates. It would then work on materializing a positive effect of the merger as soon as possible by, for example, leveraging the assets gained through the merger to boost its sales capability and reducing liabilities to enhance efficiency.

In this chapter total assets and ROA, which are key indicators of a company's performance, will be used as basic analytical elements as they were in Chap. 3. At the same time, it would be reasonable to discuss the ROA of different types of financial institutions in Japan with the objective of seeing how they could increase their ROA to a certain level. It will be necessary for financial institutions to increase assets and streamline operations in order to increase their ROA to that level. Hopefully this will promote mergers and lead to more efficient capital allocation across Japan as well as smaller earnings differences among different types of financial institutions.

[3]Consolidated earnings summary for fiscal year ending March 31, 2018 (JGAAP): (1) operating results: operating profit and ROA; (2) financial standing: total assets; (3) cash flows.

First, Sect. 1.1 will analyze the current situation based on the ROA data for different types of financial institutions. The focus will be on three public financial institutions (JP Bank, Shoko Chukin Bank, and the DBJ). We will then analyze, in Sect. 1.3, how the imbalance between assets and liabilities, a problem unique to JP Bank, will affect its bottom line when short-term and long-term interest rates go up in the future. The analysis will substantiate the urgent need for reconstituting assets. When it comes to regional financial institutions, we should focus our discussions on local reorganization, including mergers among regional banks. Therefore, Sect. 1.2 will look at statistical data to determine the size of assets regional banks should maintain after going through regional restructuring in order to achieve a decent ROA. Finally, Sect. 1.4 will analyze the trends in financial institutions by type and region. This analysis should provide important insights into regional restructuring.

1.1 Narrowing the ROA Gap Between Public and Private Financial Institutions

As shown in Fig. 4.1, the correlation between gross prefectural product and prefectural loan balance is very high at 0.949.

According to Fig. 4.2, regional banks and shinkin banks provide 80%[4] of all loans made in any rural prefecture. This high percentage figure indicates that regional financial institutions contribute greatly to the gross prefectural product. To estimate the potential increase in the prefectural loan balance if postal savings held by JP Bank were used for lending, I calculated the potential lending capacity by multiplying each prefecture's postal savings balance by the deposit-loan ratio (i.e., prefectural loan balance divided by prefectural deposit balance). When calculated using the postal savings balance of 165.8 trillion yen as of March 31, 2017, the potential lending capacity is 73.7 trillion yen.

It is quite possible that this amount will increase prefectural gross product, but the question is whether this money can really be used. The time-worn standard operating procedure has been to take locally collected funds and centrally invest them in foreign bonds and JGBs rather than letting the money work locally. This existing postal savings model or Norinchukin model must be changed. Although special public institutions reform was initiated to tackle this problem head on, post offices and agricultural cooperatives (JA) across Japan are still operating both banking and insurance businesses in order to keep their organizations afloat.

Table 4.1 shows how personal savings amounting to 241 trillion yen (accounting for 27% of Japan's personal savings total), a combined total of deposits at JP Bank and the money entrusted by JA to Norinchukin Bank, are used. As of the end of March 2017, JP Bank and Norinchukin Bank had a total of 82 trillion yen in JGBs, 43 trillion yen in foreign investment trusts, 54 trillion yen in foreign bonds, and

[4] Financial Map 2018, *Kinyu Journal* (March 2017).

Fig. 4.1 Correlation between gross prefectural product and prefecture's total loans (trillion yen). Tokyo (94/201), Osaka (38/45), Aichi (36/28), and Kanagawa (30/25) are not shown on this chart. (*Source*: Financial statements of regional banks [this can be downloaded from the electronic supplementary material])

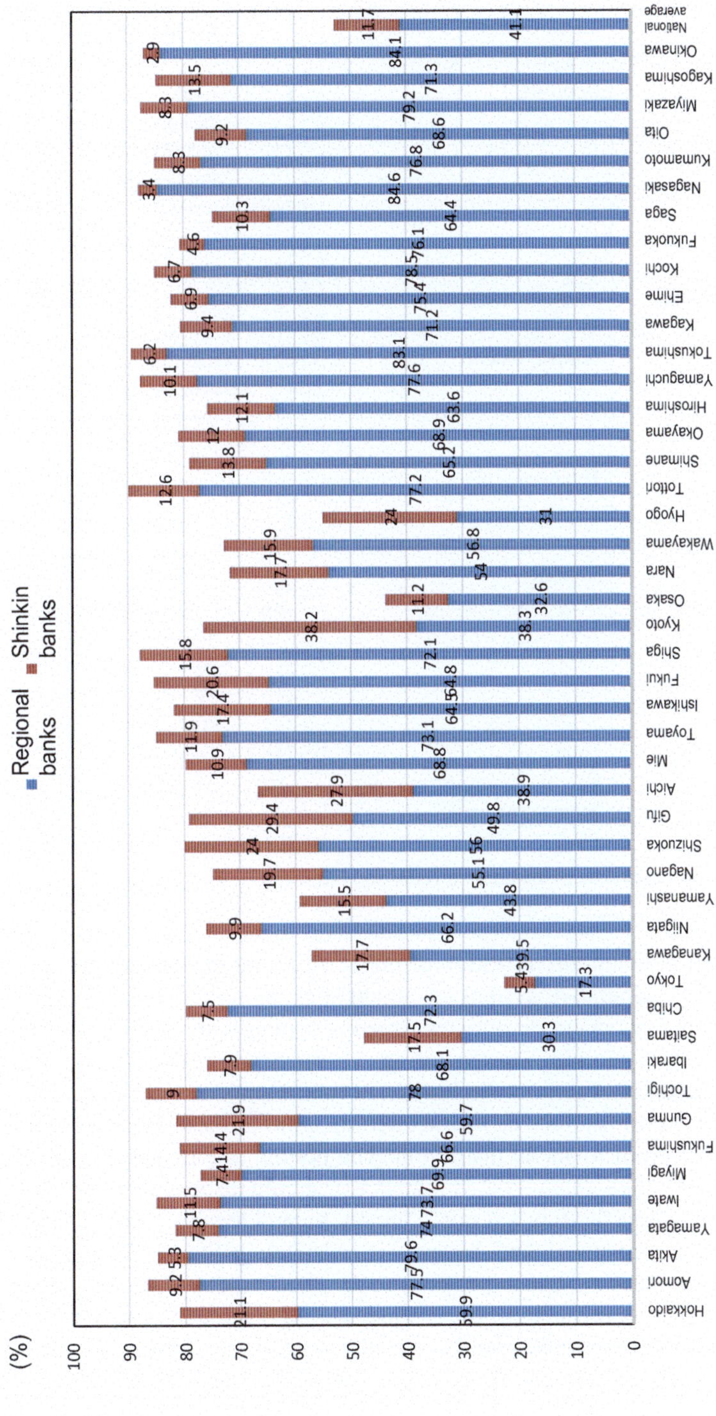

Fig. 4.2 Loan market share of regional banks and shinkin banks by prefecture, March 2017. (*Source*: Financial statements of each bank)

Table 4.1 Japan Post Bank and Norinchukin Bank (March 2017) (trillion yen)

	Interest-bearing liabilities		Earning assets	
(a) Interest-bearing liabilities and earning assets				
JP Bank	Deposits	179.4	Loans	4.1
			Japanese government bonds	68.8
			Foreign investment trusts	32.6
			Foreign bonds	20.1
	Total	179.4	Total	125.6
Norinchukin Bank	Cooperative deposits	61.9	Loans	11.9
	Negotiable certificates of deposit, others	10.3	Japanese government bonds	13.2
			Foreign investment trusts	10.0
			Foreign bonds	34.6
	Total	70.2	Total	69.7
Total		251.6		195.3
(b) Total of two banks: interest-bearing liabilities and earning assets				
JP Bank + Norinchukin Bank	Deposits	179.4	Loans	16.0
	Cooperative deposits	61.9	Japanese government bonds	82.0
			Foreign investment trusts	42.6
			Foreign bonds	54.7
	Total	241.3	Total	195.3
	Negotiable certificates of deposit, others	10.3	(Deposits with BOJ)	(51.0)
	Total	251.6	Total	246.3

Source: Financial statements of Japan Post Bank and Norinchukin Bank

16 trillion yen in loans. Privatization of public financial institutions and reforms of the agricultural cooperative system are aimed at changing this flow of funds. While the government is working on policies aimed at coping with population decline and vitalizing local economies, restructuring of financial institutions and regional restructuring needed to promote industries have not gained much ground.

Financial institutions must be restructured to optimize the share of total assets and ROA of each type of financial institution. The bottom line is that it is all about the three privatized banks. Japan Post Holdings Co. should dispose of all of its shares so that JP Bank can use the funds it raises locally to lend locally. Shoko Chukin Bank should be fully privatized and become a financial institution, equipped with a corporate governance system, operating under the Banking Act. The DBJ should compete with private megabanks on an equal footing without relying on government guarantees. These three banks could contribute to vitalizing local economies through business strategies focused on, for example, renewable energy, the "sextiary sector," healthcare, and the relocation of information technology (IT) companies. In what follows, specific road maps are laid out for the respective banks.

1.1.1 Sale of JP Bank shares

The Act for the Partial Revision of the Postal Service Privatization Act stipulates that JP Holdings must dispose of shares in postal savings bank and postal insurance companies as soon as possible while considering the two financial companies' financial standing, possible impact on ensuring basic postal services, and other relevant factors, with an eye to disposing of all shares. As of March 31, 2018, JP Holdings had a 74% stake in JP Bank, holding 3.3 billion shares. General shareholders held 0.5 billion shares, accounting for 11% of all shares. This is far from full privatization. As long as JP Holdings is a controlling shareholder with more than 50% of the shares in JP Bank, JP Bank cannot start a new business. JP Holdings' stake in JP Bank should be reduced to less than 50% as soon as possible so that JP Bank can be authorized to start a new business on a notification basis and diversify its operations to hedge risks. JP Holdings will be able to use the revenue from the sale of shares to supplement postal service operations or make investments.

1.1.2 Sale of Shoko Chukin Bank Shares

The government partially revised the Shoko Chukin Bank Limited Act in May 2015.

<Sale of government-owned shares>.

Supplementary Provisions Article 2: The government must reduce its shares in the company (one of the two privatized companies) in light of the impact its holdings may have on achieving the companies' objectives as well as market trends and dispose of all shares as soon as possible.

- Government's shareholding related to emergency lending operations

Supplementary Provisions Article 2–8: The government must hold more than a third of all outstanding shares in the company for an unspecified period in order to ensure that the company effectively conducts emergency lending operations.

- Government's shareholding related to special investment operations

Supplementary Provisions Article 2–13: The government must hold more than half of all outstanding shares in the company until the company completes special investment operations in order to ensure that the company effectively conducts said operations. The government will decide whether or not to actually sell shares in light of the impact its holdings may have on achieving the company's objectives as well as market trends, as described earlier, while taking into consideration how well the company is prepared for the sale, such as progress made on developing the necessary internal organization.

According to the provisions, Shoko Chukin Bank will not be fully privatized until it completes special investment operations in 2025. With regard to emergency lending operations, however, the government decided to review the schedule for full privatization following the bank's illicit lending problem and will make a final decision by 2022. Therefore, Shoko Chukin Bank could possibly be privatized by 2022 at the earliest. Since 53.5% of its shares are held by private investors, all it needs to do is sell the remaining 46.5% of shares held by the government. If that happens, the bank could be fully privatized ahead of schedule.

1.1.3 Sale of Development Bank of Japan Shares

While the DBJ is subject to the same provision stipulated in Article 2 of the supplementary provisions for Shoko Chukin Bank, the law does not provide a road map to full privatization since the deadline by which the government needs to sell all shares in the bank is spelled out in the fuzzy term "as soon as possible." It is high time the government revised the special laws to change the ownership of shares in the two companies.

One realistic institutional design for full privatization would be the government's selling of all shares in Shoko Chukin Bank ahead of schedule.

This section will analyze the current ROA in order to demonstrate the reasoning behind this conclusion. As shown in the list of ROAs by type of financial institution (Table 3.3), JP Bank's ROA for the fiscal year ending March 31, 2017 is low, 0.211%, which is about half of the ROA for regional banks, 0.370%. If JP Bank were fully privatized, could lend its deposits to companies, and achieved an ROA comparable to that of regional banks, its profits would double. What keeps the ROA of the three privatized banks at the low figure of 0.253% is the low ROA (0.211%) of JP Bank, which invests heavily in JGBs and foreign bonds. Despite the high ROA of Shoko Chukin Bank and the DBJ, standing respectively at 0.397% and 0.683%, the ROA of the three privatized banks drops to 0.253% when combined with JP Bank's ROA. For reference, the ROA of commercial banks is 0.389%.

As shown in Fig. 4.3a, ROA varies among different types of financial institutions. Numerical targets for the reform of special public institutions can be set with the aim of making these varied ROA levels. The ROA of different types of financial institutions from fiscal 2009 through fiscal 2016 shows that there were always certain gaps in ROA. This indicates that the revenue structure of each type of financial institution has not changed and that either horizontal or vertical restructuring of financial institutions will be necessary to change their revenue structure.

If JP Bank's ROA (0.211%), which is the lowest among all types of financial institutions, is increased by 0.119 percentage points to match the average ROA of private financial institutions (0.330%), that increase would be equivalent to a 0.25-trillion-yen increase in JP Bank's ordinary profit (i.e., 0.119% of the bank's total assets of 209 trillion yen).

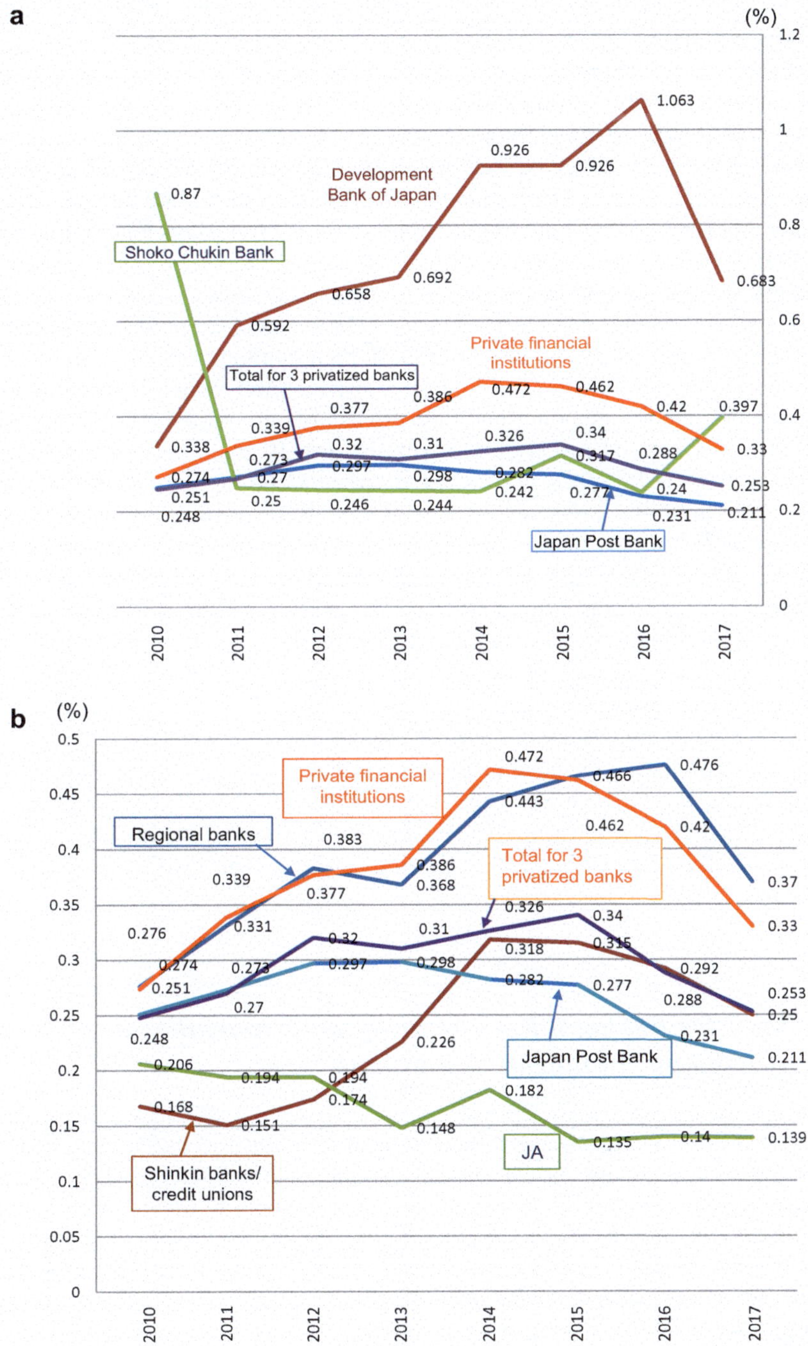

Fig. 4.3 ROA of (**a**) three privatized banks, (**b**) regional banks, by type of financial institution and optimization objective function, March 2010–2017. (*Source*: Financial statements of each bank)

If JP Bank's profitability improves, JP Holdings will be able to sell shares in the bank, whose corporate value is higher, and the government will be able to repay the national debt using the proceeds from Japan Post Holding's selling of shares. If JP Bank continues to enjoy revenue increases, that will add to the government tax revenue, contributing to the national interest.

As shown in Fig. 4.3b, the types of regional banks whose ROA for the fiscal year ending March 31, 2017, is lower than the average ROA of private financial institutions (0.330%) are shinkin banks/credit unions (0.250%), JP Bank (0.211%), and JA (0.139%).

If shinkin banks/credit unions were to match the ROA of private financial institutions, they would have to boost it by 0.080 percentage points, which would be equivalent to a 0.14-trillion-yen increase in their combined ordinary profits (i.e., 0.08% of their total assets of 172 trillion yen). For the same reason, JA needs to up its ROA by 0.191 percentage points and increase its ordinary profit by 0.22 trillion yen (i.e., 0.191% of its total assets of 115 trillion yen). JP Bank needs to increase its ordinary profit by 0.25 trillion yen, as noted earlier. If the ROAs of these three types of financial institutions are increased to match the ROA of private financial institutions, narrowing the gaps among regional financial institutions, the combined total of ordinary profits for the three types of financial institutions would go up 0.61 trillion yen. While it is especially important that JP Bank's profitability should improve, each type of financial institution should aim for an ROA of at least 0.330%. In other words, if they are unlikely to achieve this target, they will have to pursue an advantage of scale through mergers.

Note that the average ROA of regional banks is 0.370%, which is higher than the average ROA of private financial institutions, which stands at 0.330%. A number of regional banks still have an ROA that is lower than 0.330%. These banks need to optimize their ROA by boosting their bottom lines through restructuring, for example. It is crucial that these financial institutions increase their total assets to improve their ROA.

1.2 Need for Regional Restructuring and Optimal Size of Regional Financial Institutions

While the need for using ROA as a management indicator was highlighted earlier in Sect. 1.1, there is a certain correlation between the ROA and total assets of financial institutions. When JP Bank is fully privatized, it is likely to operate locally based banking services, which have always been its forte. If that happens, JP Bank will compete with regional banks and other local financial institutions while trying to find ways to also coexist with them. Regional banks are struggling to generate a profit in the current economic environment where interest rates are low. Keeping these points in mind, it is extremely important to identify the ideal future for regional financial institutions and analyze the minimum level of total assets they should maintain in order to achieve steady growth and contribute to the development of the local economy. Such an analysis should provide important insights into the study of regional financial institutions.

First, we will start by considering the government's view. In April 2018, the Working Group on Banks' Financial Intermediation for the Local Economy, with the backing of the Financial Services Agency (FSA), published a report on the challenges facing regional financial institutions and how they should compete.[5] Section 2 of this report, entitled "Competition and operational stability of regional financial institutions in the face of the declining population," discusses the contestability of the banking sector for regional banks in each prefecture (via model-based estimation). According to the estimation:

(A) *There are 13 prefectures where regional banks could survive if there were only one in each prefecture; however, they won't survive if there are two competing banks* (Hokkaido, Iwate, Yamagata, Fukushima, Ibaraki, Niigata, Nagano, Shiga, Kyoto, Hyogo, Ehime, Kumamoto, and Okinawa).
(B) *There are 23 prefectures where regional banks do not generate any profit, even though there is only one operating in each of those prefectures. Financial institutions are likely to withdraw from the market or die out in these prefectures* (Aomori, Akita, Gunma, Tochigi, Yamanashi, Gifu, Mie, Toyama, Ishikawa, Fukui, Nara, Wakayama, Shimane, Tottori, Yamaguchi, Okayama, Kagawa, Tokushima, Kochi, Oita, Miyazaki, Saga, and Nagasaki).
(C) *There are 10 prefectures where two banks could coexist* (Miyagi, Saitama, Chiba, Kanagawa, Shizuoka, Aichi, Osaka, Hiroshima, Fukuoka, and Kagoshima. Tokyo is excluded).

Altogether, the total number of prefectures comes to 47.

Given that it was released by the FSA, the report shocked the relevant industries. According to an estimation based on the model used in the report, a total of 35 regional banks, including 13 banks that fall in category A, 20 in category C, and two in Tokyo, will survive.

Next, let us take a brief look at the current status of regional banks. Regional banks are up against declining local economies due to the relocation of factories overseas on top of the depopulation that goes hand in hand with the declining birth rate and graying population. To make things worse, the Bank of Japan's prolonged low-interest-rate policy has caused regional banks' revenues from financial intermediary operations to decline. Figure 4.4 shows net interest income of regional banks and secondary regional banks. Their net interest income has continued to worsen over the last 10 years due to the zero-interest-rate policy.

---

[5] Attendees of the April 11, 2018, meeting of the Working Group on Banks' Financial Intermediation for the Local Economy: Tsutomu Muramoto, Kazuhiko Toyama, Hiroya Masuda, and five others.

Naoki Ohgo, Takashi Muraoka, and Naoyuki Yoshino from the FSA.

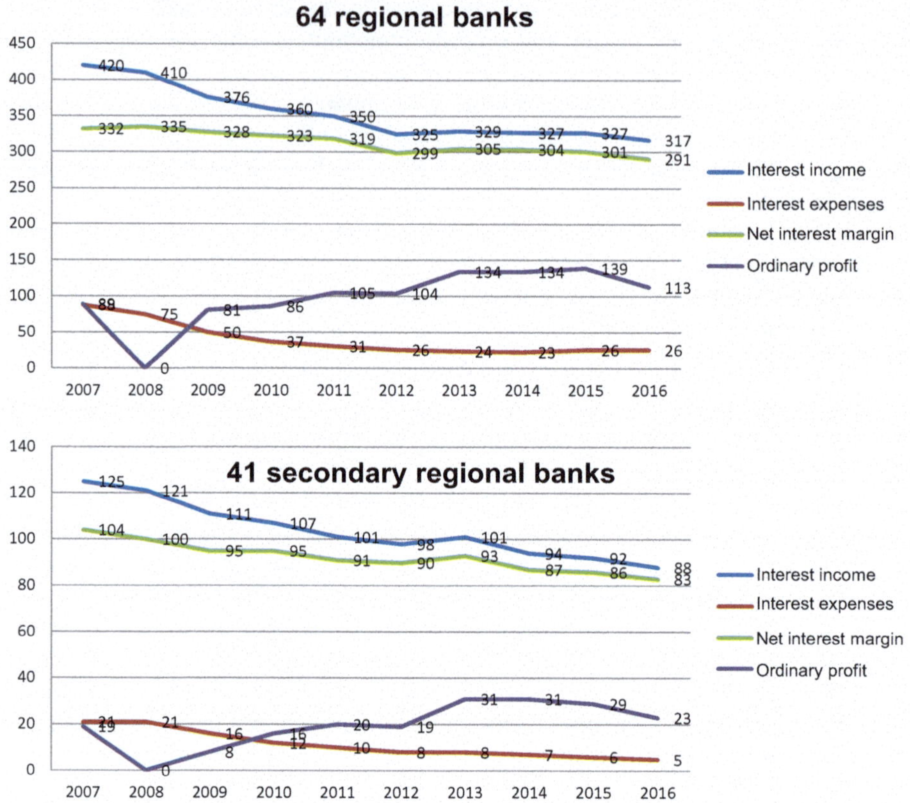

Fig. 4.4 Regional banks' net interest income over 10 years (in 10 billion yen). (*Source*: Japanese Bankers Association's financial statements by type of financial institution)

In Chap. 3, Sect. 2.3.4 of this book, I analyzed total assets and ratings of banks, estimating that the 27 banks that have already merged with other banks as well as 18 leading big banks with solid financial standings would be the only ones to survive. In this section, I will be following up on this analysis by examining the correlation between total assets and ROA as well as the correlation between total assets and operating expense ratios in order to construct a theory for analyzing the restructuring of regional banks.

The FSA's model-based analysis (the prior study) is problematic since it looks at contestability in each prefecture with a focus on depopulation. Here I will analyze contestability across broader administrative divisions (i.e., regional blocs or *doshusei*) using the economic indicators and key performance indicators of financial institutions operating within each bloc.

Table 4.2 shows historical data of economic indicators in each regional bloc, which are the primary data used in this book. Comparison of the March 2017 data with the March 2000 data reveals that there is almost no change in the percentage share for each market indicator. This is a clear reflection of the low-growth,

Table 4.2 Share of market indicators by region (%) (transition from March 2010 to March 2017)

		Population[a]	Number of companies[b]	Gross prefectural product[c]	Number of workers[c]	Personal insurance in force[d]	Bank balance[e]	Japan Post Bank	Balance of bank loans[e]	Number of branches[f]
Hokkaido	2010	4.3	4.2	3.6	4.1	3.6	3.0	4.1	2.6	5.2
	2017	4.2	4.1	3.6	3.9	3.4	2.9	4.2	2.5	5.1
Tohoku	2010	7.4	5.7	6.3	7.5	6.8	4.7	5.8	4.0	9.9
	2017	7.0	5.6	6.3	7.1	6.8	5.1	6.2	4.3	10.3
Kanto	2010	32.8	39.6	37.0	32.6	34.8	42.2	33.3	50.6	21.8
	2017	33.5	39.9	37.8	33.8	34.9	43.4	33.9	50.9	22.0
Chubu	2010	18.6	17.5	19.8	19.8	19.6	17.8	19.2	14.3	22.0
	2017	18.3	16.8	19.0	20.2	19.4	17.2	18.4	13.8	22.1
Kinki	2010	16.3	15.7	15.6	15.6	16.3	16.9	17.8	15	14.0
	2017	16.3	16.0	15.7	15.3	16.4	16.4	17.6	14.1	13.9
Chugoku	2010	5.9	5.3	5.7	6.2	5.7	5.1	6.6	4.3	8.6
	2017	5.9	5.2	5.6	5.8	5.8	4.9	6.5	4.4	8.5
Shikoku	2010	3.2	3.0	2.6	3.2	3.2	3.0	3.3	2.4	5.0
	2017	3.1	2.9	2.7	3.0	3.1	2.8	3.1	2.3	4.8
Kyushu/ Okinawa	2010	11.5	9.0	9.4	11.1	10.0	7.3	9.9	6.8	13.5
	2017	11.7	9.5	9.3	10.9	10.2	7.3	10.1	7.7	13.2

Sources: *Kinyu Journal* (December 2017)

[a]As of January 1, 2017 (Ministry of Internal Affairs and Communications); [b]March 31, 2016 (National Tax Agency); [c]Fiscal 2014 (Cabinet Office); [d]March 31, 2017 (Life Insurance Association of Japan); [e]Only domestic bank accounts as of March 31, 2017; [f]Total number of locations, including head offices, branches, and satellite offices, as of March 31, 2017

low-inflation, low-interest-rate environment. The percentage shares of rural areas in particular remained the same. On top of that, the percentage shares for basic market indicators, i.e., population, number of corporations, gross prefectural product, and the number of workers, are the same for all these areas across the board. Kanto has the highest share of finance-related market indicators, signifying an overconcentration in Tokyo.

The percentages for economic indicators in regional blocs are different from the percentages for total assets held by financial institutions in the respective regional blocs. Financial institutions in Tokyo and other urban areas have higher shares. On the flip side, since industries are dispersed in rural areas, the overconcentration of financial institutions in urban areas could be solved by spreading them out so their distribution is proportional to the distribution of industries. This analysis provides a rationale for splitting the three privatized public financial institutions into different businesses and regional companies following their full privatization, which will be described later on. If financial institutions revert to their original *raison d'être*, i.e., promoting industrial development through financial intermediary services, paradoxically the population will stop decreasing and start increasing. As I theorized earlier, optimizing the balance among different types of financial institutions means optimizing their share of total assets and ROA. In what follows, I will propose an institutional design for optimizing the percentage shares of JP Bank, Shoko Chukin Bank, and regional banks in different regional blocs.

1.2.1 Analytical Findings and Theoretical Rationale for Regional Restructuring

Figure 4.5 shows the correlation between total assets and ordinary profit of 105 regional banks for the fiscal year ending March 31, 2017.

Among 46 regional banks with total assets of less than 3 trillion yen (accounting for 44% of all regional banks) and 62 regional banks with ordinary profit of less than 0.1 billion yen (accounting for 59% of all regional banks), as many as 33 regional banks have less than 2 trillion yen in total assets and less than 50 million yen in ordinary profit. This is summarized in Table 4.3.

Four regional banks have total assets exceeding 10 trillion yen. They are the Shizuoka Bank, Bank of Fukuoka, Chiba Bank, and Bank of Yokohama, respectively generating 51.8 billion yen, 60.1 billion yen, 70 billion yen, and 87.3 billion yen in ordinary profits.

This clearly suggests that increasing total assets will lead to higher profits.

Figure 4.6 analyzes the correlation between total assets and the operating expense ratio (i.e., the ratio of operating expenses to ordinary revenue).

When total assets increase, the operating expense ratio drops, leading to a low-cost and high-operating-profit structure. While the correlation coefficient between total assets and ordinary profit is 0.973, the correlation coefficient between total assets and the operating expense ratio is merely 0.866, indicating a possible advantage of scale.

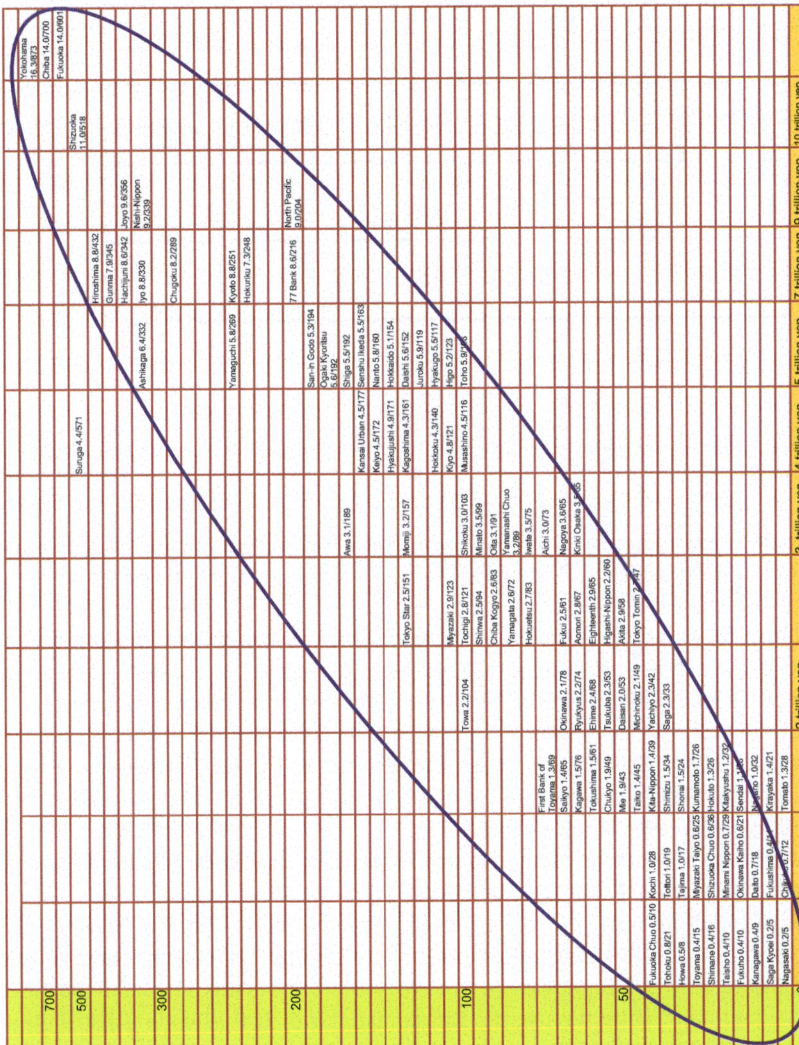

Fig. 4.5 Total assets and ordinary profit, March 2017. (*Source:* Financial statements of regional banks [this can be downloaded from the electronic supplementary material])

Table 4.3 Correlation between total assets and ordinary profit

Total assets / Ordinary profit	Less than 2 trillion yen	Less than 4 trillion yen	Less than 7 trillion yen	7 trillion yen or more
200 million yen or higher			3 banks	15 banks
100- 200 million yen		7 banks	18 banks	
50-100 million yen	4 banks	21 banks		
Less than 50 million yen	33 banks	4 banks		

To sum up, the correlation between total assets and the operating expense ratio is as shown in Table 4.4.

Of the 20 regional banks with total assets of less than 1 trillion yen, 16 (80%) have an operating expense ratio of 60% or higher. These regional banks do not have much room left for enhancing efficiency. Figure 4.7 analyzes the correlation between total assets and ROA.

This figure looks at the correlation between total assets and ordinary profit in terms of ROA, which is still significant. Therefore, the greater total assets a bank has, the higher its ROA will be, enabling the bank to enjoy an advantage of scale.

We will now take a closer look at this point. The following table shows descriptive statistics of 105 regional banks that compares the ROA of 14 banks whose total assets exceeded 7 trillion yen as of the end of March 2017 with 91 banks whose total assets were less than that figure (Table 4.5).

First, we use the F-test to evaluate the null hypothesis that the ROA distribution of the two groups is identical. The test statistic, which has an F-distribution with 13 and 90 degrees of freedom, is 1.179, so the null hypothesis can be rejected. Now we test the null hypothesis that the mean values of the two groups' ROA is the same in two cases, one where the population variance of the two groups is unknown and the other where it is identical. While we use the test statistic, which follows a t-distribution with 103 degrees of freedom under the null hypothesis, in this case the test statistic is 2.690 and the significance level is 1% (one side), rejecting the null hypothesis. Therefore, the ROA of banks that have total assets exceeding 7 trillion yen is relatively higher than the ROA of banks that do not. In addition, since there is no statistical variance of the distribution between the two groups, increasing total assets will be unlikely to cause significant differences in profitability.

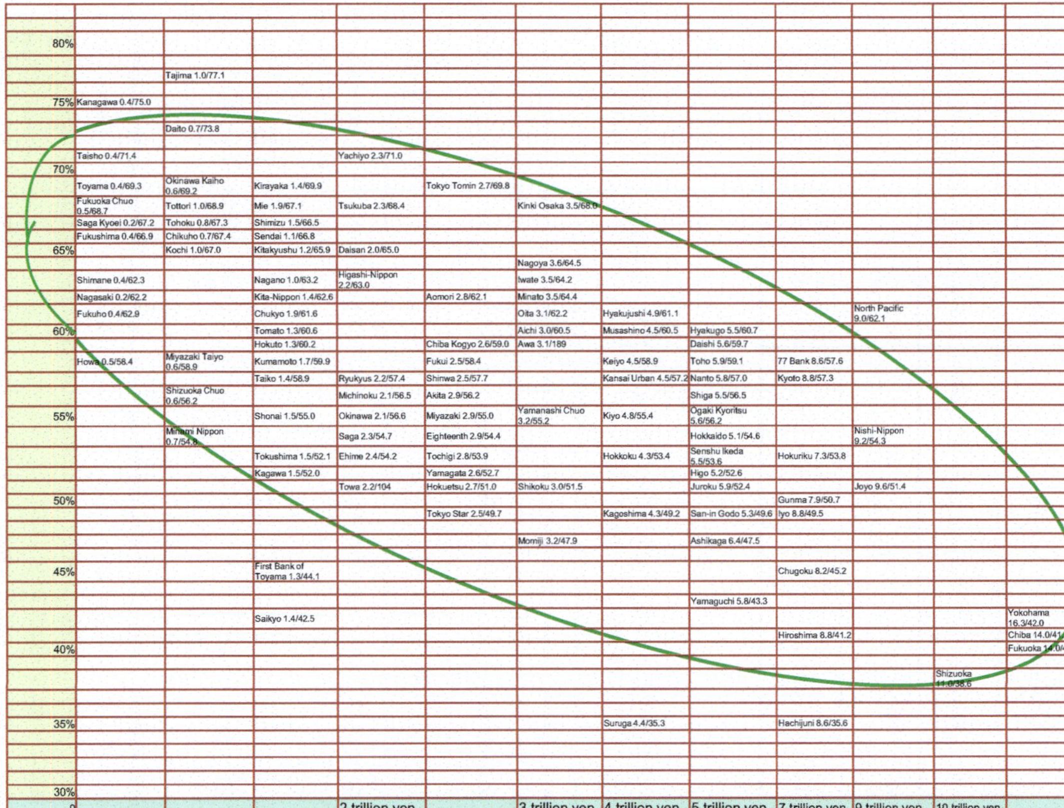

Fig. 4.6 Total assets and operating expense ratio, March 2017. (*Source*: Financial statements of regional banks [this can be downloaded from the electronic supplementary material])

Table 4.4 Correlation between total assets and the operating expense ratio

Total assets / Operating expense ratio	Less than 2 trillion yen	Less than 4 trillion yen	Less than 7 trillion yen	7 trillion yen or more
60% or more	26 banks	12 banks	3 banks	1 bank
50% - 60%	9 banks	18 banks	13 banks	6 banks
40% - 50% (14 banks)	2 banks	2 banks	4 banks	6 banks
Less than 40%			1 bank	2 banks

I then performed the same test for the 105 banks by dividing them into two group, one consisting of 28 banks with total assets of 5 trillion yen or more and the other consisting of 77 banks with total assets of less than 5 trillion yen. As a result, the null hypothesis that the mean values of the two groups' ROA is the same was not rejected. No significant difference in ROA is recognized when the threshold value is set at 5 trillion yen. This indicates that a bank needs total assets of at least 7 trillion yen if it wants to enjoy an advantage of scale.

The empirical analysis based on these three tables clearly shows that there is a correlation between total assets and the operating expense ratio as well as a correlation between total assets and ordinary profit, providing a theoretical rationale for the restructuring of regional banks. In fact, the regional banking system is drowning in banks with 105 institutions across 47 prefectures. A third of these banks have already been merged to form holding companies. In terms of market indicators, total assets of each bank need to be increased through mergers or restructuring within the same regional bloc as opposed to prefecture. As noted in the previous section, although regional banks are exposed to an interest-rate risk, their asset liability management (ALM) is sound because their short-term and long-term assets are respectively funded by short-term and long-term liabilities. Even if interest rates increase, there is no likelihood of a mismatch between short-term liabilities and long-term assets ,despite a slight time lag (Fig.4.8).

When the economy experiences sustained low growth, low inflation, and low interest rates, there is no likelihood of higher interest rates, and a bank's total assets is the sole driver of profitability. It is difficult to draw up various operating models or different scenarios.

The regional bank operating environment was artificially created via the convoy system of the FSA (Ministry of Finance) in the first place, but the government's

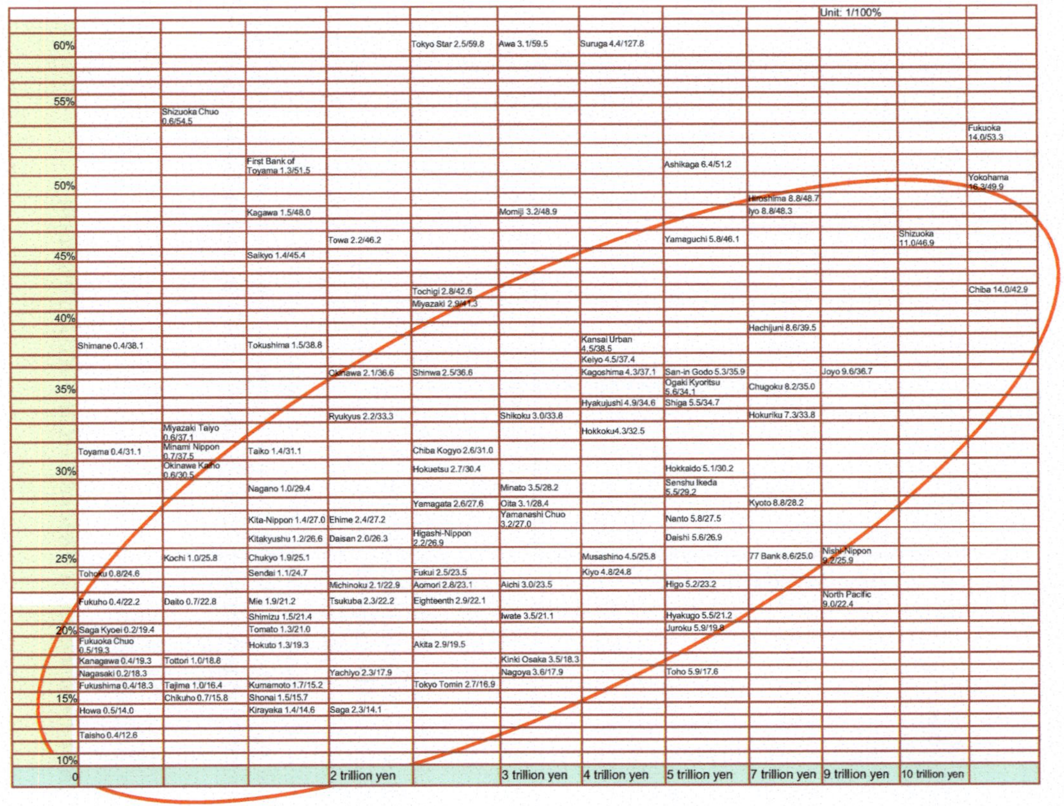

Fig. 4.7 Correlation between total assets and ROA, March 2017. (*Source*: Financial statements of regional banks [this can be downloaded from the electronic supplementary material])

Table 4.5 Optimization of total assets and ROA

Total assets	7 trillion yen or more	Less than 7 trillion yen
Number of banks	14	91
Average total assets (billion yen)	10,141.0	2680.9
Standard deviation for total assets (billion yen)	2618.6	1753.6
Average ROA (%)	0.419	0.300
Standard deviation for ROA (%)	0.176	0.1495

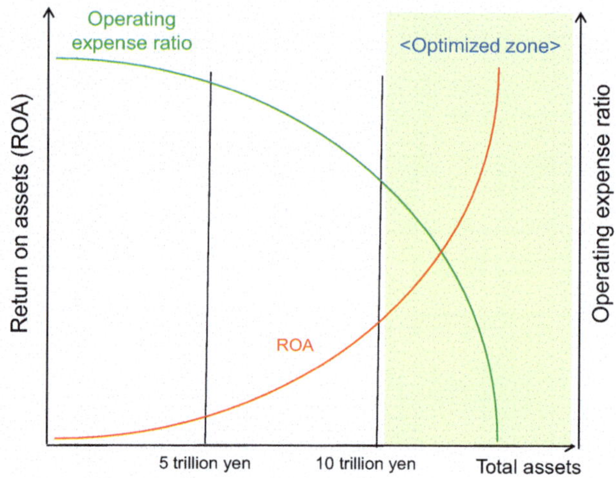

Fig. 4.8 Optimization of total assets and operating expense ratio/total assets and ROA

low-interest-rate policy has turned it into a grueling financial market that forces small financial institutions out of the picture.

While they could take certain measures that might ensure their survival, boosting their total assets is the only option left for them under the current economic environment. If they don't pare down the excessive number of banks and work to bolster their operating foundation and workforce, they won't be able to survive the competition in the new setting that is taking shape in which interest rates are climbing.

1.3 *Japan Post Bank's Interest-Rate-Risk Problem*

Earlier, in Sect. 1.2, we looked into the optimal asset size of regional financial institutions. Regional banks, one of the main actors in the regional financial sector, do not have a major problem with an asset-liability mismatch, but they do need to pursue an advantage of scale. JP Bank, another main actor, has a serious ALM problem, although it has no problem with asset size. In this section we will look into these aspects.

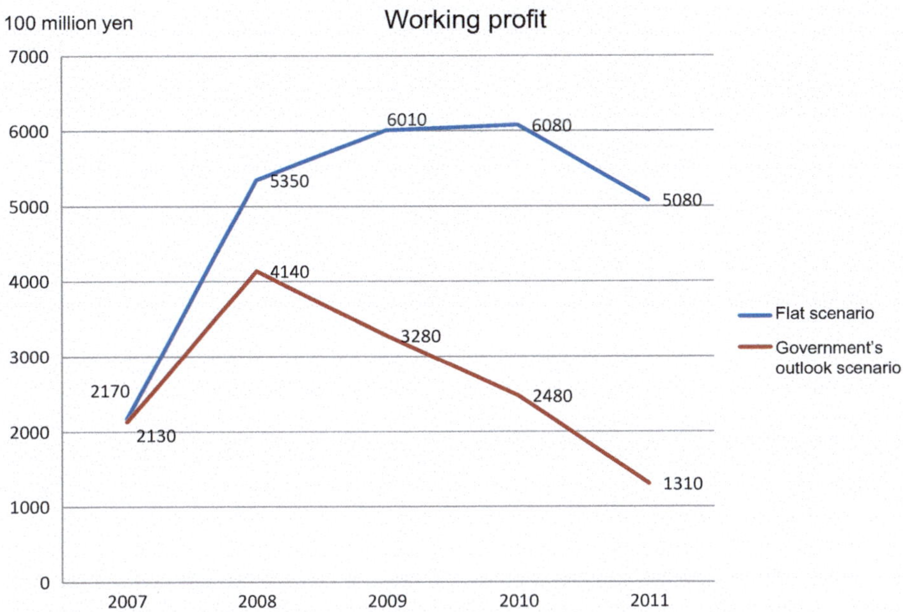

Fig. 4.9 Medium- to long-term management plan for postal savings bank under implementation plan.
The flat-interest-rate scenario assumes that the interest rate would remain what it was in December 2006 (1.7%). The government's outlook scenario assumes that the interest rate for long-term government bonds maturing in 10 years will increase to 4% 5 years after privatization
Source: Implementation plan for transferring Japan Post Operations (2007)

One of the reasons the full privatization of JP Bank and improvement to its asset portfolio are deemed pressing issues is the current economic state under which interest rates are sure to rise sooner or later. In what follows, we will review some of the events that took place in the run-up to the current economic circumstances.

On August 4, 2006, the government's Postal Privatization Committee announced an Outline of the Implementation Plan for Transferring Japan Post Operations. Attachment 4-(5) to Sect. III of the plan, outlining the successor companies, provided a financial outlook for the postal savings bank. This forecast served as JP Bank's medium- to long-term management plan beginning in October 2007 and was the first manifestation of the government's vision for the bank under its postal privatization policy. This medium- to long-term management plan was slightly revised by the government in September 2007 and released right after the establishment of JP Bank on October 1.

Figure 4.9 shows medium- to long-term (2007–2011) profit and loss projections in graphic format.

The postal savings bank's medium- to long-term management plan employs two business models. The newly established JP Bank saw interest-rate risk as the most significant of the various market risks.

Table 4.6 Structural reform and medium-term economic/fiscal outlook (approximate figures)

Fiscal year	2006	2007	2008	2009	2010	2011
Nominal growth rate (%)	2.0	2.5	2.9	3.1	3.1	3.2
Nominal GDP (trillion yen), A	513	526	541	558	576	594
Nominal long-term interest rate (%)	1.7	2.4	2.9	3.3	3.7	3.9
Consumer price (%)	0.5	1.1	1.6	1.9	2.1	2.2
Outstanding government bonds, etc. (trillion yen), B	737	758	778	801	824	848
B/A (%)	(145)	(143)	(144)	(143)	(143)	(142)

Source: Cabinet Office

On the liability side of risk management, losing postal savings, the bulk of which is fixed-amount postal savings, to other financial institutions due to a change in interest rates is a risk trigger. Since fixed-amount postal savings, featuring a fixed interest rate with a 6-month deposit period, involves the risk of fluctuating periodic profit and loss, future periodic profit and loss needs to be calculated quantitatively. On the asset side, however, the majority of assets are invested in JGBs and other securities, which is risky, since that could trigger interest-rate and price fluctuations. At about the same time this medium- to long-term outlook was announced, the government's Cabinet Office unveiled its Structural Reform and Medium-Term Economic and Fiscal Outlook at the January 18, 2006, meeting of the Council on Economic and Fiscal Policy, as shown in Table 4.6.

Since these projections are based on a scenario in which the nominal long-term interest rate would gradually increase from 1.7% to 3.9% during the period from fiscal 2006 to fiscal 2011, the same scenario was used for the implementation plan. The postal savings bank's medium- and long-term management plan was based on the government's outlook, forecasting the interest rate on long-term JGBs maturing 10 years would increase to 4% in 5 years after privatization. As noted earlier, rising interest rates will cause the liability side risk of losing fixed-amount postal savings to other financial institutions along with a mismatch between short-term liabilities and long-term assets.

This is due to the product characteristics of the fixed-amount postal savings account, which offers a fixed interest rate for a deposit period of 6 months. Once low-interest-rate, fixed-amount postal savings mature after 6 months, account holders switch to a higher fixed-interest-rate account. When funds procured at a low interest rate are invested in long-term JGBs that mature in 10 years, the bank's net interest income will decrease once account holders withdraw their savings to deposit them with another financial institution. If account holders withdraw their postal savings when the interest rate increases every 6 months, the cost of funds will rise in the short term, resulting in a likelihood of a negative spread.

Therefore, the postal savings bank's net profit was projected to decline gradually in the government's scenario shown in Fig.4.9. In other words, the government expected that the postal savings bank's financial performance would decline when the interest rate increased.

Table 4.7 Market risk exposure of Japan Post Bank

Risk assets	Interest rate risk model	Scenario
Liability side: fixed-amount postal savings	→ Higher interest rate	Substantial profit decline
	Flat interest rate	Profit decline due to loss of deposit balance
	Lower interest rate	Same as if interest rate remained the same under current circumstances
Risk assets	→ Price fluctuation risk model	Scenario
Asset side: JGBs and other receivables	Higher interest rate	Impairment loss accounted for
	Flat interest rate	No impairment loss accounted for
	Lower interest rate	

While it would be possible to imagine a scenario other than the government's to project the bank's performance against the backdrop of rising interest rates, it is as projected in the government's medium- to long-term economic and fiscal outlook.

There are two other models besides the rising-interest-rate model. The second model is based on a scenario in which the interest rate and economic conditions would remain the same. The medium- to long-term plans for the postal savings bank developed under the implementation plan were based on this flat-interest-rate scenario. This model assumes that the balance of postal savings would decline. It projects that, although the interest rate would remain the same, the balance of postal savings would decline, causing the bank's fiscal health to deteriorate.

The third model is based on a scenario in which the interest rate would drop. In reality, the interest rate on fixed-amount postal savings with a maturity period of 6 months was 0.02% in 2006 under the zero-interest-rate policy and later dropped to 0.01% when the negative-interest-rate policy was introduced. Since the interest rate is almost zero, the falling-interest-rate model is basically the same as the flat-interest-rate model under current circumstances.

On the asset side, the risk accompanying higher interest rates would be lower prices of JGBs invested in and a higher risk of price fluctuation for bonds with a longer time remaining until maturity (i.e., longer duration). Even if the bank were to hold on to JGBs until they matured, fluctuations in their prices due to a higher interest rate resulting in more than a 30% loss in market value at the end of each fiscal year would mean the bank would have to consider writing off impairment losses in order to maintain its fiscal health.

Table 4.7 is a summary of the market risks JP Bank is exposed to, which were discussed earlier.

By October 2017, a decade had passed since JP Bank was established following postal privatization. JP Bank announced its medium-term management plans every 3 years over the decade, setting a goal of maintaining at least 170 trillion yen in assets under management (mainly deposits) in its FY 2015–2017 and FY 2018–2020 medium-term management plans. These plans do not paint a clear picture about investment assets, such as how the bank plans to diversify asset management channels, but rather only cover receivables. Therefore, we will simulate JP Bank's revenues in the fiscal year ending March 31, 2019, and onward based on an analysis of past data and the current asset portfolio. In particular, we will focus on how the aforementioned duration gap between assets and liabilities will have a negative effect on revenues (Table 4.8).

(a) Balance of assets
JP Bank's assets mainly consist of deposits due from banks, JGBs, foreign bonds, foreign investment trusts, and loans. What follows is the rationale for the projections made for each asset item from March 2019 to March 2023.
Since deposits due from banks are the proceeds from JGBs purchased by the Bank of Japan, they are virtually JGBs. For this reason, I estimated the total balance of deposits due from banks and JGBs and then broke it down into JGBs and deposits due from banks. I expected the balance of deposits due from banks to gradually decrease and the balance of JGBs to increase at the same rate as their balance total would slowly climb. I assumed that, while the total balance of foreign bonds and foreign investment trusts would decrease, if they were combined with the total balance of deposits due from banks and JGBs, the total assets would remain flat at 210 trillion yen. This forecast is based on my assumption that JP Bank's capital adequacy ratio, which was low at 17.4% for the fiscal year ending March 31, 2018, would remain low.
(b) Balance of liabilities
JP Bank's balance of liabilities remained stable, standing at 190+ trillion yen from March 31, 2013, to March 31, 2018. The balance of postal savings, which account for 90% of liabilities, in particular, remained slightly below 180 trillion yen. Based on these figures, I assumed that the balance of liabilities would remain at 180 trillion yen.
(c) Yields on interest-earning assets and interest rates on interest-bearing liabilities for yen-denominated transactions (Table 4.9).

The yield on interest-earning assets for yen-denominated transactions dropped substantially from 0.90% on March 31, 2013, to 0.43% by March 31, 2018, due to low interest rates. In estimating yields on interest-earning assets for the next 5 years, I focused my attention on the percentage of outstanding JGBs, broken down by the number of years remaining to their maturity. JGBs with less than 5 years left to maturity account for 67.7% of all JGBs on average during the 11-year-period from March 31, 2008, to today, and their standard deviation was 5.2%, indicating that they remained stable over a long period of time (Table 4.10).

Since the main purpose of this analysis is to estimate the impact of interest-rate fluctuations, I assumed that the ratio of JGBs with less than 5 years left to maturity to JGBs with 5 or more years left to maturity would be 67.7% to 32.3%. To make it simple, I assumed that the yield curve would slope upward and that the yield of JGBs with less than 5 years left to maturity would be a certain percentage (60% for this analysis) of the yield of JGBs with 5 or more years left to maturity (hereinafter "Hypothesis 1").

Table 4.8 Revenue simulation of Japan Post Bank

March		2014	2015	2016	2017	2018	2019	2020	2021	2022	2023
Assets (trillion yen)	Due from banks	19.3	33.1	45.7	51.1	49.1	50	50	45	40	35
	JGBs	126.4	106.8	52.3	68.8	62.7	60	60	70	75	85
	Foreign bonds	14.5	18.8	19.8	20.1	20.2	20	20	20	20	20
	Foreign investment trusts	8.1	14	25.5	32.7	39	40	40	35	35	30
	Loans	3.1	2.8	2.5	4.1	6.1	7	8	9	10	10
Assets (trillion yen)		202.5	208.2	207.1	209.6	210.6	210	210	210	210	210
Liabilities (trillion yen)	Deposit balance	176.6	177.7	177.9	179.4	179.9	180	180	180	180	180
Liabilities (trillion yen)		191	196.5	195.5	197.8	199.1	199	199	199	199	199
Revenues (billion yen)	Interest income	1828	1893	1731	1568	1503	1425	1419	1339	1451	1475
	Interest expenses	362	357	375	349	332	387	422	446	483	512
	Net interest income, A	1466	1536	1356	1219	1171	1039	997	894	968	963
	Operating expenses, B	1095	1114	1064	1054	1043	1000	1000	1000	1000	1000
	A − B	371	422	292	165	128	39	−3	−106	−32	−37

Source: Japan Post Bank financial statements

Table 4.9 Yields on interest-earning assets and interest rates on interest-bearing liabilities for yen-denominated transactions

March		2014	2015	2016	2017	2018	2019	2020	2021	2022	2023
Domestic (%)	Yield on interest-earning assets	0.82	0.74	0.64	0.53	0.43	0.37	0.37	0.37	0.45	0.52
	Interest rate on interest-bearing liabilities	0.16	0.15	0.15	0.13	0.09	0.12	0.15	0.18	0.21	0.24
	Net interest margin	0.66	0.58	0.49	0.4	0.33	0.25	0.22	0.19	0.24	0.28
Overseas (%)	Yield on interest-earning assets	1.31	1.81	1.33	1.23	1.34	1.30	1.30	1.30	1.30	1.30
	Interest rate on interest-bearing liabilities	0.48	0.41	0.40	0.37	0.41	0.40	0.40	0.40	0.40	0.40
	Net interest margin	0.82	1.39	0.92	0.86	0.93	0.90	0.90	0.90	0.90	0.90

Source: Japan Post Bank financial statements

Table 4.10 Japanese government bonds (%) by number of years remaining to maturity

March	2014	2015	2016	2017	2018
–1 year	23.1	17.9	19.3	14.4	11.4
1–3 years	27.2	30.8	20.9	22.4	25.1
3–5 years	13.2	14.5	19.5	23.9	35.9
Subtotal	63.5	63.2	59.7	60.7	72.5
5–7 years	11.9	15.4	27.6	29.8	11.0
7–10 years	22.9	19.3	10.0	5.5	9.4
10 years –	1.6	2.1	2.7	3.9	7.2
Subtotal	36.5	36.8	40.3	39.3	27.5
Total	100.0	100.0	100.0	100.0	100.0

Source: Japan Post Bank financial statements

Table 4.11 Estimated yield on yen-denominated interest-earning assets

March	2014	2015	2016	2017	2018	2019	2020	2021	2022	2023
Less than 5 years	0.66	0.59	0.50	0.42	0.36	0.30	0.30	0.30	0.36	0.42
10 years or less	1.10	0.99	0.84	0.70	0.60	0.50	0.50	0.50	0.60	0.70
Average yield	0.82	0.74	0.64	0.53	0.43	0.37	0.37	0.37	0.45	0.52

Source: Japan Post Bank financial statements

Future yields were estimated on the basis of this hypothesis. The following discussion is only for the purpose of demonstrating the rationale for projecting future yields. We use a scenario in which the interest rate would rise by 0.2% over the next 5 years. Since our focus here is the net interest margin, based on Hypothesis 1 and the historical data of yields (on all JGBs) behind the increase in interest rates, we see that the yield on bonds with 5 or more years left to mature went from 1.10% to 0.99%, 0.84%, 0.70%, and to 0.60% during the 5 years from the fiscal year ending March 31, 2014, to the fiscal year ending March 31, 2018, dropping 0.5% over this period at an annual rate of 0.1–0.15%. Once the interest rate starts to gradually pick up, the yield on interest-earning assets should also gradually improve. With this in mind, we assumed a scenario in which the yield would slowly increase by 0.2% over the next 5 years (from the fiscal year ending March 31, 2019, through the fiscal year ending March 31, 2023), going from 0.5% to 0.5%, 0.50%, 0.60%, and to 0.70% (Table 4.11).

On the other hand, the interest rate on interest-bearing liabilities for yen-denominated transactions rises more quickly than the yield on interest-earning assets since the interest rate for fixed-amount postal savings is changed every 6 months, as mentioned earlier. While the interest rate on interest-bearing liabilities dropped over the last 5 years, falling from 0.16% to 0.15%, 0.15%, 0.13%, and finally 0.09%, we assume that it will increase over the next 5 years, rising from 0.12% to 0.15%, 0.18%, 0.21%, and finally 0.24%. We assume that the interest rate on interest-bearing liabilities will increase 0.15% over the next 5 years, which is lower than the estimated 0.2% increase in the yield on interest-earning assets over the same period, but also assume that the interest rate will immediately rise.

(d) Yields on interest-earning assets and interest rates on interest-bearing liabilities for foreign-currency-denominated transactions.

Over the past 5 years (from the fiscal year ending March 31, 2014, to the fiscal year ending March 31, 2018) the yield on interest-earning assets and interest rate on interest-bearing liabilities for foreign-currency-denominated transactions, such as foreign bonds and foreign investment trusts, remained stable at around 1.3% and 0.4%, respectively. Based on these data, we assume that both figures will remain at the same level for the next 5 years.

(Results) The results of this simulation are as shown in Table 4.8. While interest income is estimated to remain around 1.4 trillion yen during the 5-year period beginning in the fiscal year ending March 31, 2019, interest expenses are expected to increase from 387 billion yen to 512 billion yen. This means that the bank's net interest income will dip below one trillion yen at some point, and it will be unable to cover operating expenses in that same amount. As shown in the simulation, an interest-rate increase could have a profound effect on JP Bank's bottom line, even if it were small and gradual.

With regard to the interest-rate hike, in the Economic and Fiscal Projections for Medium- to Long-Term Analysis dated July 9, 2018, the government projected that the nominal long-term interest rate would remain at 0% from fiscal 2018 to fiscal 2020. It would then start gradually picking up, rising to 0.3% in fiscal 2021 and reaching 2.6% by fiscal 2025. Looking at the domestic interest rate, JP Bank, on the other hand, projects in its medium-term management plan that the interest rate for 10-year JGBs will be close to zero, at 0.13% in the fiscal year ending March 31, 2019, and 0.29% in the fiscal year ending March 31, 2021. Since there would be no market risk related to higher interest rates under the government's outlook scenario, where interest rates are almost zero, both the government and JP Bank medium- to long-term plans, offering no solution to the zero-interest-rate policy, are still fraught with problems.

Now that JP Bank has gone public, it should ensure management transparency to its shareholders, even though it is a minority and demonstrates good corporate governance as a listed company. As noted earlier, its parent company, JP Holdings, should sell its shares in JP Bank and lay out a road map to full privatization. Although it is understandable that the bank is unable to diversify its investment channels quickly, the inclination to invest in high-risk foreign bonds and increase risk assets without a full-scale risk management system needed for an institutional investor may saddle the public with a financial burden in the future. It should also take into consideration that JP Bank, with its convenient payment and settlement operations via the post office network, may have lost ground to online banking, fintech, and other types of businesses that have emerged in the market.

Therefore, to hedge interest-rate risk, JP Bank should immediately look into various scenarios based on the rising-interest-rate model, on both the liability and asset sides, and develop an ideal institutional design for each scenario. While JP Bank's interest rates as well as its portfolio of interest-bearing liabilities and earning assets remained unchanged for a decade, this means that the bank kept the public's small savings at an extremely low ROA, as shown in the analysis of ROA by type of financial institution, and contributed nothing to the national interest.

The conclusion drawn from this analysis of interest-rate risk is that the three privatized public financial institutions should pursue a scenario in which they would be fully privatized and procure funds in accordance with the Banking Act, instead of sourcing funds via fixed-amount postal savings that are protected by the special law, while diversifying their investments so that they can build an operating structure that can withstand any risk of higher interest rates.

1.4 Japan Post Bank's Credit Risk Problem

While Sect. 1.1 earlier highlighted JP Bank's interest-rate-risk problem, the bank is also facing a credit-risk problem. This section will discuss the greater credit risk JP Bank is exposed to as it seeks to quickly increase profitability after going public. The section will also analyze the credit risks of different types of financial institutions.

Looking at asset portfolios by type of financial institution, we see that the major types of investment risk are basically the risks associated with loans and securities. Loans involve a credit risk, and the bad debt ratio is used as an analysis indicator. As shown in Table 4.12 and Fig. 4.10 illustrating changes in the bad debt ratio of each type of financial institution, the bad debt ratio of private financial institutions is somewhere between 1% and 3%, whereas that of public financial institutions is high, at somewhere between 5% and 7%.

JP Bank has a loan balance of about 5 trillion yen, which is lent primarily to local governments, and therefore has no bad loans. Incidentally the bad debt ratio of the three privatized banks is in the 1–2% range, which is about the same level as private financial institutions'. As noted in the reply to recommendation 1, JP Bank's deposits are used as a source of funds for government-affiliated financial institutions. Given the fact that their bad debt ratio is in the 5–7% range, the bad debt ratio of public financial institutions that include JP Bank, which is in the 4–5% range, is rather high. The system where JP Bank raises capital (point of entry), which is then used by government-affiliated financial institutions for lending (point of exit), can be categorized as a moderate-risk, low-return scheme. In a broad sense, JP Bank is not really low-risk.

The capital adequacy ratio under the Basel Accord is used as an analysis indicator to measure the credit risk of securities.

As shown in Table 4.13 and Fig. 4.11, the capital adequacy ratios of all types of financial institutions have not changed much over the last 10 years, satisfying the Basel requirements. The capital adequacy ratio of JP Bank, however, dropped 22.64% from its level in the fiscal year ending March 31, 2015 (before it went public) to 15.78% in the fiscal year ending March 31, 2019, as shown in Table 4.8, because it shifted the focus of its portfolio from government bonds to foreign bonds and investment trusts. The sum total of its risk assets increased 34.5 trillion yen from

Table 4.12 Bad debt ratio by type of financial institution (March 2010–March 2017)

FY ending March	Commercial banks	Regional banks	Trust banks	JBA-affiliated private banks	Shinkin banks	Credit unions	JA	Depository institutions	Japan Post Bank	Shoko Chukin Bank	Development Bank of Japan	3 privatized banks, average	Japan Finance Corporation	Japan Bank for International Cooperation	Japan International Cooperation Agency (JICA)	State-owned financial institutions, average	Public financial services, average
2010	1.8	3.2	1.3	2.5	5.8	8.2	3.6	2.9	0	2	5	3.2	7.7	4.2	5.7	6.2	4.9
2011	1.8	3.2	1	2.4	6	8	3.2	2.9	0	2	1.3	1.3	8	3.5	5.6	6.2	4.1
2012	1.9	3.2	1	2.4	6.3	8.5	3.2	3	0	2.5	1.5	1.6	8.8	2.3	8.3	7.1	4.6
2013	2	3.1	1	2.3	6.4	8.4	3	2.9	0	3.3	1.2	1.8	9.5	2.3	8.2	7.1	4.8
2014	1.5	2.7	0.7	1.9	6	7.7	2.7	2.5	0	4	1	1.9	9.1	2	7.9	6.5	4.7
2015	1.3	2.4	0.5	1.6	5.5	7.2	2.5	2.1	0	4.1	0.8	1.9	8.9	1.6	7.4	5.9	4.4
2016	1.2	2.1	0.3	1.5	4.9	6.1	2.3	1.9	0	3.8	0.6	1.7	8.7	1.9	7	5.9	4.2
2017	1.1	1.9	0.3	1.3	4.3	4.6	2	1.7	0	3.6	0.5	1.3	8	1.7	6.7	5.4	3.8

Sources: Financial statements of Japanese Bankers Association, Shinkin Central Bank, Shinkumi Federation Bank, National Federation of Agricultural Cooperative Associations, and government-affiliated financial institutions

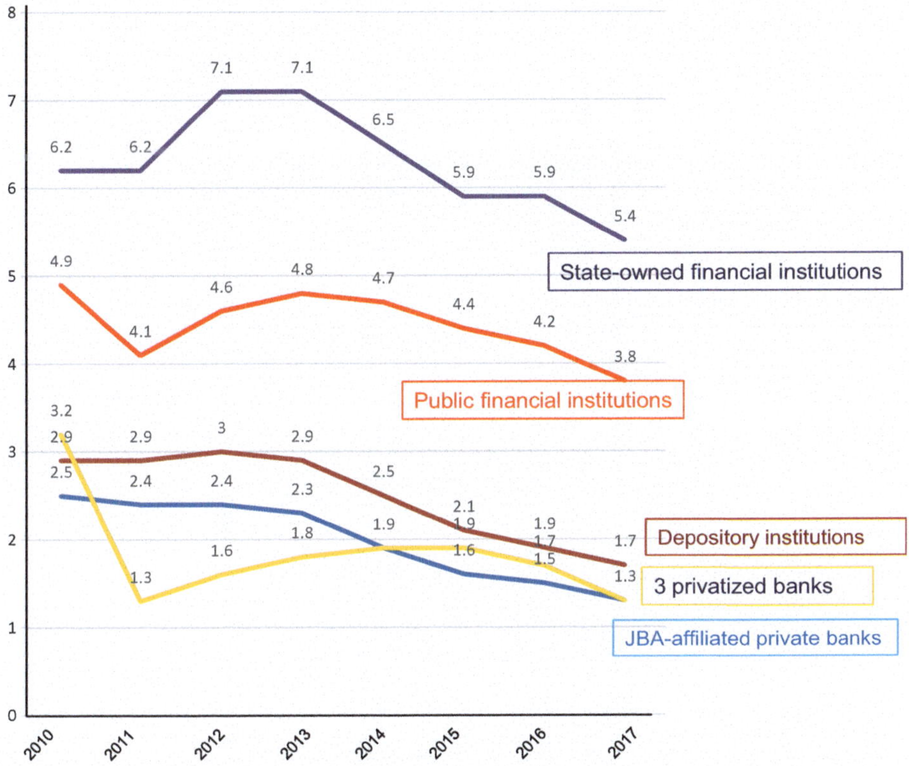

Fig. 4.10 Bad debt ratio of public and private financial institutions (FY ending March 2010–2017). (*Sources*: Financial statements of Japanese Bankers Association, Shinkin Central Bank, Shinkumi Federation Bank, National Federation of Agricultural Cooperative Associations, and government-affiliated financial institutions)

21.5 trillion yen in the fiscal year ending March 31, 2015, to 56 trillion yen in the fiscal year ending March 31, 2019.

Table 4.14 shows how JP Bank shifted from a low-risk, low-return portfolio that is heavily tilted toward government bonds to a moderate-risk, low-return portfolio that is weighted toward foreign bonds and investment trusts, and then to a high-risk, low-return portfolio. The purpose of the analysis here is to examine this unique structure, which cannot be assessed with the conventional risk-return analysis because the bank invests heavily in high-risk foreign bonds in order to maintain its dividend policy as noted in (Sect. 1.3), but that does not mean that it excludes risks from consideration. The interest-rate risk JP Bank is exposed to is as discussed in Sect. 1.3 of this book. While its credit risk has increased since it started investing more on foreign bonds in order to maintain a high dividend payout, overall ROA has declined due to the low-interest-rate policy of the government and the Bank of Japan. This is the essence of the bank's problem. On top of that, its interest-rate risk is gradually

Table 4.13 Capital adequacy ratio (March 2010–March 2019)

FY ending March	Commercial banks/trust banks		Regional banks + Saitama Resona		Shinkin banks	Credit unions	Japan Post Bank	Shoko Chukin Bank	Development Bank of Japan	Japan Bank for International Cooperation
	International standard	Japanese standard	International standard	Japanese standard						
2010	15.82		11.3		12.34	10.93	91.62	11.4	19.13	19.65
2011	17.33		11.6		12.67	11.04	74.82	12.37	20.5	21.23
2012	17.95		11.9		12.85	11.14	68.39	13.09	18.56	23.47
2013	17.45	14.7	14.3	11.2	13.04	11.3	66.04	13.51	15.02	20.02
2014	15.18	14.27	14.28	11.04	13.16	11.84	56.81	13.73	15.83	17.98
2015	15.63	13.95	14.64	10.5	13.17	12.01	38.42	13.59	16.8	14.47
2016	16.17	13.3	14.1	10.2	13.08	11.95	26.38	13.41	17.87	16.04
2017	16.29	11.88	13.94	9.86	12.77	11.78	22.22	13.16	17.47	17.12
2018	17.63	11.26	14.01	9.7	12.51	11.58	17.42	13.57	16.82	19.28
2019	17.83	10.52	13.84	9.47	–	–	15.78	13.02	16.94	–

Sources: Financial statements of Japanese Bankers Association, Shinkin Central Bank, Shinkumi Federation Bank, government-affiliated financial institutions, and FSA data

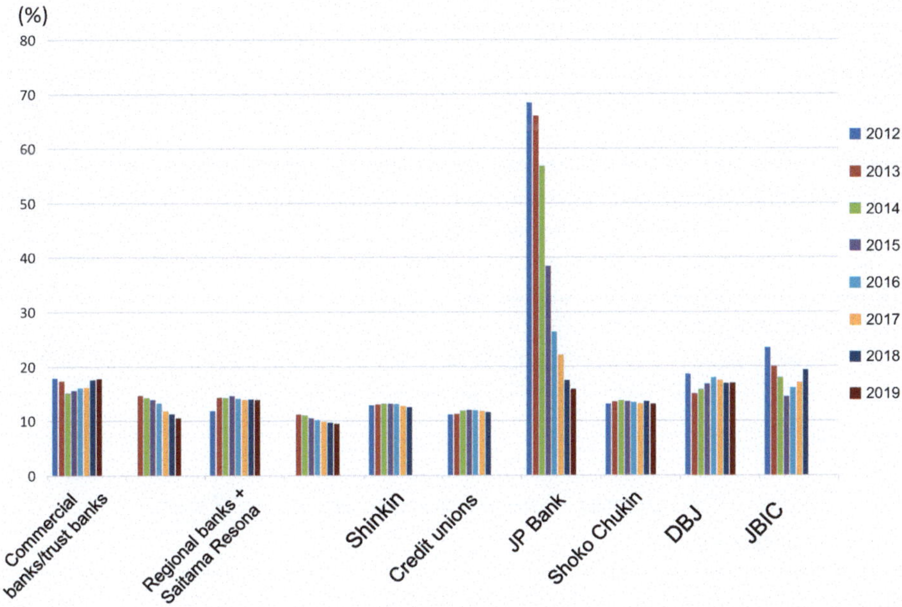

Fig. 4.11 Capital adequacy ratio, March 2012–2019. (*Sources*: Financial statements of Japanese Bankers Association, Shinkin Central Bank, Shinkumi Federation Bank, government-affiliated financial institutions, and FSA data)

Table 4.14 Japan Post Bank shifts from low-risk/low-return to high-risk/low-return

FY ending March	Capital adequacy ratio (%)	Risk assets (trillion yen)	Bad debt ratio (%)	ROA (%)	ROE (%)	Net profit (10 billion yen)	Dividend payout ratio (%)
2010	91.62	9.1	0	0.251	3.43	29	24.9
2011	74.82	11.5	0	0.273	3.56	31	25.0
2012	68.39	12.9	0	0.297	3.69	33	25.0
2013	66.04	13.8	0	0.298	4.01	37	25.0
2014	56.81	16.5	0	0.282	3.68	35	26.5
2015	38.42	21.5	0	0.277	4.37	37	54.9
2016	26.38	32.2	0	0.231	3.72	32	28.8
2017	22.22	38.8	0	0.211	3.55	31	60.0
2018	17.42	50.3	0	0.233	3.94	35	53.1
2019	15.78	56.0	0	0.177	3.01	27	70.4

Source: Japan Post Bank financial statements

increasing, and hence the importance and urgency of developing an institutional design for solving these problems must be highlighted.

In the following chapter we will examine the ideal paths the three privatized banks and regional banks should follow in light of the findings of the analyses discussed in this chapter. The problems JP Bank is facing now are low profitability and greater interest-rate and credit risks as a result of heavily investing in government bonds with the virtual existence of the mandatory deposit system. Regional banks, on the other hand, are faced with a worsening investment environment due to the low-interest-rate policy that has lasted for 10 years and are finally undergoing mergers, which did not really happen even when commercial banks transformed themselves into megabanks through mergers around 2000. There still exist more than 100 regional banks, including secondary regional banks. The analysis discussed in the previous chapter discovered that regional banks with total assets of less than 7 trillion yen have poorer operational efficiency and a much lower ROA than those with higher total assets.

This kind of an analysis of the current situation should help spark ideas on how to reorganize the three privatized banks and regional banks.

1.5 Trends in Regional Financial Institutions by Type of Business

Earlier, in Sect. 1.2, we concluded that regional financial institutions need to have total assets of 7 to 10 trillion yen in order to maintain an ROA of 0.35–0.4%. In this section we will look into the trends in deposits and loans by type of financial institution as well as by region in order to understand the current status of regional financial institutions that should be restructured. We will also examine how JP Bank's smaller market share in each region and overconcentration in Tokyo will affect the regional financial sector.

In 2015, the government formulated the Japan Revitalization Strategy[6] and identified revitalization and structural reform of regional economies as a key policy issue. Under the strategy, the government expected regional financial institutions that support regional economies to serve in a consulting role to help middle-standing SMEs and small businesses. The Liberal Democratic Party of Japan also highlighted mergers as a key option for regional financial institutions to consider under its Japan Revitalization Vision proposal.

In the Council on Economic and Fiscal Policy's 2018 Basic Policy released in June 2018, the government made the following statement: "By networking these revitalized areas, the government will correct the overconcentration in Tokyo toward the balanced development of national land appropriate to the coming era. To stop population decline and bring about regional revitalization, it is essential not only to consider policies in local government concerned, but also deepen cooperation with other local governments to promote policies having broader economic zones in mind." The government also went on to state that "To encourage local governments' ingenuity, the government will steadily and strongly promote decentralization

[6]"Revolution in productivity by investment in the future," Cabinet decision, June 2015.

reform. To improve the overconcentration in the Tokyo area, the government will enhance the functions of major regional cities,[7] and consider and prepare a definite plan of specific measures within this year in order to make those cities attractive so that the invitation of companies and expansion of local businesses invigorate business activities and attract people and universities together."

The central and local governments began thinking that local economies could not be sustained unless they began overseeing broader economic zones. They also started promoting mergers and reorganizations of regional banks in broader economic zones in order to overcome issues of overbanking and the small economic scale of areas divided by prefectural borders. These trends indicate that reasons for considering the *doshusei* system or super-regional banking system are well founded.

While the government has looked at regional economies in terms of broad economic zones, they are vaguely divided into groups of prefectures, such as Kanto and Chubu, for which no gross regional product targets have been set. Nor have policies for achieving any such targets been implemented.

Likewise, since no regional financial institutions cover a wider area, the government has only pursued financial policy targets at the individual prefecture level. In reality, however, regional banks, operating with clear performance targets, have gone beyond prefectural boundaries in mergers to form financial groups as holding companies that encompass a wider geographical swath.

Table 4.15, Fig. 4.12, and Fig. 4.13, providing the historical data of deposit and loan balances (from the fiscal year ending March 31, 2000, to the fiscal year ending March 31, 2017) and percentage shares by type of financial institution, indicate the following characteristics.

First, commercial banks, trust banks, and others significantly increased the balance of deposits (by 148 trillion yen) and decreased the balance of loans (by 44 trillion yen). Regional banks increased the balance of both deposits (by 88 trillion yen) and loans (by 57 trillion yen). There are two possible factors behind the increase in the deposit balance. One is that the declining capital (94 trillion yen) in postal savings, which had become bloated prior to the FILP reform, flowed into commercial and regional banks. The other factor is that household financial assets increased as a result of the economic recovery and were deposited with major banks. The overall balance of loans did not change much over the last 17 years as the decrease (44 trillion yen) in loans at commercial banks, trust banks, and others was transferred to regional banks (57 trillion yen). Looking at the historical data of deposit and loan balances by region and by type of financial institution shown in Table 4.17 in order to analyze this transfer of declining loans at commercial and trust banks to regional banks, one sees that 90% of the increases and decreases come from banks in the three major urban areas, i.e., Tokyo metropolitan area, Tokai, and Kinki. Figures remained flat in rural areas while loan balances at urban regional banks grew. However, since commercial banks, trust banks, and so forth increased loans overseas, where

[7]The compact city and shrinking cities.

Table 4.15 Balance and share of deposits/loans of financial institutions: March 2000, 2010, 2017, and difference between 2000 and 2017 (trillion yen)

		Commercial banks, trust banks, etc.	Regional banks	Secondary regional banks	Shinkin banks	Credit unions/ Labor Banks	JA	Japan Post Bank	Total deposits
Deposit balance	2000	283	175	60	102	31	70	260	982
	2010	344	213	57	117	33	84	168	1017
	2017	431	263	68	138	39	98	166	1203
	2017–2000	148	88	8	36	8	28	−94	221
Share of deposits	2000	28.8	17.9	6.1	10.4	3.2	7.2	26.5	100
	2010	33.8	20.9	5.6	11.5	3.2	8.3	16.5	100
	2017	35.9	21.9	5.6	11.5	3.2	8.2	13.8	100
	2017–2000	7.1	4	−0.5	1.1	0	1	−12.7	0
Balance of loans	2000	279	134	51	69	21	22	–	576
	2010	222	155	43	64	20	23	–	527
	2017	235	191	51	69	23	20	–	589
	2017–2000	−44	57	0	0	2	−2	–	13
Share of loans	2000	48.4	23.3	8.8	11.9	3.8	3.8	–	100
	2010	42	29.3	8.2	12.2	4	4.3	–	100
	2017	39.8	32.5	8.6	11.7	3.9	3.5	–	100
	2017–2000	−8.6	9.2	−0.2	−0.2	0.1	−0.3	–	0

Source: Financial statements of each bank

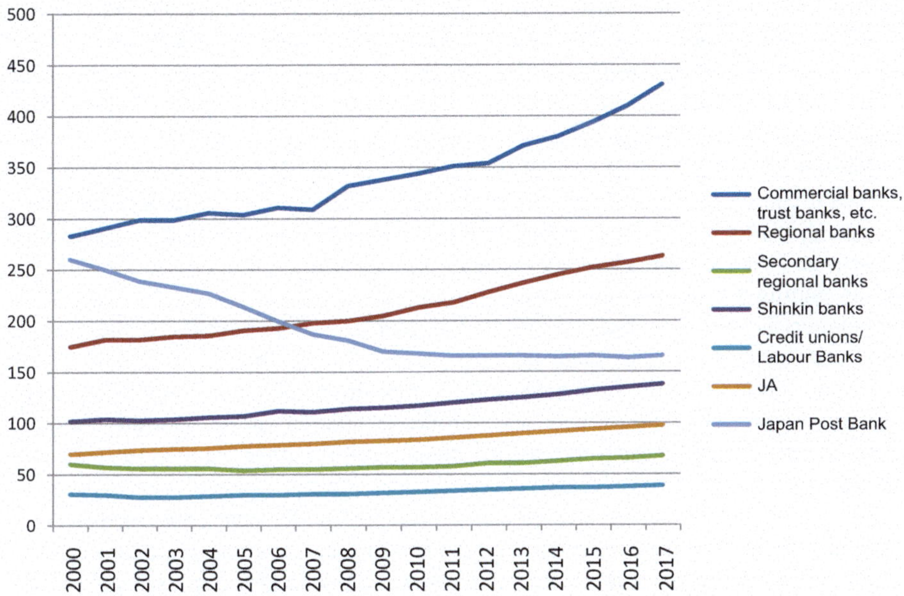

Fig. 4.12 Deposit balances, March 2000–2017 (trillion yen). (*Source*: Financial statements of each bank)

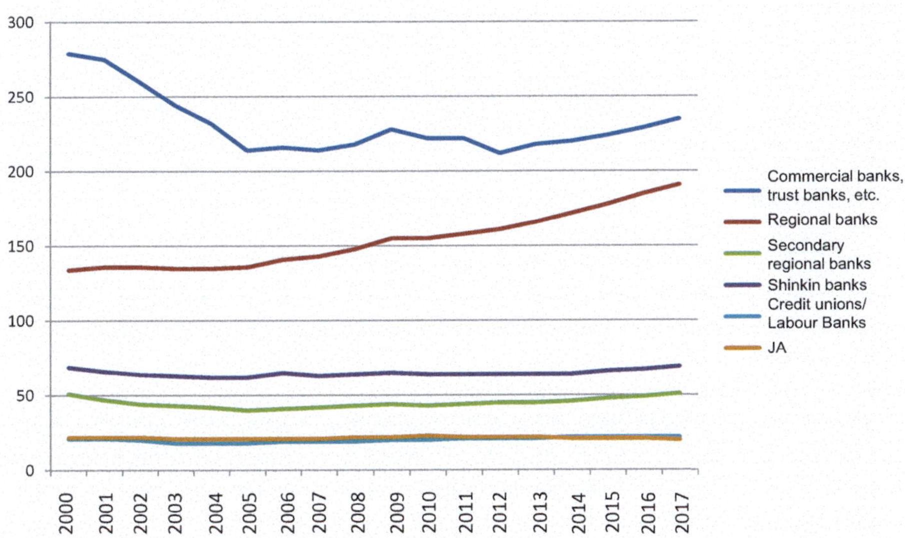

Fig. 4.13 Loan balances, March 2000–2017 (trillion yen). (*Source*: Financial statements of each bank)

profitability is high, it does not represent a simple transfer of money. For other types of financial institutions, the balance of deposits at secondary regional banks, credit unions, and Labor Banks remained flat (8 trillion yen) while the balance increased at shinkin banks (38 trillion yen) and JA (28 trillion yen) proportionately to the recent economic recovery. The loan balance remained unchanged at all types of financial institutions.

Looking at chronological changes in the percentage shares of deposits and loans by type of financial institution in Fig. 4.14 and Fig. 4.15, one sees that the balance of deposits and their percentage shares appear as gentle curves, descending for JP Bank and ascending for commercial banks, trust banks, and others overall, despite the financial crisis following the collapse of Lehman Brothers in 2008. The balance of loans and their percentage share declined at commercial banks, trust banks, and others and increased at regional banks. There was almost no change at other types of financial institutions. There was no significant change in the overall financial structure either, despite the policy-based finance reform since it failed to spark any dramatic change.

Yet commercial banks, trust banks, and regional banks are aggressively reforming their operations to cope with a shrinking and graying population, fiscal deficit, and zero-interest-rate issues that cause their financial health to deteriorate in the shadow of low growth, low inflation, and low interest rates. Other types of financial institutions whose profitability has always been low have not taken any reform initiatives. The historical data of ROA by type of financial institution tell us that if they fail to act now, they will be unable to get their business back on track. Theoretically speaking, the first step in solving this problem would be to reduce the number of regional financial institutions and increase their asset size via mergers. The second step would be to eliminate barriers between different types of financial institutions and integrate organizations of regional banks and secondary regional banks and, in addition, align the organizations of shinkin banks, credit unions, Labor Banks, and others, as well as the laws governing them to make it easier for them to merge. Japan's financial structure should be simplified by eliminating the barriers between different types of financial institutions. Financial institutions should seek holding company–based vertical integration beyond their business category or other restructuring strategies that will ensure an adequate scale of operation covering a wide geographical area.

Table 4.16 shows changes in the balance of deposits and loans at different types of financial institutions in eight areas, which have been redivided from the regional blocs defined in the Act on Promotion of Wide-Area Administration in Special Districts for Consolidated Local Governments,[8] as well as the proposed basic law for promoting *doshusei* (the regional administration system).[9]

---

[8]Act on Promotion of Wide-Area Administration in Special Districts for Consolidated Local Governments enacted on December 20, 2006.

[9]Basic Act on the Reform Aimed at a Shift to Doshusei proposed by the Liberal Democratic Party's Regional Government (doshusei) Promotion Headquarters, September 6, 2012.

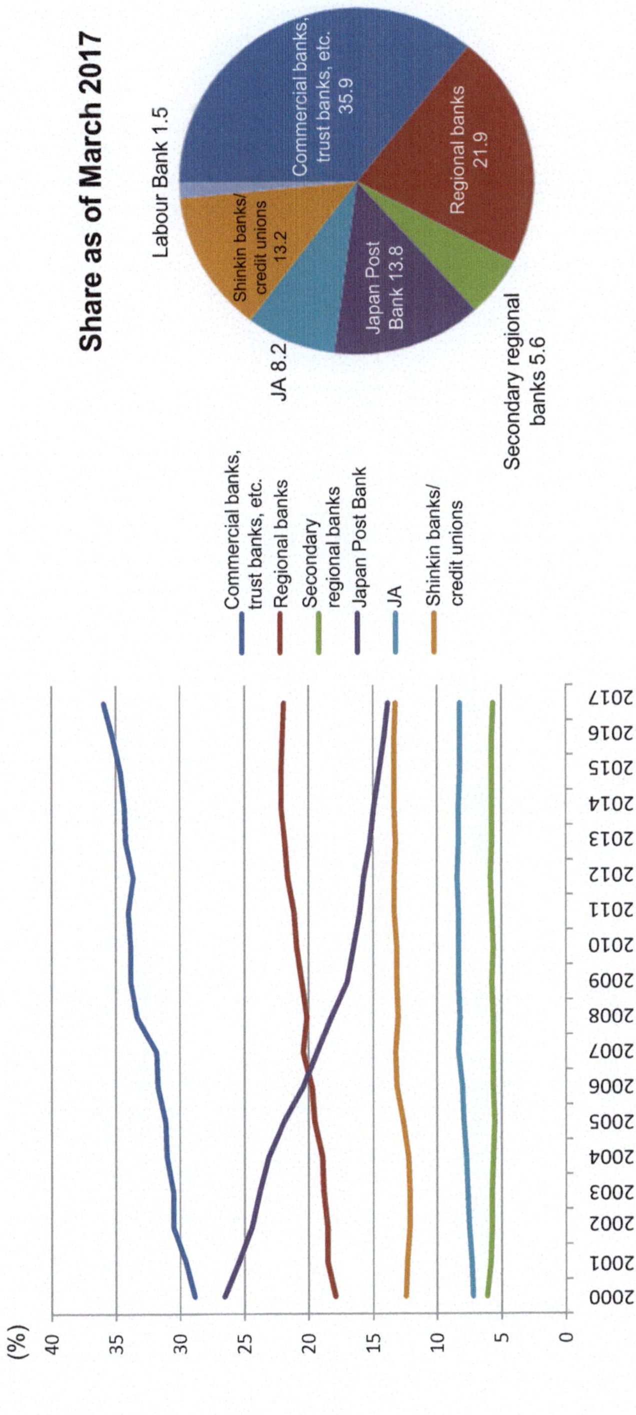

Fig. 4.14 Share of deposits by type of financial institution, March 2000–2017. (*Source:* Financial statements of each bank)

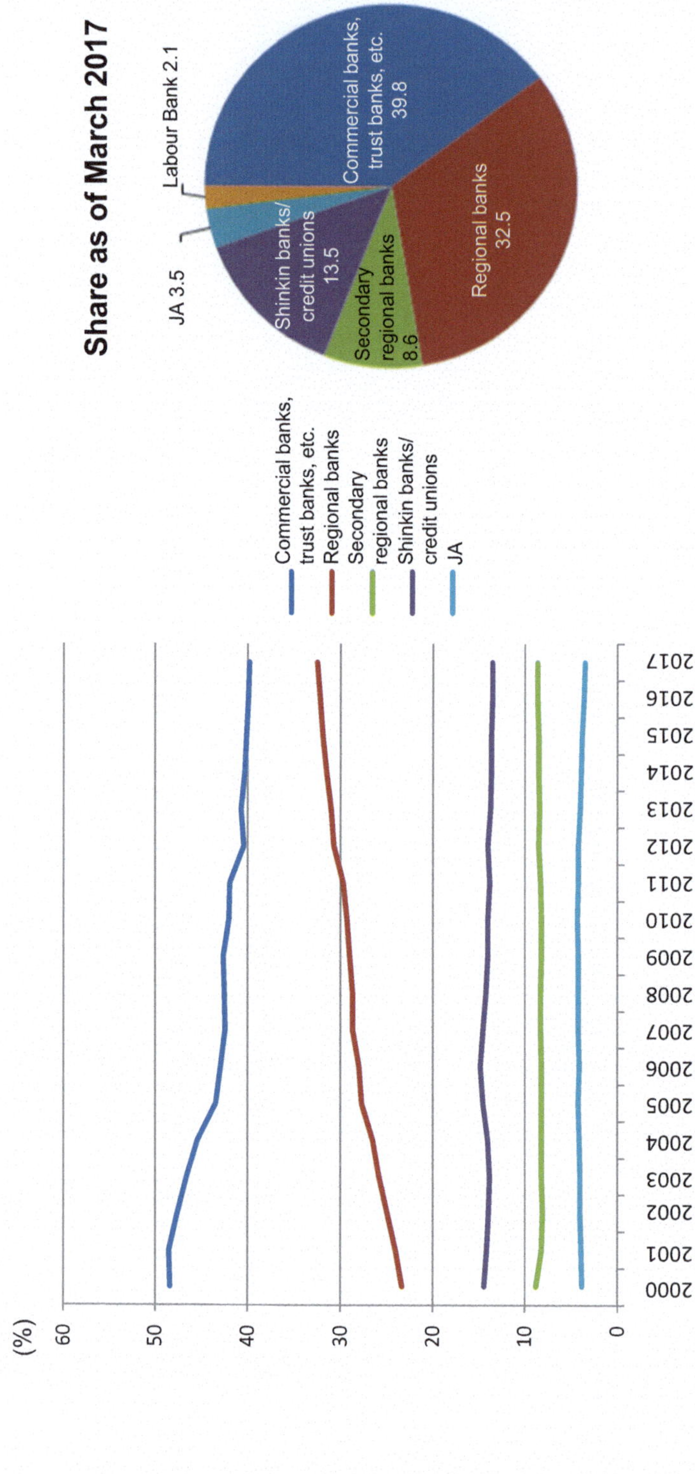

Fig. 4.15 Share of loans by type of financial institution, March 2000–2017. (*Source*: Financial statements of each bank)

Table 4.16 Balance of deposits/loans by region and type of financial institution as of March 2017, and difference from March 2000 (trillion yen)

Region		Commercial banks, trust banks, etc.	Regional banks	Secondary regional banks	Shinkin banks	Credit unions/ Labor Banks	JA	Japan Post Bank	Total deposits	Commercial banks, trust banks, etc.	Regional banks	Secondary regional banks	Shinkin banks	Credit unions/ Labor Banks	JA	Total loans
Hokkaido	Balance	2.1	5.4	8.2	7.2	1.6	3.4	6.9	34.8	1.1	3.6	5.2	3.1	1	0.7	14.7
	difference	0.3	1.2	2.5	2	0.2	1	−3.5	3.7	0.2	0.3	0.2	0	0	−0.1	0.6
Tohoku	Balance	2.4	29.3	4.8	5.3	3.1	6.5	10.2	61.6	1.6	15	3.1	2.5	1.7	1.3	25.2
	difference	0.6	12.2	0.8	1.3	0.6	1.9	−4.8	11.6	−0.4	3.1	0.3	0	−0.1	−0.5	2.4
Kanto	Balance	307.4	63.6	16.8	45	11.2	21.9	56.4	522.3	184.6	63.9	15.5	23.6	6.6	5.4	299.6
	difference	121.9	20.4	3.8	10	0.9	6.7	−22.9	140.8	−10.2	23.8	3	−0.6	−0.6	−0.4	15
Chubu	Balance	31.3	55.7	13.6	38	8.9	28.6	30.5	206.6	10.1	33.9	8.6	18.1	5.2	5.6	81.5
	difference	4	19.8	0.6	11.8	2.6	8.5	−21.0	26.3	−6.3	8.7	−0.5	1.1	0.1	−0.2	2.9
Kinki	Balance	77.7	30.5	8	28.6	6.1	16.4	29.2	196.5	31.3	23.5	7	14.7	3.7	2.6	82.8
	difference	13.3	11	−0.9	8	0.6	5.6	−19.7	17.9	−24.1	7.9	−1.8	3	−0.2	0	−15.2
Chugoku	Balance	4.1	22.4	5.8	5.9	2.8	7.2	10.7	58.9	1.9	13.6	4.2	3.2	1.9	1.6	26.4
	difference	1.6	7.1	1.6	0.9	−7	2.5	−7.5	−0.3	−0.8	1.9	0.5	−0.1	0.4	0.1	2
Shikoku	Balance	1.4	13.2	5.1	2.8	0.7	5.4	5.3	33.9	1.1	7.2	3.2	0.9	0.6	0.7	13.7
	difference	0.3	3.3	1.2	1.1	0.1	1.3	−4.7	2.6	0	1	0.2	−0.3	0.3	−0.1	1.1
Kyushu/ Okinawa	Balance	5	43	4.9	5.1	3.6	9.3	16.7	87.6	3.3	30.7	3.3	2.9	2.3	2.5	45
	difference	1.6	17.1	−2.4	0.9	0.9	2.5	−9.3	11.3	−1.4	10.5	−2.9	−0.1	0.2	0.1	6.4
Nationwide	Balance	431	263	68	138	37	98	166	1201.0	235	191	51	69	22	20	588
	difference	148	87	8	36	7	28	−94	220	−44	57	0	0	1	−2	12

Source: Financial statements of each bank

In the fiscal year ending March 31, 2017, Kanto had 43% of all deposits and 50% of all loans. Looking at the nine market indicators, such as population, number of companies, and total prefectural assets, in Table 4.17, one sees that Kanto has about a 36% share. In light of this figure, the balance of deposits and loans is quite overconcentrated in Tokyo. In comparison, the share of the deposit and loan balances is about the same as the share of market indicators in the Chubu or Kinki regions and lower in Hokkaido, Tohoku, Chugoku, Shikoku, and Kyushu. This overconcentration of financial services in Tokyo is weakening the local financial market. Taking a further look at the percentage shares by region and by type of financial institution, one sees that JP Bank and JA have a good share of deposits, respectively 15–20%, or around 10% on average, as shown in Table 4.18.

These deposits are centrally collected and invested in JGBs and foreign bonds, although not directly. Analysis of share of deposits and loans by region revealed that commercial banks, trust banks, and others procure funds locally and invest them locally. Regional banks and secondary regional banks in Tohoku, Chugoku, Shikoku, and Kyushu claim more than 50% of all deposits while the percentage is low for those in Kanto and Kinki. This composition is the same for loans at regional banks and secondary regional banks. The percentage is high for those in Tohoku, Chugoku, Shikoku, and Kyushu, at 71%, 67%, 75%, and 75%, respectively.

Compared with the share of deposits and loans in the fiscal year ending March 31, 2000, by region and by type of financial institution, the share of deposits significantly increased (10.3%) at commercial banks, trust banks, and others in Kanto, while the share decreased (10–15%) at JP Bank across Japan, as shown in Table 4.19. Regional banks' share sharply increased (15.4%) due to postdisaster reconstruction in Tohoku and accelerating reorganization of regional banks in Kyushu, while secondary regional banks and other types of financial institutions saw only minor changes in their share. As for loans, regional banks across Japan increased their share (9.2%), indicating the positive effect of their reorganization. On the other hand, commercial banks, trust banks, and so forth decreased their share (8.6%). There was almost no change at other types of financial institutions.

As discussed earlier, the analysis of current and past data has highlighted the structural problem where funds are centrally collected by JP Bank and JA in rural areas as opposed to overconcentration of financial services in Tokyo. The analysis has also proved that regional banks that reformed their operations by increasing assets via mergers over these years took the right path. According to the analysis, theoretically, secondary regional banks, which have neither a strong operating foundation nor earning power, are more likely to merge with other regional banks.

If regional banks do not secure a certain share in the financial market, they will be unable to stay afloat and will eventually need to gain market share as a new type of financial institution operating without any barriers between different types of financial institutions.

Table 4.17 Share of market indicators by region

	Population [a]	Number of companies [b]	Gross prefectural product [c]	Number of workers [c]	Compulsory personal insurance [d]	Deposits at all banks [e]	Postal savings	Loans at all banks [e]	Number of locations [f]	Average	Share in whole numbers
	125.2 million	2.755 million	513.3 trillion yen	60.2 million	861.5 trillion yen	1202.6 trillion yen	165.8 trillion yen	589.1 trillion yen	54.4		
Share (%)											
Hokkaido	4.23	4.10	3.58	3.98	3.38	2.88	4.16	2.49	5.15	3.73	4
Tohoku	7.03	5.63	6.32	7.19	6.75	5.12	6.15	4.26	10.29	6.52	6
Kanto	33.55	39.93	37.77	33.72	34.83	43.43	34.02	50.87	22.05	36.58	36
Chubu	18.29	16.84	19.05	20.09	19.44	17.16	18.39	13.83	23.16	18.47	19
Kinki	16.29	15.97	15.72	15.28	16.35	16.35	17.61	14.07	13.97	15.79	16
Chugoku	5.91	5.19	5.57	5.81	5.79	4.90	6.45	4.43	8.45	5.83	6
Shikoku	3.11	2.86	2.67	2.99	3.13	2.83	3.13	2.34	4.78	3.09	3
Kyushu/Okinawa	11.58	9.47	9.31	10.96	10.23	7.31	9.95	7.69	13.23	9.98	10

Sources: *Kinyu Journal* (December 2017)

Notes: [a]January 1, 2017 (Ministry of Internal Affairs and Communications); [b]March 31, 2016 (National Tax Agency); [c]Fiscal 2014 (Cabinet Office); [d]March 31, 2017 (Life Insurance Association of Japan); [e]Total amount of deposits and loans for domestic bank accounts only, as of March 31, 2017; [f]Including head offices, branches, and satellite offices, as of March 31, 2017

Table 4.18 Share of deposits/loans (%) by region and type of financial institution in March 2017 and differences from March 2000

		Share of deposits by type of financial institution								Share of loans by type of financial institution						
	March	Commercial banks, trust banks, etc.	Regional banks	Secondary regional banks	Shinkin banks	Credit unions/ Labor Banks	JA	Japan Post Bank	Total deposits	Commercial banks, trust banks, etc.	Regional banks	Secondary regional banks	Shinkin banks	Credit unions/ Labor Banks	JA	Total loans
Hokkaido	2017	6.1	15.5	23.6	20.7	4.6	9.7	19.8	100	7.5	24.5	35.3	21.1	6.8	4.8	100
	diff.2000	0.3	2	5.3	4	0.1	2	−13.6	0	1.2	1.3	0.1	−0.7	−0.3	−0.8	0
Tohoku	2017	3.9	47.6	7.8	8.6	5	10.5	16.6	100	6.3	59.5	12.3	9.9	6.8	5.2	100
	diff.2000	0.3	11.4	−0.2	0.6	0	1.3	−13.4	0	−2.5	7.3	0	−1.0	−1.1	−2.7	0
Kanto	2017	58.9	12.2	3.2	8.6	2.1	4.2	10.8	100	61.6	21.3	5.2	7.9	2.2	1.8	100
	diff.2000	10.3	0.9	−0.2	−0.5	−0.6	0.2	−10.0	0	−6.8	7.2	0.8	−0.6	−0.3	−0.2	0
Chubu	2017	15.2	26.9	6.6	18.4	4.3	13.8	14.8	100	12.4	41.5	10.6	22.2	6.4	6.9	100
	diff.2000	1.7	5.1	−0.7	2.7	0.7	2.5	−14.1	0	−8.5	9.4	−1.0	0.6	0	−0.5	0
Kinki	2017	39.5	15.5	4.1	14.6	3.1	8.3	14.9	100	37.8	28.3	8.5	17.8	4.5	3.1	100
	diff.2000	3.6	4.6	−1.3	3.1	0	1.7	−12.4	0	−17.2	12.8	−0.2	3.5	0.6	0.5	0
Chugoku	2017	7	38	9.8	10	4.8	12.2	18.2	100	7.2	51.5	15.9	12.1	7.2	6.1	100
	diff.2000	2.4	9.3	2	0.6	−1.4	3.4	−15.9	0	−4.3	5.8	0.1	−2.0	0.7	−0.3	0
Shikoku	2017	4.1	38.9	15.1	8.3	2.1	15.9	15.6	100	8.1	52.9	23.5	6.6	3.7	5.2	100
	diff.2000	6	7.3	2.7	2.9	0	2.8	−16.3	0	−0.6	3.7	−0.3	−2.9	1.3	−12	0
Kyushu/ Okinawa	2017	5.7	49.1	5.6	5.8	4.1	10.6	19.1	100	7.3	68.2	7.3	6.5	5.1	5.6	100
	diff.2000	1.3	15.4	−4.4	0.3	0.4	1.7	−14.7	0	−5.0	16	−8.8	−1.3	−0.3	−0.6	0
Nationwide	2017	35.9	21.9	5.6	11.5	3.2	8.2	13.8	100	39.8	32.5	8.6	11.7	3.9	3.5	100
	diff.2000	7.1	4	−0.5	1.1	0	1	−12.7	0	−8.6	9.2	−0.2	−0.2	0.1	−0.3	0

Source: Financial statements of each bank

Table 4.19 Share of deposits and loans of financial institution by region (comparison of March 2000 and 2017) (%)

Region	Share of deposits								Share of loans						
	Commercial banks, trust banks, etc.	Regional banks	Secondary regional banks	Shinkin banks	Credit unions/ Labor Banks	JA	Japan Post Bank	Total deposits	Commercial banks, trust banks, etc.	Regional banks	Secondary regional banks	Shinkin banks	Credit unions/ Labor Banks	JA	Total loans
Hokkaido	0.3	2	5.3	4	0.1	2	−13.6	0	1.2	1.3	0.1	−0.7	−0.3	−0.8	0
Tohoku	0.3	11.4	−0.2	0.6	0	1.3	−13.4	0	−2.5	7.3	0	−1.0	−1.1	−2.7	0
Kanto	10.3	0.9	−0.2	−0.5	−0.6	0.2	−10.0	0	−6.8	7.2	0.8	−0.6	−0.3	−0.2	0
Chubu	1.7	5.1	−0.7	2.7	0.7	2.5	−14.1	0	−8.5	9.4	−1.0	0.6	0	−0.5	0
Kinki	3.6	4.6	−1.3	3.1	0	1.7	−12.4	0	−17.2	12.8	−0.2	3.5	0.6	0.5	0
Chugoku	2.4	9.3	2	0.6	−1.4	3.4	−15.9	0	−4.3	5.8	0.1	−2.0	0.7	−0.3	0
Shikoku	6	7.3	2.7	2.9	0	2.8	−16.3	0	−0.6	3.7	−0.3	−2.9	1.3	−12	0
Kyushu/ Okinawa	1.3	15.4	−4.4	0.3	0.4	1.7	−14.7	0	−5.0	16	−8.8	−1.3	−0.3	−0.6	0
Nationwide	7.1	4	−0.5	1.1	0	1	−12.7	0	−8.6	9.2	−0.2	−0.2	0.1	−0.3	0

Source: Financial statements of each bank

2 Portfolio Selection of Three Privatized Banks and Regional Banks

2.1 Ideal Portfolio for Three Privatized Banks and Theoretical Problems

Financial institutions always strive for diversified portfolios that are advantageous to them in light of the security and profitability of the asset mix they own. They look for an optimal combination of low-risk, high-return investments and choose assets based on portfolio theory. As discussed in Sect. 1 of this chapter, the ROA of three privatized banks combined as well as JP Bank alone is lower than the ROA of other financial institutions (commercial banks, trust banks, and regional banks). While managing a huge amount of assets, JP Bank invests heavily in JGBs, which are safe but not so profitable, as well as foreign bonds and foreign investment trusts, which are high-yielding but subject to foreign exchange risk.

In the fiscal year ending March 31, 2017, JP Bank achieved a net interest margin of 0.40% for yen-denominated transactions (mainly JGBs) and 0.86% for foreign currency-denominated transactions (mainly foreign bonds and foreign investment trusts) (Table 4.20).

Since the bank's portfolio leans heavily toward bonds, its overall net interest margin is 0.60% and its ROA is lower than that of other types of financial institutions due to high operating expenses incurred for fund procurement.

Table 4.21 compares the balance sheets of the three privatized banks, i.e., JP Bank, Shoko Chukin Bank, and the Development Bank of Japan (DBJ). You can see the difference in asset mix between JP Bank and the other two banks.

Securities account for 66.3% of JP Bank's total assets, with 35.7% JGBs, 9.6% foreign bonds, and 15.5% foreign investment trusts. Combined with the money deposited with the Bank of Japan, which accounts for 24.4%, together it all accounts for 90.7% of total assets. The funds deposited with the Bank of Japan was originally the capital JP Bank invested in JGBs. Since this money represents the proceeds from the sale of JGBs to the Bank of Japan, which was then deposited with the Bank of Japan, it can be treated as an investment in securities. The upshot is that JP Bank's portfolio lacks balance. On the other hand, loans account for a large percentage of total assets at Shoko Chukin Bank and DBJ, at 73.2% and 80.4%, respectively. These loans made by both banks include government loans related to the emergency lending and special investment operations. When it comes to Shoko Chukin Bank,

Table 4.20 Japan Post Bank's net interest income by type of operations, FY ending March 2017 (%)

	Domestic	Overseas	Total
Yield on interest-earning assets	0.53	1.23	0.78
Interest rate on interest-bearing liabilities	0.13	0.37	0.18
Net interest margin	0.40	0.86	0.60

Table 4.21 Composition of assets and liabilities for the three privatized banks, FY ending March 2017 (%)

	Japan Post Bank	Shoko Chukin Bank	Development Bank of Japan
Cash and due from banks	24.4	13.4	6.0
Securities	66.3	12.1	10.9
JGBs, etc.	35.7	8.6	1.2
Corporate bonds	5.2	3.1	4.3
Stocks	0.1	0.7	2.4
Other securities	25.3[a]	0.7	3.0
Loans	2	73.2	80.4
Other assets	7.3	1.3	2.7
Total assets	100	100	100
Deposits	85.6	40	Receivables 18.4
Time deposits	54.3[b]	25.2	Corporate bonds 10.3
Negotiable certificates of deposit	0.5	37.1[c]	0
Borrowings	6.5	7.4	51.0
Other liabilities	1.8	8.2	2.4
Total liabilities	94.4	92.7	82.1
Total equity	5.6	7.3	17.9
Total liabilities and equity	100	100	100

Source: Financial statements of each bank
Notes:
[a]Foreign bonds 9.6, foreign investment trusts 15.5
[b]Includes 49.5% fixed-amount postal savings
[c]Receivables 4.7

since these loans include the money lent illegally under the guise of emergency lending operations, its portfolio is abnormal.

The portfolios of Shoko Chukin Bank and DBJ have a problem in that their percentage of loans is 10–15% higher than that of private financial institutions. Likewise the percentage of investments in securities at these banks is 10–15% lower than at private financial institutions. If they were fully privatized and had the ability to procure funds at their own discretion, they would be able to better manage their assets and liabilities. They must change the asset-liability portfolio of a policy-based financial institution to a private financial institution's, or otherwise they will not be able to sustain stable and profitable operations.

At JP Bank, loans account for only 2%, which is virtually nothing. The reason for this abnormally low percentage lies deep in the bank's roots. Funds raised via postal savings were mandatorily deposited with the Ministry of Finance from the Meiji period until 2001. Dubbed the government's spare wallet, postal savings were fully used by the government. Even after the abolishment of mandatory deposits and postal privatization, the Postal Privatization Committee did not spell out any policy that would approve the use of postal savings for loans to private companies.

The primary reason for this is that, although JP Bank went public, the majority of its shares are held by JP Holdings, which virtually makes the government its controlling shareholder. The condition for granting JP Bank the right to engage in lending operations is stipulated in the Postal Service Privatization Act (i.e., the government disposes of all shares in the bank). The second reason is that JP Bank lacks both the organization and personnel able to screen loans. The bank also lacks any debt-collection know-how and personnel.

After the Bank of Japan introduced quantitative and qualitative monetary easing, the Bank of Japan bought JGBs from JP Bank and deposited 51 trillion yen in proceeds into the Bank of Japan's current account (as of March 31, 2017). Under the monetary easing policy, the government planned to return this money to the market in order to boost the bank's financial intermediary operations through industrial development and trigger a 2% increase in consumer prices. While JGBs held by private financial institutions were issued for the same purpose, JP Bank is not allowed to use them for lending operations. Even if the money were to be invested in securities such as foreign bonds, it would be too risky given the bank's current portfolio. If this 51 trillion yen had been used for lending to companies under monetary easing, things would have turned out just as the government planned, but that plan in reality turned to dust.

Ever since postal services were privatized, I have claimed that the Bank of Japan should buy JGBs from JP Bank and use the proceeds to diversify investment channels in order to change JP Bank's portfolio.[10] I have proposed that JP Bank should be fully privatized as soon as possible, develop lending capability, and secure necessary personnel through a merger. I also proposed that the three privatized banks should be merged and operate under a holding company in order to equalize JP Bank's disproportionate investments in securities as well as the unbalanced lending operations at Shoko Chukin Bank and DBJ in order to balance out and optimize their portfolios. It is difficult to create optimal portfolios for them as separate entities.

The three privatized banks will need to consider a number of different scenarios for business and regional splits in order to optimize their portfolios under a holding company.

[10]"As a measure for the transitional period, the Bank of Japan should buy a certain number of long-term government bonds from JP Bank for a certain period so JP Bank can use the proceeds for operating new businesses" as written on page 138 of *Kansei kinyu kaikaku to chigin saihen* [Public financial reform and regional bank reorganization] published on March 26, 2015, by Kinzai Publishing. I suggested the same on page 13 of the class material used on December 26, 2010, in my special lecture course at Kyoto University's economics department, "Introduction to Public and Private Financial Services."

2.2 Portfolios of Different Types of Private Financial Institutions

What is the optimal portfolio the three privatized banks should pursue once they become fully privatized? To find an answer to that question, I analyzed the portfolios of different types of financial institutions in Japan (Table 4.22).

There are three possible scenarios in which the three privatized banks could select the optimal portfolio under a holding company.

In the first scenario, a portfolio is built with the combined assets of the three banks.
In the second scenario a portfolio is built after JP Bank and Shoko Chukin Bank are merged.
In the third scenario the aforementioned two banks are split into regional banks after being merged and a portfolio is built for each regional bank.

The first scenario is similar to the concept of a megabank and uses the optimal portfolio model for commercial banks and trust banks.
The second scenario uses the model for super regional banks, such as Resona Bank and Saitama Resona Bank.
The third scenario uses the model for regional banks affiliated with large or medium-sized financial groups (Table 4.23).

In the first and second scenarios, the resulting financial institution would have an asset total of 100 to 200 trillion yen. Once the three banks were merged, their combined deposits due from banks totaling approximately 60 trillion yen would have to be used mainly for loans in order to diversify assets as soon as possible and optimize their portfolio. However, the money aspect alone would remain a big challenge.

In the third scenario, the three banks' combined deposits due from banks totaling 60 trillion yen would be divided into nine banks (after they were split by region), and each bank would use 6.5 trillion yen for lending purposes. As regional banks seek merger opportunities in order to stay afloat, the newly launched regional banks would be able to tap into new capital demand while competing on an equal footing with large-scale regional banks, which have been consolidated to comply with the Antimonopoly Act. Let us take a closer look at this scenario.

Since a wide-area market gives companies more options, it attracts large corporations.

The need for wide-area regional financial institutions arises in order to mitigate overconcentration of industries in Tokyo and promote regionally dispersed industries that produce and consume locally. As a result, locally collected funds are invested locally, and the three privatized banks can become financial institutions possessing optimal portfolios.

Since the correlation between gross prefectural product and prefectural total of loans has been proven, it would follow that the three privatized banks' loans would contribute to higher prefectural as well as national GDPs. Needless to say, however,

Table 4.22 Portfolio of eight financial institutions (composition of assets and liabilities) (%)

	Commercial banks	Trust banks	Regional banks	Secondary regional banks	Shinkin banks	Credit unions	JA	Norinchukin Bank
Cash and due from banks	24.6	26.6	10.8	8.6	24	30.9	62.8	21.7
Securities	17.9	21.1	24.4	21.2	28	20.5	3.5	58.7
JGBs, etc.	2.8	5.2	11.3	8.8	11.8	7.2	2.3	12.4
Corporate bonds	1.4	1.2	4.7	5.4	10.8	8.9	1	0.4
Stocks	2.3	3.2	2.1	1.5	0.5	0.4	–	0.9
Other securities	6.1	11.5	6.2	5.5	4.9	4.5	–	42.5**
Loans	44.3	46	62	68	45.8	47.5	18.4	11.3
Other assets	13.2	6.3	2.8	2.2	2.2	1.1	15.3	8.3
Total assets	100	100	100	100	100	100	100	100
Deposits	68	49.3	81.9	88	91.2	89.2	83.4	58.5
Time deposits	18.9	33.5	31.3	41.7	55.4	65.9	55.6	51.4
Negotiable certificates of deposit	5.3	12.5	3.2	2.5	0.2	0.1	0.2	21.9
Borrowings	6.7	6.5	3	1.9	1.5	3.6	0.4	4.1
Other liabilities	15.4	26.5*	6.2	2.4	1.3	0.9	6.5	8.9
Total liabilities	95.4	94.8	94.3	94.8	94.2	93.8	90.5	93.4
Total equity	4.6	5.2	5.7	5.2	5.8	6.2	9.5	6.6
Total liabilities and equity	100	100	100	100	100	100	100	100
ROA	0.389	0.35					0.139	

Source: Japanese Bankers Association's financial statements by type of financial institution
*Includes 12.2% investment trusts
**Foreign bonds 32.7, foreign investment trusts 9.5

Table 4.23 Typical portfolios: large and medium-sized commercial banks and regional banks (%)

	MUFG Bank	Resona Bank	Bank of Yokohama	Bank of Kyoto
Cash and due from banks	23.7	22.6	19	9.3
Securities	20.7	10.5	14	32.3
JGBs, etc.	10.3	5.2	3.1	9.1
Corporate bonds	1.2	1.3	3.7	7.9
Stocks	2.2	2.6	1.2	7.9
Other securities	7	1.4	6	7.4
Loans	39.9	60.8	63	56.1
Other assets	15.7	6.1	4	2.3
Total assets	100	100	100	100
Deposits	68.2	80.6	80.3	74.9
Time deposits	18.5	18.8	19.6	28.4
Negotiable certificates of deposit	3.2	3.6	1	10.5
Borrowings	8	1	4.9	1.4
Other liabilities	15.6	10.5	8.1	4.7
Total liabilities	95	95.7	94.3	91.5
Total equity	5	4.3	5.7	8.5
Total liabilities and equity	100	100	100	100

Source: Financial statements of each bank

under this scenario, 60 trillion yen deposited with the Bank of Japan is still not used for lending, leaving a big problem yet unsolved.

2.3 *Ideal Portfolio for Regional Banks and Theoretical Problems*

The asset allocation of the 64 regional banks and 41 secondary regional banks for the fiscal year ending March 31, 2017, was about the same. The asset allocation of the 64 regional banks and 46 secondary regional banks was also similar 10 years earlier in the fiscal year ending March 31, 2007. While their total assets significantly increased, their overall portfolios remained unchanged (Table 4.24).

However, due to the prolonged zero-interest-rate policy, the ROA for each asset category is higher at banks with larger total assets and lower at banks with smaller total assets. The reason for this difference lies in their portfolios. As shown in Table 4.25, the portfolios of regional banks (except for Suruga Bank) consist of 60–70% loans, 25% securities, and 5–10% deposits with the Bank of Japan. An analysis of asset allocations at banks, by amount of total assets, was carried out and revealed that smaller banks typically invest more in loans and have a lower ROA.

Table 4.24 Regional banks' portfolios, 2017 and 2007 (%)

FY ending, March	2017		2007	
	64 regional banks	41 secondary regional banks	64 regional banks	46 secondary regional banks
Cash and due from banks	10.8	8.6	2.5	3.7
Securities	24.4	21.2	27.1	22.4
JGBs, etc.	(11.3)	(8.8)	(13.1)	(11.6)
Corporate bonds	(4.7)	(5.4)	(2.6)	(4.5)
Stocks	(2.1)	(1.5)	(3.6)	(2.5)
Other securities	(6.2)	(5.5)	(4.7)	(3.7)
Loans	62	68	64.8	69.7
Other assets	2.8	2.2	5.6	4.2
Total assets	100	100	100	100
Deposits	81.9	88	86.9	90.7
Time deposits	(31.3)	(41.7)	(38.8)	(50.8)
Negotiable certificates of deposit	3.2	2.5	2.1	1.1
Borrowings	3	1.9	0.8	0.7
Other liabilities	6.2	2.4	4.5	2.5
Total liabilities	94.3	94.8	94.3	95
Total equity	5.7	5.2	5.7	5
Total liabilities and equity	100	100	100	100

Source: Japanese Bankers Association's financial statements by type of financial institution

Table 4.25 Regional banks' ROA and asset allocation by total asset amount (%), FY ending March 2017

Total assets (trillion yen)	No. of banks	ROA	Loans	Securities	Funds deposited with BOJ
10 trillion yen or more	4	0.483	66.2	15.2	14.7
7–10	10	0.349	60.7	26.3	10.1
5–7	14	0.319	60.8	26.1	10.5
3–5	17	0.316	62.3	26.4	8.5
2–3	22	0.305	64.2	24.6	9.0
1–2	20	0.282	67.5	23.6	6.6
Less than 1 trillion yen	17	0.271	69.1	20.9	7.9

Source: Financial statements of 104 regional banks (Suruga Bank, not included)

According to this analysis, a portfolio that is ideally profitable and safe for a regional bank with total assets of 7 trillion yen or more consists of 60% loans, 25% securities, and 10% deposits with the Bank of Japan (which are virtually securities), for a total of 95%, with the remaining 5% made up of net and other assets.

As long as the zero-interest-rate policy is in effect, however, regional banks will have difficulty ensuring income through financial intermediary operations due to the low interest rate and low profit margin. While the assets deposited with the Bank of Japan were originally safely invested in JGBs, once they pursue profitability, it would be best to promote industrial development and create demand for funds so they can invest the money deposited with the Bank of Japan into making loans. As discussed in Sect. 1 of this chapter, an increase in loans within a prefecture will result in an increase in gross prefectural product, a win-win scenario. When investing funds in securities, regional banks should invest in municipal bonds and corporate bonds of local companies.

Reorganization of regional banks should occur in such a way that many regional banks are placed under holding companies and optimize their portfolios as consolidated corporate groups. The ideal model for an optimal portfolio would be one that ensured safety and profitability through diversification. On the other hand, smaller regional banks, which have already invested more than 70% of their assets in loans and lack the expertise for investing in securities, still face a problem since their portfolios will be more difficult to optimize.

In this chapter, we analyzed the three privatized banks and regional banks by looking at total assets and ROA of different types of financial institutions. We also analyzed the interest-rate risk and portfolio of JP Bank. While these are all interrelated, analyzing each aspect quantitatively enabled us to identify the problems facing these banks. Keeping the findings of these analyses in mind, we will discuss institutional designs for the three privatized banks as well as reorganized regional banks in the following chapter.

References

Financial Map 2018 (2017) *Kinyu Journal*, suppl. The Japan Financial News Co., Ltd., Tokyo

Japan Post Holdings (2007) *Nippon yusei kosha no gyomu tou no shokei ni kansuru jisshi keikaku* [Implementation plan for transferring Japan Post operations]. https://www.yuseimineika.go.jp/iinkai/dai26/siryou1_2.pdf.

Kinzai Institute for Financial Affairs, Inc., ed. (2011) *Kinyu Zaisei Jijo* 62, no. 37, October 3

Uno, Akira (2015) *Kansei kinyu kaikaku to chigin saihen* [Public financial reform and regional bank reorganization]. Kinzai Institute for Financial Affairs, Inc., Tokyo

Chapter 5
Institutional Designs for the Reorganization of the Three Privatized Banks and Regional Banks

1 Ideal Path and Institutional Design for Three Privatized Banks

Centralized and bloated, public financial organizations have become too big to efficiently deploy their human and physical resources in an effort to get people to deposit their savings in a network of small branches that stretches across Japan. Public financial services lack the know-how to deal with risks and bad loans because they are protected by a government guarantee or automatic government guarantee when investing funds. That's why they fail to operate as financial institutions in the true sense.

Since October 2007, the process of fully privatizing the three privatized banks has not made any progress, and the government has presented neither a clear road map nor a vision for the banks after their full privatization. In my book *Kansei kinyu kaikaku to chigin saihen* [Public financial reform and regional bank reorganization], which was published in March 2015, I presented a framework for public financial institutions after their full privatization based on an innovative simulation. In this chapter, I will construct a theory that provides the basis for an institutional design that will resolve the current situation based on the analysis of current data as discussed in the previous chapter while keeping in mind future financial conditions. We will look at the changes in society over time to examine a more realistic future for the three privatized banks and their institutional design.

Electronic supplementary material The online version of this chapter (https://doi.org/10.1007/978-981-15-1408-1_5) contains supplementary material, which is available to authorized users.

A. Uno, *Japan Post Bank*, https://doi.org/10.1007/978-981-15-1408-1_5

1.1 *Visions for Three Privatized Banks*

1.1.1 Basic View

(A) **Financial sector view of the future of Japan Post Bank submitted to the government Postal Privatization Committee**

Article 19 of the Postal Service Privatization Act requires the Postal Privatization Committee to comprehensively review the progress of postal privatization every 3 years and submit its observations to the prime minister. The law also requires that the committee be notified if any measures are taken based on its observations. Over the last 10 years since privatization commenced, the Postal Privatization Committee has asked the Japanese Bankers Association, Regional Banks Association of Japan, and other banking associations for their opinions about the progress every 3 years, but the response is always the same, meaning not much progress has been made.

The committee[1] obtained the latest responses, summarized in what follows, from these banking associations in October 2017.

[Regional Banks Association of Japan View] (based on document submitted to committee)

- Basic philosophy and viewpoint
  Article 2 of the Postal Service Privatization Act
  The law requires that the postal service take measures necessary to ensure that it plays on an equal footing with competing businesses while paying attention to the impact it may have on the sound development of local economies as well as the market. In light of this requirement, the following three points of view are important.

(a) Ensuring fair competition

- As long as the government maintains ties with JP Bank by indirectly holding its shares, JP Bank is not competing with private financial institutions on an equal footing.
- We are extremely disappointed that the government has not clearly indicated a specific road map for fully privatizing JP Bank, i.e., selling all its shares (requesting early implementation of Article 7 of the Postal Service Privatization Act).
- Listing of both the parent company and its subsidiary may threaten the interest of minority shareholders of the subsidiary (JP Bank). Therefore, all shares of the two financial companies should be sold as soon as possible.

---

[1]Solicitation of Public Comments: Interviews with Relevant Organizations, 176th Postal Privatization Committee Meeting, October 26, 2017 - Japanese Bankers Association, Second Association of Regional Banks, National Association of Shinkin Banks, National Central Society of Credit Cooperatives, and Norinchukin Bank.

(b) Downsizing operations to an optimal level

- JP Bank has a balance of deposits that is greater than that of any financial institution in the world.
- When there is no clear path to full privatization, raising the deposit cap further will increase the risk of expanding operations and may saddle the public with a financial burden in the future.
- Although we believe that JP Bank's aim of being an institutional investor is desirable, the scale of its operations must be controlled to a level where risk management is possible (concern about increasing overseas investments).

(c) Coexistence with local communities and user convenience

- We recognize the significance of JP Bank and private financial institutions working together toward vitalizing local economies, enhancing user convenience, and so forth. To coexist with JP Bank, however, private financial institutions should be allowed to compete with it on an equal footing.

The Japanese Bankers Association and the Second Association of Regional Banks also expressed opinions similar to these.

(B) The Ministry of Economy, Trade and Industry Set up an expert panel to examine reform measures for Shoko Chukin Bank and started looking into fully privatizing the bank

In October 2017 the Ministry of Economy, Trade and Industry, Ministry of Finance, Financial Services Agency, and Ministry of Agriculture, Forestry and Fisheries took administrative disciplinary action[2] against Shoko Chukin Bank in connection with its illicit lending practices. An expert panel was established to look into reform measures for Shoko Chukin Bank and met seven times. In its January 2018 interim report, the panel made proposals on steps that Shoko Chukin Bank should take. The panel recommended that the bank reorganize its board of directors so that outside directors would make up the majority and have a third-party committee supervise its management in order to enhance governance. The panel also proposed that the bank look into a future business model and focus on helping SMEs turn around or sustain their businesses while nurturing companies with low credit-worthiness but good growth potential. The panel stated that the bank should decide on making the move to full privatization in light of the outcome of its reform efforts over the next 4 years. Then the bank stop practicing of amakudari (retired bureaucrats of Ministry of Economy, Trade and Industry take office there) and appointed a president from the private sector instead.

---

[2]October 25, 2017 administrative order based on Articles 59 and 24 of the Shoko Chukin Bank Limited Act

The panel was established on November 17, 2017 at the direction of the Minister of Economy, Trade and Industry. Chaired by Yusuke Kawamura, the panel consists of nine other members.

After meeting seven times, the panel submitted an interim report on January 11, 2018.

(C) Future operations of Development Bank of Japan

The Act on the DBJ Inc. was partially revised in May 2014 following a review conducted at the end of fiscal 2014. The revision is described in detail in Chapter 3, 4-7.

While maintaining its policy on disposing of all shares in the DBJ, against the backdrop of a changing economic landscape, the government has failed to specify when it plans to fully privatize it. Article 2 of the revised law's supplementary provisions requires the government to reduce its shares in the company in light of the impact its holdings may have on achieving the company's objectives (special investment and emergency lending operations) as well as market trends and dispose of all shares as soon as possible.

The provisions concerning the disposal of government-owned shares stipulated in the Shoko Chukin Bank Limited Act are identical to those stipulated in the Act on DBJ Inc. The Shoko Chukin Bank Limited Act may be handled separately depending on the recommendations of the expert panel looking into reform measures for Shoko Chukin Bank.

1.1.2 Lessons from NTT's Postprivatization Restructuring: A Privatization Success Story

In 1952 the Ministry of Posts and Telecommunications established Nippon Telegraph and Telephone Public Corporation (NTT) as an entity dedicated to telecommunications operations. The purpose of setting up this state-run corporation was to meet the increasing demand for telephone services and operate the business in a corporate style.

In 1985 the ministry privatized the public corporation and made it a stock company, believing that operational independence would make it an efficient and innovative organization. However, the government imposed the requirement that NTT's shares had to be held by the state, so it was not fully privatized and still remained a special corporation. The reasons for doing that included the fact that NTT was Japan's core telecommunications company and that telephone service is a universal service.

Privatization of NTT opened the gates of the telecommunications market to private companies and brought the vitality of the private sector into the market. The government took the following actions with regard to privatizing NTT and its operations.

- **Actions taken with regard to the change in the governing law**

  (i) Drastically revising the financial and accounting systems due to the shift from the NTT Act to commercial, tax, and other laws
  (ii) Reviewing labor-management relations due to the shift from the public corporation law to the three labor laws

- **Revising organizational structure, for example, for competition and revitalization purposes**

  (i) Shifting from a function-based organization to a business division system in November 1985
  (ii) Revising the personnel system (shifting to the merit pay system in which employee salaries are not based on position)
  (iii) Increasing efficiency by expanding into a new business arena and outsourcing head office operations

- **Basic reorganization policy**

  (i) NTT was split into a long-distance communications company and two regional communications companies all operating under a pure holding company.
  Each company operated as a financially independent company.
  (ii) The long-distance communications company was to operate as a private company that provides interprefectural communications services with the potential of expanding into the international communications business.
  (iii) The regional communications companies were made responsible for ensuring telephone services in the respective areas they covered. NTT East was to cover Hokkaido, Tohoku, Kanto, Tokyo, and Shinetsu, and NTT West Tokai, Kansai, Chugoku, Shikoku, Kyushu, and Okinawa.
  (iv) NTT Communications was to provide interprefectural communications services in Japan and expand into the international communications business.
  (v) The holding company was to operate as a special corporation responsible for fundamental research and development. The long-distance communications company and regional communications companies were made responsible for applied research and development closely related to their business operations.
  (vi) Ensuring that the long-distance communications company and regional communications companies could compete on an equal footing.
  (vii) The Ministry of Posts and Telecommunications was responsible for coordinating government functions to implement special measures in relation to antitrust, commercial, and other laws as well as consolidated taxation and other tax measures.

- **Proposal for reorganizing NTT**

While the Ministry of Posts and Telecommunications was initially tasked with formulating a vison for NTT by 1989, it extended the deadline to 1995 and finalized a reorganization policy in December 1996.

The main point of the company split was that NTT's holding company was designed to be a pure holding company. A pure holding company is a company that does not operate its own business but only oversees its affiliates.

– **Reorganization**[3]

In 1999, 14 years after its privatization, NTT was reorganized to become a pure holding company in order to increase the efficiency of its bloated organizational operations, respond to every customer need, and promote fair competition. NTT expanded into the international communications business to meet the public's diverse telecommunications needs. As shown in Fig. 5.1, business companies were established as financially independent companies operating under a holding company. NTT was split into the holding company, NTT East, and NTT West, which were special corporations, as well as three stock companies. These were NTT Data, NTT DoCoMo, and NTT Communications. Since NTT Data and NTT DoCoMo had already been separated in 1988 and 1992, respectively, NTT Communications was the only stock company that was separated then.

Consequently, both operating income and net income doubled after business operations were split under a holding company.

– **What the reorganization did**

Splitting NTT's bloated organization into different types of companies, as well as into regional companies, resulted in deregulating the industry, making it more competitive, and expediting NTT's decision-making process. In the end, reorganization transformed NTT into a comprehensive communications company providing both domestic and international services and made it a financially sound corporate group, contributing to the national interest by lowering telecom rates, and providing Internet accessibility, for example.[4]

Norio Wada, who was at the helm of NTT then and navigated the shift to a holding company through a company split and restructuring, said, "NTT is like a huge forest. Since it's so big, it's impossible to make quick decisions and can in no way compete in the global telecom industry. In breaking it up into smaller companies, like groves that make up a forest, we should respect the independence of each company and meet societal demands." Wada took charge of the holding company after NTT's reorganization. In May 2018 Wada was awarded the Grand Cordon of the Order of the Rising Sun in recognition of his contribution in spearheading NTT's reorganization, which in turn brought about a structural change in the Japanese society and led to Japan's economic development. This is a testament to the significance of NTT's restructuring.

---

[3]Nippon Telegraph and Telephone Corp. report on privatization and reorganization of NTT, June 16, 2004

Annual Report 2014: "Major Transformations," pp. 177–133

Annual Report 2017: "NTT Group's Process of Self-Transformation," pp. 1–13

[4]On page 262 of his book *NTT mineika no kozai* [Pros and cons of NTT's privatization], published in January 2006 by Nikkan Kogyo Shimbun, Masaki Kanzaki writes, "It had been pointed out since 1995 that liberalization had not made the market competitive, and that's why NTT was split into regional communications companies as well as a long-distance and international communications company operating under a holding company in 1999." Then NTT president, Norio Wada, emphasized that the move dispersed the power of the giant.

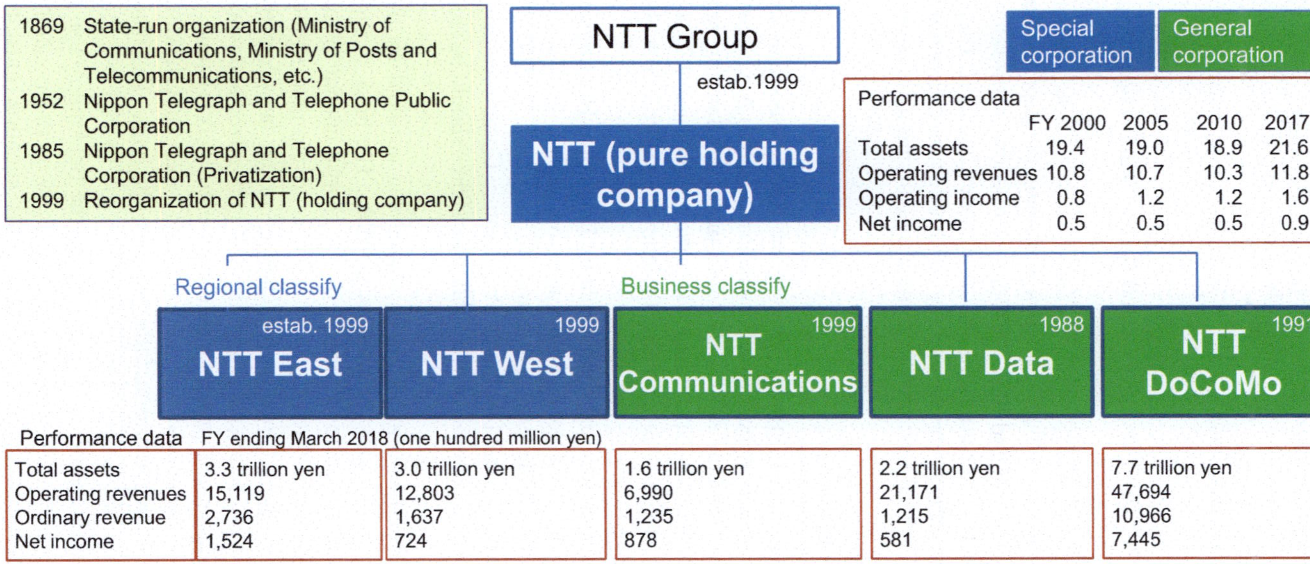

NTT Group's business results data 1985, 99, 2017 (one hundred million yen)

	1985 Privatized	1999	2017	1999/ 1985 (%)	2017/ 1999 (%)
Operating revenues, a	50,914	100,187	113,910	196	113
Operating income, b (b/a, %)	7,677 (15.0)	8,238 (8.2)	15,398 (13.5)	107	186
Net income, c (c/a, %)	1,857 (3.6)	2,990 (3.0)	8,001 (7.0)	161	267
Shareholders' equity	35,118	60,146	90,525	171	150

Fig. 5.1 NTT Group reorganization

The three privatized banks remain bloated organizations 10 years after becoming special corporations. They are still operated in the same way they used to be. To change this situation, we will discuss the future of these three privatized banks by looking at the example of NTT, which was in a similarly bad situation and successfully got out of it by reforming its operations.

1.1.3 Steps to an Ideal Path for the Three Privatized Banks: Theoretical Rationale for Ch.4

Below are five steps to solve various problems, such as narrowing the gaps in total assets and return on assets (ROA) among different types of financial institutions, solving the current interest rate risk and portfolio selection issues facing JP Bank, and narrowing the gaps among regional banks as they go through reorganization. These steps were developed in light of the views presented by banking associations and successful past cases.

(A) **Establishing Competitive Equality**

- Establishing competitive equality means placing the three banks that are governed by special laws, such as the Postal Service Privatization Act, Shoko Chukin Bank Limited Act, and the Act on DBJ Inc., under the Banking Act, which governs private banks, and specifying when the government will sell all of its shares (reducing to less than a third at the minimum) through public offerings to fully privatize them.
- JP Bank should reduce the controlling shares held by Japan Post Holdings to less than 50% as soon as possible and start new businesses in order to diversify operations. It should develop a medium- to long-term plan for its operations after full privatization. (The Postal Privatization Committee originally specified in the implementation plan that all bank shares should be sold by October 2017.)
- Shoko Chukin Bank should sell 46.5% of its shares that are held by the government to general shareholders as soon as possible. The bank is supposed to finalize the way it should be operated and chart a course to full privatization in 4 years' time, which is by 2022. The government should revise the Shoko Chukin Bank Limited Act, change current laws, clearly indicate how the bank should be operated after it is fully privatized and when it will dispose of all its shares, and present a road map to the bank's listing. It is obvious that the 2017 loan fraud scandal involving emergency lending operations was a result of neglecting to fully privatize the bank. The bank should also be freed from the restrictions imposed by the special law that limit the bank's scope of operations and placed under the Banking Act so it can compete with private banks on an equal footing, otherwise its operations will continue to put pressure on private banks. This situation must be changed, and the bank should change its asset portfolio so it places more

of an emphasis on lending to middle-standing SMEs to benefit local industrial development.

- The DBJ is governed by a special law and is in competition with commercial banks, trust banks, and others. It should stop receiving an automatic government guarantee, be privatized, and placed under the Banking Act so it will not put pressure on private financial institutions. At the same time, as a practical measure, the government should stipulate current provisions concerning special investment and emergency lending operations in the supplementary provisions as temporary legislation. The government should also specify when it will sell off its shares in the bank and present a road map to its listing. The bank should maintain a portfolio that's comparable to those of commercial banks and trust banks to ensure an equal footing with them.
- Fully privatizing the three privatized banks will make Japan's financial market more open and free (i.e., private financial institutions accounting for 95% of total assets).

(B) **Downsizing Operations to an Optimal Level**

- JP Bank's total assets, amounting to 210 trillion yen exceed the total assets of megabanks in Japan. Operating a nationwide branch network, JP Bank is in intense competition with regional banks in raising funds. The bank remains bloated, with its balance of deposits being unchanged for 10 years after privatization. Unable to make agile decisions, it maintains the status quo while still facing a large interest-rate risk and portfolio selection problem, which were theoretically identified. To break free from this situation, JP Bank should learn some lessons from NTT's successful reorganization and downsize its total assets of 210 trillion yen through restructuring, i.e., breaking up its operations into different businesses and regional companies.
- Specifically, following NTT's reorganization model, total assets of the three banks that are to be fully privatized, amounting to 238 trillion yen, should be placed under a pure holding company. JP Bank and Shoko Chukin Bank should then merge and establish regional banks operating in different regional administrative blocs (*doshu*). The total assets of regional banks should be maintained at 7 trillion yen or more (which is a theoretically identified value). Regional banks should be divided into eight new banks operating in eight regional administration blocs, each with total assets of 7 to 80 trillion yen. This will divide them into profitable regional banks with an optimal asset size based on the theoretical value obtained from the correlation between total assets and ROA. The post office network's payment and settlement operations, standard administrative operations, and system management operations should be spun off into an online banking business and placed under a holding company.

(C) Integrating Fund Raising and Investment Organizations (Developing Lending Capability)

- It has been proven with theoretical values that the financial industry is more concentrated in Tokyo than other industries. This overconcentration is the result of a failure to invest locally collected funds locally. It is mostly attributable to the system in which the funds of JP Bank and the Japan Agricultural Cooperative (JA) are centrally collected but not invested locally. JP Bank has not diversified its operations since it still lacks lending and risk management capabilities even 10 years after its privatization. The second best way to solve this problem would be utilizing Shoko Chukin Bank's 100 branches across Japan that are equipped with lending and risk management capabilities. While small regional banks operating in areas with an excessive number of banks have been merged into financially stable regional banks, JP Bank too can acquire regional banks via a bailout takeover if it becomes a private bank governed by the Banking Act. JP Bank can also take over excess personnel (especially lending personnel) from the reorganized regional banks. Merging JP Bank, Shoko Chukin Bank, and some regional banks that share a mutual interest will diversify their operations and could serve as a way to optimize the ROA by type of financial institution.

(D) Enhancing User Convenience

- Raising and investing funds locally can increase transactions with a wide variety of customers, including local independent businesses, SMEs, middle-standing companies, and individual customers. The online settlement bank, in particular, can horizontally connect with new regional banks that have been set up in different regional blocs to provide the same service across Japan, which is JP Bank's strength. The bank can use fintech, IoT, AI, and so forth for online banking as well as big data for banking operations through the use of its ATM network.
- Putting the DBJ under a holding company will enable the banking group to take advantage of its international operations, transactions with large corporations, and investment banking business across the group.
- The amount of assets belonging to companies operating under the holding company will be optimized while the total assets of the entire group remain the same. The share of total assets among different types of financial institutions will also be optimized, and the ROA gaps among financial sectors and regions will be narrowed, enabling financial institutions to compete on an equal footing.

(E) Regional Coexistence and Coprosperity

- The regional banks created as a result of the merger between JP Bank and Shoko Chukin Bank will compete with the banks that have increased their assets and formed into *doshu* through a reorganization of regional banks that will compete on an even playing field. This will create an environment that will ensure their coexistence and coprosperity.

- The regional banks created as a result of the merger between JP Bank and Shoko Chukin Bank would provide an alternative choice for customers in a regional administration bloc where there were only a few regional banks operating as a result of a reorganization (such as Kyushu) and would be a way to avoid breaching antitrust laws, as pointed out by the Japan Fair Trade Commission. As indicated by the analysis of total assets of different types of financial institutions, regionally distributed fund raising will put a stop to overconcentration of financial institutions in Tokyo and transform the financial system into a more regionally distributed one.
- If the government shifts away from the conventional notion of gross prefectural product and sets gross domestic product (GDP) targets on the basis of *doshu*, it will accelerate decentralization and end overconcentration in Tokyo. These *doshu* will have the same level of power as EU countries and become the driving force behind increasing Japan's GDP. If the DBJ leverages its organization-wide strengths to enhance its overseas transactions, it will help increase Japan's gross national income (GNI). According to its 2018 Basic Policy, the government will correct overconcentration in Tokyo by networking the revitalized areas to achieve balanced development of national land appropriate for the coming era. The aforementioned financial reform can help the government realize this vision.

1.1.4 Basic Design Based on the Five Steps

To resolve various issues facing Japan's financial system, we will look into a new fundamental design based on the five steps that can be used as a foundation for the future as well as the government's September 2004 institutional design for postal reform and the June 2006 institutional design for policy-based finance reform.

[Basic Vision]

(i) Full privatization of JP Bank, Shoko Chukin Bank, and the DBJ is a must (i.e., they will become privately owned and operated financial institutions). Upon the initial public offering, the government will reduce its stake in these banks from the less than 50% it now holds to less than a third and specify when it will dispose of all shares.

(ii) These banks will operate under the principle of raising and investing funds locally to contribute to local finance.

(iii) JP Bank and Shoko Chukin Bank will engage in commercial banking operations while the DBJ will generally engage in investment banking operations.

(iv) Japan Post's post office network should be used for payment and settlement operations.

(v) JP Bank should enhance its management transparency and become financially sustainable.

[Prerequisites for JP Bank and three postal services]

(i) The postal service should be run by the government. It should be clearly specified that postal service is the only universal service.
Mail and parcel delivery (including international distributions) businesses should also be operated by the government.
(ii) The telegram business should be transferred to NTT, and postal money orders should be phased out since JP Bank has joined the Japanese Banks' Payment Clearing Network.
(iii) JP Bank, which operates the postal savings business, should be fully privatized to eliminate automatic government guarantees and pressure on private financial institutions. The number of directly managed branches should be increased from the current 233 to 1000–1500 (about the same number as the number of post offices with mail collection and delivery functions) by establishing regional banks. The number of branches to be directly managed by each regional JP Bank company should be around 100.
(iv) Japan Post Life Insurance, which operates the postal life insurance business, should eventually be fully privatized.
(v) Post offices operated by agents should be allowed not only to act as the agencies of JP Bank and Japan Post Life Insurance but also to operate other businesses after a specified period of time has passed. Both JP Bank and Japan Post Life Insurance should be allowed to use other types of businesses as their agencies. Deregulating agency requirements will ensure transparency of agency fees through competition.
(vi) While following the road map to full privatization, JP Bank should shift away from investing operations that place too much emphasis on Japanese government bonds and be allowed to start new businesses so it can diversify operations. Regulations on business operations imposed by the Postal Service Privatization Act should be lifted, and JP Bank should be governed by the Banking Act so it can compete with private banks on an equal footing.

- The bank should focus on over-the-counter sale of government bonds to individual customers, home loans, and loans to SMEs to enhance profitability.
- It should start providing loans to middle-standing companies and listed companies as soon as it is ready and restructure its portfolio to make it comparable to the portfolios of commercial banks, trust banks, and large regional banks in order to enhance profitability.
- While the Bank of Japan (BOJ) buys a certain amount of long-term Japanese government bonds from JP Bank to cope with the transitional period, it should use the proceeds (funds deposited with the BOJ) for new business operations.

[Prerequisites for Shoko Chukin Bank]

While the Ministry of Economy, Trade and Industry claims that it will make a final decision concerning the future and full privatization of Shoko Chukin Bank by 2022, the government should revise the current Shoko Chukin Bank Limited Act, place it under the Banking Act, and set a schedule for its full privatization. This will finalize the road map to privatization.

[Prerequisites for the DBJ]

The government should revise the current Act on DBJ Inc. and place the bank under the Banking Act. It should then set a schedule for its full privatization and finalize the road map. Then it should determine the portfolio selection for the bank.

1.2 Vision for Restructuring the Three Privatized Banks

The theoretical values obtained through the examinations in Chap. 4 revealed that JP Bank's assets should be divided into optimal amounts in order to optimize the percentage of total assets held by the bank. The more urgent problem is that JP Bank is exposed to a huge interest-rate risk. The risk on the asset management side as well as the peculiar way funds are collected (via fixed-amount postal savings) makes its liability-side risk big as well. This risk will be triggered by a hike in interest rates once the current zero-interest-rate policy ends, and it will rock the operational foundations of JP Bank. JP Bank cannot solve this problem by maintaining the status quo, so it will soon have to change its operational structure to manage interest-rate risk. On top of that, the unbalanced portfolio selection of the bank has long been a stumbling block to better profitability and makes its operations rigid. Getting the bank on track to better financial health will require an overhaul of the operations of the three privatized banks.

We can learn from the cases of public organizations that were successfully privatized or those that were successfully transformed following privatization. These organizations include JR and NTT, whose bloated operations were divided into separate regional entities by function. Following in the footsteps of these companies should put the three privatized banks on the right path.

Although the Council on Economic and Fiscal Policy discussed privatizing JP Bank and dividing it into separate companies at its 24th meeting, held in 2004, when it presented the basic policy for postal privatization, the council decided to postpone the move.

As noted earlier, NTT is an example of a public organization that was split into regional companies after privatization. After it was privatized in 1985, two of its functions were separated, one becoming NTT Data in 1988 and the other becoming NTT DoCoMo in 1992. The company was then split into regional companies, NTT East and NTT West, in 1999.

Japanese National Railways was also privatized in 1987 and was divided into 12 different companies. The company's passenger rail operations were divided into six regional companies based in Hokkaido, East Japan, Tokai, West Japan, Shikoku, and Kyushu.

Privatization and split-ups of the two companies enabled them to optimize their assets, enhance operational efficiency, and significantly reduce their workforces. Blue-chip companies created as a result of the company split later went public and brought a huge windfall in sales profits and dividend revenues to the government. Operating in the black, these blue-chip companies also increased the government's tax revenues. In addition to these benefits, privatization and company splits resulted in enhanced customer service and turned labor unions that had morphed into political players into organizations that built harmonious labor-management relations, all of which was welcomed by the public. Japanese National Railways, a state-run company whose deficit was going to end up as a public financial burden, was transformed into blue-chip corporations (under the Japan Railways or JR brand), enabling the government to reap substantial amounts of tax revenues and proceeds from the sale of shares.

By going private and splitting their operations by function and region, NTT and JR rid themselves of the burdens they were saddled with as public corporations, such as organizational and operational problems as well as labor-management issues and the problem of labor unions becoming political organizations. These successful examples suggest that the reform of public financial services proposed through postal and policy-based finance reforms should focus on splitting the operations of public financial institutions by business and region to optimize their asset size and enhance their operational efficiency, just as JR and NTT experienced after their privatization and splits.

In the latter part of this chapter this will be referred to as the vision for restructuring the three privatized banks under a holding company.

Scenario 1: NTT model

The three privatized banks are placed under a new holding company after full privatization. Then the following steps are taken.

(i) JP Bank's payment and settlement function, systems function, and others are spun off as a new online banking business.
(ii) JP Bank and Shoko Chukin Bank are merged and split into eight regional banks (super-regional bank vision).
(iii) The DBJ is placed under the holding company to serve an investment banking function.

[Basic framework]

(i) Group size: Combined total assets of JP Bank, Shoko Chukin Bank, and the DBJ, totaling 238 trillion yen as of the fiscal year ending March 31, 2017, are placed under a pure holding company.

(ii) Form: The holding company is named YSD Financial Group, using the initial of each bank's name (Y stands for Yucho Ginko, the Japanese name of JP Bank).
(iii) Restructuring: JP Bank is responsible for payment and settlement operations as well as standard administrative operations. Systems operations are split off as a newly established network company (named the YSD Network Bank).

  - JP Bank and Shoko Chukin Bank are merged after their operations have been split up. They are split into eight regional companies operating under the name YSBC Regional Bank (super-regional bank).

Indicators for the merger between JP Bank and Shoko Chukin Bank (as of March 31, 2017)

Company overview	JP Bank	Shoko Chukin Bank
Branches	234	100 in Japan, 4 overseas
Employees	12,965	4102

Number of Shoko Chukin shares issued

- Common stock: 2,156,531,448 shares (approx. 2.2 billion shares)
- Capital: 218.6 billion yen
- Breakdown by stockholder: Share unit number = 1000 shares
- Government 46.53%, financial institutions 2.92%, general corporations 49.94%, individuals 0.61% (Table 5.1).

When merged with Shoko Chukin Bank, JP Bank, whose profitability is low, can provide loans, and its ROA improves to 0.221%. Yet this ROA figure is still much lower than regional banks' ROA, which stands at 0.370%. If its portfolio for lending were enhanced, there would be much more room for improving profitability. Other advantages of the merger include that the bank will be able to operate nationwide and acquire lending capabilities, management transparency will be ensured, and the bank will have a risk management system. The Development Bank of Japan will become a private bank known as DBJ and be placed under the YSD umbrella (Table 5.2).

The ROA of the three privatized banks is 0.253%, which is still lower than regional banks' ROA standing at 0.370%.

When launched, the YSD Financial Group's total assets are comparable to megabanks' total assets, but its profitability is low and it needs to change its asset portfolio to sustain its operations as a listed company. It may have to shrink its assets by reducing marketable securities in the process of qualitative transformation. The group will not necessarily represent a threat to other financial institutions. It and the holding company together will be named the YSD Financial Group (Fig. 5.2).

Table 5.1 Total assets and profitability of YSBC

	JP Bank	Shoko Chukin Bank	YSBC total
Balance sheet, March 31, 2017 (trillion yen)			
Cash and deposits	51.2	1.7	52.9
Securities	138.8	1.5	140.3
Loans	4.1	9.3	13.4
Other assets	15.4	0.3	15.7
Total assets	209.5	12.8	222.3
Deposits	179.4	5.1	184.5
Bonds, etc.	18.3	6.8	25.1
Total liabilities	197.7	11.9	209.6
Total net assets	11.8	0.9	12.7
Liabilities/net assets	209.5	12.8	222.3
Income statement April 1, 2016–March 31, 2017 (100 million yen)			
Ordinary profit	4420	508	4928
Net income	3122	324	3446
ROA (%)	0.211	0.397	0.221

Table 5.2 Total assets and profitability of YSD Financial Group

	DBJ Bank	YSBC total	YSD FG
Balance sheet March 31, 2017 (trillion yen)			
Cash and deposits	1.0	52.9	53.9
Securities	1.8	140.3	142.1
Loans	13.2	13.4	26.6
Other assets	0.4	15.7	16.1
Total assets	16.4	222.3	238.7
Deposits	0	184.5	184.5
Bonds, etc.	13.4	25.1	38.5
Total liabilities	13.4	209.6	223.0
Total net assets	3.0	12.7	15.7
Liabilities/ net assets	16.40	222.3	238.7
Income statement April 1, 2016–March 31, 2017 (100 million yen)			
Ordinary profit	1138	4928	6066
Net income	802	3446	4248
ROA (%)	0.683	0.221	0.253

[Reasons for business and regional splits]

- Splitting off payment and settlement operations, standard administrative operations, and systems operations enables the group to efficiently maintain and manage the post office network while enhancing the efficiency of backyard operations of JP Bank and Shoko Chukin Bank. In the future the post office network will be made available for use by other business operations to

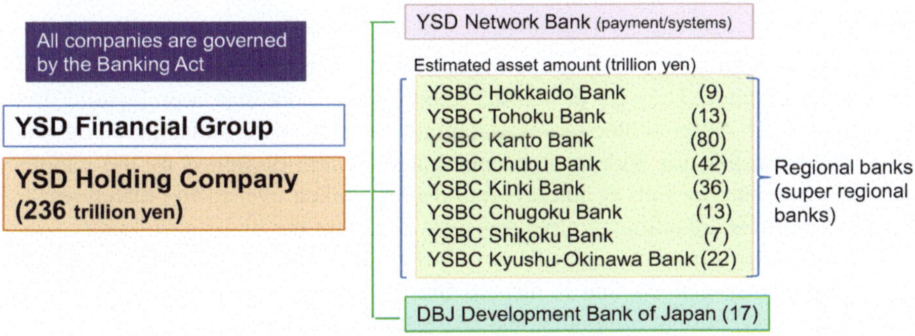

Fig. 5.2 Reorganization of the three privatized banks under a holding company. Y: Japan Post Bank, S: Shoko Chukin Bank, D: DBJ Development Bank of Japan

enhance customer convenience and provide the banks with new profit opportunities.

- A merger between JP Bank and Shoko Chukin Bank brings fund raising and investment operations under one roof. The fact that JP Bank will gain lending and risk management capabilities, in particular, is a big plus.
- Next, dividing the banks' bloated assets into regional companies downsizes these banks, which is the biggest factor for ensuring the kind of fair competition private banks desire. Optimizing the scale of operations enables them to make quick decisions.
- Large-scale regional banks encompassing a wide geographical area (YSBC Kanto, YSBC Chubu, YSBC Kinki, and YSBC Kyushu) can expand into overseas markets in Asia and elsewhere. It has already been proven that an operating foundation encompassing a wide geographical area can be expanded through aggressive M&A and restructuring without waiting for the government to implement the *doshusei* (regional administration) system. YSBC Hokkaido, YSBC Tohoku, YSBC Chugoku, and YSBC Shikoku operate as wide-area regional banks with total assets of about 10 trillion yen and will compete with large regional banks to be created through reorganizations. However, they can take over the surplus workers and branches of regional banks as a result of these reorganizations.
- It has been verified that companies affiliated with NTT have enjoyed better financial performance since its privatization and reorganization. While the three privatized banks' ROA is currently low at 0.253%, it can be increased to the ROA level of wide-area large regional banks (0.429% at the Bank of Fukuoka and 0.533% at the Bank of Yokohama).

Reference Data: [Outline of the Basic Law for Promoting *Doshusei* (Regional Administration System) Proposed by the Liberal Democratic Party]

[Definition]

Doshu are regional administrative blocs whose names contain either *do* (circuit) or *shu* (state). They cover a wider geographical area than a prefectural division. Each regional bloc serves as a broad-based local administrative body and is responsible for wide-area administrative affairs (assigned by the national government) as well as administrative affairs taken over from prefectures.

Municipalities are administrative divisions based on the divisions of a city (*shi*), town (*machi* or *cho*), and village (*mura* or *son*). Each municipality is a basic administrative body that is responsible for administrative affairs taken over from conventional municipal and prefectural governments.

[Basic Concept (Excerpt)]

(i) The government should change the centralized system and build a decentralized system based on *doshu* and municipalities in light of the division of roles between the central and local governments.

(ii) The central government's roles should be limited as much as possible to administrative affairs that pertain to the foundation of the nation's existence, management of national crises, protecting the lives, health, and property of citizens when its involvement is necessary, and development of an economic foundation, as well as truly national affairs, in order to consolidate and enhance national functions.

(iii) National affairs other than those specified in (iii) should be delegated to *doshu*. *Doshu* should take charge of some of the conventional national functions and be established as internationally competitive regional administrative bodies.

(iv) Overconcentration in Tokyo should be eased so that diverse and vigorous local economic zones can be created.

[Proposed *Doshusei*]
Organization

- About 10 *doshu* will be created across Japan.
- Prefectural divisions will be abolished.
- Current municipal divisions will remain as municipalities.

Heads and assemblies

- The assembly of each *doshu* will be composed of those elected from the constituencies of the current corresponding prefectural divisions.
- The head of each *doshu* will be directly elected by its residents.

Taxation and financial systems

- Systems will be designed according to the division of roles between national and local governments.
- A fiscal equalization system will be implemented.
  (*Source*: Outline of the basic law for promoting

doshusei (the regional administration system) proposed by the Liberal Democratic Party in September 2012)

[Quantitative Rationale for Business and Regional Splits]

(i) Table 5.3 shows market indicators that provide the basis for regional split proposals. It lists eight regions' percentage shares for the market indicators that are based on the nine regional economic statistics categories, including, for example, population, number of corporations, gross prefectural product, and number of workers.
When converted to whole numbers, the average percentage shares of the nine categories are 4% for Hokkaido, 6% for Tohoku, 36% for Kanto, 19% for Chubu, 16% for Kinki, 6% for Chugoku, 3% for Shikoku, and 10% for Kyushu and Okinawa.

(ii) Table 5.4 shows the combined balance sheets of JP Bank and Shoko Chukin Bank by item, which are divided into different regions using these regional percentage shares in whole numbers. The balance sheet of each of the eight regional banks of the two merged banks would initially look like this (although their initial total assets and liabilities actually vary depending on the number of customers each one has).

<<Examination of a Case Scenario Based on the Simulation of Regional Banks after Restructuring: YSBC Kinki Bank>>

The six prefectures of the Kinki region developed institutional designs based on specific policy proposals when they formed the Union of Kansai Governments and seek to reform the governance structure based on the *doshusei* administrative system toward decentralization via the Osaka Metropolis plan.

In light of these developments in the Kinki region's wide-area administrative systems, we will look at a case scenario for YSBC Kinki, the YSD Financial Group's regional bank operating in the Kinki region. We will then apply Kinki's process to seven other regions to develop a vision for reorganization in the respective regions.

As shown in Table 5.5, the combined total of gross prefectural product for the Kinki region was 81 trillion yen in fiscal 2015, which accounted for 15.7% of the national total. To sustain a 3% nominal growth rate to achieve a nominal GDP of 600 trillion yen by 2020 as targeted by the government, the Kinki region's gross prefectural product must increase by 14 trillion yen to hit the 95 trillion yen target. As of March 31, 2017, deposits and savings in the Kinki region totaling 114 trillion yen are mainly invested in marketable securities by the central government. Although the investment yield is partially returned to the Kinki region, its strategic goal for the growth of gross prefectural product will not be achieved unless the growth strategy aimed at locally investing locally raised funds is implemented. In particular, since deposits at JP Bank totaling 29 trillion yen are not used locally, once

Table 5.3 Base data (theoretical values) for regional split simulation. Method of regional split: Scenario 3, to regionally divide the combined balance sheets of Japan Post Bank and Shoko Chukin Bank in proportion to the percentage share of each region, that share was calculated based on the following data

	Population (million)	Number of companies (thousand)	Gross prefectural product (trillion yen)	Number of workers (million)	Compulsory personal insurance (trillion yen)	Deposits at all banks (trillion yen)	Postal savings (trillion yen)	Loans at all banks (trillion yen)	Number of locations	Average	Share in whole numbers
Hokkaido	5.3 4.23%	113 4.10%	18.4 3.58%	2.4 3.98%	29.1 3.38%	34.6 2.88%	6.9 4.16%	14.7 2.49%	2.8 5.15%	3.73%	4%
Tohoku	8.8 7.03%	155 5.63%	32.4 6.32%	4.3 7.19%	58.2 6.75%	61.6 5.12%	10.2 6.15%	25.1 4.26%	5.6 10.29%	6.52%	6%
Kanto	42.0 33.55%	1100 39.93%	193.9 37.77%	20.3 33.72%	300.7 34.83%	522.3 43.43%	56.4 34.02%	299.7 50.87%	12.0 22.05%	36.58%	36%
Chubu	22.9 18.29%	464 16.84%	97.8 19.05%	12.1 20.09%	167.5 19.44%	206.4 17.16%	30.5 18.39%	81.5 13.83%	12.6 23.16%	18.47%	19%
Kinki	20.4 16.29%	440 15.97%	80.7 15.72%	9.2 15.28%	140.9 16.35%	196.7 16.35%	29.2 17.61%	82.9 14.07%	7.6 13.97%	15.79%	16%
Chugoku	7.4 5.91%	143 5.19%	28.6 5.57%	3.5 5.81%	49.9 5.79%	59.0 4.90%	10.7 6.45%	26.1 4.43%	4.6 8.45%	5.83%	6%
Shikoku	3.9 3.11%	79 2.86%	13.7 2.67%	1.8 2.99%	27.0 3.13%	34.1 2.83%	5.2 3.13%	13.8 2.34%	2.6 4.78%	3.09%	3%
Kyushu Okinawa	14.5 11.58%	261 9.47%	47.8 9.31%	6.6 10.96%	88.1 10.23%	87.9 7.31%	16.5 9.95%	45.3 7.69%	7.2 13.23%	9.98%	10%
Nationwide total	125.2 100%	2755 100%	513.3 100%	60.2 100%	861.5 100%	1202.6 100%	165.8 100%	589.1 100%	54.4 100%	100%	100%

Sources:
Kinyu Journal (December 2017); (1) population as of January 1, 2017 (Ministry of Internal Affairs and Communications); (2) number of companies as of March 31, 2016 (National Tax Agency); (3) gross prefectural product and the number of workers for fiscal 2014 (Cabinet Office); (4) personal insurance in force as of March 31, 2017 (Life Insurance Association of Japan); (5) total amount of deposits and loans for domestic bank accounts only as of March 31, 2017; (6) total number of locations, including head offices, branches, and satellite offices, as of March 31, 2017

Table 5.4 YSBC bank balance sheet divided into eight regions based on regional share (trillion yen). Steps to creating data: (1) use combined balance sheets as base data, as proposed in Scenario 3; (2) use percentage share of eight regions (in whole numbers) calculated on basis of market indicators; (3) divide each balance sheet item into eight regions based on percentage share (as shown in the following table); (4) outcome is the initial balance sheets for super-regional banks in the eight regions

Item	FY ending March 2017 *	Hokkaido 4%	Tohoku 6%	Kanto 36%	Chubu 19%	Kinki 16%	Chugoku 6%	Shikoku 3%	Kyushu-Okinawa 10%	Item	FY ending March 2017 *	Hokkaido 4%	Tohoku 6%	Kanto 36%	Chubu 19%	Kinki 16%	Chugoku 6%	Shikoku 3%	Kyushu-Okinawa 10%
Cash and deposits due from banks	53.0	2.1	3.2	19.1	10.0	8.5	3.2	1.6	5.3	Deposits	184.5	7.4	11.0	66.4	35.0	29.5	11.0	5.6	18.4
Securities	140.3	5.6	8.4	50.5	26.7	22.4	8.4	4.2	14.0	Bonds	4.7	0.2	0.3	1.7	0.9	0.7	0.3	0.1	0.5
JGBs	69.7	2.8	4.2	25.1	13.2	11.1	4.2	2.1	7.0	Borrowings	1.4	0.04	0.06	0.4	0.2	0.2	0.06	0.04	0.1
Local bonds	1.3	0.05	0.08	0.5	0.3	0.2	0.08	0.02	0.1	Other liabilities	19.4	0.8	1.2	7.0	3.7	3.1	1.2	0.6	1.9
Corporate bonds	11.3	0.5	0.7	4.1	2.1	1.8	0.7	0.3	1.1	Liabilities	210	8.4	12.5	75.5	39.8	33.5	12.5	6.4	20.9
Other	53.0	2.1	3.2	19.1	10	8.5	3.2	1.6	5.3										
Loans	13.4	0.5	0.8	4.8	2.5	2.2	0.8	0.4	1.3	Capital	3.7	0.15	0.22	1.13	0.7	0.6	0.22	0.11	0.37
Other assets	15.2	0.6	0.9	5.5	2.9	2.4	0.9	0.5	1.6	Surplus, etc.	5.9	0.23	0.35	2.12	1.12	0.94	0.35	0.18	0.59
Fixed assets	0.4	0.01	0.02	0.14	0.07	0.06	0.02	0.01	0.04	Net assets	12.7	0.6	0.8	4.5	2.4	2.1	0.8	0.3	1.3
Total assets	222.3	8.9	13.3	80.0	42.2	35.6	13.3	6.7	22.2	Liabilities + net assets	222.7	8.9	13.3	80.0	42.2	35.6	13.3	6.7	22.2

*Balance sheet figures are the total for Japan Post Bank and Shoko Chukin Bank

Systems-related assets will be transferred to YSD Network Bank when it is split off

Table 5.5 Simulated reorganization of YSBC Bank and regional banks in Kinki region as a model case. New growth strategy target for Kinki region: 95 trillion yen by FY 2020 (GDP of 600 trillion yen)

Prefecture	Gross product (trillion yen) FY 2015, A	2020 new growth strategy target (trillion yen), B (B − A)	Market indicators: Population (million)	Number of companies (thousand)	Number of workers (million)
Shiga	5.9 (7.3%)	6.9 (+1.0)	1.4	21	0.6
Kyoto	10.0 (12.4%)	11.8 (+1.8)	2.5	56	1.2
Osaka	37.9 (46.9%)	44.5 (+6.6)	8.6	229	4.2
Hyogo	19.8 (24.5%)	23.3 (+3.5)	5.5	99	2.3
Nara	3.5 (4.3%)	4.1 (+0.6)	1.4	19	0.5
Wakayama	3.6 (4.6%)	4.4 (+0.8)	1.0	16	0.4
Total	80.7 (100%)	95 (+14.3)	20.4	440	9.2

Target setting: Infrastructure development (e.g., airports, roads); gross prefectural product based on FY 2015 Cabinet Office data

YSBC Kinki Bank is established and achieves an average loan-deposit ratio of 49% for the Kinki region, 14 trillion yen of loans can be invested locally. Although this requires the Kinki region to have a growth industry, applying the theory discussed in the previous chapter shows that a 14-trillion-yen increase in loans will bring Kinki's gross prefectural product up and enable the region to achieve its goal.

(a) Overview of Japan Post Bank and Other Financial Institutions in Kinki Region

Table 5.6 shows the balances of deposits and loans at financial institutions in the Kinki region by prefecture. As of March 31, 2017, the total amounts of deposits and loans at all financial institutions in the Kinki region were 196 trillion and 82 trillion yen, respectively. Excluding the deposit balance of 29 trillion yen at JP Bank, the loan-deposit ratio is low, at 49%. By prefecture, the ratio is high in Osaka, at 57%, but other prefectures' figures are below 50%, with Shiga's figure standing at 49%, Kyoto 47%, Hyogo 43%, Nara 37%, and Wakayama 34%. Loan amounts have not increased due to relocation of companies headquartered in the Kyoto-Osaka-Kobe area to Tokyo as well as the relocation of factories overseas. Looking at the data by type of financial institution, one sees that major banks, such as commercial banks, have collected 77 trillion yen from local depositors but are lending only 31 trillion yen (making their loan-deposit ratio a low 40.3%). On the other hand, regional banks are doing well with a loan-deposit ratio of 79%. This can be deemed an adverse effect of the overconcentration of commercial banks in Tokyo. Osaka's plan to rehost an expo in 2025 is expected to help the city regain economic power.

Table 5.6 Kinki's financial institutions' balance of deposits and loans (FY ending March 2017) (trillion yen)

	Shiga		Kyoto		Osaka		Hyogo		Nara		Wakayama		Total	
	Deposits	Loans	Deposits	Loans	Deposits	Loans	Deposits	Loans	Deposits	Loans	Deposits	Loans	Deposits	Loans
Major banks, etc.	0.3	0.1	6.0	1.9	51.9	22.9	16.4	5.4	2.3	0.7	0.8	0.3	77.7	31.3
Regional banks	4.3	2.5	6.5	3.7	9.8	11.5	2.8	2.7	4.1	1.9	3.0	1.2	30.5	23.5
Secondary regional banks	1.0	0.7	0.3	0.3	3.0	3.4	3.4	2.4	0.1	0.1	0.2	0.1	8.0	7.0
Shinkin banks	1.2	0.7	7.0	3.9	9.3	5.1	8.6	4.0	1.4	0.6	1.1	0.4	28.6	14.7
Credit unions/ Labour Banks	0.3	0.2	0.5	0.3	3.0	2.0	1.8	0.9	0.2	0.1	0.3	0.2	6.1	3.7
JA	1.6	0.2	1.3	0.2	4.8	0.6	5.7	1.1	1.4	0.3	1.6	0.2	16.4	2.6
Japan Post Bank	1.7	—	3.7	—	12.4	—	7.7	—	2.1	—	1.6	—	29.2	14.3*
Total	10.5	4.4	25.4	10.3	94.3	45.6	46.4	16.6	11.6	3.6	8.7	2.4	196.5	82.8

Source:
Kinyu Journal (2017). Deposit and loan figures are for bank accounts only. Figures for major banks are the totals for commercial banks, trust banks, and other banks
Note: Figures may not add up precisely to the totals due to rounding
*Making YSBC Kinki Bank a super-regional bank will increase its funds by 14+ trillion yen
Excluding Japan Post Bank loan-deposit ratio 49%

(b) JP Bank's Competition with Regional Banks in the Kinki Region

Table 5.7 compares JP Bank and regional banks in the Kinki region in terms of deposit and loan balances and number of branches by prefecture as of March 31, 2017.

JP Bank's deposit balance is 29 trillion yen, while regional banks' deposit balance is 38 trillion yen. Since the regional banks' deposit balance includes 7 trillion yen deposited with their branches outside the Kinki region, the total of deposits at 10 regional banks in the Kinki region comes to 31 trillion yen, which is about the same as JP Bank's deposit balance. Their loan balance of 30 trillion yen, after the loan balance at their branches outside the Kinki region totaling 11 trillion yen is deducted, is 19 trillion yen, which indicates that they are doing their part to invest locally raised funds locally.

(c) YSBC Kinki Bank (Super-Regional Bank) Created via Privatization and Company Split

In reality, YSBC Kinki Bank has to either have its government bonds redeemed by the government or sell them to the BOJ in order to create funds for lending, but it can use 8.2 trillion yen (Kinki's 6% share) of the 51 trillion yen JP Bank deposited with the BOJ for lending purposes.

- When it comes to the number of branches in the Kinki region, JP Bank has 44 locations under its direct management and 3384 outlets operated by its agents whereas, 10 regional banks have a combined total of 1258 locations. If these regional banks are consolidated into three banking groups as a result of reorganization, each group will have roughly 400 branch locations. That means YSBC Kinki Bank should increase its directly managed branches to about 200. The postal service already operates about 200 post offices with mail collection and delivery functions in the Kinki region, which have enough space for them to be converted into YSBC Kinki Bank's directly managed branches and could also hire more workers. Regional banks in the Kinki region have 21,190 employees. Two of these banks are expected to be culled as a result of reorganization, and about 1000 workers are expected to lose their jobs. Therefore, the number of employees who will face redundancy should be less than the number of people who will be hired by YSBC Kinki Bank. On top of that, Kinki's postal savings operations can be easily split to form YSBC Kinki Bank because they have been conducted via independent organizations with sales and administrative systems all handled by the Kinki Postal Services Bureau.
- While there could be cause for concern that, once launched, YSBC Kinki Bank would become a competitor of local regional banks, it will gradually lose its assets since it holds a huge amount of government bonds. Regional banks must expand their operations through mergers beyond prefectural borders to enjoy economies of scale if they want to stay afloat. For decentralization purposes, the Kinki region should ideally have three to four local financial institutions competing with one another, and that should help revitalize its economy.

Table 5.7 Loan (trillion yen) and branch number of Japan Post Bank and regional banks in Kinki region (March 2017)

					Number of branches			
	JP Bank	Regional banks			JP Bank			
Prefecture	Deposit balance	Deposit balance, A	Loan balance, B	Loan-deposit ratio, B/A (%)	Total	Directly managed branches	Agencies	Regional banks
Shiga	1.7	5.3	3.2	60.4	259	1	258	160
Kyoto	3.7	6.8	4.0	58.8	472	4	468	162
Osaka	12.4	12.8	14.9	116.4	1108	24	1084	478
Hyogo	7.7	6.2	5.1	82.2	956	12	944	268
Nara	2.1	4.2	2.0	47.6	318	2	316	107
Wakayama	1.6	3.2	1.3	40.6	315	1	314	83
Total	29.2	38.5	30.5	79.2	3428	44	3384	1258

Source: *Kinyu Journal* (2017)

Table 5.8 YSBC Kinki Bank and regional banks' reorganization in Kinki (FY ending March 2017) (trillion yen)

	YSBC Kinki Bank's initial balance sheet	Regional banks				
		Shiga Bank	Bank of Kyoto	Kansai Mirai FG (Kinki Osaka/ Kansai Urban/ Minato Bank)	Senshu Ikeda/ Nanto/ Kiyo Bank	Total
Cash and deposits due from banks	8.5	0.5	0.8	1.2	2.1	4.7
Securities	22.4	1.5	2.9	1.4	3.9	9.9
(JGBs)	(11.1)	(0.4)	(0.8)	(0.5)	(1.1)	(2.8)
Loans	2.2	3.5	5.0	8.8	9.9	28.3
Other	2.4	0.1	0.2	0.2	0.3	0.9
Total assets	35.6	5.5	8.9	11.6	16.2	43.8
Deposits	29.5	4.5	6.6	10.4	13.4	36.4
Other liabilities	4.0	0.4	1.5	0.7	2.2	5.1
Total liabilities	33.5	5.2	8.1	11.1	15.5	41.5
Total net assets	2.1	0.4	0.8	0.5	0.7	2.3
Total liabilities and equity	35.6	5.5	8.9	11.6	16.2	43.8

Source: Financial statements of regional banks

When established though the aforementioned process, YSBC Kinki Bank will initially have the balance sheet shown in Table 5.8. (A combined balance sheet of regional banks and secondary regional banks in the Kinki region, which has been created on the basis of Table 5.8, is also shown in what follows for comparison purposes.)

The bank will start off with total assets of 36 trillion yen. As a result of the merger with Shoko Chukin Bank, YSBC Kinki Bank will be staffed with personnel needed for lending operations and also have former Shoko Chukin employees responsible for SME loans.

- Comparing YSBC Kinki Bank's balance sheet and the combined balance sheet of 10 regional banks in the Kinki region as of March 31, 2017 (Table 5.8) shows that their assets are about the same. The difference between YSBC and regional banks is that instead of lending, it uses its funds for government bonds and other securities. Since personal savings in the Kinki region are not directly used for loans to local industries but instead invested in government bonds, the bank is not building credit.
- In estimating the revenues of YSBC Kinki Bank established through privatization and regional split, 49.9 billion yen, which is 16% (i.e., the percentage share of the Kinki region) of JP Bank's net profit of 312.3 billion yen for the fiscal year ending March 31, 2017, can be regarded as its net profit, as shown in Table 5.9. The Kinki region's 10 regional banks, on the other hand, generated a combined total of 94.2 billion yen in net profit, which is 1.8 times larger than YSBC Kinki Bank's net profit, according to their balance sheets for the fiscal year ending

Table 5.9 Simulated regional bank reorganization in Kinki: income statement (March 2017) (10 billion yen)

	Kyoto + Shiga			Kansai Mirai FG				Senshu Ikeda + Nanto+ Kiyo				
	Kyoto	Shiga	Total	Kinki Osaka	Kansai Urban *	Minato*	Total	Senshu Ikeda	Nanto	Kiyo	Total	Total
Ordinary revenue	10.2	7.4	17.6	5.9	7.7	5.3	18.9	8.8	7.4	6.7	22.9	61.9
Ordinary expenses	7.7	5.5	13.2	5.2	6.0	4.3	15.5	7.1	5.8	5.5	18.5	49.2
Ordinary profit	2.5	1.9	4.4	0.7	1.8	1.0	3.4	1.6	1.6	1.2	4.4	12.6
Net profit	1.8	1.4	3.2	0.8	1.4	0.7	2.8	1.1	1.2	1.0	3.3	9.4

*Secondary regional banks

Source: Financial statements of regional banks

Japan Post Bank income statement (10 billion yen)

	JP Bank profit and loss	Kinki's 16% share
Ordinary revenue	189.7	30.4
Ordinary expenses	145.5	23.3
Ordinary profit	44.2	7.1
Net profit	31.2	5.0

ROA (%)

Kansai Mirai Bank	0.296
Kinki total	0.287
JP Bank Kinki	0.198

Profit and loss figures of current JP Bank after it is regionally split

  March 31, 2017 (Table 5.9). The ROA for the same fiscal year is 0.296% at Kansai Mirai Financial Group and 0.287% for all regional banks in the Kinki region, both of which are low. When simulated using the region's percentage share for JP Bank based on its total assets of 35.6 trillion yen and ordinary profit of 70.7 billion yen, its ROA is even lower at 0.198%. This profitability gap is deemed to come from the difference in their loan balances.

  While JP Bank invests postal savings in government and foreign bonds to generate profits at a low net interest margin that exposes it to risk, it can improve its portfolio and increase profits if it merges with Shoko Chukin Bank and uses more funds for lending.

- Some may be concerned about whether JP Bank will really be able to use funds for lending, but based on the knowledge I gained through my career in the banking industry, serving as the head of the business planning department and general manager of three branches, commercial banks with a financial intermediary function can endlessly create lending opportunities by matchmaking companies they do business with. I experienced real joy working in the financial industry through mediating business deals across the globe and helping emerging companies go public. It gave me the sense that I played a part in supporting national and local economies.

<<Simulation of Eight YSBC Regional Banks across Japan>>

To summarize the vision for the YSD Financial Group's YSBC regional banks (super-regional banks), I compiled the initial balances of the eight YSBC regional banks, which were calculated according to the same steps used for YSBC Kinki Bank (Table 5.10).

Their balances can be simulated in the same way as I did with YSBC Kinki Bank since mergers and reorganizations of regional banks beyond prefectural borders have also been occurring in regions other than Kinki. The Fukuoka Financial Group based in the Kyushu region was created as a result of a merger among three regional banks in Fukuoka, Nagasaki, and Kumamoto Prefectures. The Kyushu Financial Group

Table 5.10 Simulation of regional YSBC banks after restructuring based on March 2017 figures (trillion yen)

	Regional YSBC banks' balance sheets			
YSBC	Total assets	Securities	Loans	Deposits
Hokkaido	8.9	5.6	0.5	7.4
Tohoku	13.3	8.4	0.8	11.0
Kanto	80.0	50.5	4.8	66.4
Chubu	42.2	26.7	2.5	35.0
Kinki	35.6	22.4	2.2	29.5
Chugoku	13.3	8.4	0.8	11.0
Shikoku	6.7	4.2	0.4	5.6
Kyushu/Okinawa	22.2	14.0	1.3	18.4

Source: Financial statements of regional banks

was formed after banks in Kagoshima and Kumamoto Prefectures were merged. In the Kanto region the Concordia Financial Group was established as a result of a merger between banks in Kanagawa and Tokyo. Mebuki Financial Group was formed through a merger between banks based in Tochigi and Ibaraki. Other reorganizations and mergers have been carried out in the Tohoku, Chubu, and Chugoku regions as well, making it possible for us to do simulations. (Further details will be discussed later on.)

Simulating the unforeseen future of privatized public financial services by analyzing actual mergers and reorganizations of private banks means simulating how the ROA of each type of financial institution can be optimized through restructuring the three privatized banks.

Below are two other possible scenarios, though unrealistic, in which JP Bank avoids the risk of remaining in operation while maintaining its current assets.

Possible institutional designs

JP Bank becomes fully privatized and expands operations targeting individuals and SMEs ⇒ becoming a retail bank, reducing the current asset size

Integrating the three privatized banks after their full privatization

JP Bank, the DBJ, and Shoko Chukin Bank merge after full privatization ⇒ becoming a megabank

Scenario 2: Vision for specializing in retail banking (online banking for payment and settlement operations)

If JP Bank continues to maintain a huge amount of assets and restricted business operations, it is likely to face a larger interest-expense risk due to the huge amount of assets it holds as well as a risk associated with investing in government and foreign bonds. Even if the bank places more emphasis on doing business with individual customers, its profitability will decline because it will find it difficult to reduce the ratio of operating expenses to ordinary revenue.

As social infrastructure for online banking via smartphones, tablets, and computer terminals develops, and as other industries enter the retail banking (transaction banking) market through the use of fintech, banks like JP Bank that have large-scale computer systems and branch networks will lose their competitive edge.

If JP Bank wants to continue independently operating in the retail banking market, it will have to transform itself into a bank driven by IoT, AI, and big data. The good news is that both megabanks and emerging retailers are still new to the market. JP Bank has 60 million customers, almost half of Japan's population, which gives the bank a leg up over other banks, but its current system supporting enormous customer data is too big and will cost the bank too much both in terms of personnel and infrastructure to shift to a new technology. Therefore, JP Bank will not be able to survive by retail banking alone.

Although an online bank will be established as a result of the restructuring of the three privatized banks, this bank will only provide transaction banking services even if its operations are retail oriented since it mainly provides settlement services. The online bank, whose primary source of income will be fees, will be agile and able to remain in business by focusing on online banking only.

Scenario 3: Vision for creating a megabank through a merger of JP Bank, DBJ, and Shoko Chukin Bank

Focusing on making a shift from public to private, postal reform and policy-based finance reform aim to fully privatize JP Bank, the DBJ, and Shoko Chukin Bank. When combined, their total assets come to 238 trillion yen (as of the fiscal year March 31, 2017), which is far larger (about 1.5 times) than the assets of the Bank of Tokyo-Mitsubishi UFJ, Sumitomo Mitsui Banking Corporation (SMBC), and Mizuho Bank, respectively standing at 204 trillion yen, 162 trillion yen, and 162 trillion yen. The three banks' combined loan balance is 26 trillion yen, which is about a third of the loan balance at the Bank of Tokyo-Mitsubishi UFJ, SMBC, and Mizuho Bank, respectively standing at 82 trillion yen, 75 trillion yen, and 71 trillion yen. The reason for this gap is the difference in the amount of government bonds and foreign bonds held by each bank. It's not easy for them to change their portfolios.

To realize this megabank vision, the first thing the three privatized banks must do is build a lending capability so their earnings structure can be shifted from one that focuses on interest from securities to one that focuses on revenues from commercial banking operations. They must shift to an earning structure that can sustain their publicly listed status and develop a personnel and risk management capability so they can compete with other megabanks. Even if their assets become comparable to those of megabanks when they merge, it will be difficult to build a strong operating foundation through efficient fund raising and lending alone. Aiming to become a huge bank that combines a megabank and Norinchukin Bank does not mean eliminating bloated pubic financial services and pressure on private financial services. It is also likely that the megabank created through a merger of the three privatized banks will not be able to sustain its listed status due to an earnings structure that is exposed to major risks such as an interest-rate risk related to fixed-amount postal savings. Therefore this scenario is not very feasible.

2 Future of Regional Bank Reorganization and Institutional Design

2.1 *Visions for Reorganizing Regional Banks*

Section 2.3 of Chap. 3 discusses in detail the visions of the Financial Services Agency and the Regional Banks Association of Japan concerning the reorganization of regional banks. A third of the 105 regional banks have already undergone some form of merger and reorganization. The chapter also theoretically explains why it is important for regional banks to merge or reorganize within broader administrative divisions and maintain assets needed to achieve a certain ROA level after reorganization.

In fact the BOJ's zero-interest-rate policy and powerful negative-interest-rate policy have weakened the financial health of regional banks, and their profitability is going downhill. Slightly less than a third of regional banks are small with a low rating and must find some kind of management strategy that will keep them afloat. A little over a third of regional banks are of sound financial health and are actively looking into ways to expand operations. This is summarized in Table 5.11.

- According to the Financial Services Agency's April 2018 model-based estimation, regional banks in 20 prefectures (under the current prefectural system) will die out in the future market due to the declining as well as aging population.
  On top of that, according to "*Rokaru keizaiken no kasegu chikara soshutsu* [Building earning power in local economies]" released by the Ministry of Economy, Trade and Industry, an analysis found a correlation between the total assets held by regional banks and their net profit. The analysis compares average financial results for fiscal 2013 between regional banks whose total assets exceed 10 trillion yen and all regional banks. Total assets and net profit of regional banks with total assets worth more than 10 trillion yen were respectively 3.5 and 4.7 times higher than the average for all regional banks.
- Looking at the preceding table by bank shows that among the banks that are operated in the same way as usual, 15 have total assets of less than 7 trillion yen with a rating of BBB or below, while 26 have the same level of assets with a rating of A− to A. These 41 banks are likely to be absorbed and merged into another bank in the future, although they could survive under a holding company. Small banks that were merged with other banks have already succumbed to the same fate, and 17 banks whose assets and rating are at the same level as these 41 banks are likely to be absorbed by another bank. This will leave us with 30 listed regional banks.
  When estimated on the basis of regional banks' combined total assets for the fiscal year ending March 31, 2017, amounting to 386 trillion yen, the number of regional banks whose assets total 10 trillion yen will be reduced to about 40, while the number of regional banks whose assets total 15 trillion yen will be around 25. While this simulation is based on a simple division of total assets, the basic indicators banks currently use for making merger and reorganization decisions are still total assets and ROA (plus rating) shown in their earnings summaries.
- The BOJ's drastic monetary easing as well as Abenomics have been the driving forces behind the ongoing depreciation of the yen, hikes in share prices, and thriving economy. However, these policies differ from the structural reforms implemented by the Koizumi Cabinet, such as the postal reform and policy-based finance reform.
  If the government were to launch another "arrow" under Abenomics that would go hand in hand with its growth strategy, it should be aimed at aggressively implementing the structural reform of local financial services, especially regional

Table 5.11 Mergers and reorganizations among 91 listed regional banks (March 31, 2016). Correlation between regional banks' assets and rating

	Long-term rating as of April 2017	BBB⁻ – BBB	A⁻ – A	A⁺ – AA	Total
Merged/ reorganized banks	Total assets of 7 trillion yen or more	–	1 bank	3 banks	4 banks
	Less than 7 trillion yen	7 banks	10 banks	6 banks	23 banks
	Total	7 banks	11 banks	9 banks	27 banks
Banks operated in the same way as usual	Total assets of 7 trillion yen or more	–	1 bank	8 banks	9 banks
	Less than 7 trillion yen	15 banks	26 banks	14 banks	55 banks
	Total	15 banks	27 banks	22 banks	64 banks
Total		22 banks	38 banks	31 banks	91 banks

Table 5.11 Suppl Correlation between regional banks' assets and rating

1. Reorganized regional banks

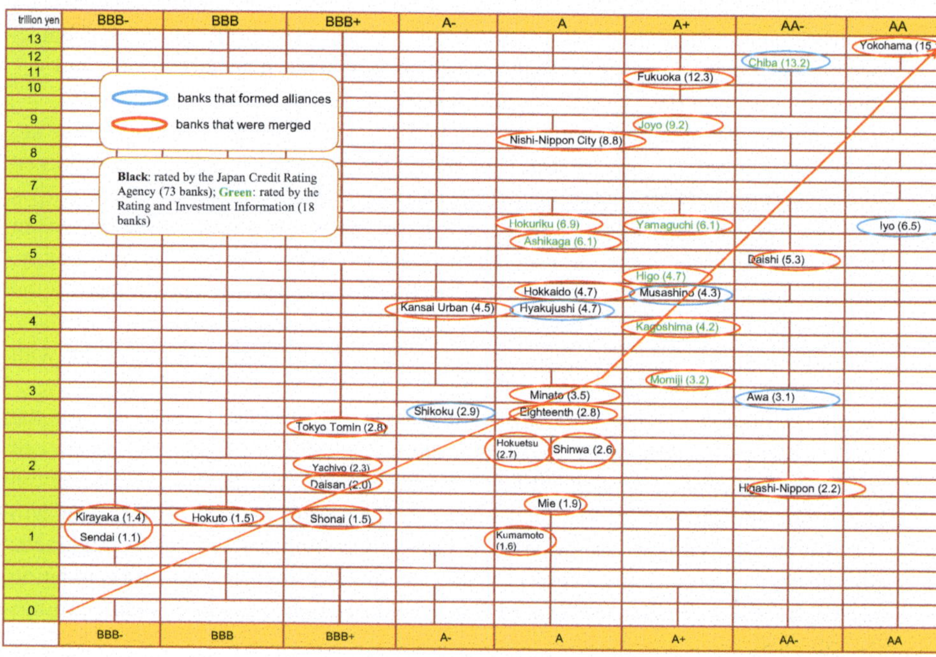

(continued)

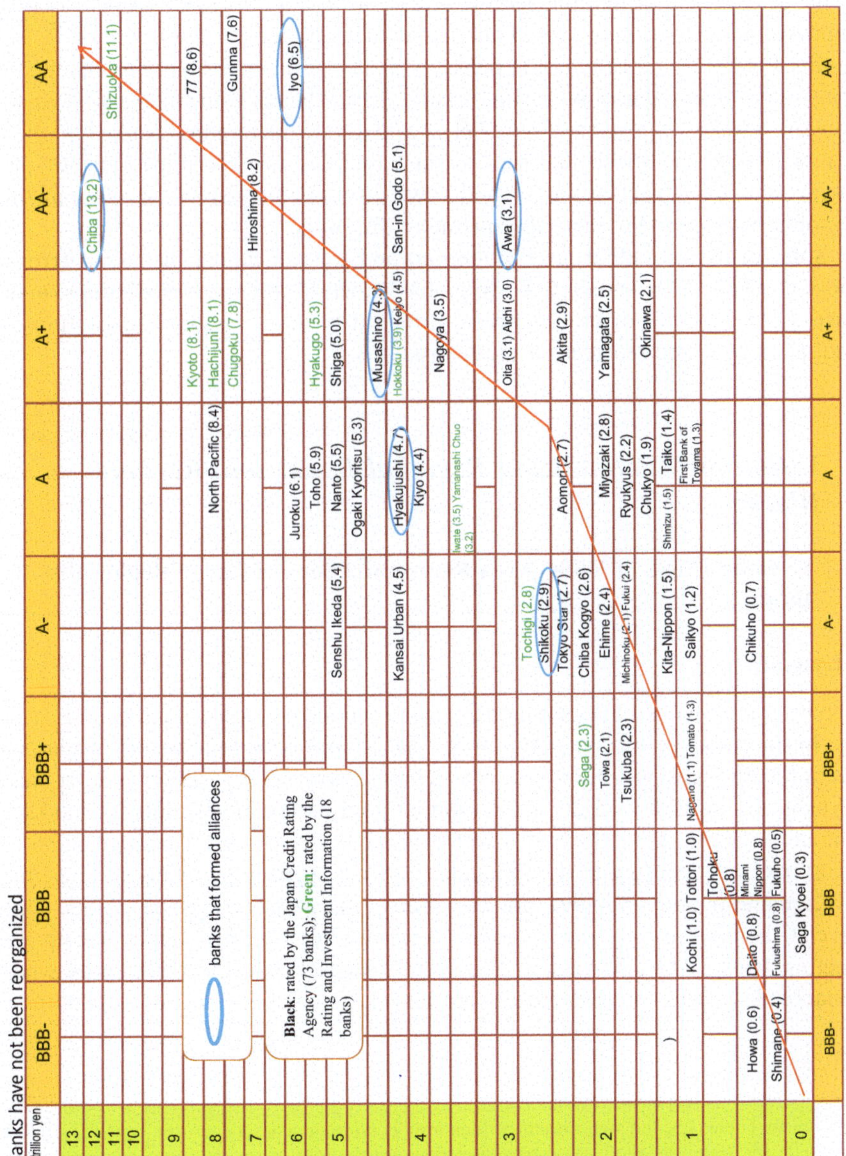
2. Banks have not been reorganized
trillion yen
BBB-
BBB
BBB+
A-
A
A+
AA-
AA
banks that formed alliances
Black: rated by the Japan Credit Rating Agency (73 banks); Green: rated by the Rating and Investment Information (18 banks)
Chiba (13.2)
Shizuoka (11.1)
77 (8.6)
Kyoto (8.1)
Hachijuni (8.1)
North Pacific (8.4)
Chugoku (7.8)
Gunma (7.6)
Hiroshima (8.2)
Iyo (6.5)
Juroku (6.1)
Toho (5.9)
Hyakugo (5.3)
Senshu Ikeda (5.4)
Nanto (5.5)
Shiga (5.0)
Ogaki Kyoritsu (5.3)
Musashino (4.3)
San-in Godo (5.1)
Kansai Urban (4.5)
Hyakujushi (4.7)
Hokkoku (3.9)
Keiyo (4.5)
Kiyo (4.4)
Nagoya (3.5)
Iwate (3.5)
Yamanashi Chuo (3.2)
Oita (3.1)
Aichi (3.0)
Awa (3.1)
Tochigi (2.8)
Shikoku (2.9)
Tokyo Star (2.7)
Aomori (2.7)
Akita (2.9)
Saga (2.3)
Chiba Kogyo (2.6)
Miyazaki (2.8)
Yamagata (2.5)
Towa (2.1)
Ehime (2.4)
Tsukuba (2.3)
Michinoku (2.1)
Fukui (2.4)
Ryukyus (2.2)
Chukyo (1.9)
Okinawa (2.1)
Kita-Nippon (1.5)
Shimizu (1.5)
Taiko (1.4)
Kochi (1.0)
Tottori (1.0)
Nagano (1.1)
Tomato (1.3)
Saikyo (1.2)
First Bank of Toyama (1.3)
Tohoku (0.8)
Howa (0.6)
Daito (0.8)
Minami Nippon (0.8)
Chikuho (0.7)
Shimane (0.4)
Fukushima (0.8)
Fukuho (0.5)
Saga Kyoei (0.3)
13
12
11
10
9
8
7
6
5
4
3
2
1
0

banks, as proposed by the government and the Liberal Democratic Party and restructuring financial institutions aimed at expanding their operations in order to help local companies grow and go global.

As evident from the mergers carried out in the past, since listed financial institutions disclose their financial statements by following the same accounting standard required by the Detailed Regulations of the Banking Act, their accounting items can be combined without any problem when multiple banks merge. The Bank of Yokohama has the largest assets among all regional banks, totaling approximately 16 trillion yen. This means that no monster bank will arise as a result of the merging of regional banks. This is a good opportunity to change the long-standing practice of protecting small regional banks with small assets via the convoy system. I'll just spell it out below and divide the regional banks into those that will sink and those that will swim based on five classifications[5] of past mergers and reorganizations. I will then discuss my vision for reorganizing regional banks into broader administrative divisions.

Some of the individual cases of mergers and reorganizations discussed here are those that have been agreed to between banks, while others are predictions on the basis of an analysis of trends among different types of financial institutions as well as merger and reorganization theory.

2.2 *Vision for Reorganizing Regional Banks into Regional Blocs*

2.2.1 Existing Cases of Wide-Area Reorganizations of Large Regional Banks

(A) **Kyushu**

The Kyushu region has 11 regional banks and 7 secondary regional banks, for a total of 18. In the fiscal year ending March 31, 2017, combined total assets of regional banks in Kyushu was 59 trillion yen, which breaks down to 3.2 trillion yen per bank.

Kyushu accounts for 15.2% of combined total assets of all regional banks in Japan, and its ROA, at 0.335%, is lower than the 0.354% overall average ROA for regional banks. According to the Financial Services Agency's model-based estimation, Kumamoto and Okinawa are the prefectures where regional banks could survive if there were only one in each prefecture but wouldn't make it with two competing banks. Oita, Miyazaki, Saga, and Nagasaki are the prefectures where regional banks would not generate any profit even if there were only one operating in

[5]As shown in Table 3.5, the five classifications are: 1. wide area/asset increase type, 2. adjacent prefectures/asset increase type, 3. adjacent prefectures/bailout type, 4. same prefecture/asset increase type, and 5. same prefecture/bailout type.

each of these prefectures. Fukuoka and Kagoshima are the prefectures where two regional banks could coexist.

- As shown in Table 5.12, combined total assets of banks operating under the Fukuoka Financial Group (including the Eighteenth Bank) are 21 trillion yen, accounting for 36.1% of total assets in the Kyushu region. When combined, ordinary profit of the Fukuoka Financial Group's four banks comes to 78.7 billion yen, with an ROA of 0.371%, which is relatively high. The financial group operates in the three prefectures of Fukuoka, Kumamoto, and Nagasaki, covering a wide area of operation. Once the group builds a solid operating foundation in northern Kyushu, it will have the potential to expand into ASEAN and other overseas countries by taking advantage of its proximity. If the group enhances operating efficiency by effectively using the 3747 employees of the three banks operating under its umbrella (1051 employees at Kumamoto Bank, 1387 employees at Shinwa Bank, and 1309 employees at the Eighteenth Bank), it will have great potential to grow into a banking group with total assets of 20 trillion yen, even though each of the affiliated banks currently has total assets of less than 3 trillion yen.
- The Kyushu Financial Group is a 10-trillion-yen banking group operating Kagoshima Bank (with total assets of 4.3 trillion yen and ROA of 0.371%; note that, henceforth, figures in parentheses denote total assets, ROA, and number of employees for fiscal year ending March 31, 2017) and Higo Bank (5.2 trillion yen, 0.232%) under a holding company.
  The two banks decided to merge with a vision of implementing a locally based business model over a wide area that crosses prefectural borders while addressing the issue of a declining population. These banks, operating on a similar scale, can work together to enhance operating efficiency and help revitalize the local economy of southern Kyushu.
- Nishi-Nippon City Bank merged eight companies, including the Bank of Nagasaki, which is a secondary regional bank, as well as credit card, securities, and credit guarantee companies, to form Nishi-Nippon Financial Holdings.
  The Kyushu region still has Oita Bank (3.2 trillion yen, 0.284%) in Oita Prefecture and Miyazaki Bank (3 trillion yen, 0.413%) in Miyazaki Prefecture. These banks will eventually have to merge with another bank since, according to the model-based estimation, Oita and Miyazaki were found to be the prefectures where regional banks would not generate a profit even if there were only one operating in each of those prefectures. Nishi-Nippon City Bank could be a merger candidate for both banks.

  Otherwise, operating in neighboring prefectures at a similar scale, they could merge under a holding company just as the Kyushu Financial Group was formed. The Nishi-Nippon Financial Holdings could also take over secondary regional banks in Oita and Miyazaki (Howa Bank: 0.6 trillion yen, 0.140%, 497 employees; Miyazaki Taiyo Bank: 0.7 trillion yen, 0.371%, 628 employees) to expand operations.

Table 5.12 Simulated regional bank reorganization in Kyushu (March 2017) balance sheet

	Fukuoka FG (trillion yen)					Kyushu FG (trillion yen)			Nishi-Nippon FH (trillion yen)		
	Fukuoka	Kumamoto	Shinwa	Eighteenth	Total	Higo	Kagoshima	Total	Nishi-Nippon City	Nagasaki	Total
Securities	2.5	0.3	0.7	1.0	4.5	1.6	1.0	2.6	1.7	0.0	1.7
(JGBs)	(1.3)	(0.2)	(0.6)	(0.4)	(2.5)	(0.7)	(0.3)	(1.0)	(0.6)	0.0	(0.6)
Loans	8.9	1.2	1.5	1.5	13.1	3.1	3.1	6.2	6.6	0.2	6.8
Other	2.6	0.2	0.4	0.4	3.6	0.6	0.2	0.8	0.9	0.1	1.0
Total assets	14.0	1.7	2.6	2.9	21.2	5.3	4.3	9.6	9.2	0.3	9.5
Deposits	9.6	1.4	2.2	2.5	15.7	4.3	3.6	7.9	7.4	0.2	7.6
Other liabilities	3.8	0.2	0.2	0.3	4.5	0.7	0.4	1.1	1.3	0.1	1.4
Total liabilities	13.4	1.6	2.4	2.8	20.2	5.0	4.0	9.0	8.7	0.3	9.0
Total net assets	0.6	0.1	0.1	0.2	1.0	0.3	0.3	0.6	0.5	0.0	0.5
Total liabilities and equity	14.0	1.7	2.6	2.9	21.2	5.3	4.3	9.6	9.2	0.3	9.5
Income statement (ten billion yen)											
Ordinary revenue	17.3	2.4	3.6	4.3	27.6	7.7	7.3	15.0	13.6	0.5	14.1
Ordinary profit	6.0	0.3	0.9	0.7	7.9	1.2	1.6	2.8	3.4	0.05	3.4
Net income	4.4	0.15	0.74	0.52	5.8	0.87	1.08	1.95	2.51	0.04	2.55
ROA (%)	0.429	0.152	0.366	0.221	—	0.232	0.371	—	0.367	0.183	—

Source: Financial statements of regional banks

- While there is no specific scenario for reorganizing regional banks in Kyushu, options are few. Banks operating under three or four holding companies would compete against one another to dominate the market. As for Okinawa, the combined total assets of its three regional banks amount to 4.7 trillion yen. A reorganization could take place with the Bank of the Ryukyus at the center.
- Just as with the Kinki region discussed earlier, the Kyushu region would have YSBC Kyushu-Okinawa Bank (with total assets of 22 trillion yen) operating under the YSD Financial Group, which would happen through a restructuring. Holding the same amount of assets as Fukuoka Financial Group, it would compete with three to four financial groups of regional banks in Kyushu on an equal footing.

  Even if other regional banks in Kyushu had an oligopoly, YSBC Kyushu-Okinawa Bank would serve as an alternative bank for local customers, dispelling the Japan Fair Trade Commission's concerns.

  Chikuho Bank (0.7 trillion yen, 0.158%, 594 employees), Saga Kyoei Bank (0.3 trillion yen, 0.194%, 408 employees), and Minami Nippon Bank (0.8 trillion yen, 0.375%, 658 employees) could be merged into YSBC Kyushu-Okinawa Bank, and the merger would be beneficial to both sides. Such a merger would give YSBC Kyushu-Okinawa Bank the financial foundation and organizational capability needed for lending operations and enable it to quickly diversify its portfolio, making it comparable to those of large regional banks (Table 5.13).

(B) **Kinki Region**

As shown in Table 5.14, the total assets of 10 regional banks in the Kinki region amounted to 44 trillion yen for the fiscal year ending March 31, 2017, with 7 regional banks holding 35 trillion yen and 3 secondary banks 8.6 trillion yen.

The Financial Services Agency released its model-based estimation in April 2018. According to the estimation, Shiga, Kyoto, and Hyogo are the prefectures where regional banks could survive if there were only one in each prefecture but wouldn't survive if there were two competing banks. Nara and Wakayama are the prefectures where regional banks would not generate any profit, even if there were only one operating in each prefecture. Using this model as a reference, I will look at every angle as I simulate possible reorganizations of regional banks in light of what I know as well as actual reorganizations that have already taken place in the region.

- On September 26, 2017, Kansai Mirai Financial Group (12 trillion yen, 0.293% – three banks combined) began phasing in a merger that will make Kinki Osaka Bank (3.5 trillion yen, 0.183%) and Kansai Urban Banking Corporation (4.6 trillion yen, 0.385%) in Osaka Prefecture as well as Minato Bank (3.5 trillion yen, 0.282%) in Hyogo Prefecture its wholly owned subsidiaries. Kinki Osaka Bank and Kansai Urban Banking Corporation were merged in April 2019. Resona Holdings and SMBC are major shareholders of the Kansai Mirai Financial Group, each holding a 51% and 22.3–26.3% stake.

  This means that SMBC gave up Kansai Urban Bank and Minato Bank, with which it has strong capital and personal relationships, to the Kansai Mirai

Table 5.13 Regional bank reorganization and YSBC Kyushu-Okinawa Bank in Kyushu/Okinawa (March 2017)

Balance sheet (trillion yen)					
YSBC Kyushu-Okinawa Bank Initial		Fukuoka FG	Kyushu FG	Nishi-Nippon FH	Total
14.0	Securities	4.5	2.6	1.7	13.1
(7.0)	(JGBs)	(2.5)	(1.0)	(0.6)	(5.5)
1.3	Loans	13.1	6.2	6.8	37.9
6.8	Other	3.6	0.8	1.0	7.6
22.2	Total assets	21.2	9.6	9.5	58.6
18.4	Deposits	15.7	7.9	7.6	46.9
2.5	Other liabilities	4.5	1.1	1.4	8.6
20.9	Total liabilities	20.2	9.0	9.0	55.5
1.3	Total net assets	1.0	0.6	0.5	3.1
22.2	Total liabilities and equity	21.2	9.6	9.5	58.6

Japan Post Bank income statement (10 billion yen)		
	JP Bank profit and loss	Kyushu/Okinawa's 10% share
Ordinary revenue	189.7	18.9
Ordinary profit	44.2	4.4
Net profit	31.2	3.1

Income statement (10 billion yen)			
	Fukuoka FG	Kyushu FG	Nishi-Nippon FH
Ordinary revenue	27.6	15.0	14.1
Ordinary profit	7.9	2.8	3.4
Net income	5.8	1.95	2.55

Source: Financial statements of regional banks

Financial Group that is controlled by Resona Holdings. Forty years ago I worked full-time on making arrangements for merging Kansai Bank, which later became Kansai Urban Bank, with Sumitomo Bank. I was working on the frontlines of a merger between Daiwa Bank (later Resona Bank) and Sumitomo Bank (later SMBC) that eventually fell through. I was also involved in the merger between Sakura (later SMBC) and Sumitomo Banks. In light of what we know about how the Kansai Mirai Financial Group was formed as well as past events, this reorganization suggests three things. First, the three banks decided that they would not be able to survive with the amounts of assets they had on hand. Second, SMBC and Resona Holdings saw the three banks as playing second fiddle to their wholesale banking operation as it shifted the focus away from retail banking. When it comes to SMBC, in particular, no other megabank can beat its strategy as its operations span Shiga, Osaka, and Hyogo Prefectures. Third, megabanks concentrate on overseas strategies so they can beat the competition in the global market, knowing that they are required to comply with international banking regulations, unlike regional banks, which follow domestic standards.

Table 5.14 Simulated regional bank reorganization in Kinki (March 2017) balance sheet. Mergers by region and financial group (trillion yen)

	Holdings or merger			Kansai Mirai FG				MUFG-affiliated				
				Resona-affiliated		SMBC-affiliated						
	Shiga	Kyoto	Total	Kinki Osaka	Kansai Urban*	Minato*	Total	Senshu Ikeda	Nanto	Kiyo	Total	Kinki total
Cash and deposits due from banks	0.5	0.8	1.3	0.4	0.4	0.4	1.2	0.7	0.7	0.7	2.1	4.7
Securities	1.5	2.9	4.3	0.7	0.2	0.5	1.4	1.0	1.7	1.3	4.0	9.9
(JGBs)	(0.4)	(0.8)	(1.2)	(0.3)	(0.0)	(0.2)	(0.5)	(0.1)	(0.6)	(0.4)	(1.1)	(2.8)
Loans	3.5	5.0	8.5	2.4	3.9	2.5	8.8	3.8	3.3	2.8	9.9	28.3
Other assets	0.1	0.2	0.3	0.1	0.1	0.1	0.2	0.1	0.1	0.1	0.3	0.9
Total assets	5.5	8.9	14.4	3.5	4.6	3.5	11.6	5.6	5.8	4.9	16.2	43.8
Deposits	4.5	6.6	11.2	3.2	4.0	3.2	10.4	4.8	4.7	3.8	13.4	36.4
Other liabilities	0.4	1.5	2.1	0.2	0.4	0.2	0.7	0.5	0.8	8.0	0.2	5.1
Total liabilities	5.2	8.1	13.3	3.4	4.4	3.4	11.2	5.3	5.5	4.6	15.6	41.5
Total net assets	0.4	0.8	1.1	0.2	0.2	0.1	0.5	0.2	0.3	0.2	0.7	2.3
Total liabilities and equity	5.5	8.9	14.4	3.5	4.6	3.5	11.6	5.6	5.8	4.9	16.2	43.8

*Secondary regional banks

Note: Taisho Bank was merged into TOMONY HD. Tajima Bank may not survive

Source: Financial statements of regional banks

- In Nara and Wakayama, two other prefectures in Kinki, Nanto Bank (5.8 trillion yen, 0.275%) and Kiyo Bank (4.8 trillion yen, 0.248%) may be culled since these two prefectures were found in the model-based estimation to be the ones where regional banks would generate no profit even if there were only one operating in each of the prefectures. MUFG Bank, which has long maintained close ties with both banks as a shareholder, will have no choice but to take the initiative in restructuring the banks while keeping an eye on future developments at Kansai Mirai Financial Group. MUFG Bank, which also has a stake in the Osaka-based Senshu Ikeda Bank (5.6 trillion yen, 0.292%), may look into the possibility of integrating these three banks in order to bolster its operations in Osaka, Nara, and Wakayama (16 trillion yen, 0.274% – three banks combined).
- In Shiga and Kyoto Prefectures, Shiga Bank (5.5 trillion yen, 0.347%) and Bank of Kyoto (8.9 trillion yen, 0.282%) have respectively established a firm position as regional financial institutions. As the model-based estimation suggests, the Bank of Kyoto may take the lead in a reorganization designed to spur economic growth in the Kyoto-Shiga area.

  The Bank of Kyoto has been behind the growth of some world-renowned blue-chip corporations. Kyoto is home to 21 manufacturers listed on the First Section of the Tokyo Stock Exchange, including Omron, Murata Manufacturing, Murata Machinery, Horiba, Rohm, Kyocera, Nidec, and Wacoal. Having developed unique industries through collaboration with the academic sector, Kyoto-based companies have built up an expertise in manufacturing over the years and have always had their eye on overseas markets. Today many of them have half of their assets outside Japan and generate more than half of their revenues overseas. These companies have helped stimulate the local economy by remaining headquartered in Kyoto. The Bank of Kyoto must further increase its total assets and ROA in order to raise and use funds locally through financial intermediary operations and achieve further growth.
- The simulation found that regional banks in the Kinki region could be consolidated into three to four groups in light of the analysis of their current financial standing.

(C) Kanto

The Kanto region has 9 regional banks and 7 secondary regional banks, for a total of 16. The combined total assets in the region amount to 84 trillion yen, with each bank holding 5.2 trillion yen on average. Six banks have already undergone reorganization.

Kanto's combined total assets of 84 trillion yen account for 21.8% of all bank assets in Japan. Boasting an ROA of 0.423%, regional banks in Kanto enjoy the highest profitability in Japan.

According to the model-based estimation, Ibaraki is one of the prefectures where regional banks could survive if there were only one in each prefecture. Gunma and Tochigi are the prefectures where regional banks would generate no profit even if there were only one operating in each of those prefectures. Saitama, Chiba, and

Kanagawa could have two regional banks competing with each other. Tokyo is the exception.

- In northern Kanto, Ibaraki Prefecture's Joyo Bank (9.7 trillion yen, 0.367%) and Tochigi's Ashikaga Bank (6.5 trillion yen, 0.512%) merged to create a holding company, Mebuki Financial Group (16 trillion yen, 0.425%). MUFG Bank, a major shareholder of both banks who has long ties with both through related businesses and provided Ashikaga Bank with financial support to help it write off its bad debts, played a part in the merger. It makes sense that a megabank would develop strong ties with regional banks to build a strong operational foundation. Gunma Bank (8 trillion yen, 0.432%), another regional bank in northern Kanto, has strong ties with SMBC through stockholding and related operations, and their moves toward reorganization are something to take note of. Since Gunma Bank focuses on the Tokyo market, Kiraboshi Financial Group, which was formed as a result of the merger between Tokyo Tomin Bank (2.8 trillion yen, 0.169%) and Yachiyo Bank (2.3 trillion yen, 0.179%), could remerge with Gunma Bank.
- Chiba Bank (14 trillion yen, 0.499%) based in eastern Kanto has formed a business alliance with Saitama's Musashino Bank (4.5 trillion yen, 0.258%). Given the proximity of the Tokyo market, it makes perfect sense for Chiba Bank to try to form a 20-trillion-yen banking group operating under a holding company.
- In southern Kanto, Concordia Financial Group was established via the merger between the Bank of Yokohama (16.4 trillion yen, 0.533%) and Higashi-Nippon Bank (2.2 trillion yen, 0.267%). According to the Kanagawa-based Bank of Yokohama, it made the merger decision in light of abundant business opportunities in the Tokyo market with an eye toward bolstering lending operations through Higashi-Nippon Bank.
- While a vision for the reorganization of regional banks in Kanto is almost in view, what remains to be seen is where the three megabanks' financial groups that compete mainly in Kanto, as well as Resona Holdings, will go with their domestic strategies for reorganizing regional banks, for example, as they keep their sights on the global financial market (Tables 5.15 and 5.16).
- If the YSD Financial Group's YSBC Kanto Bank (80 trillion yen, 0.221%) and the DBJ DBJ (16 trillion yen, 0.683%) are formed as a result of the restructuring of the three privatized banks and enter the Kanto market, they will compete with regional banks on an equal footing under the Banking Act since they will no longer receive automatic government guarantees. The YSBC Kanto Bank will be able to leverage the functions transferred from Shoko Chukin Bank to increase lending to middle-standing companies and SMEs. Its entry will not crowd the field all that much since the Tokyo market is broad. If the bank successfully expands its lending operations, it has good potential to become a megabank comparable to Resona.

The DBJ will suffer from losing government backing when it comes to competing with megabanks. However, it will have the ability to turn a profit since it deals mainly with blue-chip companies. Since its total assets do not measure up to those of

Table 5.15 Simulated regional bank reorganization in Kanto (FY ending March 2017)

	Mebuki FG			Tokyo Kiraboshi FG			Concordia FG		
Balance sheet (trillion yen)	Ashikaga	Joyo	Total	Tokyo Tomin	Yachiyo*	Total	Higashi-Nippon*	Yokohama	Total
Securities	1.4	2.8	4.2	0.5	0.6	1.1	0.4	2.3	2.7
(JGBs)	(0.3)	(0.9)	(1.2)	(0.3)	(0.1)	(0.4)	(0.1)	(0.5)	(0.6)
Loans	4.3	6	10.3	1.8	1.6	3.4	1.7	10.3	12
Other	0.8	0.9	1.7	0.5	0.1	0.6	0.1	3.8	3.9
Total assets	6.5	9.7	16.2	2.8	2.3	5.1	2.2	16.4	18.6
Deposits	5.3	8.2	13.5	2.3	2.2	4.5	1.9	13.2	15.1
Other liabilities	0.9	0.9	1.8	0.4	0	0.4	0.2	2.2	2.4
Total liabilities	6.2	9.1	15.3	2.7	2.2	4.9	2.1	15.4	17.5
Total net assets	0.3	0.6	0.9	0.1	0.1	0.2	0.1	1.0	1.1
Total liabilities and equity	6.5	9.7	16.2	2.8	2.3	5.1	2.2	16.4	18.6
Income statement (10 billion yen)									
Ordinary revenue	9.8	14.1	23.9	4.3	3.6	7.9	3.8	24.6	28.4
Ordinary profit	3.3	3.7	7.0	0.5	0.4	0.9	0.6	8.7	9.3
Net profit	2.4	2.4	5.1	0.3	0.4	0.6	0.4	6.1	6.5
ROA (%)	0.512	0.367	0.425	0.169	0.179	0.174	0.267	0.533	0.501

Source: Financial statements of regional banks

Table 5.16 Regional bank reorganization in Kanto and YSBC Kanto Bank (March 2017)

Balance sheet (trillion yen)					
YSBC Kanto Bank's initial balance sheet		Mebuki FG	Tokyo Kiraboshi FG	Concordia FG	Total
50.5	Securities	4.2	1.1	2.7	16.8
(25.1)	(JGBs)	(1.2)	(0.4)	(0.6)	(4.6)
4.8	Loans	10.3	3.4	12.0	55.9
24.7	Other	1.7	0.6	3.9	11.4
80.0	Total assets	16.2	5.1	18.6	84.1
66.4	Deposits	13.5	4.5	15.1	70.9
9.1	Other liabilities	1.8	0.4	2.4	8.5
75.5	Total liabilities	15.3	4.9	17.5	79.4
4.5	Total net assets	0.9	0.2	1.1	4.7
80.0	Total liabilities and equity	16.2	5.1	18.6	84.1

Japan Post Bank income statement (10 billion yen)		
	JP Bank profit and loss	Kanto's 36% share
Ordinary revenue	189.7	68.3
Ordinary profit	44.2	15.9
Net profit	31.2	11.2

Income statement (10 billion yen)			
	Mebuki FG	Tokyo Kiraboshi FG	Concordia FG
Ordinary revenue	23.9	7.9	28.4
Ordinary profit	7.0	0.9	9.3
Net profit	5.1	0.6	6.5

Source: Financial statements of regional banks

the megabanks, it's crucial that the bank create synergy with YSBC regional banks through, for example, YSD Group's overseas expansion or through investment banking business, which deals with large corporations and blue-chip companies.

2.2.2 Reorganization of Regional Banks into Other Regional Blocs

Section 2 of the April 2018 Financial Services Agency report, pertaining to competition and operational stability of regional financial institutions in the face of a declining population, discusses the contestability of the banking sector for regional banks in each prefecture (via model-based estimation). I used this material in the previous section when looking into institutional designs for regional banks across Japan. Having looked at mergers that already took place in Kyushu, Kinki, and Kanto, I will simulate a reorganization of regional banks in the remaining five regions (Hokkaido, Tohoku, Chubu, Chugoku, and Shikoku), out of the eight regions across Japan. In doing so, I will look at trends in each prefecture and each bank in light of what I have learned through my work and classify the merger process into five types based on the prefectural data provided in the model-based estimation.

Since reorganization of regional banks is still at the half-way point in these five regions, the simulation should use specific total assets and ROA targets set for each region based on the theory for reorganizing regional banks. The views presented in what follows concerning reorganization are inferences based on the circumstances of individual banks.

(A) **Hokkaido**

Regional banks in Hokkaido have combined total assets of 14 trillion yen, which account for 3.7% of the national total, and their ROA is low at 0.252% on average. The market is oligopolized by Hokkaido Bank (5 trillion yen, 0.302%) and North Pacific Bank (9 trillion yen, 0.224%). Hokkaido Bank merged with the geographically distant Hokuriku Bank (7 trillion yen, 0.338%) to establish a holding company, Hokuhoku Financial Group. After taking over the Hokkaido operations of the failed Hokkaido Takushoku Bank in 1998, Hokuyo Bank became the largest bank in Hokkaido. In 2001, it formed Sapporo Hokuyo Holdings jointly with Sapporo Bank, a secondary regional bank, before finally merging with Sapporo Bank in 2008. The reorganization of regional banks in Hokkaido can be deemed to have been completed.

- Once YSBC Hokkaido Bank is established as a result of restructuring the three privatized banks, it will have total assets of 8 trillion yen. While Hokkaido accounts for 3.6% of Japan's GDP, it accounts for 2.8% in terms of deposits and loans. Since financial institutions still have room to increase their share of the market, the entry of YSBC Hokkaido Bank will change the dynamics of this oligopolistic market where two banks dominate, making it competitive. This might increase the kind of lending that would facilitate a shift from agriculture to the so-called sextiary sector and benefit tourism, renewable energy, and other sectors to revitalize the local economy (Table 5.17).

(B) **Tohoku**

The Tohoku region can be geopolitically divided into three prefectures located along the Pacific Ocean and another three located along the Sea of Japan. The first group has eight regional banks with combined assets of 23 trillion yen, while the latter has seven regional banks with combined assets of 15 trillion yen. Together the region has assets totaling 38 trillion yen, or 9.9% of the national total, with a low ROA of 0.219%. According to the model-based estimation, Aomori and Akita are the prefectures where regional banks would generate no profit even if there were only one operating in each of those prefectures. Iwate, Yamagata, and Fukushima are the prefectures where regional banks could survive if there were only one in each prefecture but would not survive if there were two competing banks. While secondary regional banks in the Tohoku region have been undergoing reorganizations in order to stay afloat, other regional banks have not changed. Once earthquake reconstruction comes to an end, the depopulation issue will be spotlighted. This will lead to reorganizations of regional banks across prefectural boundaries, as indicated in the model estimation.

Table 5.17 Regional bank reorganization in Hokkaido and YSBC Hokkaido Bank (March 2017)

Balance sheet (trillion yen)

YSBC Hokkaido Bank's initial balance sheet		Hokuhoku FG (Hokkaido)	North Pacific	Total
5.6	Securities	1.0	1.7	2.7
(2.8)	(JGBs)	(0.4)	(6.0)	(1.0)
0.5	Loans	3.3	6.1	9.4
2.7	Other	0.8	1.3	2.1
8.9	Total assets	5.1	9.1	14.2
7.4	Deposits	4.5	8.1	12.6
1.0	Other liabilities	0.4	0.6	1.0
8.4	Total liabilities	4.9	8.7	13.6
0.5	Total net assets	0.2	0.4	0.6
8.9	Total liabilities and equity	5.1	9.1	14.2

Japan Post Bank income statement (10 billion yen)

	JP Bank profit and loss	Hokkaido's 4% share
Ordinary revenue	189.7	7.6
Ordinary profit	44.2	1.8
Net profit	31.2	1.3

Income statement (10 billion yen)

	Hokkaido	North Pacific	Total
Ordinary revenue	7.9	12.0	19.9
Ordinary profit	1.5	2.1	3.6
Net profit	1.1	1.6	2.7
ROA (%)	0.302	0.224	–

Source: Financial statements of regional banks

- Akita Prefecture's Hokuto Bank (1.3 trillion yen, 0.193%, 911 employees) and Yamagata Prefecture's Shonai Bank (1.5 trillion yen, 0.157%, 894 employees) merged to establish FIDEA Holdings. Yamagata Prefecture's Kirayaka Bank (4 trillion yen, 0.146%, 997 employees) and Miyagi Prefecture's Sendai Bank (1.1 trillion yen, 0.247%, 704 employees) merged to form Jimoto Holdings. However, both companies have total assets of less than 3 trillion yen, with a low ROA and small workforce. This means they will have to seek further merger opportunities.
- Aomori and Akita are the prefectures where regional banks would not generate a profit even if there were only one operating in each of the prefectures. Working against this backdrop, Aomori Bank (2.9 trillion yen, 0.231%), Akita Bank (3 trillion yen, 0.195%), and Iwate Bank (3.5 trillion yen, 0.211%) formed a business alliance to enhance efficiency by consolidating their standard administrative operations, information systems, and other units with an eye to the future. If these three banks merge to form a holding company, it will become a 10-trillion-yen regional banking group.

- While regional banks might survive in Yamagata and Fukushima if there were only one in each prefecture, Yamagata Bank (2.6 trillion yen, 0.276%) will have to seek a merger opportunity with a regional bank outside the prefecture to expand operations since secondary regional banks in Yamagata have already merged. Fukushima-based Toho Bank (6 trillion yen, 0.176%) should consider partnering with a secondary bank in northern Kanto when seeking a merger opportunity since the two secondary regional banks in Fukushima have total assets of less than 1 trillion yen (Fukushima Bank: 0.8 trillion yen, 0.183%, 540 employees, Daito Bank: 0.8 trillion yen, 0.228%, 540 employees).
- Since, according to the model-based estimation, Miyagi can have two competing regional banks, the 77 Bank (8.6 trillion yen, 0.250%) has the potential to grow into a 10-trillion-yen bank by itself.
- YSBC Tohoku Bank, established via restructuring, will have total assets of 13 trillion yen, with deposits totaling 2.6 trillion yen in Miyagi and 2.5 trillion yen in Fukushima. The bank should be able to compete with regional banks for the time being if it increases lending in Miyagi and Fukushima (Table 5.18).

Table 5.18 Regional bank reorganization in Tohoku and YSBC Tohoku Bank (March 2017)

Balance sheet (trillion yen)

YSBC Tohoku Bank's initial balance sheet		Iwate/ Aomori/ Akita Group	Yamagata Bank	77 Bank	Toho Bank	Total
8.4	Securities	3.2	0.7	3.2	1.5	11.7
(4.2)	(JGBs)	(1.0)	(0.3)	(1.2)	(0.6)	(4.1)
0.8	Loans	5.0	1.7	4.5	3.2	21.7
4.1	Other	1.2	0.1	0.9	1.3	4.6
13.3	Total assets	9.4	2.6	8.6	6.0	38.0
11.0	Deposits	7.8	2.2	7.4	5.2	32.6
1.5	Other liabilities	1.1	0.2	0.7	0.6	3.6
12.5	Total liabilities	8.9	2.4	8.1	5.8	36.2
0.8	Total net assets	0.5	0.2	0.5	0.2	1.8
13.3	Total liabilities and net assets	9.4	2.6	8.6	6.0	38.0

Japan Post Bank income statement (10 billion yen)

	JP Bank profit and loss	Tohoku's 6% share
Ordinary revenue	189.7	11.4
Ordinary profit	44.2	2.7
Net profit	31.2	1.9

Income statement (10 billion yen)

	Iwate/Aomori/Akita Group	Yamagata Bank	77 Bank	Toho Bank
Ordinary revenue	12.2	3.9	9.6	6.5
Ordinary profit	2.0	0.7	2.2	1.1
Net profit	1.5	0.5	1.7	0.7
ROA (%)	–	0.276	0.250	0.176

Source: Financial statements of regional banks

While there are a number of small, low-revenue regional banks in Tohoku, YSBC Tohoku Bank can benefit from merging with these banks in order to diversify its operations and build a foundation and capability for lending operations. YSBC Tohoku Bank should play a vital role in improving the regional ROA in place of regional banks, which will be the key to bolstering the local economy.

(C) **Chubu**

The Chubu region can be geopolitically divided into three economic zones. They encompass 10 prefectures, i.e., Koshinetsu (Niigata, Yamanashi, and Nagano), Tokai (Shizuoka, Aichi, Gifu, and Mie), and Hokuriku (Toyama, Ishikawa, and Fukui). There are 6 regional banks in Koshinetsu (23 trillion yen, 0.325%), 12 in Tokai (48 trillion yen, 0.393%), and 6 in Hokuriku (16 trillion yen, 0.329%). When combined, the total assets of all 24 banks amount to 86 trillion yen, 22.5% of the national total, with an average ROA of 0.363%. According to the model-based estimation, Niigata and Nagano are the prefectures where regional banks could survive if there were only one in each prefecture. Yamanashi, Gifu, Mie, Toyama, Ishikawa, and Fukui are the prefectures where regional banks would generate no profit even if there were only one operating in each of those prefectures, indicating that most prefectures have weak economic bases. Aichi and Shizuoka are the prefectures where two banks could coexist.

- In Tokai, Mie Prefecture's Mie Bank (2 trillion yen, 0.218%) and Daisan Bank (2 trillion yen, 0.263%) have already merged to operate under San ju San Financial Group. Since SMBC was involved in this merger, the financial group seems to have a vision for expanding operations in Mie and Aichi in the future that includes merging with secondary regional banks based in the city of Nagoya. Mie Prefecture has another regional bank, Hyakugo Bank (6 trillion yen, 0.212%).

  Looking to enter the Nagoya market, Ogaki Kyoritsu Bank (5.6 trillion yen, 0.341%) and Juroku Bank (6 trillion yen, 0.198%) in Gifu Prefecture may seek out mergers with secondary regional banks in Nagoya. There are various possible scenarios. Shizuoka Bank (11 trillion yen, 0.469%) is a Tokyo-oriented bank and has a good financial standing, so it has good growth potential even if it does not strike any merger deal. Suruga Bank (4.5 trillion yen, 1.278%) may be able to get back on its feet depending on how its illicit lending scandal goes, but its future remains uncertain.
- In Koshinetsu, Daishi Bank (5.6 trillion yen, 0.269%) and Hokuetsu Bank (2.7 trillion yen, 0.304%), both based in Niigata Prefecture, have agreed to merge and form a holding a company. While the merger of the two banks based in the same prefecture follows the model-based estimation exactly, the decision to merge was actually made before the estimation was published. While Nagano Prefecture's Hachijuni Bank (8.6 trillion yen, 0.395%) is likely to survive on its own, Yamanashi Prefecture's Tokyo-leaning Yamanashi Chuo Bank (3.3 trillion yen, 0.270%) is likely to be merged into a regional banking group in Kanto when it becomes difficult to keep its head above water.

- In Hokuriku, Toyama Prefecture's Hokuriku Bank (7 trillion yen, 0.338%) has already partnered with Hokkaido Bank to build a stronger operating foundation. The future of regional banks in the area depends on which direction Ishikawa Prefecture-based Hokkoku Bank (4.3 trillion yen, 0.325%), another regional bank in Hokuriku, goes in when reorganizing itself with secondary regional banks in Toyama Prefecture and small regional banks in Fukui Prefecture.
  As noted earlier, regional banks in the Chubu region could undergo different types of reorganization in three areas, but we should also anticipate a scenario where banks merge further afield, across prefectural boundaries.
- If formed as a result of restructuring, YSBC Chubu Bank would operate across a broader area and have combined total assets of 40 trillion yen. This figure would include a deposit balance totaling 31 trillion yen, which can be divided into 20 trillion yen in Tokai, 7 trillion yen in Koshinetsu, and 4 trillion yen in Hokuriku. YSBC Chubu Bank will have to develop a lending capability mainly in Nagoya to help middle-standing companies and SMEs as well as the agriculture, forestry, and fisheries industries thrive while coexisting with regional banks. Like other YSBC regional banks, YSBC Chubu Bank should be able to build up the foundation, workforce, and other features needed for lending operations via mergers with small, low-profitability regional banks. This will enable the bank to improve its ROA and diversify its portfolio (Table 5.19).

(D) **Chugoku**

The nine regional banks in the Chugoku region have combined total assets of 35 trillion yen, accounting for 9.3% of the national total. Their ROA is relatively high at 0.411% on average. According to the model-based estimation, there are no prefectures where regional banks could survive if there were only one in each prefecture. Shimane, Tottori, Yamaguchi, and Okayama are the prefectures where regional banks would not generate a profit even if there were only one operating in each of those prefectures. Hiroshima alone is a prefecture where two regional banks could coexist.

- The region can be geopolitically divided into two areas, one situated along the Sea of Japan and the other along the Seto Inland Sea. Since the model-based estimation found that regional banks in Shimane and Tottori Prefectures, which are located on the Sea of Japan side, would not generate any profit even if there were only one operating in each prefecture, they should look for merger opportunities beyond their prefectural borders. In fact, San-in Godo Bank (5.4 trillion yen, 0.359%), headquartered in Shimane Prefecture, operates in both prefectures. If it were to merge with other regional banks, such as Shimane Bank (0.4 trillion yen, 0.381%) and Tottori Bank (1 trillion yen, 0.188%), in order to bail them out, and such a merger violated antimonopoly law, that's where the YSBC Chugoku Bank would come into play.
- Yamaguchi Bank (5.8 trillion yen, 0.461%), located on the Seto Inland Sea side, has already partnered with Momiji Bank (3.2 trillion yen, 0.489%), based in adjacent Hiroshima Prefecture, and Kitakyushu Bank (1.2 trillion yen, 0.266%),

Table 5.19 Regional bank reorganization in Chubu and YSBC Chubu Bank (March 2017)

Balance sheet (trillion yen)

YSBC Chubu Bank's initial balance sheet		Koshinetsu (Niigata/ Nagano/ Yamanashi)	Tokai		Hokuriku (Toyama/ Ishikawa/ Fukui)	Total
			Shizuoka/ Aichi	Gifu/ Mie		
26.7	Securities	7.2	4.5	5.9	3.9	21.5
(13.2)	(JGBs)	(3.0)	(1.2)	(1.7)	(1.6)	(7.4)
2.5	Loans	12.7	18.2	13.5	9.8	54.2
13.0	Other	2.9	3.7	1.7	2.8	11.1
42.2	Total assets	22.8	26.4	21.1	16.5	86.8
35.0	Deposits	18.3	23.0	18.1	13.4	72.9
4.8	Other liabilities	3.1	1.5	1.8	2.3	8.6
39.8	Total liabilities	21.4	24.5	19.9	15.7	81.5
2.4	Total net assets	1.4	1.9	1.2	0.8	5.3
42.2	Total liabilities and equity	22.8	26.4	21.1	16.5	86.8

Japan Post Bank Income Statement (10 billion yen)

	JP Bank profit and loss	Chubu's 19% share
Ordinary revenue	189.7	68.3
Ordinary profit	44.2	15.9
Net profit	31.2	11.2

Source: Financial statements of regional banks

based in Fukuoka Prefecture, to form Yamaguchi Financial Group, covering a broad geographical area.

Okayama Prefecture-based Chugoku Bank (8.2 trillion yen, 0.250%) could survive on its own, but, looking ahead, it should seek merger opportunities with secondary regional banks in neighboring prefectures in order to expand its business turf.

Hiroshima Bank (9 trillion yen, 0.487%), with its potential to grow and survive on its own, should increase its assets to achieve further growth.

– Although its operations cover a wide geographical area, YSBC Chugoku Bank has a mere 13 trillion yen in assets. Out of its deposit balance of 11 trillion yen, 9 trillion yen comes from the three prefectures located on the Seto Inland Sea side. The bank should develop lending capacities mainly in the city of Hiroshima, where the market is big, and work with an eye toward building a solid business foundation in the prefectures situated along the Seto Inland Sea.

Since there are only a few small regional banks in the Chugoku region, YSBC Chugoku Bank will have to develop lending capabilities on its own.

(E) Shikoku

There are four regional banks (with combined total assets of 18 trillion yen) and four secondary regional banks (with combined total assets of 6.7 trillion yen). Altogether the eight regional banks have total assets of 25 trillion yen, which account for 6.4% of the national total. Standing at 0.415%, their ROA is relatively high.

According to the model-based estimation, Kagawa, Tokushima, and Kochi are prefectures where regional banks would not generate any profit even if there were only one operating in each of these prefectures. Ehime is the only prefecture that falls into the category of a prefecture where regional banks could survive if there were only one in each prefecture.

- Two secondary regional banks, Kagawa Bank (1.6 trillion yen, 0.480%) and Tokushima Bank (1.6 trillion yen, 0.388%), merged to establish TOMONY Holdings, which later acquired the Osaka-based Taisho Bank (0.5 trillion yen, 0.126%).
- While other regional banks have not undergone any reorganizations, four regional banks, i.e., Awa Bank (3.2 trillion yen, 0.595%), Hyakujushi Bank (5 trillion yen, 0.346%), Iyo Bank (6.8 trillion yen, 0.483%), and Shikoku Bank (3 trillion yen, 0.338%), formed a loose alliance to enhance efficiency by integrating their standard administrative operations. It is possible that the alliance may develop into a merger in the future. Although they operate in four geopolitically divided areas, they can overcome geographical barriers through the use of information technology.

  There is also the possibility of the two banking groups taking over secondary regional banks.
- YSBC Shikoku Bank will have total assets of 7 trillion yen and operate across all prefectures in the Shikoku region. Its deposit balance of 4.5 trillion yen in prefectures situated on the Seto Inland Sea accounts for 85% of all its deposits. To avoid violating antimonopoly law, YSBC Shikoku Bank will have to look into ways to improve its ROA and portfolio by considering mergers with Ehime Bank (2.5 trillion yen, 0.273%, 1383 employees) and the Bank of Kochi (1.1 trillion yen, 0.258%, 852 employees), although this will depend on which reorganization scenario regional banks in Shikoku choose (Tables 5.20 and 5.21).

Reorganizations of regional banks in the Kanto, Kinki, and Kyushu regions were already simulated in the previous section based on actual mergers that took place.

We have so far simulated possible mergers among the two different types of financial institutions in eight regions while taking note of ongoing reorganizations as we looked for a path to coexistence and coprosperity for the three privatized banks and regional banks based on an analysis of the current financial conditions of financial institutions by type discussed in Chap. 3 and the merger and reorganization theory for different types of financial institutions discussed in Chap. 4. The results of the simulation are summarized in Table 5.22.

Table 5.20 Regional bank reorganization in Chugoku and YSBC Chugoku Bank (March 2017)

Balance sheet (trillion yen)

YSBC Chugoku Bank's initial balance sheet		Tottori/ Shimane Group	Three Yamaguchi FG banks	Hiroshima Bank	Chugoku Bank	Total
8.4	Securities	2.2	1.9	1.8	2.7	15.9
(4.2)	(JGBs)	(1.0)	(0.5)	(0.8)	0.9	(5.4)
0.8	Loans	3.8	6.8	5.6	4.4	36.3
4.1	Other	0.8	1.5	1.4	1.2	8.2
13.3	Total assets	6.8	10.2	8.8	8.3	60.4
11.0	Deposits	5.2	8.5	7.0	6.2	48.2
1.5	Other liabilities	1.2	1.1	1.4	1.6	8.6
12.5	Total liabilities	6.4	9.6	8.4	7.8	56.8
0.8	Total net assets	0.4	0.6	0.4	0.5	3.6
13.3	Total liabilities and equity	6.8	10.2	8.8	8.3	60.4

Japan Post Bank income statement (10 billion yen)

	JP Bank profit and loss	Chugoku's 6% share
Ordinary revenue	189.7	11.4
Ordinary profit	44.2	2.7
Net profit	31.2	1.9

Income statement (10 billion yen)

	Tottori/ Shimane Group	Three Yamaguchi FG banks	Hiroshima Bank	Chugoku Bank
Ordinary revenue	10.1	14.8	13.5	12.5
Ordinary profit	2.3	4.6	4.3	2.9
Net profit	1.5	3.2	3.0	1.9
ROA (%)	–	0.447	0.487	0.350

Source: Financial statements of regional banks

3 Reorganizing the Three Privatized Banks and Reorganizing Regional Banks into Regional Blocs for Coexistence and Coprosperity

The Fiscal Investment and Loan Program (FILP) reform, policy-based finance reform, and postal privatization that were carried out in the 2000s were a series of fiscal reforms aimed at making the Japanese financial market free, fair, and efficient.

Table 5.21 Regional bank reorganization in Shikoku and YSBC Shikoku Bank (March 2017)

Balance sheet (trillion yen)

YSBC Shikoku Bank's initial balance sheet		Awa Bank	Hyakujushi Bank	Iyo Bank	Shikoku Bank	Total
4.2	Securities	1.1	1.4	1.7	1.0	6.9
(2.1)	(JGBs)	(0.3)	(0.4)	(0.6)	(0.3)	(2.0)
0.4	Loans	1.8	2.8	4.0	1.7	14.7
2.1	Other	0.2	0.7	1.1	0.3	3.0
6.7	Total assets	3.2	4.9	6.8	3.0	24.6
5.6	Deposits	2.7	4.0	5.0	2.6	19.8
0.8	Other liabilities	0.2	0.6	1.2	0.3	3.3
6.4	Total liabilities	2.9	4.6	6.2	2.9	23.1
0.3	Total net assets	0.3	0.3	0.6	0.1	1.6
6.7	Total liabilities and equity	3.2	4.9	6.8	3.0	24.7

Japan Post Bank Income Statement (10 billion yen)

	JP Bank profit and loss	Shikoku's 3% share
Ordinary revenue	189.7	5.7
Ordinary profit	44.2	1.3
Net profit	31.2	0.9

Income statement (10 billion yen)

	Awa Bank	Hyakujushi Bank	Iyo Bank	Shikoku Bank
Ordinary revenue	5.4	8.2	9.9	4.8
Ordinary profit	1.9	1.7	3.3	1.0
Net profit	1.2	0.9	2.1	0.7
ROA (%)	0.595	0.346	0.483	0.338

Source: Financial statements of regional banks

Postal privatization was aimed at creating a mechanism that would alter the monetary supply system in the Japanese economy and channel financial capital to sectors with higher growth potential. The mechanism that keeps a huge amount of money outside the market blocks an efficient flow of funds and could have an adverse effect on the Japanese economy. On top of that, the fact that these funds are automatically guaranteed by the government makes the playing field for private financial institutions woefully uneven.

To find ways to solve these problems facing Japan's private and public financial services, the previous chapter analyzed total assets and ROA at different types of financial institutions in Japan to develop a theory for creating an optimal balance among and within different types of financial institutions. The analysis proved that the portfolio makeup of each type of financial institution was crucial to rectifying the correlation between total assets and ROA in order to narrow the gaps among and within different types of financial institutions.

A survey of Japan's financial landscape reveals an overabundance of regional banks that have all been hindered by a protracted low-interest-rate policy along with

Table 5.22 (Final) Theoretical values for YSBC regional banks (super-regional banks) and reorganized regional banks across Japan (FY ending March 2017, trillion yen). 35 regional banks + 8 YSBC banks, 43 banks in total

Regional bank mergers, consolidations, and reorganizations	Total assets	Loans	Deposits
North Pacific	9.1	6.1	8.1
YSBC Hokkaido	8.9	0.5	7.4
3 banks in Iwate/Aomori/Akita	9.4	5.0	7.8
Yamagata	2.6	1.7	2.2
77	8.6	4.5	7.4
Toho	6.0	3.2	5.2
YSBC Tohoku	13.3	0.8	11.0
Mebuki FG	16.2	10.3	13.5
Tokyo Kiraboshi FG	5.1	3.4	4.5
Concordia FG	18.6	12.0	15.1
Gunma	8.0	5.2	6.5
Chiba	14.0	9.3	11.6
YSBC Kanto	80.0	4.8	66.4
Daishi, Hokuetsu FG	8.5	4.7	6.9
Hachijuni	8.6	4.9	6.4
Shizuoka	11.0	8.0	9.3
Suruga	4.5	3.3	4.1
San ju San FG	4.0	2.6	3.5
Hyakugo	5.5	2.9	4.6
Juroku, Ogaki Kyoritsu	11.6	7.9	10.1
Hokuhoku (Hokuriku + Hokkaido) FG	12.4	7.7	10.6
Hokkoku	4.3	2.3	3.2
YSBC Chubu	42.2	2.5	35.0
Shiga	5.5	3.5	4.5
Kyoto	8.9	5.0	6.7
Kansai Mirai FG	11.6	8.8	10.4
Senshu Ikeda/Nanto/Kiyo	16.2	9.9	13.4
YSBC Kinki	35.6	2.2	29.5
San-in Godo	5.4	2.8	4.0
Yamaguchi FG	10.2	6.8	8.5
Hiroshima	8.8	5.6	7.0
Chugoku	8.3	4.4	6.2
YSBC Chugoku	13.3	0.8	11.0
Iyo/Shikoku	9.8	5.7	7.6
Awa/Hyakujushi	8.1	4.6	6.7
YSBC Shikoku	6.7	0.4	5.6
Fukuoka FG	21.2	13.1	15.7
Kyushu FG	9.6	6.2	7.9
Nishi-Nippon FH	9.5	6.8	7.6
Oita/Miyazaki	6.2	3.6	4.9
Okinawa (3 banks)	5.0	3.5	4.5
YSBC Kyushu-Okinawa Bank	22.2	1.3	18.4

Source: Financial statements of regional banks

JP Bank, which is exposed to interest-rate risks both on the asset and liability sides because it heavily invests its huge amount of fixed-amount postal savings in securities.

The first and second sections of this chapter focused on these two types of financial institutions, which are currently viewed as the most problematic among all the types of financial institutions in Japan, looking at them in specific ways and with an eye toward reorganizing the three privatized banks and regional banks. The sections then discussed institutional designs for them, such as organizational structures and types of M&A.

These two institutional designs were developed with the aim of achieving coexistence and coprosperity of local financial institutions. We defined basic requirements for achieving coexistence and coprosperity.

First, the total assets of the banks should be regionally combined or divided so that they are appropriate for the market in order to allow them to compete on an equal footing.

Second, banks should be merged to increase their total assets to a certain level in order to narrow ROA gaps.

Third, the proportion of loans provided by regional banks should be optimized through mergers, and the banks to be created as a result of regionally dividing the three privatized banks should take over regional banks' employees whose jobs have been made redundant.

Shown below are the basic data used for developing institutional designs in the first and second sections of Chap. 5 based on the theory and positive analysis discussed in Chap. 4 (Table 5.23).

Combined total assets of financial institutions in Japan amount to 1640 trillion yen. Their ROA on average is 0.315%. It should be noted that, as shown earlier, private financial institutions have a higher ROA than public financial institutions (see Table 3.3 for changes in ROA for reference). Narrowing this ROA gap between public and private financial institutions is what was meant by the catchphrase "Leave to the private sector what it can do." These data also remind us of the hefty task of reducing the share of assets held by public financial institutions, which tip the scales when looking at it in comparison to other advanced countries. The data also indicate the differences in the portfolios of public and private financial institutions.

Table 5.24 and Tables 5.25, 5.26, 5.27 show how the three privatized banks can coexist and coprosper with regional banks through restructuring and reorganization in regional blocs.

These tables show how the two types of banks, one public and the other private, can coexist in regional blocs when they are restructured, regionally divided and reorganized via mergers after the three privatized banks are fully privatized. The key to realizing coexistence is strengthening their financial intermediary operations to increase lending. As shown in these figures and tables, once their assets are optimized so they can compete on an equal footing, coexistence of the two types of financial institutions will boost their financial intermediary operations, which will lead to coprosperity.

Table 5.23 Basic data for examining optimal portfolio and ROA by type of financial institution (FY ending March 2017, trillion yen (%)

	Private financial services		Public financial services		
	(percentage breakdown)	Regional banks	3 privatized banks	(percentage breakdown)	Total (percentage breakdown)
Deposits due from banks	321	39	54	60	381
	(23.8)	(10.1)	(22.5)	(20.4)	(23.2)
Securities	26	92	142	142	408
	(19.7)	(23.8)	(59.2)	(48.5)	(24.9)
Loans	646	244	26	69	715
	(47.9)	(62.2)	(10.8)	(23.5)	(43.6)
Other assets	114	11	18	22	136
Total assets	1347	386	240	293	1640
	(100)	(100)	(100)	(100)	(100)
Deposits	1014	321	184	184	1198
	(75.3)	(83.2)	(76.7)	(62.8)	(73.0)
Other liabilities	251	43	40	76	327
Net assets	82	22	16	33	115
	(6.1)	(5.7)	(6.7)	(11.3)	(7.0)
Total liabilities and net assets	1347	386	240	293	1640
	(100)	(100)	(100)	(100)	(100)
ROA	0.330%	0.370%	0.253%	0.215%	0.315%

The preceding six figures and tables (a summary of Sects. 1 and 2 of Chap. 5) provide a recipe for coexistence and coprosperity. The recipe based on these six figures and tables provides guidelines for seeing how small local banks that do not survive can be absorbed and leveraged by looking at total assets of YSBC regional banks, which are formed by dividing the three privatized banks' assets by region, as well as regional banks that survive through reorganization. This is the first step.

The second step is where banks expand lending once their operations are strengthened and increase their total assets to help correct the overconcentration of banks in Tokyo and achieve the balanced development of national land. YSBC regional banks then draw from Table 5.26 to determine ROA targets as they work to raise their ROA, standing at 0.221% in the fiscal year ending March 31, 2017, to match regional banks' average ROA of 0.370% by implementing measures to narrow gaps in each region. Once ROA gaps among different regions and banks are narrowed, the ROA of regional financial institutions will increase. This will result in increased GDP and tax revenues in each region.

In the final step, Table 5.27 provides a recipe for simulating the number of regional bank employees, whose jobs are made redundant as a result of a merger or reorganization, who can be taken in by YSBC regional banks.

These employees can be divided into 123,967 employees of 59 regional banks to survive and 44,866 employees of 46 regional banks to be merged or reorganized as simulated in Sects. 1 and 2 of Chap. 5. Regional banks taken over by another bank

Table 5.24 Banks to survive and to be merged/culled after simulation

Area	Prefecture	Bank, total assets (trillion yen)/ROA (%)	
		To survive (59 banks)	To be merged or culled (46 banks)
Hokkaido	Hokkaido	Hokkaido 4.0/0.302	
		North Pacific 9.1/0.224	
Tohoku, Japan Sea side	Akita	Akita 2.9/0.195	Hokuto 1.3/0.193
	Aomori	Aomori 2.9/0.231	Michinoku 2.1/0229
	Yamagata	Yamagata 2.6/0.276	Kirayaka 1.4/0.146
			Shonai 1.5/0.157
Tohoku, Pacific side	Fukushima	Toho 6.0/0.176	Daito 0.8/0.228
			Fukushima 0.7/0.183
	Iwate	Iwate 3.5/0.211	Kita-Nippon 1.4/0.270
			Tohoku 0.8/0.246
	Miyagi	77 bank 8.6/0.250	Sendai 1.1/0.247
Kanto	Chiba	Chiba 14.0/0.499	Chiba Kogyo 2.7/0.310
			Keiyo 4.6/0.374
	Gunma	Gunma 7.9/0.432	Towa 2.2/0.462
	Ibaraki	Joyo 9.7/0.367	Tsukuba 2.4/0.222
	Kanagawa	Yokohama 16.3/0.533	Kanagawa 0.5/0.193
	Saitama		Musashino 4.5/0.258
	Tochigi	Ashikaga 6.5/0.512	Tochigi 2.8/0.426
	Tokyo	Tokyo Tomin 2.8/0.169	Tokyo Star 2.5/0.598
		Higashi-Nippon 2.2/0.267	
		Tokyo Star, Yachiyo 2.3/0.179	
Chubu/Hokuriku	Fukui		Fukuho 0.5/0.222
			Fukui 2.6/0.235
	Ishikawa	Hokkoku 4.3/0.325	
	Toyama	Hokuriku 7.3/0.338	First Bank of Toyama 1.3/0.515
			Toyama 0.5/0.311
Chubu/Koshinetsu	Nagano	Hachijuni 8.6/0.395	Nagano 1.1/0.294
	Niigata	Daishi 5.6/0.269	Taiko 1.4/0.311
		Hokuetsu 2.7/0.304	
	Yamanashi		Yamanashi Chuo 3.3/0.270
Chubu/Tokai	Aichi		Aichi 3.1/0.235
			Chukyo 1.9/0.251
			Nagoya 3.6/0.179
	Gifu	Juroku 6.0/0.198	
		Ogaki Kyoritsu 5.6/0.198	
	Mie	Daisan 2.0/0.263	
		Hyakugo 5.5/0.212	
		Mie 1.9/0.218	
	Shizuoka	Shizuoka 11.0/0.469	Shimizu 1.6/0.531
		Suruga 4.5/1.278	Shizuoka Chuo 0.7/0.545

(continued)

Table 5.24 (continued)

Area	Prefecture	Bank, total assets (trillion yen)/ROA (%)	
		To survive (59 banks)	To be merged or culled (46 banks)
Chugoku	Hiroshima	Hiroshima 8.8/0.487	
		Momiji 3.2/0.489	
	Okayama	Chugoku 8.2/0.350	Tomato 1.3/0.210
	Shimane	San-in Godo 5.4/0.359	Shimane 0.4/0.381
	Tottori		Tottori 1.0/0.188
	Yamaguchi	Yamaguchi 5.8/0.461	Saikyo 1.4/0.454
Kinki	Hyogo	Minato 3.5/0.282	Tajima 1.0/0.164
	Kyoto	Kyoto 8.9/0.282	
	Nara	Nanto 5.8/0.275	
	Osaka	Kinki Osaka 3.5/0.183	Taisho 0.5/0.126
		Kansai Urban 4.6/0.385	
		Senshu Ikeda 5.6/0.292	
	Shiga	Shiga 5.5/0.347	
	Wakayama	Kiyo 4.9/0.248	
Shikoku	Ehime	Iyo 6.8/0.483	Ehime 2.5/0.272
	Kagawa	Hyakujushi 4.9/0.346	Kagawa 1.6/0.480
	Kochi	Shikoku 3.0/0.338	Kochi 1.1/0.258
	Tokushima	Awa 3.2/0.595	Tokushima 1.6/0.388
Kyushu	Fukuoka	Fukuoka 14.0/0.429	Chikuho 0.8/0.158
		Nishi-Nippon City 9.2/0.367	Fukuoka Chuo 0.5/0.193
		Kitakyushu 1.2/0.266	
	Kagoshima	Kagoshima 4.3/0.371	Minami Nippon 0.8/0.375
	Kumamoto	Higo 5.3/0.232,	
		Kumamoto 1.7/0.152	
	Miyazaki	Miyazaki 3.0/0.413	Miyazaki Taiyo 0.7/0.371
	Nagasaki	Eighteenth 2.9/0.221	
		Nagasaki 0.3/0.183	
		Shinwa 2.6/0.366	
	Oita	Oita 3.2/0.284	Howa 0.6/0.140
	Saga		Saga 2.3/0.141
			Saga Kyoei 0.3/0.194
Okinawa	Okinawa	Okinawa 2.1/0.366	
		Okinawa Kaiho 0.7/0.305	
		Ryukyus 2.2/0.333	
Total assets		312 trillion yen	73 trillion yen

Note: Banks operating under a holding company retain their current name, while others will be absorbed by another bank sometime in the future. The number of banks will eventually decline. Their combined total assets will remain as is

Table 5.25 Number of banks and their total assets after reorganization of the three privatized banks and regional banks in regional blocs (FY ending March 2017)

Total assets		Hokkaido	Tohoku	Kanto	Chubu	Kinki	Chugoku	Shikoku	Kyushu/ Okinawa	Total
Regional YSBC banks trillion yen (%)		8.9 (4.00)	13.3 (6.00)	80 (36)	42.2 (19)	35.6 (16)	13.3 (6)	6.7 (3)	22.2 (10)	222.2 (100)
Regional banks*	Hokkaido	2/14.2								
		0								
	Tohoku		6/26.6							
			9/11.5							
	Kanto			8/61.9						
				8/22.2						
	Chubu				12/65.3					
					12/21.5					
	Kinki					8/42.2				
						2/1.6				
	Chugoku						5/32.7			
							4/3.0			
	Shikoku							4/17.9		
								4/6.8		
	Kyushu/ Okinawa								14/51.5	
									7/7.1	
	National total	2/14.2	6/26.6	8/61.9	12/65.3	8/42.2	5/32.7	4/17.9	14/51.5	59/312.3
		0	9/11.5	8/22.2	12/21.5	2/1.6	4/3.0	4/6.8	7/7.1	46/73.7
		2/14.2	15/38.1	16/84.1	24/86.8	10/43.8	9/35.7	8/24.7	21/58.6	105/386.0
		3.70%	9.90%	21.80%	22.50%	11.30%	9.20%	6.40%	15.20%	100%
Regional YSBC banks and regional banks		2/23.1	7/51.4	9/164.1	13/129.0	9/79.4	6/49.0	5/31.4	15/80.8	67/608.2
		3.80%	8.50%	26.90%	21.20%	13.10%	8.10%	5.20%	13.30%	100%

*Figures in upper row are for banks likely to survive; figures in lower row are for banks likely to be merged

Table 5.26 ROA by regional bloc after reorganization of the three privatized banks and regional banks (FY ending March 2017)

ROA (%)		Hokkaido	Tohoku	Kanto	Chubu	Kinki	Chugoku	Shikoku	Kyushu/ Okinawa	National total
Regional YSBC banks		0.221	0.221	0.221	0.221	0.221	0.221	0.221	0.221	0.221
Regional banks*	Hokkaido	0.253								
		0								
	Tohoku		0.223							
			0.21							
	Kanto			0.445						
				0.364						
	Chubu				0.395					
					0.291					
	Kinki					0.29				
						0.177				
	Chugoku						0.419			
							0.305			
	Shikoku							0.441		
								0.346		
	Kyushu/Okinawa								0.349	
									0.207	
	National total	0.253	0.219	0.423	0.369	0.287	0.406	0.415	0.335	0.354
		35.7 billion yen	834	3565	3206	1255	1501	1025	1923	13,666

*Figures in *upper row* are for banks likely to survive; figures in *lower row* are for banks likely to be merged

Table 5.27 Number of employees by regional bloc after reorganization of the three privatized banks and regional banks (FY ending March 2017)

		Hokkaido	Tohoku	Kanto	Chubu	Kinki	Chugoku	Shikoku	Kyushu/ Okinawa	National total
Regional YSBC banks		684 (4%)	1024 (6%)	6144 (36%)	3242 (19%)	2730 (16%)	1024 (6%)	513 (3%)	1706 (10%)	17,067 (100%)
Regional banks*	Hokkaido	5301								
		0								
	Tohoku		10293							
			7364							
	Kanto			21920						
				12189						
	Chubu				26249					
					12737					
	Kinki					20143				
						1047				
	Chugoku						10719			
							2619			
	Shikoku							7573		
								4212		
	Kyushu/ Okinawa								21766	
									4701	
	National total	5301 (3.10%)	17,657 (10.50%)	34,109 (20.20%)	38,986 (23.10%)	21,190 (12.50%)	13,338 (7.90%)	11,785 (7.00%)	26,467 (15.70%)	168,833 (100%)
		0	7364	12,189	12,737	1047	2619	4212	4701	44,866

*Figures in upper row are for banks likely to survive; figures in lower row are for banks likely to be merged

initially go under a holding company but likely cease to exist in the future. Naturally their employees may become subject to layoffs or early retirement. Out of 44,866 employees, those who get hired by YSBC banks or other banks are likely to be lending personnel. If 30% of them, or 13,500 employees, are re-employed by YSBC regional banks, the remaining 31,366 employees will lose their jobs. Since there are eight regions, the number would be 2000–6000 people per region. Surviving regional banks and other types of financial institutions should be able to absorb them. The impact on local economies should be minimal, although quality may remain an issue.

In this section, we looked at institutional designs for restructuring the three privatized banks and reorganizing regional banks into regional blocs. We then analyzed the regional distribution of total assets, ROA, and the workforce at each bank, which was identified through institutional designs, and provided a recipe. Using the recipe to implement these institutional designs will breathe new life into the Japanese economy. This will ultimately lead to higher GDP and GNI as well as increased tax revenue that will in turn pave the way to better national fiscal health.

4 Effect of Total Optimization via Reorganization of the Three Privatized Banks and Regional Banks: How It Will Restore Japan's Fiscal Health

The history of the preprivatization era discussed in the first section of Chap. 1 teaches us an important lesson. Following the launch of the postal savings system in 1875, the Industrial Bank of Japan, a special bank that can be thought of as the predecessor of the DBJ, was established via the industrial loan program in 1902. In 1936 Shoko Chukin Bank was established as a special public institution. These public financial services were a government-led initiative designed to raise a small amount of funds to be provided to state-owned corporations and SMEs.

Mounting public debt in the face of growing postal savings during and after the war led to the collapse of national finances, a lesson we can learn from. In Sect. 2 of the same chapter, I pointed out that the public debt and postal savings grew after the economic bubble burst in the late 1990, just as they did during and after the war, and that the nation's fiscal health was still declining today. Looking at the analysis of outstanding government bonds and gross national product in wartime/postwar Japan published by the BOJ's Research Bureau in 1966, I discovered some similarities in the relationship between the government debt and postal savings balance following the bursting of the economic bubble. I pointed out these similarities during a class I conducted at Kyoto University in the 2013 autumn semester.

As shown in Table 5.28, Hitotsubashi University Professor Makoto Saito discusses these similarities in his study *Herikoputa mane to ijigen kinyu kanwa no hikaku ko* [Comparative study on helicopter money and new quantitative and qualitative monetary easing measures] (August 2016). As a point of fact, the

Table 5.28 Similarities between current and wartime/postwar financial conditions

(1) Wartime/postwar financial condition (hundred million yen)

<Interval>	End of FY 1930	FY 1936 <6 years>	FY 1944 <8 years>	FY 1949 <5 years>	FY 1959 <10 years>
Government debt, A	68	113	1519	2908	4598
Long-term domestic bonds	44	92	1067	2908	4598
Nominal GNP, B	138	178	745	33,752	133,772
A-B ratio (%)	49.3	63.5	204.0	8.6	3.4
Balance of postal savings, D	23.4	34.8	303.7	1220	9866
D-B ratio (%)	16.9	19.6	40.6	3.6	7.3

Source:
Honpo shuyo keizai tokei [Major Japanese economic statistics] Bank of Japan Statistics Bureau
The table on the left is taken from Bank of Japan's Research Bureau (1966) *Waga kuni no kinyu seido* [The Japanese financial system], p. 67
Data for the balance of government debt and postal savings were added by author

(2) Financial condition during lost two decades following collapse of economic bubble (trillion yen)

<Interval>	End of FY 1997	FY 2003 <6 years>	FY 2011 <8 years>	FY 2016 <5 years>	FY 2026 <10 years>
Government debt, A	373	630	865	1012	1178[a]
Outstanding government bonds	257	456	669	845	1178
Nominal GNP, B	521	501	470	539	732[b]
A-B ratio (%)	72	125	184	188	160
Balance of postal savings, D	240	227	175	179	179
D-B ratio (%)	46.0	45.3	37.2	33.2	24.4

Table on left was created by author based on same time intervals used in table shown above
[a]*Source*: Jan. 2018 data published by Abe Cabinet
[b]*Source*: Medium- and Long-term Economic and Fiscal Management Plan, Council on Economic and Fiscal Policy, Cabinet Office. 13.6% of GDP if general expenditure remains 100 trillion yen

similarities identified by Professor Saito and me are identical. The only difference is in the thrust of our arguments. I pointed to the ratio of the postal saving balance to GDP as well as the way postal savings are used as problems and proposed that JP Bank should be fully privatized and governed by the Banking Act in order to resolve these problems. Professor Saito, on the other hand, focused on solutions to restore Japan's financial health and argued that the Japanese government should use tax revenues to pay down its debt.

In Chap. 2, we identified the steps to reforming Japan's financial system, which has been distorted by excessively bloated public financial services, to create a free and fair market by reforming the FILP as well as special public institutions. The chapter concluded that, once the three privatized banks are fully privatized, 95% of financial institutions in Japan will be privately operated and governed by the Banking Act, allowing them to compete on an equal footing. We then obtained the theoretical values that would be the targets for optimizing the percentage shares of total assets and ROA of different types of financial institutions by increasing the ROA of banks whose ROA is low with an eye toward optimizing the financial sector as a whole.

Chapter 3 analyzed the percentage shares of total assets and ROA of different types of financial institutions to assess postprivatization trends and examined ways to optimize them in order to propose a vision for their future operations.

The chapter suggested that, in light of the lessons learned from the preprivatization era, the government should stop providing the three privatized banks with automatic guarantees and fully privatize them in order to prevent them from becoming overly bloated. In capping off this argument, the chapter presents a road map for fully privatizing JP Bank and Shoko Chukin Bank. The chapter analyzes past and present data of regional banks, whose number totals a whopping 105, to demonstrate that the gaps among regional banks should be narrowed. It also analyzes the trends among other types of financial institutions, including commercial banks, trust banks, shinkin banks, JA, and state-owned financial institutions, to find theoretical values for ideal ROAs that would contribute to the national interest.

In Chap. 4, we looked at ways to narrow the gaps among different types of financial institutions as well as among individual banks in terms of their assets and profitability in order to create a free, fair, and efficient financial market and developed an optimization theory based on the findings. First of all, the optimization theory focuses on the percentage share of total assets held by private and public financial institutions. The theory proposes that the three privatized banks should be fully privatized so that 95% of all assets would be held by private financial institutions. If the bulk of assets were held by private financial institutions and used for local finances, gross prefectural product would increase. The correlation between gross prefectural product and prefectural loan balance is very high at 0.949, indicating that regional financial institutions contribute greatly to the gross prefectural product. Second, the theory explores increasing the low ROA of the three privatized banks to a decent level and indicates possible solutions to narrowing the gaps among different types of financial institutions, which have not changed for years. Third, it's about optimizing the percentage share of total assets and ROA of banks within each type of financial institution in order to improve their operations and profitability. By demonstrating the correlation between total assets and operating expense ratio as well as ROA, for example, the theory proved that a bank must have a certain amount of assets in order to ensure an optimal ROA. Fourth, the theory proves that JP Bank should improve and optimize its portfolio selections both on the asset and liability sides since our analysis found that the bank was exposed to a high interest-rate risk, especially in the event or rising interest rates, and proposed a direction in which it should be headed. It also suggested that small regional banks too need to change their portfolios through mergers or reorganizations.

In light of the historical background discussed in Chaps. 1, 2, 3 and 4, we looked into a theory for reorganizing the three privatized banks and regional banks after analyzing the data. Chapter 5 then laid out institutional designs for reorganizing the three privatized banks and regional banks based on this theory and positive analysis.

A decade ago I formulated an implementation plan for privatizing JP Bank and developed an institutional design for the sole purpose of privatizing the bank with the firm belief that a shift in structure from public to private is the only way to create a free, fair, and efficient financial market in Japan. Looking at ways to complete the privatization of postal services and policy-based financial institutions, I later presented a road map to full privatization at a special lecture course I taught at Kyoto University. In March 2015 I published a book, *Kansei kinyu kaikaku to chigin saihen* [Public financial reform and regional bank reorganization], in which I proposed institutional designs for reorganizing the three privatized banks and regional banks. While the goal of these institutional designs was the same as the original goal of the implementation plan for full privatization, the institutional designs turned out to be more complex than originally believed because they addressed the challenge of regionally dividing the three privatized banks and reorganizing regional banks. Fortunately, I believe I was able to come up with an innovative policy by leveraging the experience I had gained through working on mergers at Sumitomo Bank as well as working at the Office for Privatization of Japan Post.

In developing the institutional designs discussed in Chap. 5 of this book, I looked at societal changes from historical and fundamental perspectives and addressed the public economic interest. To design a mechanism that would achieve that public economic interest, I developed a theory and conducted a positive analysis. Working in the public economic interest, which could be rephrased as the public and private interest, means achieving coexistence and coprosperity of the reorganized three privatized banks and regional banks to promote the growth of the Japanese economy as well as GDP and GNI.

Following the introduction of the postal savings system in 1875, mandatory deposits of postal savings with the Ministry of Finance's Deposits Section began in 1878, and this mandatory deposit system remained in force until 2001, when it was abolished. Over these 125 years, the postal savings system supported Japan's FILP and policy-based financial institutions. We can learn a valuable lesson from the history of the postal savings system, which was used to pay off the public debt during World War II and led to the collapse of the national finances after the war. Today Japan's public debt exceeds one quadrillion yen, and household financial assets totaling 1.8 quadrillion are automatically guaranteed by the government.

Figure 5.3 shows the flow of this money. It illustrates the flow of funds of households, private financial institutions, the BOJ, and the government based on their balance sheets for the fiscal year ending March 31, 2017.

As shown in the figure, the money deposited by households across Japan with different types of private banks is used for financial intermediary operations. Consideration of the figure with a focus on uses other than loans to private companies reveals that household deposits and savings are used for household loans, government and foreign bonds, and funds deposited with the BOJ, indicating that they are used to repay government debt. Our analysis found that JP Bank and JA, which function as centralized intermediaries in this system, are not generating much of a profit.

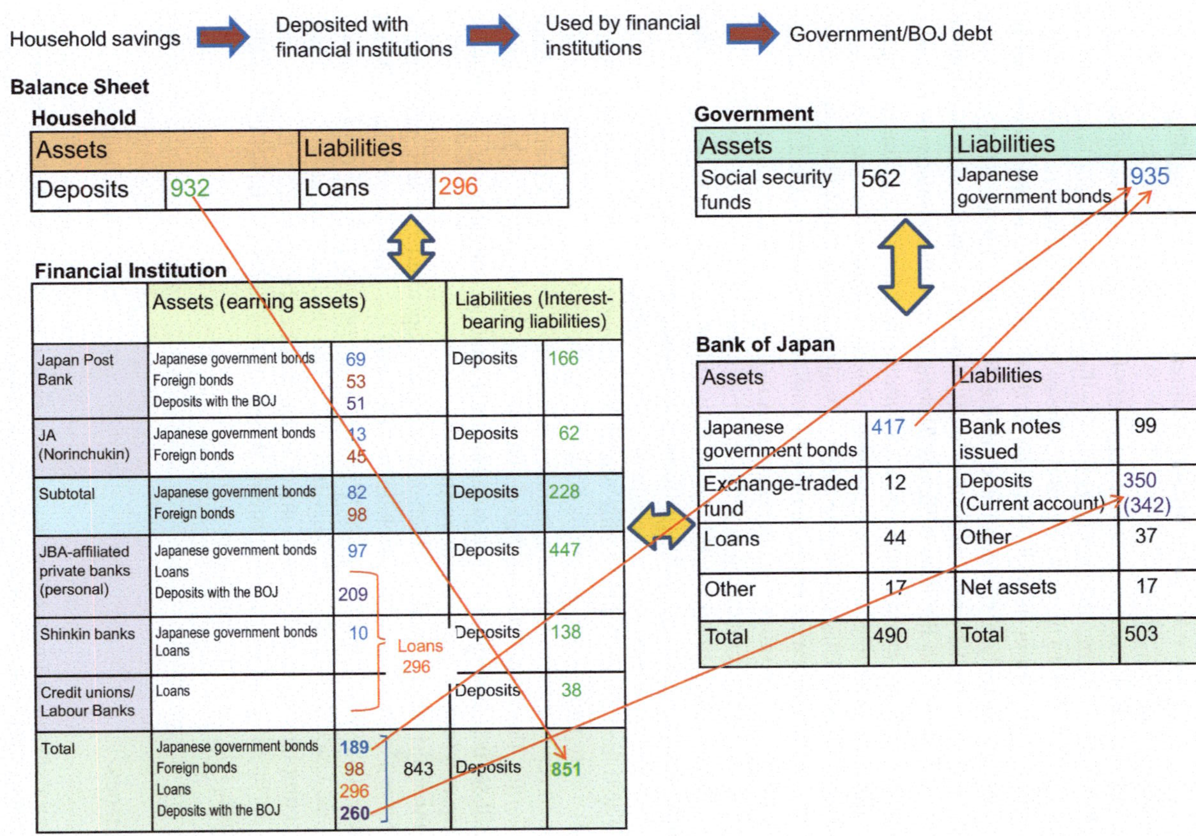

Fig. 5.3 Balance sheet of households, financial institutions, BOJ, and government (trillion yen): How household savings are used (FY ending March 2017). (*Source*: Bank of Japan and Ministry of Finance data)

In other words, if postal savings, agricultural cooperative savings, and private bank savings deposited with the BOJ or invested in Japanese government bonds are creating a low-profit economy, household deposits and savings should be optimized through the restructuring of public and private financial institutions that are financial intermediaries working in the public economic interest to generate higher profits that will benefit society as a whole.

Although the BOJ has purchased government bonds that have been issued as a monetary easing measure, the proceeds from selling the government bonds owned by banks do not flow into the real economy. The money instead gets reinvested to the tune of 350 trillion yen in deposits with the BOJ. Comparison of the flow of postal savings totaling 51 trillion yen deposited by the JP Bank with the BOJ, which are invested in government bonds, with mandatory deposits, reveals that this flow of money is very similar to the flow of funds deposited with the Ministry of Finance, which were invested in government bonds. Although the Ministry of Finance and the BOJ are different organizations, they are both closely connected to the government and its fiscal policies. That is why the three privatized banks should be restructured so that the 51 trillion yen currently deposited with the BOJ can be used for lending; otherwise, they will be unable to generate funds in the public economic interest. The three privatized banks' expansion into the lending market is the key to the BOJ's exit strategy. The best step to take would be to fully privatize them as soon as possible (by selling all shares through public offerings as required by law).

If the economy grows, the government's tax revenue will increase, leading to healthy fiscal management and turning around the general account, and the national debt will be repaid. If the nation is to survive, the government should use tax revenues to repay the national debt, which Hitotsubashi University Graduate School of Economics Professor Makoto Saito claims is the top priority for Japan, while household savings and deposits are automatically used as collateral for government debt, supplementing Japan's creditworthiness.

The three privatized banks, which are privately operated but still government owned, have a unique fund flow mechanism that Japan has maintained since its Meiji era, where the money comes from JP Bank and goes to policy-based financial institutions. Once these banks are fully privatized and the reorganization of regional banks is complete, financial institutions in Japan will be able to narrow the gaps and achieve an optimal balance among them. When all this happens, Japan will finally have a free, fair, and efficient financial market.

References

Bank of Japan's Research Bureau (1966) *Waga kuni no kinyu seido* [The Japanese financial system]

Saito, Makoto (2016) *Herikoputa mane to ijigen kinyu kanwa no hikaku ko* [Comparative study on helicopter money and new quantitative and qualitative monetary easing measures]. Chuo Koron, August

Uno, Akira (2015) *Kansei kinyu kaikaku to chigin saihen* [Public financial reform and regional bank reorganization], Kinzai Institute for Financial Affairs Inc., Tokyo

Afterword

In April 2003 I became the chairman of SMBC Consulting, which was established as a result of a merger between the Sakura Institute of Research and Sumitomo Business Consulting. In looking back, I see that it was this opportunity that provided the impetus to write an economics book. Back then I would give lectures and seminars to corporate executives, many of which were on economy and finance. I had many opportunities to meet famous scholars and bureaucrats and exchange opinions on various topics with them. Some of the scholars I met include University of Tokyo Professors Hiroshi Yoshikawa, Toshihiro Ihori, and Motoshige Ito. I also had the opportunity to meet Haruhiko Kuroda, current Bank of Japan governor (then a Ministry of Finance officer), Eisuke Sakakibara (also then a Ministry of Finance officer), and other bureaucrats on several occasions. All of them had authored books and papers that were included among the number of books I had to read as part of my job. After working in the private sector for so long, I finally got my first look at how scholars and bureaucrats worked, and I learned a lot. Since many of the seminars and lectures focused on administrative and fiscal reforms, postal privatization, and policy-based finance reform, I learned how economics was applied in the process of crafting government policies.

On January 10, 2006, I got a phone call from the president of Japan Post Holdings. He told me to quit my job a month from then, on February 16, and come work for Japan Post on the 20th. Although I had unofficially told him about what I wanted to do, the phone call came out of the blue right after the New Year holiday. It was the beginning of my multistage[1] life. My career path veered away from a private-sector megabank and toward a public-sector financial institution, i.e., Japan Post Bank, the organization at the heart of postal privatization. As someone who had witnessed firsthand how public financial institutions were given an

[1]Dr. Lynda Gratton, author of *The 100-Year Life: Living and Working in an Age of Longevity*, says in the age of the 100-year life, people live a multistage life with two or three careers instead of a three-stage life of education, work, and then retirement.

A. Uno, *Japan Post Bank*, https://doi.org/10.1007/978-981-15-1408-1

advantage over private financial institutions under special laws, I was determined to reform the financial sector from behind enemy lines as I took heart in former Prime Minister Koizumi's catchphrase "shift from public to private."

Assigned to the Office for Privatization of Japan Post, I first developed an implementation plan, in which I presented a vision for fully privatizing the postal savings bank by September 2017, 10 years after its initial privatization. Although the bank was privatized in October 2007, the privately operated stock company was still government owned and was not really privatized. Since the government was still involved (via a guarantee), it was going nowhere, and the organization itself was still bloated, a lingering problem for Japan Post Bank.

Working for this privately operated but government-owned stock company at my new life stage, I met many talented people and learned about a decision-making process that was markedly different from how decisions are made in the private sector. The difference was that the law always comes first in a nation governed by law. I learned that if you want to start something new or make a change, you have to change the law and the government.

Serving as the director in charge of new businesses, I developed institutional designs for new businesses, such as credit card and variable-annuity businesses, for which it was necessary to obtain the approval of politicians and bureaucrats. This gave me a wealth of experience in, for example attending council meetings and being called to give unsworn testimony in the Diet. It was this experience that really helped me construct a solid and well-substantiated theoretical foundation as well as institutional designs contained in this book.

In November 2008, I was given an opportunity to conduct a special lecture course on postal privatization at the Graduate School of Economics, Kyoto University, and taught the course in the 2009 autumn semester. I switched over to the academic sector believing that I could move policy forward by using my private-sector expertise to say the right thing and develop the right institutional designs. I had to submit a syllabus right away and managed to cobble together the contents of the 15-h course. I have put together 10 syllabi so far, and I always devise ways to help students understand how my institutional designs are theoretically developed using various kinds of data. I resigned from Japan Post Bank in June 2009 and moved on to the third stage of my multistage life encompassing the private, public, and academic sectors. Immediately after that, the Democratic Party became the ruling party following the election, in which voters were asked to choose the political party they wanted to put in power. The election results turned back the clock of privatizing public financial institutions and blocked the path to taking them public.

In March 2011, however, Japan faced a national crisis in the wake of the Great East Japan Earthquake and the subsequent nuclear accident in Fukushima. The burden of tax hikes to fund reconstruction efforts fell on the public's shoulders. Seeing reconstruction-related laws making progress at a snail's pace, I published articles in Nikkei Online and *Kinyu Zaisei Jijo*, making logical proposals for an institutional design, which could be deemed an extralegal measure. In the articles I argued that the Japan Post Holdings Group's capital reserve should be returned to the government through a share buyback and used to fund reconstruction.

These articles generated a lot of interest and, in swaying the media and lawmakers, paved the way for the addition of Article 14 to the supplementary provisions of the Act on Special Measures for Securing Financial Resources Necessary to Implement Measures for Reconstruction following the Great East Japan Earthquake (the Reconstruction Funding Act). This law, which was enacted in November 2013, stipulated that approximately 4 trillion yen from the sale of Japan Post shares were to be spent on repaying reconstruction bonds. After the Liberal Democratic Party came back to power in December 2014, the ruling party took up the plan to take the three Japan Post Group companies public off the ground and laid out a road map to listing them on the first section of the Tokyo Stock Exchange in November 2017.

My career encompassing the private, public, and academic sectors made me see economics in a whole new light. In Japanese, economics originally meant "manage the country and save the people." I believed that the study of economics should contribute to society in both theory and practice. In other words, I was committed to applying the theory I developed through my career in the private, public, and academic sectors to developing policies and institutional designs. In March 2015, following the enactment of the Reconstruction Funding Act, the Kinzai Institute for Financial Affairs published *Kansei kinyu kaikaku to chigin saihen* [Public financial reform and regional bank reorganization], a book I wrote upon the advice of Kazuhiro Ueta, the former dean of the Faculty of Economics, Kyoto University. It is an academic work that puts the theory of "managing the country and saving the people" into practice.

Back then, although the date for listing Japan Post Bank shares had been set, there was no prospect of taking Shoko Chukin Bank and the Development Bank of Japan public. Their privatization plans were rolled back due to emergency lending operations, among other factors. I penned the book with the aim of helping the government break free of this situation by presenting policies and institutional designs for the full privatization of the three privatized banks as well as their future operations. I also aimed to propose a drastic institutional design for reorganizing regional banks, which was also on Japan's political agenda.

Since the negative-interest-rate policy was introduced in January 2016, structural change has been occurring among Japanese financial institutions, as seen in the accelerating regional banks' move toward reorganization in response to Shoko Chukin Bank's illegal lending problem and declining regional bank revenues. I believe that my book had some positive effect on moving forward the reorganization of regional banks, which increased their total assets in regional blocs. In 2016 the book was added to the collections of various university libraries, including Stanford University, Harvard University, Columbia University, Cornell University, and Dartmouth College, as well as the Library of Congress in the U.S. and the National Library of China. In 2017 it was added to the University of California, San Diego library. When viewed from the outside, Japan's public financial system looks peculiar, and my oft-quoted book seems to be recognized as the go-to guide for insight into this unique system.

After the book was published, I received an offer from the Financial Services Agency and the Japan International Cooperation Agency (JICA) in August 2016 to speak about Japan's financial system (public and private) at a financial training session hosted by both agencies for top officials of finance ministries, central banks, and other institutions of developing countries. Similar training sessions were held over the last 3 years and attended by 57 people from 45 countries. At every session participants asked me about an English version of my book or other books on the same topic. I told Masahiko Mori, president of DMG Mori Co., for which I serve as a senior executive fellow, about this, and he kindly agreed that his company would translate my book into English and publish it. The publishing process is now under way.

Having been added to the collections of libraries of major countries and universities, my book has generated interest in advanced countries as people wonder how Japan's unique public financial services, unlike any other in the world, have supported Japan's rich economy. Many of the officials from developing countries who participated in the aforementioned financial system training expressed interest in learning about the present status and future of Japan's unique financial system that has fueled the country's astonishing economic growth since the end of World War II. I thought that the best way to answer the question on how Japan's financial system works would be in the de facto universal language. I also thought that if a book about Japan's financial system was translated into English and added to library collections, it would serve as a useful reference for many people, especially for those in developing countries working on their own financial systems.

The 2018 autumn semester marked the 10th year my special lecture course, "Introduction to Public and Private Financial Services," has been taught since it was first offered in the 2009 autumn semester at the Faculty of Economics, Kyoto University. Over the years, the course has been offered 10 times and a total of 1137 students have taken it, with 681 students earning credit for it. The course's final exam consisted of essay questions (for which students were asked to choose a certain number of questions to answer). One of the questions was on how public financial institutions should be operated after their full privatization. Seventy-four percent of students who answered the question opted for breaking them up into regional organizations to downsize their assets to an optimal level and allow them to compete with regional banks on an equal footing.

The bottom line of this book is that reorganizing the three privatized banks and regional banks will change the composition of financial institutions in Japan by type and lead to total optimization. The data on the share of total assets and return on assets (ROA) by type of financial institution provide a rationale for this theory. To verify whether total optimization is achieved, I estimated optimal figures for each bank based on their past data and changed the composition of financial institutions by type. If the share of total assets by type of financial institution is optimized through mergers or vertical integration between different types of financial institutions, and if ROA is optimized overall as a result, the structure of financial institutions in Japan will be optimized.

Postal savings, agricultural cooperative savings, and private bank savings deposited with the Bank of Japan or invested in Japanese government bonds have resulted in a low-profit economy. As a concrete measure, household deposits and savings should be optimized through the restructuring of public and private financial institutions that are financial intermediaries in order to create a high-profit economy. I strongly hope that this concrete measure will materialize the proposal for restoring Japan's fiscal health made by Makoto Saito, the Hitotsubashi University Graduate School of Economics professor who argued in his study that the Japanese government should use tax revenues to repay its bond debt.

In my multistage life encompassing the private, public, and academic sectors, I have implemented concrete knowledge-based measures for solving problems in the private sector, acquired practical public sector experience in formulating rules and systems designed to create social change, and learned how to formulate theory through an understanding of history and analyzing the current situation in the academic sector. Leveraging the basic knowledge gained at Sumitomo Bank and SMBC Consulting and my experience in postal privatization at Japan Post Holdings, as well as teaching and writing papers at Kyoto University, I finally completed two books that have been translated into English. I will continue to do my part to ensure that the theory and institutional designs laid out in this book will not have been proposed in vain but will end up being put into practice.

August 15, 2019 Akira Uno

Bibliography

Council on Economic and Fiscal Policy. "Basic Policy on the Privatization of the Japan Post." September 10, 2004. https://www5.cao.go.jp/keizai-shimon/english/publication/pdf/040922japanpost.pdf.

Council on Economic and Fiscal Policy. "Basic Policy on the Reform of Policy-based Finance." November 22, 2005. https://www5.cao.go.jp/keizai-shimon/english/publication/pdf/051129basic_policies.pdf

Kanzaki, Masaki. *NTT mineika no kozai* [Pros and cons of NTT's privatization]. Tokyo: The Nikkan Kogyo Shimbun, Ltd., 2006.

Miwa, Ryoichi (1993) *Gaisetsu Nihon Keizaishi: Kingendai* [Overview of the modern economic history of Japan]. Tokyo Daigaku Suppankai

Morimune, Kimio, Nobuhiko Terui, Mitsuru Nakagawa, Haruhisa Nishino, and Eiji Kurozumi. *Tokeigaku* [Statistics: Data Science for Social Studies]. Tokyo: Yuhikaku Publishing Co., Ltd., 2008.

Negishi, Yasuo. *Gendai potoforio riron koza* [Lecture on modern portfolio theory]. Tokyo: Kinzai Institute for Financial Affairs, Inc., 2006.

Nomura Institute of Capital Markets Research. Chiho sosei ni idomu chiiki kinyu [Regional financial institutions' challenges to local economic revitalization]. Tokyo: Kinzai Institute for Financial Affairs, Inc., 2015.

Okubo, Yutaka, ed. *Jissen Ginko ALM* [Practical bank ALM]. Tokyo: Kinzai Institute for Financial Affairs, Inc., 2006.

Saito, Makoto. *Kiki no ryoiki* [Crisis zone]. Tokyo: Keiso Shobo, 2018.

Sato, Takafumi, ed. *Bazeru II to ginko kantoku* [Basel II and banking supervision]. Tokyo: Toyo Keizai Inc., 2008.

Takigawa, Yoshio. *Yusei mineika no kinyu shakaigaku* [Sociology of finance for postal privatization]. Tokyo: Nippon Hyoron Sha Co.,Ltd., 2006.

Tang, Cheng. *Chugoku no chochiku to kinyu* [Savings and finance in China]. Tokyo: Keio University Press, 2005.

Togashi, Naoki (2009) *Kinyu daitogo jidai no riteru senryaku* [Retail strategy in the era of financial mergers]. Diamond, Inc. Tokyo.

Tohara, Tsuneko. *Koteki kinyu no kaikaku: Yubin chokin mondai no hensen to tenbo* [Public finance reform: Postal savings' past problems and future prospects]. Tokyo: Association of Agriculture and Forestry Statistics, 2001.

Yoshida, Kazuo. *Ginko saisei no bijon* [A vision for bank reorganization]. Tokyo: Nippon Hyoron Sha, 2000.

A. Uno, *Japan Post Bank*, https://doi.org/10.1007/978-981-15-1408-1

The manufacturer's authorised representative in the EU is Springer Nature Customer Service Centre GmbH, Europaplatz 3, 69115 Heidelberg, Germany. If you have any concerns regarding our products, please contact ProductSafety@springernature.com

Printed and bound by CPI Group (UK) Ltd, Croydon, CR0 4YY
23/09/2026
02221549-0001